Mississippi Nights: A History of The Music Club in St. Louis

By

Garrett and Stacy Enloe

In memory of Steve Duebelbeis
1950 – 2019

Editors: Angela Sebben and Greg Kessler

Interior design: Angela Sebben

Cover design: Kim Wagoner

Cover photo courtesy of Kel Midthnaetitulla

Mississippi Nights diagram by Lauren Gornik (Lgornikart.com)

Selections from interviews have been edited for clarity and continuity. While all attempts have been made to verify information provided in this publication, neither the Author nor the Publisher assumes any responsibility for errors, omissions, or contrary recollections of stories volunteered for inclusion herein. In addition, all efforts have been made to accurately credit contributions including stories, photos, flyers, posters, and other materials.

ISBN 978-1-7372031-0-0 (hardback)

ISBN 978-1-7372031-1-7 (paperback)

MississippiNights.com

First Edition

CONTENTS

PREFACE

Garrett Enloe grew up in a household filled with music. His mother worked at Now and Then Records, and their house had a plethora of records and music memorabilia, including a jukebox that played 45s. His parents took him to his first concert in 1979, Beatlemania at the American Theater, when he was five years old.

Stacy Shelton also grew up in a household filled with music. Her parents were avid KSHE-95 listeners, and her mother often took her to the radio station in Crestwood, Missouri, to buy concert tickets or collect prizes that she had won from radio contests. Stacy's parents took her to several outdoor music events before she attended her first "real" concert with her mom and aunt at the The Arena in 1984 — Van Halen.

The two met while waiting in line at the American Theater to see Jackyl in 1994, but didn't start dating until after running into each other at two more concerts. They bonded over their love for music and married in 2000. The couple cut the wedding cake to "The Lumberjack" by Jackyl.

Sixteen years later, Stacy's mom talked the couple into attending a trivia night for the St. Louis Classic Rock Preservation Society. One of the items up for silent auction was a section of the Mississippi Nights awning. They were far from the winning team that night, but Garrett won the bid on the Mississippi Nights awning.

Excited about adding this rare piece to his music memorabilia collection, Garrett decided to start a Mississippi Nights Fan Page on Facebook for people to share their memories of the legendary venue.

Within two years, the fan page had grown to about 2,000 members. The outpouring of love for Mississippi Nights was immense. Garrett concluded that he had to write a book to chronicle this iconic venue and preserve its memory. Knowing the gravity of the project, Stacy initially resisted, but eventually joined him on the journey.

Stacy, age 5.

Garrett, about age 3.

And what an interesting journey it has been! Owner Rich Frame and former employees welcomed the couple with open arms into the Mississippi Nights family. Garrett received the Jerry M. Cook Award from the St. Louis Classic Rock Preservation Society for his work preserving the memory of Mississippi Nights. The St. Louis History Museum approached Garrett to lend the awning and other St. Louis music memorabilia to their 2021 special exhibit, "St. Louis Sound." The couple has received an outpouring of support, encouragement, and excitement from Mississippi Nights fans, who have eagerly awaited this book.

Garrett and Stacy Enloe

WELCOME TO MISSISSIPPI NIGHTS

Los Angeles had the Whiskey a Go Go, Troubadour, and The Roxy Theater.

New York City had CBGB, Studio 54, and the Palladium.

St. Louis had Mississippi Nights.

Mississippi Nights, appropriately promoted as "The Music Club of St. Louis," operated from 1976 until 2007 and was located in the historic Laclede's Landing section of downtown St. Louis at 914 North 1st Street.

To get to Mississippi Nights, you drove past the Gateway Arch grounds, under the ornate arches of the Eads Bridge, over several blocks of cobblestone streets and past century-old buildings that once housed fur traders, slaughterhouses, and dry goods warehouses. The old, weathered brick building had character with its arched doorways and windows. The color variation in the bricks suggested that once there were more windows and doors, removed for unknown reasons. The Eads Bridge, spanning the mighty Mississippi River, could be seen from the parking lot on the south side of the building.

Upon entering the wooden door on the right, you were in a vestibule surrounded by signed 8x10 band photographs in black frames. To the left, past the second door, were a couple of video games, a pinball machine, a cigarette machine, some round, white-topped tables with black, wooden chairs, a small bar in the corner, and another set of doors that sometimes opened to accommodate large crowds. It was a short walk forward to have your ID checked, hand stamped, and ticket torn.

To the right was the bar with wood paneling up the back wall, neon beer signs, and open shelves of liquor and glasses. Following a sloped walk down past two tiers of additional tables and chairs on the left (the first tier also housed the sound mixer), the walkway opened, revealing restrooms and the underage section (the raised area often referred to as the "kiddie corral") on the right, and to the left was the dance floor and stage.

ANGELA PRADA* REMEMBERS...

Mississippi Nights was lightning in a bottle. Having worked there, I have to say everyone felt they were part of the show, not just watching it. There was a true sense of community and a love of music between patrons, staff, and the bands. No one complained about it being hot, crowded, smoky, or that they were eating popcorn out of a trash can. They were there to see the show.

*Mississippi Nights' Server

M. NIGHTS
YOU GUYS RULE
THANKS A LOT

The stage was covered with parquet flooring and elevated about three-and-a-half feet off the floor. A small walkway to the right of the stage led to the back door and, behind the building, steep metal steps where the bands loaded out their equipment at the end of the night. (Fortunately for the crew, they were able to load in through the front door into the empty venue in the morning.) Sometimes, metal barricades blocked the front of the stage, but often you could press yourself right up against this platform in front of your favorite band.

Several factors contributed to the longevity and popularity of Mississippi Nights. They did an excellent job of booking shows and showcased a variety of music genres, unlike many clubs that catered to one genre. The sound system was incredible, appealing to the audiences and the musicians. The staff was welcoming and made the club feel like a second home to many. Finally, you were able to get up-close and personal with the bands — in front of the stage as they played, at the bar while they drank, or outside as they came and went.

Being the best place to experience music in St. Louis for so many years, countless people forged new relationships and memories at Mississippi Nights. Many concertgoers developed friendships that would last a lifetime with the staff or fellow patrons. Some went to the club on first dates or even met their spouses there. The memories run the gamut from meeting bands, the friendly staff, amazing performances, and crazy incidents (some involving liquor).

Mississippi Nights was a treasure in St. Louis. Unfortunately, as time passes, memories fade. Losing the treasured *Music Club of St. Louis* to fading memories would be a tragedy. So, we preserve those memories and the music that Mississippi Nights produced for thirty years with this book.

CHUCK MCPHERSON* REMEMBERS...

What was special about Mississippi Nights? The people. The atmosphere. The smell. The experience. You could not only see a good show but meet the artist. It was seeing up-and-coming bands before everyone else, as well as bands on the way down. It was all-ages shows in a bar atmosphere. I was underage and limited to the floor and the side of the stage for much of my time there, but it didn't matter. To borrow the phrase, it was the most magical place on earth. Mississippi Nights was one of the places where I spent much of my mid-teens to early adult years. I made friends at the club that I still have to this day. It's a place I will never, ever forget. No other club can compare. 914 North 1st Street will be in my heart until the day I die.

*Mississippi Nights Patron

The only music I don't think we did was opera.
-- Owner Rich Frame

History of 914 North 1st Street

Laclede's Landing lies north of the Gateway Arch and Eads Bridge, the only remaining section of St. Louis' nineteenth-century commercial riverfront. Designed by Pierre Laclede and Auguste Chouteau in 1763, Laclede's Landing was built a year before the city was named St. Louis. By 1840, the riverfront was lined with steamboats. Laclede's Landing included a mill, a foundry, shops, and homes of those who owned businesses in the area. The riverfront served as an outdoor center to transfer freight and passengers.

The street that would include Mississippi Nights was first named "La Grande Rue." This was Americanized and renamed North Main Street in 1804, following the Louisiana Purchase of 1803. Maps dating from 1822 show each block separated into numbered sections. Section 24 at the corner of Cherry Street and North Main Street stood vacant in 1822. The date the Mississippi Nights building was built is unclear. When historian and author of *The Lost St. Louis Riverfront,* Thomas Grady, was shown an artist's rendition of the building, he observed, "The building has a triple gabled roof. My guess is it was built circa 1838."

The street numbering system in St. Louis changed in 1867, and for the first time, maps charted 918 North Main Street, which eventually became the Mississippi Nights parking lot. In the year 1868, plots 914 and 916 are documented. The street name alternated between Main Street and 1st Street for many years before the street officially became North 1st Street by city ordinance in 1881.

Before 914 North 1st Street became Mississippi Nights, the building housed various businesses. The walls that would eventually see early shows by legendary bands like The Police, AC/DC, and Nirvana once housed syrup, fireworks, pallets of paper, burlap bags, and two post-Civil War butcheries.

Illustration by Rob Zlich, www.robsportraits.com

1867: Pork Packers

Although the building may date as early as the 1830s, the first confirmed business in the Mississippi Nights building does not appear in records until 1868. James Reilley & Co. Pork Packers may have lasted for less than a decade, but the business is responsible for one of the signature features of the club, the floor that began to slope as you passed the ticket window. Documents from 1868 declare the building was owned by James Reilley, David A. Spellen, and Michael McEnnis. The 1874 book *St. Louis: The Commercial Metropolis of the Mississippi Valley* contains an advertisement for James Reilley & Co. Pork Packers, located at 914, 916, and 918 North Main Street. "Pork Packers" is a euphemism for a slaughterhouse or meat processing facility. The building's signature slanted floor, eventually bordered by the bar and the over-21 seating section, was designed to drain blood from animal carcasses.

In *Pictorial St. Louis: The Great Metropolis of the Mississippi Valley,* an 1875 Topographical Survey, artist Camille N. Dry crossed St. Louis in a hot air balloon and captured downtown city life, producing detailed drawings of buildings, horse-drawn carriages, trains, ferries, the new Eads Bridge, and for the first time, the building at 914 North Main Street.

Pictorial St. Louis took two years to complete and is arguably the most impressive perspective map ever made.

In August 1879, James Reilley's body was found in the Mississippi River near Kimmswick, Missouri. The *St. Louis Globe-Democrat* reported, "It was a suicide while laboring under temporary aberration of mind." His pork processing company closed a short time later, but the sloping floor would remain a century later.

JAMES REILLEY.   D. A. SPELLEN.

JAMES REILLEY & CO.,

PORK PACKERS,

AND

PROVISION MERCHANTS,

914, 916 & 918 North Main Street,

ST. LOUIS, MO.

1875 Building Number 80 is the Mississippi Nights building. Photo from *Pictorial St. Louis* Survey. Arrow points to future Mississippi Nights building.

1884-1893: Nine Years of Sweetness

The C. D. Chase Syrup Company opened in 1884 at 914 and 916 North 1st Street. Their slogan was: "Best syrup made from the whitest crystals of rock candy." They sold five varieties of syrup: Windsor Maple, Boston Club, Rock Candy, Sugar Loaf, and Royal Drips. The company closed in 1893. Maybe the company's pledge of $1,000 in gold "for the detection of the slightest adulteration in any of these syrups" put them out of business after only nine years.

Behind the Mississippi Nights building in 1890.

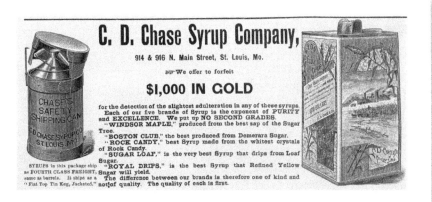

5

1902-1911: Back to Bacon

At 914 North 1st Street, Joseph P. Funk & Co. opened another beef and pork packing company in 1902. As their packing predecessor, they too closed shop after nine years in 1911.

1912-1922: Short-lived Occupancies

From 1912 to 1913, United States Fireworks Co. occupied 916 North 1st Street.

Another fleeting business in the building was Commercial Paper Stock Co. They utilized the building from 1921 to 1922.

1957 National Bag Company. Photo provided by Missouri History Museum. Photo by Lloyd Spainhower. Arrow points to future Mississippi Nights building.

1923-1969: It's in the Bag

In 1923, the National Bag Company moved into 914 (and plots 916 and 918) North 1st Street to manufacture burlap bags.

Around 5 p.m., July 31, 1954, lightning struck the building, and the fire burned for almost an hour and a half before it was contained. The smoke was so dense that riverboats stopped to watch. The *St. Louis Post-Dispatch* reported, "Seven firemen were treated at City Hospital for minor cuts and bruises and smoke inhalation. Damage to the bag company was severe but not total."[a] Company owner, Ben Samuels, was at a country club for dinner when the fire was reported. He learned about the fire on the radio later that evening.

The fire caused $39,000 in damage (approx. $403,493 in 2022 dollars). The National Bag Company continued business for fourteen more years, closing in 1968.

(a) *Newspapers.com, St. Louis Post-Dispatch, 01 August 1954, pg. 3, http://stltoday.newpapers.com/image/139741842 (28 December 2018)*

Early 1960s aerial photo from north of Eads Bridge. Arrow points to future Mississippi Nights building.

1969: Our Mysterious Johnny

On June 6, 1969, a "sing and dance bar" called Stage Door opened at 914 North 1st Street. The advertisement claimed that the bartender was Johnny Brock, brother of Cardinal's Hall of Fame left fielder Lou Brock. When we contacted Lou Brock Jr., in hopes of getting more information on The Stage Door, he responded with the following:

About Johnny Brock, when he died recently, I got calls giving condolences for a passing uncle. However, I've never heard of Johnny Brock, and there is not a "Johnny" in our family. If he had a younger brother named Lou, just know it was not Lou, my father. So, there's no information to give you other than people told me he said my dad was his brother. The ad you sent is the first evidence beyond that hearsay.

It is unclear whether this was a case of estranged brothers or a bard trying to capitalize on a famous name. If it was the latter, the attempt failed. The Stage Door closed in October 1969, after only three months.

Vacancy at 914 North 1st Street

On May 10, 1970, a four-alarm fire broke out in the vacant building, and the roof collapsed. No one was injured. The cause of the fire was never determined. The building remained vacant for the next four years.

900 block of North 1st Street in 1972. Photo courtesy of *St. Louis Post-Dispatch.*

1974-1975: In Walks Ellis Salem

Ellis Salem (originally from Louisville) opened up a nightspot on the landing called River Rat. There was nothing on the landing entertainment-wise in those days. The only thing on The Landing was rats... hence the name. He believed the landing had the potential to be a mecca for entertainment.

Pat Liston — Mama's Pride

In 1974, Ellis Salem hired James Trout to help remodel the fire-damaged building at 914 North 1st Street. The two completed the entire project by themselves, including a window in the back that offered a view of the Mississippi River. Pat Liston, vocalist and guitarist of Mama's Pride, remembers Ellis Salem sprayed vermiculite on the ceilings for soundproofing, the first step for making great sound. The most notable feature of the new club, at least for the bands, was Trout's partially-stripped 1958 Mark II Jaguar on blocks in place of a couch in the artists' dressing room. The bands liked to drink beer in it. Trout also added six-foot movie posters to the walls around the club. "They were mine, and I donated them to the cause," Trout explains, "since we couldn't afford anything else." Terrie Cooksey Snyder, an early patron, remembers the club:

> *River Rat looked like a warehouse, with big hooks and chains hanging from the ceiling. The ceiling wasn't as low as it was in the later years. The stage was a foot off the ground. With no chairs to sit on, you sat on the concrete floor that sloped towards the stage. The bar was a long piece of plywood sitting on barrels. I think it had one pinball machine. The place was very bare and dark. There was nothing else on that street but warehouses, and the only streetlight was a bulb on a pole out in front. There were no parking lots, so you just parked on the street. It was kind of creepy. It wasn't bad, just scary down by that river without lighting.*

1974 advertisement. Courtesy of Pat Liston.

James Trout "worked the door, worked the bar, and closed most nights [while] Ellis wrote the ads, hired the bands and managed payroll." He recalls, "Saturdays, we were packed. Weekdays, we were pretty empty." Trout's dedication was rewarded with an offer from Salem of a future partnership in the club.

"[Ellis Salem's] dream was to attract national talent," says Trout. "Big names were willing to play for local rates. The warehouse district on the big river was a big draw." National acts like Ginger Baker, Heartsfield, and Fats Domino played at River Rat. Some local bands began their careers at River Rat, becoming national acts like Mama's Pride, The Outlaws, and Grinderswitch. The arrival of River Rat and subsequent revival of Laclede's Landing was celebrated in the *St. Louis Post-Dispatch*:

> *After hearing all the grandiose ideas for Laclede's Landing for years, there's something paradoxical about finding a nightspot in the midst of those warehouses on [North] 1st Street called the River Rat. The club is a warehouse decorated in early fat Crayola and furnished in impoverished Spartan. It costs $1 to enter, and there's a person to check IDs for age. (September 27, 1974)*

> *Another nighttime establishment already opened on the outer edge of the area is the River Rat, serving up live Southern blues and rock in a raunchy, border town environment. Owner Ellis Salem says the riverfront is the most natural of scenes for this kind of entertainment. (November 10, 1974)*

Mama's Pride made the biggest splash out of all the local bands that played River Rat. They also credited Ellis Salem with helping them get signed to Atlantic Records. Singer and guitarist Pat Liston remembers:

> *I had been living in Los Angeles from '69 to '72. In 1972 I came back to St. Louis to put together Mama's Pride with my brother Danny and Max Baker. I immediately took the band back to LA, and we played six nights a week for almost two years before we came back to St. Louis. St. Louis was a great market, but it was a small pond, and we always wanted more. We started working at [Salem's] club. He brought in great acts like Heartsfield and The Outlaws (before their first LP release). Ellis loved our band ... [and] connected us with a booking agent named Steve Cole out of Louisville, Kentucky. Steve booked us all over the south. In Augusta, Georgia, Alan Walden saw us and signed us. Alan managed The Outlaws and Lynyrd Skynyrd. He was the brother of Phil Walden, President of Capricorn Records. Alan got us signed to Atlantic Records less than a year later. We'd have never gotten that deal without Ellis Salem getting that ball rolling.*

River Rat closed in 1975, setting the stage for a bigger club to come. Between the closing of River Rat and the opening of the next club, the three-story building at 918 North 1st Street was demolished and became a parking lot.

1975: Another Attempt to Find Gold

In November 1975, the second club to last a mere three months opened at 914 North 1st Street: On the Rox. Brother Bait, Coal Kitchen, and Iron Butterfly are the only bands confirmed to have played On the Rox.

1976: Jackpot

Mississippi Nights opened in 1976.

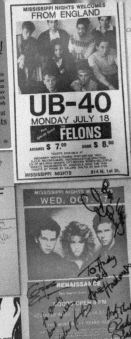

MISSISSIPPI NIGHTS WELCOMES
FROM ENGLAND

UB-40

FELONS

MONDAY JULY 18

ADVANCE **$7.00** DOOR **$8.00**

MISSISSIPPI NIGHTS 914 N. 1st St.

METAL CHURCH

LIVE IN CONCERT

MONDAY NOV. 18

Mississippi Nights

Metal Child Enterprises, Ltd.

MERCYFUL FATE

Tues Oct 30
Mississippi Nights

John Cale

THE VELVET UNDERGROUND

The Return of
COWBOY MOUTH

Live at The Music Club in St. Louis- Mississippi Nights
Tickets are $20 flat and are onsale now
This is an ALL AGES EVENT!!!!
Mississippi Nights 914 N.First St 63102 314.421.3853

LEFTOVER SALMON

FRIDAY MARCH 31, 2000

MISSISSIPPI NIGHTS

DOORS @7PM SHOW @8PM

TICKETS $15 ALL AGES

FERRARI

LIVE @ MISSISSIPPI NIGHTS

MISSISSIPPI NIGHTS
WED. OCT.

RENAISSANCE

DOORS OPEN 8 PM

EXCITER

VIOLENCE AND FORCE

U.S. ATTACK

IN CONCERT!

Wednesday, February 26

welcomes

Phantom, Rocker & Slick

MISSISSIPPI NIGHTS
914 N. First

THE B'zz

MISSISSIPPI NIGHTS
TUE. MAR. 8

AVAILABLE ON **EPIC** RECORDS & TAPES

Wednesday, June 24, 1992
at
THE FLAMING LIPS
—AND—
THE URGE

MISSISSIPPI NIGHTS
THE MUSIC CLUB IN ST. LOUIS

NEW YEARS EVE PARTY

with **BIG FUN**

MONDAY DECEMBER 31

MISSISSIPPI NIGHTS

PHISH

MISSISSIPPI NIGHTS
914 N. FIRST ST. · LACLEDE'S LANDING

FRIDAY, DECEMBER 4

MISSISSIPPI NIGHTS WELCOMES

WED. MAY 9

A IN CONCERT
RECORDING ARTIST

RATT

With Special Guest
TALAS

DOORS OPEN 8 PM
Admission **$5.00**
AT THE DOOR

LIMITED # OF SEATS AVAILABLE
FOR UNDER 21

MISSISSIPPI NIGHTS   914 N. First St.
LACLEDE'S LANDING   421-3853

JASON & THE SCORCHERS

THUR. MAR. 22
MISSISSIPPI NIGHTS

New Album Available on Records & Tapes

---

mae

CIRCA SURVIVE
MUTEMATH
THE WORKING TITLE

Thursday October 20, 2005
@Mississippi Nights

An evening with

RATDOG

playing 2

BOB WEIR · ROB WASSERMAN
JAY LANE · MARK KARAN
JEFF CHIMENTI · KENNY BROOKS

FRIDAY MARCH 22

MetroTix MISSISSIPPI NIGHTS
914 N.1st St. St.Louis-MO

SLAYER

MISSISSIPPI NIGHTS

Doors 7:00 $18 adv.
August 18
All Ages Welcome
Show 8:00 $20 d.o.s.

Fight

Featuring Rob Halford

with Monster Voodoo Machine

MISSISSIPPI NIGHTS

Friday, June 23, 1995

Doors 8:00 Show 9:00
All Ages Welcome
Tix are $14 in advance and $16 day of show
Tickets go on sale Wednesday, May 10th
at all 49 Tickets Now locations

SUMMER SHOWDOWN

featuring

Murder City Players

also
THE UNCONSCIOUS

JUNE 27

MISSISSIPPI NIGHTS
914 N. FIRST 421-3853

Brothers in Arms

MISSISSIPPI NIGHTS

WELCOMES FROM EDINBURGH, SCOTLAND

the PROCLAIMERS

Mon., March 13th

at MISSISSIPPI NIGHTS
914 N. FIRST STREET · LACLEDE'S LANDING
DOORS 8 PM SHOWTIME 9 PM ALL AGES

FOR MORE INFO PLEASE CALL 421-3853

Jonathan Richman

PLUS THE

MORELLS

MISSISSIPPI NIGHTS

LACLEDE LANDING ST. LOUIS MISSOURI
WEDNESDAY, MAY 5, 1982 $4.00 AT THE DOOR

Vintage Vinyl & KWMU 90.7 Welcome
Africa's Reggae Superstar
Direct from the Ivory Coast

ALPHA BLONDY

AND THE
SOLAR SYSTEM

WED · MARCH 16 · 9 PM
AT THE NEW
MISSISSIPPI NIGHTS

BRUCE COCKBURN

Mississippi Nights
Monday, April 24
9 pm

Mississippi Nights

ARROW MEMPHIS

Every Tuesday
thru Saturday Night

Tuesday is LADIES NIGHT

HARP Attack

Featuring the Finest Harp Players in the Midwest
with very special guest artist Howard Levy
in a Blow by Blow Assault on the City of St. Louis

Sat, April 3, 1993

MISSISSIPPI NIGHTS

Food Provided by Chef Dennis Connolly

Noon 'til 2 AM $10 Adv. / $12 Day of Show
Tickets available thru Diatix, Mississippi Nights

---

the DEL-LORDS

THURSDAY, JUNE 12

at MISSISSIPPI NIGHTS

ALL AGES ADMITTED

BURNING SPEAR and the BURNING BAND

WED. AUGUST 17

MISSISSIPPI NIGHTS
914 N. FIRST ST. LACLEDE'S LANDING
ALL AGES WELCOME

ULTRAMAN

DAZZLING KILLMEN

ALL AGES · $5.00

8 PM
MONDAY DECEMBER 30

MISSISSIPPI NIGHTS

Red Hot Chili Peppers

with BLANK SPACE

Wed
Dec. 4th

$5 cover

doors open 8pm

Mississippi Nights 421-3853
914 N. 1st

STEVE BOB & RICH

THOSE GUYS FROM KANSAS CITY, MO.

WEDNESDAY SEPT. 25

ALL AGES WELCOME

CHECK OUT OUR NEW AND IMPROVED UNDER 21 SECTION

BIGGER & BETTER $3.00 COVER

$1.00 OFF WITH COLLEGE I.D.

CATCH THEIR ALBUM
"BALLS"
ON BAT RECORDS

914 N. FIRST 421-3853

---

judge nothing

AT MISSISSIPPI NIGHTS
ON SEPT. 19
ALL AGES

FINALLY

The Eyes AT MISSISSIPPI NIGHTS

SAT. JUNE 24th

W/Special Guest: The Nukes

THE EIGHTIES ARE OVER.
WELCOME TO THE NINETIES.

WMRY-101

WELCOMES

THE BEARS

Featuring ADRIAN BELEW

$10

WEDNESDAY, SEPTEMBER 14

MISSISSIPPI NIGHTS

MISSISSIPPI NIGHTS PRESENTED
KDHX 88.1 FM

TUESDAY, FEBRUARY 21

COWBOY JUNKIES

FRIDAY MAY 12
DOORS OPEN 8 PM

OLIVER SAIN'S

26th Year SOUL REUNION

FEATURING

FRIDAY MAY 12
DOORS OPEN 8 PM

MISSISSIPPI NIGHTS
914 North 1st Street

THIS JUST IN...

ulcer

THE OTHER WORLD
FRIDAY, NOVEMBER 16

AND DON'T FORGET...
MISSISSIPPI NIGHTS
WEDNESDAY, NOVEMBER 15
WITH MARILYN MANSON AND CLUTCH.

THE DILLMAN BAND

TO RIDE

velvet elvis

MISSISSIPPI NIGHTS BY THE YEARS

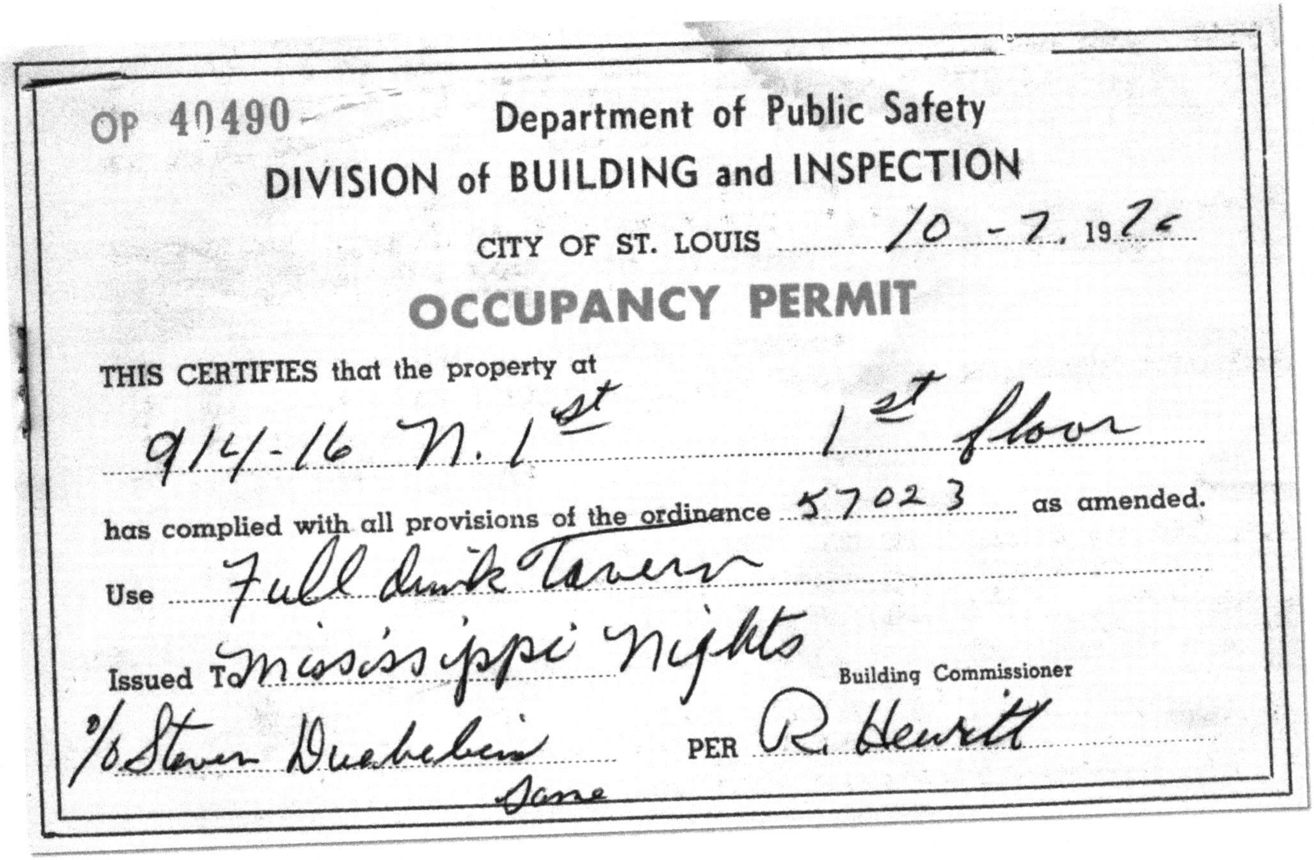

OP 40490 — Department of Public Safety
DIVISION of BUILDING and INSPECTION
CITY OF ST. LOUIS _10 - 7, 19 76_

OCCUPANCY PERMIT

THIS CERTIFIES that the property at

_914-16 N. 1st_ _1st floor_

has complied with all provisions of the ordinance _57023_ as amended.

Use _Full drink Tavern_

Issued To _Mississippi Nights_

% Steven Duebbein
Jane

Building Commissioner

PER _R. Hewitt_

LEASE OF BUSINESS PROPERTY

This Lease entered into this First day of

September, 1976, by and between WAMSER AND FERMAN INVESTMENT CO.,

a partnership, Lessor, and STEVEN D. DUEBELBEIS, and MISSISSIPPI

NIGHTS, INC., a corporation, both of St. Louis, Missouri, Lessee;

WITNESSETH:

The Lessor hereby leases to the Lessee and the Lessee

hereby takes from the Lessor as Lessee upon the following terms

and conditions:

The premises designated as 914-916 North First
Street and being a part of the building located
in block 17 of the City of St. Louis, Missouri,
at 914-916 North First Street and last occupied
by ROXY, INCORPORATED under lease from the Lessors
herein, and the parking lot designated as 910; also

14

1976

The Birth of Mississippi Nights

Steve Duebelbeis was a fan of live music in St. Louis before he left for Drury College in Springfield, Missouri, in the mid-1970s. Duebelbeis quickly noticed clubs in Springfield booked original acts such as Ozark Mountain Daredevils and Granny's Bathwater, a far cry from the cover bands back home in St. Louis at places like The Rusty Springs Saloon near Kingshighway and Manchester. The bands Duebelbeis saw in Springfield had no reason to travel north to St. Louis to play with a legion of cover bands. If a band was not popular enough to fill places like the Kiel Auditorium, they had every reason to skip St. Louis. Duebelbeis, along with his friend Tom Duffy, saw an opening in the St. Louis scene and made a plan. They returned to St. Louis to open a smaller venue for local and national bands who played original music, like the ones they saw in Springfield. Duebelbeis and Duffy shared a love for music as well as experience in the restaurant industry. They made great partners with complementary experience and personalities (Duebelbeis, a go-getting visionary, and Duffy, a practical businessman).

The pair looked at several locations around St. Louis, including a shuttered post office in south St. Louis and a former 1920s speakeasy in West County. Tom Duffy had seen shows at On the Rox and suggested 914 North 1st Street to Steve Duebelbeis. On August 30, 1976, they bought the building and founded the Mississippi Nights Corporation. Duebelbeis was the president and treasurer, with skills in networking, and Duffy was the vice president, secretary, and in charge of operations. Over the next six weeks, they cleaned up and repaired the building and installed new production equipment, including a custom sound system with a 24-track Tascam board, which was unusual at the time.

Originally, Duebelbeis wanted to call the club "The Do Drop In." But, thankfully, he began thinking about the Mississippi River right outside and that the club would be open at night, and he settled on "Mississippi Nights."

On October 11, 1976, Mississippi Nights opened with a cover charge of $1.50. The first act to perform was the 1932 Ballroom Blues Band, an eight-piece jazz, rock, and rhythm and blues ensemble. Duebelbeis was a jazz fan, so it was the perfect first show. The band even managed to pull off a jazzed-up version of The Osmond's "I'm Living for the Love of You."

Another early show was Al Stewart, touring on his 1976 hit song, "Year of the Cat." Although the details are lost, this was the first artist showcase concert at Mississippi Nights, gaining exposure for a rising artist. The show was a great success for both Al Stewart and Mississippi Nights. So, labels took note of the venue with the fantastic location and sound system.

Over the next two years, business was great for the club. Duffy says, "Local bands... offered to play for nothing sometimes because of the systems we had and exposure to the record companies." In addition, national bands who hadn't hit it big and needed a mid-sized venue found Mississippi Nights a bright spot on Midwest tours. Contemporary Productions helped to book many of these bands. The club filled a much-needed void in the St. Louis music scene.

CONTEMPORARY PRODUCTIONS

Steve Schankman and Irv Zuckerman founded Contemporary Productions in 1968. By 1976, they were booking bands and events such as Grateful Dead, the Rolling Stones, and Superjam (a day-long event at Busch Stadium featuring Jefferson Starship, Fleetwood Mac, Jeff Beck, and Ted Nugent). Tom Duffy recalls having a fantastic working relationship with the production company. Contemporary brought national acts (and audiences) to Mississippi Nights, and Mississippi Nights provided Contemporary the perfect place to test up-and-coming acts that they couldn't book at larger venues. Contemporary brought future superstars to Mississippi Nights, such as INXS, Lita Ford, Smithereens, Ratt, Saxon, Concrete Blonde, and Joe Satriani.

Contemporary Productions expanded to ten other states and businesses besides concert promotion: managing bands, promoting other events, pairing bands with corporate sponsors, forming online ticket sales companies, and creating Riverport Amphitheatre in 1991. In 1997, Schankman and Zuckerman sold Contemporary Productions to corporate concert conglomerate SFX. Three years later, SFX sold the company to a larger corporate concert conglomerate, Clear Channel Communications. Contemporary Productions was renamed Live Nation in 2005.

MISSISSIPPI NIGHTS on Laclede's Landing
brings you a Special Night with

AL STEWART

one night only—Mon. Dec. 13
tickets 3⁰⁰ in advance, 4⁰⁰ at the door—doors open at 7 PM
(this is not a GTA Production)

Ad appeared in the
St. Louis Post Dispatch,
Sunday, December 5, 1976.

Courtesy of Tom Duffy.

16

REAL ROCK RADIO KSHE-95

Radio stations are an inextricable part of rock 'n' roll concert promotion. From the beginning, St. Louis radio and Mississippi Nights shared a mission to spread the gospel of live music.

Originally known as "The Lady of FM" in 1961, KSHE-95 began life in a Crestwood, Missouri, basement, playing all classical and later a mix of classical and easy listening music. Fans were invited to drop by the station and leave their favorite records for DJs to play. But, unsurprisingly, the format failed to find an audience or attract advertisers.

In 1964, Century Broadcasting bought KSHE (minus the basement). A few years later, program director Shelly Grafman convinced Century to change KSHE's format to rock 'n' roll. By November 1967, KSHE had changed its format and joined a list of underground rock stations, and today, 55 years later, holds the record for being the longest continuous rock station in the world.

Throughout its over sixty years, KSHE has and still sponsors live shows at the biggest venues in St. Louis. The KSHE name is attached to legendary places, such as Kiel Opera House, the Checkerdome, and the American Theater. However, KSHE also promoted concerts at Mississippi Nights, including The Outfield, Joe Satriani, The Fixx, The Fabulous Thunderbirds, JJ Cale, and Mr. Big. Many events promoted by KSHE had prices that ended in 95 to promote the station. For instance, a ticket to see Pat Benatar in 1979 cost $3.95. Occasionally, KSHE shows at Mississippi Nights were free, such as the station's 22nd birthday party in 1989 featuring Atlanta Rhythm Section.

KSHE-95, like Mississippi Nights, elicits an uncommon loyalty from its fans and artists. J.D. Blackfoot played Mississippi Nights in 1976 and 1977. He returned to St. Louis in 1982 to record a live album at Kiel Opera House sponsored by KSHE. The album's back cover featured a glowering Blackfoot in a KSHE shirt. When J.D. Blackfoot returned to Mississippi Nights in 1992, he recounted his past with the club and the radio station during the show.

Other stations promoted shows at Mississippi Nights as well: KWK (T.S.O.L.), KDHX (EEK-a-Mouse, Jimmy Cliff), WSIE (Dead Milkmen and Buck Pets), KPNT (Matthew Sweet), and WMRY (The Replacements). While several of these stations are a thing of the past, like Mississippi Nights itself, KSHE-95 still promotes concerts around St. Louis and is the longest-running rock 'n' roll radio station in the United States.

KSHE·95
REAL ROCK RADIO
St. Louis

J.D.Blackfoot

18

1977

A Rumble from Down Under

Of all the shows to have taken place at Mississippi Nights, August 9, 1977, might be the most surprising. If you spent any time waiting in the foyer of Mississippi Nights, you likely stared at the wall of autographed 8x10s regretting all the shows you that you were too young or too broke to attend. Among those photos was the snarling face of Angus Young. How many people stood in that foyer asking themselves *how did a multi-platinum selling band play on that small stage, and I never knew about it?*

When AC/DC arrived on the St. Louis riverfront, they had three records in their discography, but this was only their ninth concert in America. The day started badly when the AC/DC crew took little care loading in the band's equipment. Among other things, they were running amps into the walls of the ten-month-old club. Steve Duebelbeis had to tell the crew to cool down to protect the new venue.

The opening act was Roto the Wonder Band. By accounts of several concertgoers, AC/DC delighted the crowd. During his guitar solo, Angus Young jumped off the stage and planted a kiss on audience member Kim Starr's mouth, all while not missing a note.

After the concert, a few people stayed behind to party with the band, including record executive Sam Kaiser. "Every town had local females who would come out in force for the buzz bands," Kaiser explains, "and AC/DC was a major buzz band."

St. Louis had strict liquor laws and rules dictating closing times for clubs. At 1 a.m., establishments had to stop serving alcohol, and by 1:30 a.m., everyone except the staff had to exit the building. The police made sure these laws were upheld.

At 1 a.m., the staff tried to eject some ladies from the club. Sam Kaiser witnessed the whole thing, recalling, "Bon Scott voiced his objections. Angus Young joined in, getting into a shouting match with a bouncer twice his size. The bouncer laughed at Angus and shoved him hard. Angus reached back and clocked him, and [the bouncer] dropped to the floor."

Concert August 9, 1977. Courtesy of Sam Kaiser.

It was a short brawl, and the venue had some minor damage: busted chairs, tables, and broken glasses. However, the most severe damage was probably to the ego of the bouncer dropped by a school-boy uniform-wearing Aussie who probably weighed 110 pounds soaking wet. The band wound up taking the ladies back to their hotel.

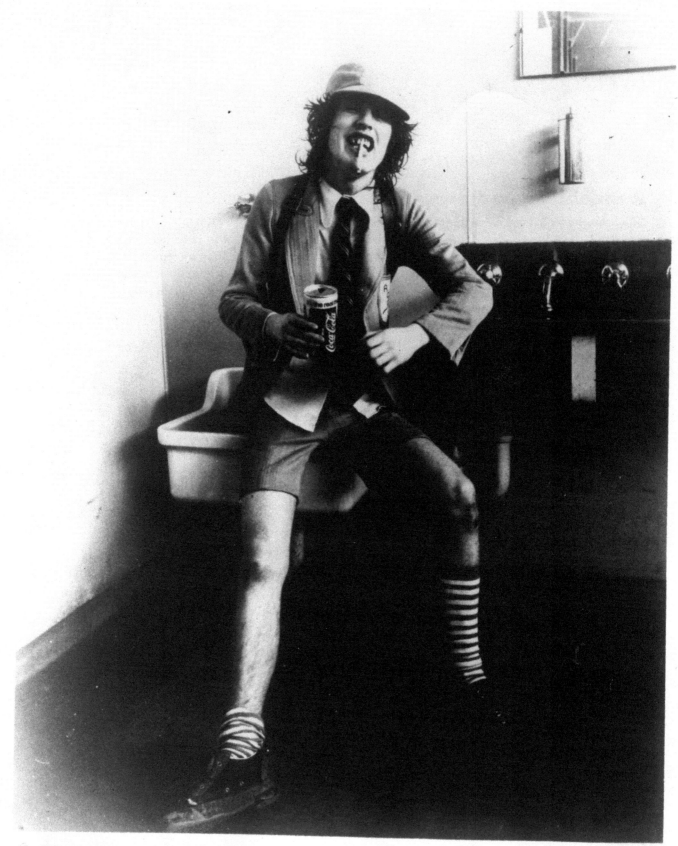

AC/DC

AMERICAN TALENT INTERNATIONAL LTD
888 SEVENTH AVENUE   (212) 977-2300
NEW YORK, N.Y. 10019

ATI

Concert August 9, 1977. Courtesy of Rich Frame.

Shortly after, Kaiser returned to Mississippi Nights with other bands. "I apologized to Steve [Duebelbeis]," Kaiser says about AC/DC. "He never held a grudge over that incident. He was a great guy, 100 percent classy and very easy to work with."

AC/DC was paid $400 for the gig. When they returned to St. Louis two years later, the band played Kiel Auditorium, moving on to a larger venue just like Duebelbeis and Duffy imagined bands should. Now, AC/DC is one of the most successful rock 'n' roll bands of all time, selling over 200 million albums worldwide.

Riverfront Times

Founded by Ray Hartmann in 1977, *Riverfront Times* is a free weekly newspaper in the St. Louis area, focusing on music, theater, arts, fashion, dining, and local politics.

Mississippi Nights was represented very well in the *Riverfront Times*. "We used to get the center spread outside right for the old bar ad that we ran," says Mississippi Nights manager, Tim Weber. "Ray Hartmann told me that we got [the prime space] because we were their first advertiser."

At one point, *Riverfront Times* would raise the advertising rates for Mississippi Nights. However, Rich Frame pointed out that many people picked up the *Riverfront Times* just to find out what was playing at Mississippi Nights. So the magazine agreed to keep the old rate.

Years later, *Riverfront Times* again informed Mississippi Nights that they were raising the advertising rates. Tim Weber thought the club didn't need the *Riverfront Times*, and they should pull their business. He came up with a plan to check his theory: Weber had the box office ask everyone that came in to buy tickets where they had heard about the show. As it turned out, about 92 percent of the people said, "the *Riverfront Times*." Weber promptly told Frame that they needed more money to pay the *Riverfront Times*.

The *RFT* moved into the digital age with a website that updates daily with blogs and photo galleries, and they still release print issues. Many newspapers, magazines, and fanzines have come and gone; *Riverfront Times* is still going strong.

Concert March 11, 1977. Courtesy of Tom Duffy.

FULL MOON CONSORT

Dwight Twilley, November 2, 1977.
Photo by Tom Duffy.

Concert June 23, 1977. Courtesy of Greg Bishop.

MORNINGSTAR

Sonny Terry & Brownie McGhee

apa
AGENCY FOR THE PERFORMING ARTS, INC.
New York   Chicago   Beverly Hills   Miami   San Juan

Concert November 9, 1977. Courtesy of Tom Duffy.

Concert November 12, 1977. Courtesy of Tom Duffy.

BRIAN AUGER

WARNER/REPRISE

Concert March 22, 1977. Courtesy of Tom Duffy.

Wolfgang
BILL GRAHAM MANAGEMENT
201 Eleventh Street San Francisco CA 94103
(415) 864-0815

23

JAN HAMMER

TONY SMITH   STEVE KINDLER   FERNANDO SAUNDERS

JAN HAMMER GROUP

Concert September 7, 1977. Courtesy of Tom Duffy.

A LOGO IS BORN

The club was open for a few months when Duebelbeis decided it needed a logo. He hired a hippie who hung around the club to create the logo. The club traded a wrought-iron elevator gate for the logo artwork. Sadly, the original drawings have disappeared.

MISSISSIPPI NIGHTS

24

1978

The Bad Habits of Michael Stipe

In 1977, the short-lived band Bad Habits formed in Illinois with guitarist Joe Haynes, future R.E.M. frontman Michael Stipe, bassist Buddy Weber, and drummer Jim Warchol. According to Warchol's records, the band played four gigs: August 21, 1978, at the Jefferson Barracks Annex; October 27, 1978, at the Collinsville Vandalia Gym; November 8, 1978, at the Madison Illinois Recreation Center; and November 13, 1978, at Mississippi Nights, opening for Rockpile featuring Dave Edmunds and Nick Lowe.

"Around the beginning of November 1978, Joe, guitarist extraordinaire, songwriter, founder of Bad Habits, announced to the band that somehow he managed to get us a gig at Mississippi Nights," says Warchol. "We were all excited. There was some trepidation about how Mike would perform, as he was very shy. But he did great! His shyness kept him from speaking much, if at all, between songs," Warchol remembers. "Somehow, we managed to screw up the sequence of the song list, and I played some songs fast, but otherwise, it went well. The crowd seemed to enjoy themselves."

Joe Haynes, Michael Stipe, Jim Warchol, and
Buddy Weber of Bad Habits, November 13, 1978.   Photo by John Korst.

25

Dave Edmunds and Nick Lowe of Rockpile, November 13, 1978.
Photo by John Korst.

In May 1977, not long after Stipe graduated from Collinsville High School, his family moved to Georgia. Near the end of 1978, Stipe decided to join his family in Georgia. That was the end of Bad Habits.

Haynes and Warchol joined another band for a couple of years. Warchol says, "It was during this time that Joe was still in contact with Mike. So, he would update me on Mike's new band, called "R.E.M.""

"Strange name, I thought," Warchol says, "Joe would say things like, 'Mike's band is starting to play shows around the south,' 'R.E.M. was recently named best new band in New York,' and 'R.E.M. has recorded an EP, and it's getting airplay on college radio.' Then, it snowballed — R.E.M. on Letterman, R.E.M. opening for The Police, and then, R.E.M. on the cover of *Rolling Stone* billed as *America's Best Rock and Roll Band*."

In 2019, Warchol formed a R.E.M. tribute band called Rabbit Ear Movement. "We were scheduled at Blueberry Hill [in St. Louis' University City Loop], opening for Miserable Now (The Smiths Tribute band)," remembers Warchol. "Our singer, and R.E.M. superfan, David Taylor, asked if we could do a Bad Habits reunion at that show." Guitarist Haynes agreed to play, and bassist Bill Dechand of Rabbit Ear Movement was set to fill in for Buddy Weber, who couldn't be located. Warchol contacted Stipe's assistant Amy through email, and she agreed to forward the Bad Habits Reunion invitation to the singer. "I made sure she knew we [the band members] would make $40 each that night," says Warchol. "In the end, Mike didn't show up. I guess he didn't need the $40."

Coal Kitchen

Rob Newhouse has been part of the Midwest music scene for over forty years. In 1972, the Chicago native joined the Spoon River Band on guitar, along with vocalist Connie Fairchild (Fairchild), Michael O'Hara (The Sheiks), and Dave Torretta (The Sheiks). Next, he founded Ace with Steve Scorfina (REO Speedwagon, Pavlov's Dog). Then, in 1976, he joined Andre Mossotti, Bobby Carlin, Carla Peyton, and Pauli Carman in Coal Kitchen. The band signed with Sony in 1977 and released *Thirsty or Not...Choose Your Flavor.*

Newhouse remembers playing all the hot spots around St. Louis in the 1970s and 1980s: River City Music Room, The 5th House, Muddy Waters, 4th and Pine, Bahama Cay, and Heartbreak Hotel. He even remembers performing at On the Rox. Between Coal Kitchen and his later band The Elvis Brothers, Newhouse played Mississippi Nights fifty times. He says, "Mississippi Nights was my favorite venue in St. Louis, in my favorite part of the city, with the best owners and the best crowds — great memories."

One Mississippi Nights show that sticks out in his memory was November 9, 1979, when Coal Kitchen opened for a new national act, Pat Benatar. Newhouse remembers saying, "I never heard of him." But, by the end of the evening, he was amazed by the up-and-coming female rocker Benatar and "especially dug Neil Giraldo on guitar."

Unbeknownst to the band, Coal Kitchen's song "Keep on Pushing" was sampled by Salt-N-Pepa on their Grammy-nominated song "Push It" in 1987. Many years later, Newhouse was browsing internet sites about song samples when he was surprised to see the name of his former band.

Beginning in 1981, Newhouse spent two decades playing in the legendary Elvis Brothers. (See the 1985 section for story). He currently plays with The Charming Axe.

1978 shirt courtesy of Pam Wheatley.
Photo by Matt Albers. Model Merril Barden.

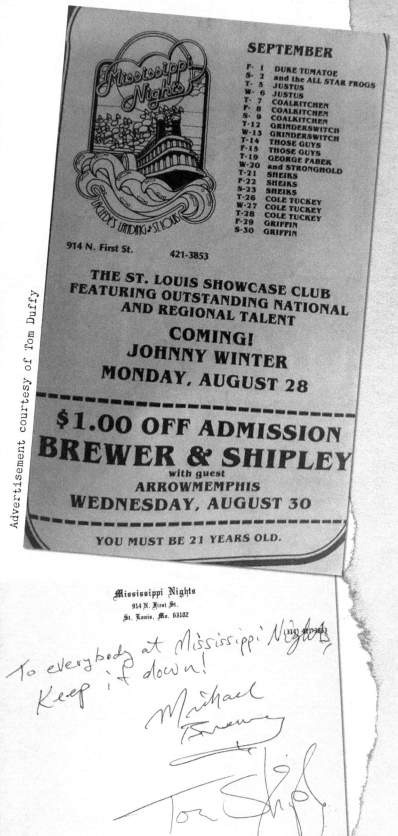

SEPTEMBER

F- 1	DUKE TUMATOE and the ALL STAR FROGS
S- 2	JUSTUS
T- 5	JUSTUS
W- 6	JUSTUS
T- 7	COALKITCHEN
F- 8	COALKITCHEN
S- 9	COALKITCHEN
T-12	GRINDERSWITCH
W-13	GRINDERSWITCH
T-14	THOSE GUYS
F-15	THOSE GUYS
T-19	GEORGE FABEK and STRONGHOLD
W-20	SHEIKS
T-21	SHEIKS
F-22	SHEIKS
S-23	SHEIKS
T-26	COLE TUCKEY
W-27	COLE TUCKEY
T-28	COLE TUCKEY
F-29	GRIFFIN
S-30	GRIFFIN

914 N. First St.   421-3853

**THE ST. LOUIS SHOWCASE CLUB
FEATURING OUTSTANDING NATIONAL
AND REGIONAL TALENT
COMING!
JOHNNY WINTER
MONDAY, AUGUST 28**

**$1.00 OFF ADMISSION
BREWER & SHIPLEY**
with guest
**ARROWMEMPHIS
WEDNESDAY, AUGUST 30**

YOU MUST BE 21 YEARS OLD.

Mississippi Nights
914 N. First St.
St. Louis, Mo. 63102
(314) 421-3853

To everybody at Mississippi Nights
Keep it down!

Michael Brewer

Tom Shipley

MICHAEL SEIBERT* REMEMBERS...

In 1978, Heart and Queen played back-to-back nights at the Checkerdome [known as The Arena after 1983]. Queen performed on Thanksgiving night. I was only 15 at the time. My friend and I decided to find out where the bands were staying. We found a limo driver who gave us a lead, and we ended up at a hotel downtown. They were not there, but another driver told us that the bands were partying at Mississippi Nights. Being minors, we couldn't get in the club, so we cased the place, noticing a bunch of limos parked behind the venue.

After standing outside for around half an hour, Heart came down the back stairs. They were incredibly gracious, and we had a nice chat with them. Then, to my surprise, Brian May of Queen came down. I approached him and asked for his autograph. I still remember him saying, "Certainly," in his British accent. Then, Freddie Mercury came down the stairs. Unfortunately, his bodyguards forced us to leave. I was amazed that only a couple of fans were waiting for the bands. It was well worth getting grounded for a couple of weeks! [November 23, 1978]

*Mississippi Nights patron

11-23-78

Heart and Queen visit Mississippi Nights, November 23, 1978.
Courtesy of Tom Duffy.

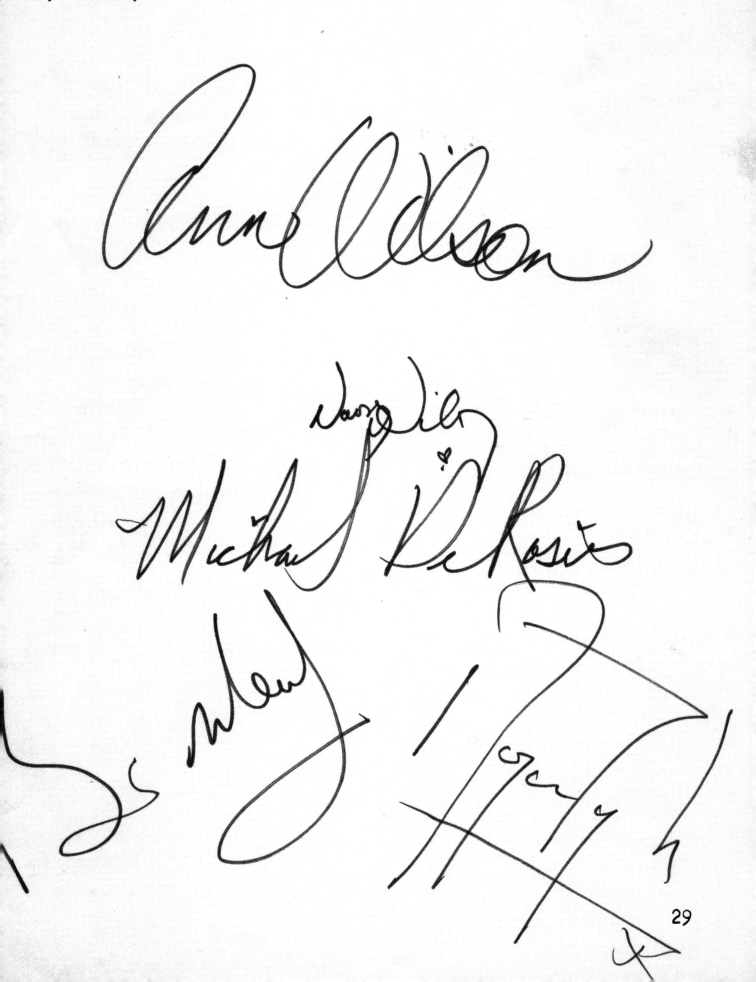

29

Griffin, October 27, 1978
Photo by Greg Bishop

Rockin' on the River
at Mississippi Nights

The following is the August schedule of performances at Mississippi Nights, in Laclede's Landing, 914 N. First St. August 1 & 2: Grinderswitch; August 3, 4 & 5: Griffin; August 8, 9 and 10: Cole Tuckey; August 11 & 12: George; August 15: Snail & Zazz; August 16: Buck Acre/Arrow Memphis: August 17, 18 & 19: St. Louis Sheiks; August 22: From This Moment On; August 23: Charlie Musselwhite/F.T.M.O.; August 24: From This Moment On; August 25 & 26: Those Guys; August 28: An Evening with Johnny Winter; August 29: Griffin; August 30: Brewer & Shipley; August 31: Duke Tomatoe & the All-Star Frogs.

This calendar is as accurate as possible at the time of printing. For an update, please call 421-3853. On Tuesdays and Wednesdays there is no cover charge, except for special attractions. On Thursdays there is no charge for women.

Courtesy of Tom Duffy.

BONNIE BRAMLETT

PERSONAL MANAGEMENT BY:
Barnett Enterprises
24149 Califa Street
Woodland Hills, CA. 91367
(213) 999-1430

variety artists international, inc.
4120 Excelsior Boulevard
Minneapolis, Minnesota 55416
612/925-3440 - Telex 29-0755

Bonnie Bramlett Concert April 19, 1978.
Courtesy of Tom Duffy.

11-1-78

JLH
JOHN Lee HOOKer

Papa John Creach, March 15, 1978.
Photo by Tom Duffy.

30

9/13/78
TO MISSISSIPPI
THANK YOU FOR A
GREAT EVENING.
"GYPSY"

Courtesy of Tom Duffy.

Bobby (T.) Torello
Johnny Winter
Jon Paris
PREMIER TALENT

Johnny Winter Concert July 28, 1978.
Courtesy of Tom Duffy.

This Week in St. Louis

SEPTEMBER 23 - 29, 1978

Bluegrass, jazz or swing, Cole Tuckey can do it all and will be performing September 26, 27 and 28 at St. Louis' hottest night spot, Mississippi Nights, located in Laclede's Landing at 914 N. First St., downtown. 421-3853.

To MISSISSIPPI Nights...
Don't forget to
Boogie
THANK Gregg Allman

To Tom, Steve, & all our friends at Mississippi Nights

The Ozarks

Supe du Jour

Autographs courtesy of Tom Duffy.   **31**

Player Concert November 29, 1978. Courtesy of Tom Duffy.

Oh! these mississippi nights!!

PETER BECKETT   RONN MOSS   J.C. CROWLEY   JOHN FRIESEN

Player

RSO Records, Inc.

Lenny White Concert November 14, 1978. Courtesy of Tom Duffy.

TO
TOM
AND THE
MISSISSIPPI NIGHTS
PEOPLE
THANX
AND
GOODLUCK

LENNY WHITE

32

The first known appearance of the Mississippi Nights logo (*Key Magazine*), March 10, 1978. Courtesy of Tom Duffy.

Mississippi Nights

See Page 6 for

LIVE ENTERTAINMENT
Weekend cover $2; Tue., Wed. no cover
Thurs. - Ladies Night
IN LACLEDE'S LANDING
914-16 N. First St.   421-3853

1979

Game of Musical Venues Leads to Lawsuit

Concerts don't always come off as planned. Sometimes bands don't show up, and occasionally, shows are moved to larger or smaller venues to accommodate a change in the band's current popularity. Mississippi Nights saw its share of cancellations and changes throughout the years. Scheduling changes at The Chase Park Plaza Hotel caused the Oingo Boingo show, slated for the hotel's Khorassan Ballroom, to be moved to Mississippi Nights at the last minute in 1989. Motorhead and Angelic Upstarts canceled for visa reasons. Oasis canceled because the Gallagher brothers had a fight and nixed the entire tour. Ziggy Marley, Nuclear Assault, and Sir Mix-a-Lot were also called off for various reasons.

Every rescheduled event results in some disappointed fans, but only one rescheduled event involving Mississippi Nights resulted in a lawsuit. On April 21, 1979, British glam band Roxy Music was scheduled to play at Kiel Opera House, a 3,000-seat theater on Market Street in downtown St. Louis. Although the band had been together since 1972, they had yet to catch on with American audiences, and poor ticket sales caused Contemporary Productions to move the show to Mississippi Nights. The Atlantics opened for Roxy Music, and by all accounts, the show was successful for the club.

Bryan Ferry of Roxy Music, April 12, 1979. Photo by Debby Mikles.

But back in 1979, St. Louis liquor laws prohibited anyone under 21 from entering Mississippi Nights. This created a problem when Roxy Music moved to Mississippi Nights because minors could not attend. However, refunds were issued for anyone under the age of 21.

On June 3, 1979, the *St. Louis Post Dispatch* reported that the father of 19-year-old Jean Donnelly, who had bought a ticket to see Roxy Music at the Kiel Opera House, sent a letter of intent to sue Contemporary Productions. The night of the concert, Jean Donnelley took the bus to Mississippi Nights to see the show and was turned away at the door for being underage. She was refunded $7.50 for the ticket, but to her father's horror, she was not refunded the 50¢ service charge or the 50¢ bus fare to and from the venue. As a result, John Donnelly Esq. asked for one dollar in actual damages and $4,999 in punitive damages.

Contemporary responded to the letter by pointing out that Miss Donnelly could have returned the ticket through the mail, saving the bus fare. So, they offered to settle the matter out of court for 80¢. John Donnelly says, "I'd had enough. Here we are trying to teach our kids morality, and they see big business can do anything it wants to them. My view is that Jean entered into a contract with Contemporary Productions when she bought her ticket, and by moving the concert, they broke their part of the contract."

The matter was either settled out of court or dropped entirely.

Calling All Sheik Freaks

Michael J. O'Hara performed at Mississippi Nights more than fifty-seven times with his band, The Sheiks, and even played the predecessor club at the same location, On the Rox.

The Sheiks had amazing energy — rock 'n' roll with hints of funk. Their large following of dedicated fans in St. Louis was known as the Sheik Freaks.

O'Hara's interest in music started at an early age. His father was a minister, and O'Hara began performing in his Baptist Church. He wrote his first song at age six on his parents' piano.

O'Hara joined David Torretta in the Spoon River Band in 1972. In 1974, following some lineup changes, they decided they needed a new moniker.

"[Drummer] Rob Sanders came up with The Sheiks as a name...and that I wear the headgear of a sheik like Rudolf Valentino from the 1920s movies," O'Hara says. The new style not only helped brand The Sheiks, but it also solved O'Hara's problem of his sweat causing his afro to fall into his eyes while performing.

The Sheiks: Rob Sanders, Michael J. O'Hara, Nick Ferber, and Mary Dunard. Courtesy of Tom Duffy.

The Sheiks played all around St. Louis in the 1970s and the early 1980s. The band relocated to New Orleans in 1979, coming back to St. Louis on occasion for a week of shows at various venues, including Mississippi Nights.

On March 16, 1979, The Sheiks played with an unknown British band with no following in St. Louis. The Police were touring for their second album, *Reggatta de Blanc,* when they opened for The Sheiks at Mississippi Nights. Most Sheiks Freaks arrived late to their shows, missing the opening band. Thus, only twenty-five people were early enough that night to see The Police in their first performance in St. Louis.

David Johansen Concert, November 19, 1979. Photo by John Korst.

Wade Brooks with Randy Hanson of Tribute to Jimi Hendirx under the original Mississippi Nights awning (below) and performing (right), August 4, 1979. Photos by Tracey Rayfield.

34

STEVE PICK REMEMBERS...

Jet Lag[a] was born because of a Ramones concert at Mississippi Nights in late 1979. Through a series of improbable events, I wound up interviewing the band before that show. Then, John "The Mailman" Korst took one spectacular photo of the Ramones. Like peanut butter and chocolate coming together, the interview and photo forced us to start a magazine.

We figured we'd cover all the local punk and new wave bands we liked and all the amazing records and touring bands happening at the time. With help from a few others -- most notably Tony Renner, Tony Patti, Cat Pick, Joe Williams, and Toby Weiss -- *Jet Lag* soldiered on for ten years.

The first issue came out in February 1980. Duwan Dunn drew the artwork for the cover in the car on the way to the printer. The last issue, published in 1990, was a full-sized tabloid newsprint with lots of photos, ads, and articles. In between, *Jet Lag* included articles, opinions, and interviews about the music our contributors loved, primarily rock 'n' roll, but also jazz, R&B, some hip-hop, some country, and lots of punk.

Jet Lag was a labor of love. Nobody got paid, and all the ads were sold simply to raise enough money to print the next issue. And heck, it put me on the tour bus with The Go-Gos, who threatened to tie me and my friends up and kidnap us to Chicago! Alas, we didn't go.

(a) Jet Lag *was published by Steve Pick and John "The Mailman"* Korst *from 1980 to 1991. By early 1982,* Jet Lag *was published monthly by Mailman Products of St. Louis.* Jet Lag *included local band and concert reviews, book and record reviews, advertising, and a calendar of local concerts.*

Ramones, November 26, 1979 Photos by John Korst.

Courtesy of Jim Agnew.

The Retros, November 26, 1979 Photo by John Korst.

35

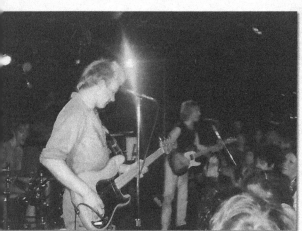

The Police, March 16, 1979.
Photos by Debby Mikles.

Sting

Stewart Copeland

Local legend claims that Sting was observed outside the club before their gig, trying to lure people inside. After their set, the band decided to check out The Sheiks. They sat to the right side of the stage behind a pony wall. As he often did during performances, O'Hara hopped off the stage to that pony wall. Sting was so impressed with O'Hara's performance that he allowed his enthusiasm to get the better of him and grabbed at O'Hara's legs. When Sting didn't listen to O'Hara's pleas to let go, O'Hara tried wiggling free, accidentally kicking Sting in the neck.

Fast forward to mid-January 1991. Monica Reed, Sting's background vocalist, invited O'Hara to sing backing vocals for Sting on *Saturday Night Live*. O'Hara worried Sting might recognize him and remember the kick from a decade earlier. During the first song of the rehearsal, Sting kept looking back at O'Hara. After the song, Sting told the audience about the incident at Mississippi Nights, pointing at O'Hara. Later, Sting asked O'Hara why he had kicked him, and O'Hara explained the situation. They both apologized.

In the mid-1980s, O'Hara realized that he needed to quit the sex and drugs of the rock 'n' roll lifestyle before it killed him. So he quit cold turkey and has been clean since 1988. Today, as a minister, he uses his story to help people with addiction.

These days, he's still rocking 'n' rolling. O'Hara performs as The Sheiks regularly in Louisiana, although he is the only original member, and road trips to play in St. Louis every few years.

Mississippi Nights

Thurs. Mar. 1	Domino		Sat. Mar. 17	St. Louis Sheiks
Fri. Mar. 2	Domino		Sun. Mar. 18	
Sat. Mar. 3	Domino		Mon. Mar. 19	
Sun. Mar. 4			Tues. Mar. 20	John Mayall /Street Corner Symphony
Mon. Mar. 5			Weds. Mar. 21	Sonny Terry & Brownie McGhee
Tues. Mar. 6	Cole Tuckey		Thurs. Mar. 22	Nite Life
Weds. Mar. 7	Cole Tuckey		Fri. Mar. 23	Nite Life
Thurs. Mar. 8	Cole Tuckey		Sat. Mar. 24	Nite Life
Fri. Mar. 9	Cole Tuckey		Sun. Mar. 25	
Sat. Mar. 10	Cole Tuckey		Mon. Mar. 26	James Walsh Gypsy Band
Sun. Mar. 11			Tues. Mar. 27	To Be Announced
Mon. Mar. 12			Weds. Mar. 28	Tantrum
Tues. Mar. 13	Poco/Fast Break		Thurs. Mar. 29	Boom Town Rats/Griffin
Weds. Mar. 14	Poco/Fast Break		Fri. Mar. 30	Griffin
Thurs. Mar. 15	Good Rats/St. Louis Sheiks		Sat. Mar. 31	Griffin
Fri. Mar. 16	Police/St. Louis Sheiks			

In Laclede's Landing
914 N. First St.

For More Information
421-3853

On Tuesdays and Wednesdays there is no cover charge, except for special attractions. On Thursdays there is no charge for women.

This calendar is as accurate as possible at the time of printing. For an accurate update, please call 421-3853.

Mississippi Nights advertisment. Courtesy of Dennis McCarthy.

Bob Geldof and
Garry Roberts of
Boomtown Rats,
Mach 29, 1979.
Photo by
Debby Mikles.

Bugs Henderson,
Oct. 5, 1979.
Photo by
Tracey Rayfield.

GAS SHORTAGE = REVENUE SHORTAGE

The summer of 1979 ushered in a 12-month gas shortage due to decreased oil output in the wake of the Iranian Revolution. With skyrocketing gasoline prices and rationing in some states, few bands toured. So, Mississippi Nights no longer attracted showcases. Local bands filled the gaps, but advertising costs and other expenses piled up for Mississippi Nights.

The Records,
Sept. 25, 1979.
Photo by John Korst.

jazz came calling on Laclede's
ding Thursday night. Yes, it was just
typical Thursday night when you
d walk up old First Street and hear
bie Hancock.

Herbie Hancock?

Yes, jazz luminary and keyboard
z kid Herbie Hancock brought his
d of all-stars and played a club on
waterfront. Actually, it wasn't any
club, it was Mississippi Nights, a
b that is rapidly becoming one of the
st showcase clubs for national acts
he country.

Hancock's band was chock full o
sicians who are recording stars
ir own right. There was Benn
upin on reeds and percussi
phonse Mouzon on drums and Webst
wis on keyboards. Rounding out the
e-up were Paul Jackson on bass and
y Obiedo on guitar.

When they all played at full crank,

Mississippi Nights
914 N. First St.
St. Louis, Mo. 63102

(314) 421-3853

To Mississippi Nights,
Thank you for a
great time,
Herbie
Hancock

of two shows the
monumental and entirely
man had more rhythm in his hands and
foot than a thousand Ginger Bakers a-

ELVIN BISHOP

Elvin Bishop concert Feb. 6,
1979. Herbie Hancock concert
March 29, 1979. Autographs
courtesy of Tom Duffy.

37

Goodbye Steve and Tom. Hello Rich.

In 1979, Rich Frame was a contractor and real estate investor remodeling a club at 724 North 1st Street on Laclede's Landing called Muddy Waters. An acquaintance of Frame's, an accountant who worked with Mississippi Nights, told him that Steve Duebelbeis and Tom Duffy were ready to sell Mississippi Nights and suggested he buy it. Rich Frame admits that he wasn't interested in owning a bar, but he thought it was a good investment. So in December 1979, Rich Frame bought Mississippi Nights. The original owners of Mississippi Nights stayed involved in the St. Louis entertainment scene: Duebelbeis opened Bingham's restaurant at 900 North 1st Street in 1981, and Tom Duffy went into the corporate restaurant business.

Frame closed on the property on December 20, 1979. Before selling the bar, the original owners had promised the waitresses a raise which Frame wasn't willing to give. "The first night I took ownership, the waitresses all quit." Eventually, most of them returned, many of the waitresses becoming good friends with Frame.

Tom Duffy in Mississippi Nights office in 1979. Photo published in the *South Side Journal*.

1980

the group that played at Spanky's is now "Our Gang"

the **NEW** Mississippi Nights presents

ZANE GREY

Starting Feb. 29 (Tues.-Sat. 9-1 p.m.)

- No Cover Charge
- More Seating
- More Footstompin'

we're lookin' for people who 'give a hoot...and a holler!

New Owner and New Business Model

For about six months, the club continued as a rock bar. In 1979, the country was knee-deep in the *Urban Cowboy* movement. A big country music fan, Frame decided to follow the honky-tonk trend and converted Mississippi Nights into a country music bar. Wooden spool tables, horse wallpaper, and a riding bull provided the country-western feel. Zane Grey, the house band, provided the country-western sound.

Frame made another change contrary to how most clubs ran in those days: he collected a cover charge for house bands like Zane Grey and Arrow Memphis. The move was risky for the club, but it worked.

According to Frame, during those two years as a honky-tonk bar, Mississippi Nights was second only to Busch Stadium in draft beer sales in St. Louis. And where there's beer, there're fights. Art Dwyer of The Soulard Blues Band remembers, "When they went through their cowboy phase and had the bull in there, it was fist fight city. I wouldn't go in there." More fights broke out at Mississippi Nights during the country music years than later.

Fidelipac cartridge used for radio broadcasts. From the collection of the St. Louis Classic Rock Preservation Society. Photo by Garrett Enloe.

Mary Fowler and Rich Frame. Photo by Andy Mayberry.

MARY FOWLER FRAME REMEMBERS...

After my first couple nights as a waitress at Mississippi Nights, they told us not to let anyone except employees in the waitress station. One evening, a man started coming up, and I said, "I'm sorry, sir. You can't come up here." He turned around and walked away.

Then, one of the waitresses said, "Do you know what you just did?"

I said, "No."

She said, "You kicked the owner out of the waitress station."

I thought, "Oh, no! There goes my job."

[The two started dating in 1982 and were married in 1995.]

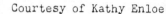

Courtesy of Kathy Enloe

From the collection of Garrett Enloe.

ROB HILL* REMEMBERS...

I went to a lot of concerts in the '70s into the early '80s. They were at the Mississippi River Festival, the Kiel, the Arena, and everywhere in between, but some of the most memorable were the shows at Mississippi Nights. One that stands out was The Homegrown Harvest Band. I worked at the hospital in Granite City with the bass player, Dave Jones (R.I.P.). He was a bass player at heart but could play a guitar "like a ringin' a bell." So they let Dave cut loose with some heavy blues on his Gibson Marauder at the end of the show.

*Mississippi Nights patron

40

1981

Crystal Craig riding the bull.
Courtesy of Crystal Craig.

Arrow Memphis

In 1976, Steve Williams (vocals, keys), Glen Harris (guitar), Bob Jones (bass) left the band Woodrose and started the country-rock band Arrow Memphis. They added Denny Knott (fiddle), Terry Petty (steel guitar), and Gary "Stix" Maxwell (drums) to complete the band.

Arrow Memphis played covers by bands such as Allman Brothers, The Band, Jackson Browne, and Loggins and Messina, as well as original songs. "Not a lot of people wanted to hear that stuff back then," notes Steve Williams. "We just played what we wanted." For example, he says, "We'd play a song off a record that wasn't very popular. It wasn't the hit..."

Petty quit the band, and Charlie Morris stepped in on guitar before releasing their self-titled record in 1980.

In 1981, the music scene caught up with Arrow Memphis' style. "When the *Urban Cowboy* scene caught on, all of a sudden we were asked to be the house band at Mississippi Nights," Williams says. By this time, guitarist Bill Engel had replaced Morris.

Artwork from the back of 1981 shirt. From the collection of Crystal Craig.

"[Mississippi Nights] had that electronic bull in the corner," remembers Williams. "I'd be playing a song, and all of a sudden, I'd hear someone kicking the side of the bull — boom, boom, boom. It sounded just like the kick drum. So you had to be careful not to follow the beat of the bull and pay attention to what the drummer was doing." Besides causing rhythm difficulties, it's a safe bet that many bands had to compete with that mechanical bull for the crowd's attention.

Arrow Memphis also opened shows at Mississippi Nights for national acts like Rodney Crowell, Leon Russell, Rosanne Cash, and Tanya Tucker.

1981 Mississippi Nights shirt from the collection of Crystal Craig. Model Ruth Guerri.

Concert August 1, 1981.
Courtesy of Rich Frame.

41

All-Woman Rock Band Lures Gawker

By Dick Richmond
Of the Post-Dispatch Staff

...tion to the number of men in rock music,
...just a few females. An all-woman band like
...o's is a novelty. Consequently, for the
...nitial St. Louis appearance in a concert at
... Nights on Wednesday evening, the place
...d with gawking people. Everyone was on
... or the show just to see what they'd do.
...g that way, people really don't get to see
... These girls are fairly tiny and with lots of
...front, it made it tough on those at the rear.
... women, who range in age from 22 to 27,
...ve in a rock-music sort of way. It was
...orth all the rubbernecking that was going

review/rock

result, no one knew whether they were good.
The women played mostly hard-rock mate...

...on.
Belin...

The...
Caffe...
Wied...

The...
row h...
drum...
could...
song...

...er the Go-...
The Run...
rs, all s...
f media a...
the same...

...ld make

oct. JET LAG #20
50¢
75¢
OUT OF
TOWN
Some people call this a rock 'n' roll magazine

OTWAY/BARRETT

THE GO-GO'S

Charlotte Caffey and
Belinda Carlisle
(right, above) and
Jane Wiedlin and
Gina Schock (right,
below) of The Go-Go's,
in concert on
September 16, 1981.
From *Jet Lag* magazine
published October 1981.

favorite positions of an all girl band

The bus exploded as all five Go-Go's shouted in unison, "Men who drink gin!"

At one point, the bus inched up a couple of feet and Jane announced, "We're taking you to Chicago." This seemed perfectly amenable to your three reporters, believe me.

After Jane then asked us our names and we politely revealed them, Belinda Carlisle, the dynamic singer with great stage pres-... ence, said, "Now we're going to tie you up and humiliate you!"

Once again the bus exploded as all persons aboard shouted in unison, "Yeah!!!"

Tony Patti voiced the question that was uppermost on many male fans minds all night: "What's your favorite position?"

Jane shouted, "On the kitchen table!!"

Belinda said, "Missionary position."

Kathy Valentine, the bass player, adopted a robotic monotone to say, "Rear entry for maximum stimulation."

Eventually, the Go-Go's noticed that John the Mailman really was a mailman. Gina really liked that. "What a great fucking job!" she said. "If this one ever fails, I'd like to be a mail lady and just walk around and deliver mail all day."

Jane said, "I want to be a short-order cook."

Gina added, "Or else I'd like to ride in a caboose for the rest of my life."

"I want to be a wife and a mother like I was meant to be."

"So why aren't you?" I asked.

« From the October
1981, issue of
Jet Lag magazine.
Belinda Carlisle on
cover (above, left).

CH1118L
G.A. GEN ADM ADULT
EVENT CODE SECTION ROW SEAT ADMISSION
$5.00 $6.00 .00
PRICE
G.A.
PP SECTION 2X
GEN ADM ROW SEAT
CTS1123
A111681

IN CONCERT
CANNED HEAT
SOMERVILLE-SCORFINA BAND
MISSISSIPPI NIGHTS
LACLEDE'S LANDING
WED NOV 18, 1981 11:00PM

Courtesy of Ed Seelig.

Riot concert February 21,
1981. Photo by Tim Hasenstab.

42

Don McLean concert December 15, 1981. Courtesy of Rich Frame.

DON McLEAN

HERBERT S. GART MANAGEMENT, INC.
101 West 57th Street, Suite 2A
New York, New York 10019
(212) 765-8160

THE RAINBOW COALITION

millennium
RECORDS
Manufactured and Distributed by RCA R...

1982

Pat Hagin. Photo by Rose Pinkas.

Enter Pat Hagin

Pat Hagin learned to tend bar down the street from Mississippi Nights at the Old Spaghetti Factory at 727 North 1st Street. Later, he worked in the basement of Brinkers Club in a venue called Orval Fingers. During his time at Orval Fingers, Hagin began booking bands. The first two he ever booked were Soulard Blues Band and Tommy Bankhead and His Blues Eldorados.

Hagin began working at Mississippi Nights in April 1980 as a bartender, eventually moving up to head bartender. Mississippi Nights was still a country bar at the time. In the fall of 1982, Hagin was promoted to manager. By the end of the year, the honky-tonk bar had run its course. This was a turning point for the venue. He says, "We started dabbling in concerts." The club began to shift away from the house band formula, as Hagin and Frame worked together to book more national acts. Mississippi Nights returned to Steve Duebelbeis' 1976 vision of showcasing a variety of genres of national and local shows.

RICKY NELSON

Ricky Nelson concert March 11, 1982. Courtesy of Rich Frame.

HISTORY COMES TO ST. LOUIS

FROM ENGLAND!

THE PROFESSIONALS

FEATURING

EX- Sex PISTOLS

STEVE JONES & PAUL COOK

THUR. MAY 20

MISSISSIPPI NIGHTS

DOORS OPEN 8:00 $4.00 AT THE DOOR

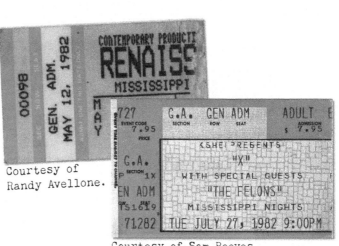

Courtesy of Randy Avellone.

CONTEMPORARY PRODUCTI
RENAISS
MISSISSIPPI

GEN. ADM. MAY 12, 1982

KSHE PRESENTS
"X"
WITH SPECIAL GUESTS
"THE FELONS"
MISSISSIPPI NIGHTS
TUE JULY 27, 1982 9:00PM

Courtesy of Sam Reeves.

43

Mississippi Nights exterior.
Photo by Andy Mayberry.

Mississippi Nights staff shirt courtesy
of Andy Mayberry. Model Merril Barden.

Chubby Checker concert March 15, 1982. Courtesy of Rich Frame.

Courtesy of Wendy Fitzgerald.

Smutty Smiff of The Rockats,
October 5, 1982. Photo by
Debby Mikles.

CHUBBY CHECKER

Personal Management
Tony DeLauro
212-757-7374

44

KSHE·95 WELCOMES
LIVE IN CONCERT!

JOHNNY WINTER

DECEMBER 20th — 9:00 P.M.
MISSISSIPPI NIGHTS

914 N. 1st STREET — "ON THE LANDING"
TICKETS ON SALE NOW! $8.50
NO AGE RESTRICTIONS!

Tickets available at Backstage Records, Spectrum, Co-op Records, Record Works, Music Vision — River Roads, Knight Amusement, West End Wax, Mississippi Nights Box Office or DIALTIX — 644-1700.

A Contemporary Production

FM 106 KWK AM 13.8
WELCOMES
IN CONCERT
For a Rare St. Louis Performance
At Mississippi Nights

JOE COCKER

Plus Special Guest

THURSDAY, JULY 8th
DOORS OPEN AT 8:00 P.M.

Tickets available at Backstage Records, Spectrum, Ye Olde Record Shoppe, Co-Op Records — Granite City, Record Works — Belleville, Mississippi Nights Box Office or tickets by phone by calling DIALTIX at 644-1700 or call 421-3853.

ADULT
ADMISSION
8.50

JW1220
EVENT CODE
$ 8.50
PRICE

SECTION
OVER   21

CONTEMPORARY PRODUCTIONS

JOHNNY WINTER
***

G.A.
SECTION

GEN ADM
ROW   SEAT
CTS1525

MISSISSIPPI NIGHTS
914 N. FIRST ST.
MON DEC 20, 1982 9:00PM

PP   2X

A12 682

Mississippi Nights exterior.
Photo by Andy Mayberry.

Mississippi Nights —
thanks for spreading the news!!

HUEY LEWIS AND THE NEWS

Chrysalis

45

TONY PATTI* REMEMBERS...

The Dead Kennedys show, 1982... Along the south wall in the back, the kiddie corral faced the stage. There was a railing holding in the teeming hordes of youth, including many belligerent bullies longing for a mosh pit. When the music started, a large, adolescent male with hob-nailed soles on his perfect, punk rock boots jumped into the air off the railing and landed directly on top of my head with both feet, crushing me to the ground. He hurt quite a few people with that stunt.

Sometime afterward, I sat outside the back door with Jello Biafra [lead singer of The Dead Kennedys] drinking a beer, as he offered his sympathy, and we looked in disbelief at the crazy crowd of new punks trying to kill each other in the pit. "The mosh pits in San Francisco are much more civilized," I complained. He agreed. [August 4, 1982]

*Mississippi Nights patron

Courtesy of Todd Aadmire.

DEAD KENNEDYS

MISS. NITE
AUG. 4 9PM
with
RUDE PETS &
AVON LADIES
tix at: vintage vinyl
west end wax

St. Louis Post-Dispatch, Sunday July 25, 1982.

KSHE-95 PRESENTS IN CONCERT
Los Angeles' Finest "X"
with "RED ROCKERS" & "FELONS"
TUESDAY, JULY 23 AT 9 P.M.
AT MISSISSIPPI NIGHTS (914 N. 1st St. on Riverfront)
TICKETS AVAILABLE AT MISSISSIPPI NIGHTS,
KSHE RADIO, ORANGE JULIUS, SPECTRUM
DON'T MISS IT! BE A PART OF THE
MOST VISUALLY EXCITING SHOW YOU'LL SEE
KCFV WELCOMES
"DEAD KENNEDYS"
WITH RUDE PETS & AVON LADIES
WEDNESDAY, AUG. 4 AT 9 P.M.
— at —
MISSISSIPPI NIGHTS (914 N. 1st St. on Riverfront)
CALL 421-3853 FOR INFO

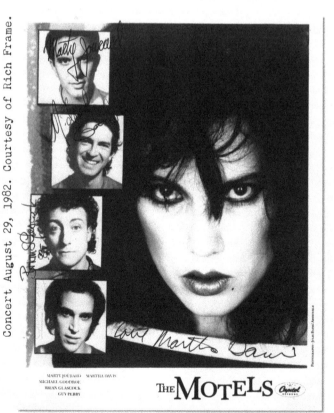

Concert August 29, 1982. Courtesy of Rich Frame.

MARTY JOURARD MARTHA DAVIS
MICHAEL GOODROE
BRIAN GLASCOCK
GUY PERRY

THE MOTELS

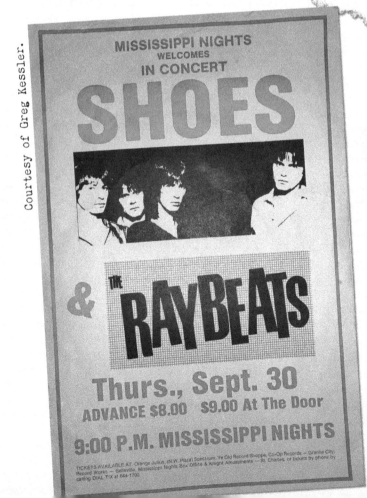

Courtesy of Greg Kessler.

MISSISSIPPI NIGHTS
WELCOMES
IN CONCERT
SHOES
& THE
RAYBEATS
Thurs., Sept. 30
ADVANCE $8.00 $9.00 At The Door
9:00 P.M. MISSISSIPPI NIGHTS
TICKETS AVAILABLE AT: Orange Julius (N.W. Plaza) Spectrum, Ye Old Record Shoppe, Co-Op Records — Granite City; Record Works — Belleville, Mississippi Nights Box Office & Knight Amusements — St. Charles, or tickets by phone by calling DIAL TIX at 644-1700.

1983

Pat Lacey. Photo by Andy Mayberry.

The Grandmother of Rock 'n' Roll

Pat Lacey's name is connected with Mississippi Nights more than anyone who worked there in the club's thirty-year history. She began her association with the club by taking her daughter Sarah and her friends to concerts at Mississippi Nights. On the night of the X show, October 24, 1983, while conversing with Rich Frame, he asked Lacey if she knew of anyone who would want an office job at the club. Frame knew she worked as a nurse, so he was surprised when she responded, "Yes, me!" With her husband laid off and their daughter Susan in college, Lacey needed another job to make ends meet.

Lacey admits she did a terrible job in her interview with Rich Frame. She kept reinforcing that she didn't have any experience and was uncertain she could do the job. However, with his knack for reading people, Frame had the confidence in Lacey that she lacked, and he hired her on the spot. Frame speaks of Lacey with reverence. "She did everything," he asserts. She juggled nursing and rock 'n' roll for four years before leaving her nursing job to dedicate her time to the club.

Lacey broke down her duties. "I wrote the checks, sold tickets, did the inventory and the ordering. I did the pouring costs, which was how much we spent on alcohol and whether we made a profit or not, and I did the same thing with shows. When Patrick [Hagin] left [in 1990], I stepped in and took on a lot more. I was doing everything that he did: doing the contracts, going to the bank, making sure the shows were advanced, so that we knew what time bands were coming in and what time they wanted to be fed, etc.," Lacey says. "I was the den mother there. I took care of the bands. A lot of them became my friends."

"Lacey had many jobs," says manager Tim Weber (1998-2007), "but arguably her most important job was to advance the shows." She organized hospitality events for bands and their crews, including solving problems

Courtesy of Sam Reeves.

MISSISSIPPI NIGHTS PRESENTS
X
ST. LOUIS, MO
24 1983 | MONDAY 8:00 PM MUST BE 21 YEARS
ADVANCE $7.00
DAY/SHO $8.00
GEN. ADM. 0431

MARK VONDRASEK* REMEMBERS...

I went to see X [a punk rock band] with my friend Liz in 1983. We were in the underage section, dancing and jumping to the music. About 35 minutes into X's set, part of the riser collapsed. Liz got the worst of it and fell through. An ambulance came and picked her up. She broke her arm. [Ken Krueger of the band Ferrari (and later, Big Fun) was there to see the show and went with Liz to the hospital that night.]

I remained at the concert and was invited to go on X's bus afterward. We were having a pleasant time when singer Exene Cervenka arrived and promptly told everybody to get off the bus. Interesting night indeed. [October 24, 1983]

*Mississippi Nights patron

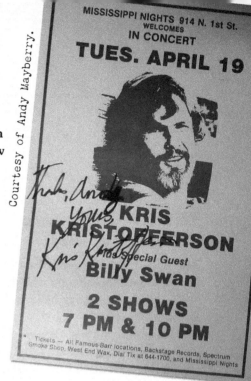

Courtesy of Andy Mayberry.

MISSISSIPPI NIGHTS 914 N. 1st St.
WELCOMES
IN CONCERT
TUES. APRIL 19

KRIS KRISTOFFERSON
Special Guest
Billy Swan

2 SHOWS
7 PM & 10 PM

Tickets — All Famous-Barr locations, Backstage Records, Spectrum Smoke Shop, West End Wax, Dial Tix at 644-1700, and Mississippi Nights

before they arrived. "She'd call up and say, 'Do you really need four gallons of hummus?' She was able to do it in the nicest possible way so that every band that showed up was in a good mood when they got there," Weber says. "If you screw that up, every band shows up in a shitty mood, and the days are wrecked. So, that tiny little thing of making the bands understand ahead of time that they were going to be cared for at least gave you a running shot to start every day pretty good." Lacey made the bands happy, everyone's job more manageable, and Mississippi Nights more successful.

"Absolutely nobody tops the legend that is Pat Lacey," proclaims Mississippi Nights patron Chuck McPherson. "She was the heart and soul of the club. [...] She always treated me and my friends like her children. She got to know us on a first-name basis and was supportive of us in our love for music."

Michael Hutchence of INXS, August 31, 1983. Photos by Laurie Richardson.

Patron Michelle Weber Rigden says, "Pat Lacey was my Concert Mom. She was so kind and nurturing, but I also knew she would take my ass out if I misbehaved as a minor."

Patron Wade Monnig says, "Pat Lacey was always amazing, always so nice and sweet. I'd always go see The Alarm at Mississippi Nights, not just because they were a great band [but] because Pat was so passionate about them. I wanted to support her!"

Lacey decided to retire the year she turned 65, thinking that's just what you do at age 65, and at the end of 2002, she did.

In May 2003, Lacey entered Mississippi Nights with a gift of strawberry shortcake for the staff. She quickly learned that her replacement was having problems managing the office. For example, he wrote checks out for every invoice without checking if they were already paid. Before long, Mississippi Nights had substantial credits with the vendors. Tim Weber asked Lacey to return, and she agreed to come back two days a week. After that, she didn't think of retiring from Mississippi Nights again and worked

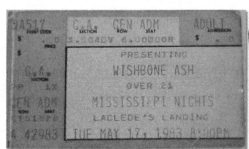

Courtesy of Lou Babinga.

Wishbone Ash, May 17, 1983.
Photo by Randy Avellone.

there through February 2007. "The Nights officially closed at the end of January, but I needed to clean out the office," she remembers.

At eighty-four-years-old in 2022, Lacey wishes she could still be working at her beloved Mississippi Nights.

"[Pat Lacey] was the grandmother of rock 'n' roll," says Tim Weber. "She cared more about more people and more bands than anybody I've ever met in my life." He adds, "I still get tour managers at the Old Rock House that remember Pat Lacey."

Steve Marriot, September 15, 1983.
Photo by John Neiman.

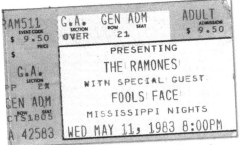
Courtesy of Stephanie VonDrasek.

EVENT OF 1983
Pat Benatar
HBO Video
Viewing,
November 2.

Wednesday
2
PAT BENETAR
VIDEO
HBO - ROCKBILL

TIM MULLEN* REMEMBERS...

[Stevie Ray Vaughan] wasn't a big show. It was in the old room before it was enlarged [more about the expansion in the 1988 section]. I think we only had about 90 people in the place. The [club] manager introduced me to the tour manager and said to go ahead and take care of the band at the bar that night. All 90 people stood there during the show with their mouths opened, astounded by Stevie. At the end of the night, he came to the bar and ordered a drink and started to get money out. I said, "No, that's okay. It's on us."

I went to wait on somebody else, and there's a $5 bill on the bar. One of my favorite memories is that Stevie Ray Vaughan tipped me $5, and that would be equivalent to at least a $10 tip now [2007].[a] [June 29, 1983]

Barback/bartender in 1977 and the bartender/head bartender from 1980 to 2007.

(a) Taken from an interview in unreleased film footage.

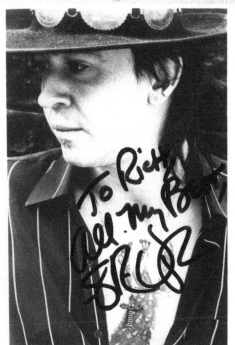
Photo Credit: Stephanie Chernikowski
Courtesy of Rich Frame.
STEVIE RAY VAUGHAN

49

Faustus

According to records, Faustus played Mississippi Nights many times in the club's early days — thirty-nine shows.

The band formed in 1974 and soon released a single with "Come on Down," with the B-side "Days of Swashbuckling" in 1978, an LP titled *Tonight at the Movies* in 1983, and another single in 1984 with "Hope You'll Never Find Another" with the B-side "Amnesia." Faustus broke up in 1985 but returned to Mississippi Nights for a reunion show in 1994.

Faustus Shirt courtesy of Andy Mayberry. Model [...]

Courtesy of Andy Mayberry.

Courtesy of Greg Kessler.

Courtesy of Andy Mayberry.

Courtesy of Robert Buescher.

Courtesy of Tracey Rayfield.

Concert 1983. Courtesy of Rich Frame.

George Duke and Stanley Clarke

Courtesy of Kathy Enloe.

50

Will Big Fun never cease?

Big Fun: The House Band That Packed the House

No band played Mississippi Nights more than Big Fun, performing over 400 times. Although their first show wasn't until 1985, the band members already had a long history with the club that stretched back to the 1970s and River Rat.

In 1974, future Big Fun guitarist Maurice Cooksey was playing with Asylum. Although the then-teenage Cooksey had already played gigs around town, Asylum's show at River Rat was his first time playing on Laclede's Landing. Asylum was one of the few local bands performing original music, challenging since most bars and clubs in St. Louis then only booked cover bands. River Rat was more open to bands playing original material. The cover charge was $1.

A few years later, Asylum relocated to Texas. In August of 1977, they played a show at Texas Electric Ballroom opening for Australian newcomers AC/DC.

Meanwhile, Ken Krueger booked concerts all over St. Louis with Continental Productions, a subsidiary of Contemporary Productions. One of his first bookings for Mississippi Nights was Meatloaf in 1977, and he also put Talking Heads on their calendar in 1979.

Asylum broke up in 1979 after the disappointment of being booked and subsequently dropped from an eight-date ZZ Top tour in favor of Point Blank from Irving, Texas. Cooksey returned to St. Louis and formed Ferrari with Ken Krueger (vocals), Gary Savage (guitar), and Scotty Valentine (drums).

Ken Krueger in Ferrari, October 12, 1984.
Photos by Patricia Fitzgerald.

BE AT MISSISSIPPI NIGHTS ON NEW YEARS EVE OR I'LL BLOW UP YOUR PLANET!

HE'S NOT KIDDING, FOLKS!
NEW YEAR'S EVE PARTY 1984
WITH FERRARI AT
MISSISSIPPI NIGHTS.

TICKETS $25.00 PER PERSON
INCLUDES OPEN BAR,
BUFFET DINNER, CHAMPAGNE
AND PARTY FAVORS.
BUY A TICKET AND
HELP SAVE OUR PLANET!
MISSISSIPPI NIGHTS   914 N. FIRST St.
LACLEDE'S LANDING   421-3853

Courtesy of
Kim McKinney.

For a few years, Ferrari dominated the St. Louis scene. They played Mississippi Nights eighty-eight times, sometimes for a week straight. Then, after five years and a couple of drummer changes, Ferrari was burnt out and split up in 1984.

Maurice Cooksey developed a friendship with Rich Frame, the owner of Mississippi Nights. Cooksey worked at Peaches Records on Hampton Avenue. Frame called him from time to time to ask about new bands he considered bringing to Mississippi Nights. Reaching out to local record stores was a common way Rich Frame and Pat Hagin researched bands before booking them. The Psychedelic Furs (April 5, 1983) is an example of a band that was booked thanks to Cooksey. The recommendation was excellent, considering the concert almost sold out.

Although he wasn't an official employee, Krueger made Mississippi Nights a second home. Sometimes, Krueger handled production, lighting, sound, and loading in and out for the venue.

In January 1985, shortly after Ferrari disbanded, Krueger formed Big Fun with Greg Moore (keyboard, guitar, sax), Jim Callahan (guitar and vocals), Stefan Ruprecht (bass), and Rob Hoover (drums and keyboard). When the band needed to replace their second guitarist, Liam Christie (aka Bill Christie), Krueger thought of Cooksey and asked him to join.

Krueger and Cooksey's relationship with Rich Frame paid off. Big Fun became Mississippi Nights' house band, playing the club 417 times and bringing in 1,000 to 1,500 people whenever they played. Krueger attributes the band's drawing power to their rule against playing any music aired on St. Louis commercial radio. "We sort of became a college radio station for a lot of people," he explains.

Big Fun released two albums: *Big Fun* in 1987 and *Well Well Well* in 1989. They had many member changes over their nine years, but Krueger and Cooksey remained the constants. Big Fun officially disbanded in 1990 but returned to Mississippi Nights in later years to perform reunion shows.

Black Flag, July 26, 1984. Photo by Ted Barron.

DAN OTTOLINI* REMEMBERS...

The first time I saw Black Flag was at Mississippi Nights in '84. I was fourteen or fifteen, and it was as if the circus had just rolled into town. It was $3 to get in. Out front, the skaters were doing boneless ones [skateboarding tricks], waiting for the doors to open. Black Flag was loud! I don't recall any other band being that loud at Mississippi Nights. [July 26, 1984]

*Mississippi Nights patron

52

After Big Fun, the members remained a part of the Mississippi Nights family. Krueger played in Heads Above Water, and Cooksey was briefly in the band. Heads Above Water played Mississippi Nights twenty-six times during 1991 and 1992.

Maurice Cooksey estimated he was in the crowd for over 150 concerts at Mississippi Nights.

Ken Krueger played 531 concerts at Mississippi Nights, worked there (even helping with a remodel in 1988), and attended as many concerts as possible. Krueger says, "I was at Mississippi Nights almost every night."

Krueger also produced two Mississippi Nights Reunion shows at Delmar Hall: the first on March 29, 2018, and the second on January 5, 2019.

KSHE-95 WELCOMES
MICHAEL SCHENKER GROUP
***
MISSISSIPPI NIGHTS
DOORS OPEN AT 8:00PM
THURSDAY FEBRUARY 23, 1984

Courtesy of Tracey Rayfield.

PRESENTING
FOGHAT
***
MISSISSIPPI NIGHTS
8:00PM
TUESDAY MARCH 20, 1984

Courtesy of George Eichelberger.

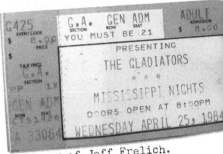

PRESENTING
THE GLADIATORS
***
MISSISSIPPI NIGHTS
DOORS OPEN AT 8:00PM
WEDNESDAY APRIL 25, 1984

Courtesy of Jeff Frelich.

Arrow
Memphis

538-7087
549-7097

Courtesy of Greg Bishop.

KCFV (METAL MANIA) WELCOMES
ACCEPT
SPECIAL GUEST EXODUST
MISSISSIPPI NIGHTS
DOORS OPEN AT 8:00PM
THURSDAY MAY 24, 1984

Courtesy of Tracey Rayfield.

ROB WAGONER* REMEMBERS...

The Ramones in 1984 at Mississippi Nights was my loudest concert of all time. I could not hear for four days. The band brought in arena gear, amplifiers that went from one end of the stage to the other. Amps were also situated in the underage section, where I was seated. I am sure I lost some hearing due to that show. [December 12, 1984]

*Guitarist of White Suburban Youth, Ultraman, Snake Ranch, Bent, Adoring Heirs, and bassist of Spacetrucker

ars nova

Ars Nova concert October 19, 1984.
Courtesy of Greg Bishop.

KWMU & JET LAG WELCOME
THE RAMONES
PLUS SPECIAL GUEST
MISSISSIPPI NIGHTS
DOORS OPEN AT 8:00PM
WED DECEMBER 12, 1984

Courtesy of Daniel Durchholz.

53

(left) Grim Reaper in concert October 4, 1984.
(below) Nick Bowcott. Photos by Patricia Fitzgerald.

PATRICIA FITZGERALD* REMEMBERS...

I photographed Grim Reaper at Mississippi Nights on October 4, 1984. The band Megalith opened the show. The Grim Reaper lineup that night was singer Steve Grimmet, guitarist Nick Bowcott, bassist Dave Wanklin, and drummer Lee Harris. I loved the concert and knew I was getting some really good shots.

After the show, the band was hanging around, signing autographs, and posing for photos. Someone told me Nick Bowcott's mother was in charge of their fan club and gave me her home address in England. I mailed her some of my best photos, and the next thing I knew, they were featured on the back of Grim Reaper's next album, *Fear No Evil*. Notice Nick Bowcott is wearing a KSHE T-shirt in the photo.

*Photographer

THIS ENTITLES BEARER TO $1.00 OFF ADMISSION TO THE GRIM REAPER CONCERT AT MISSISSIPPI NIGHTS THURSDAY OCT 4.

MUSIC VISION

MICHAEL KUSMANOFF* REMEMBERS...

I came early to the landing to see Spirit at Mississippi Nights in 1984. I went into Sundecker's a few doors down and ran smack dab into Randy California, the vocalist. I greeted him, but he was rude and pushed me aside, saying he needed to get going. Thankfully, behind him was Ed Cassidy, the drummer.

I asked if he was "The Commander," a reference to an album they made a few years back.

He humbly said, "Yes."

He shook my hand and left. R.I.P to both of them. [October 18, 1984]

*Mississippi Nights patron

54

TONY P. PONA* REMEMBERS...

I worked at Mississippi Nights for ten years, so I have many memories of the place. One that stands out is the night of Alvin Lee when Bon Jovi's Richie Sambora was sitting stage right in a packed house. I believe they were playing in town the same week of Alvin Lee, got in early, and were bummin' in the city. *Absolutely* every lady in the place knew who Sambora was. He was just there to see Alvin Lee. I worked secondary security. We kept the public away from Sambora (for the most part). He did sign and take a few pics, though. [October 31, 1984]

* Mississippi Nights stagehand/ security

G.A. - GEN ADM · ADULT
SECTION ROW SEAT ADMISSION
$10.00 OVER 21 $10.00
KSHE 95 WELCOMES
ALVIN LEE
PRODUCED BY CONTEMPORARY
MISSISSIPPI NIGHTS
HALLOWEEN NIGHT
WED OCT 31, 1984 9:00PM

Courtesy of Mark Ponder.

A ROCK 'N ROLL FALL to Remember at MISSISSIPPI NIGHTS

TICKETS ON SALE NOW!!!

KSHE REAL ROCK RADIO

ALVIN LEE
In Concert
HALLOWEEN NIGHT—OCTOBER 31
Doors Open 8 PM

— *also see* —

RENAISSANCE
In Concert
NOVEMBER 7
Doors Open 8 PM

— and... —

KSHE REAL ROCK RADIO

ROBIN TROWER
In Concert
NOVEMBER 13 & 12
Doors Open 8 PM

Tickets on sale at: Mississippi Nights, West End Wax, Smoke Shop, Record Works—Belleville, Record Company—Granite City & Edwardsville, Fast Ed's, Knight Amusement, Record Caravan or call DIALTIX 644-1700.

Courtesy of Randy Avellone.

EVENTS IN 1984

Duran Duran Video Viewing

The Police Video Viewing

David Bowie Video Viewing

Jet Lag's 4th Anniversary Party

Hullabaloo Party

JIM DANDY'S
Black Oak Arkansas

Personal Manager
John Courville

Sound Engineer
David Horan

TCI 200 West 57th Street New York, NY 10019 (212) 582-9681

NEW IMAGE PUBLIC RELATIONS

Courtesy of Rich Frame

Jim Dandy of Black Oak Arkansas, June 4, 1984.
Photo by Patricia Fitzgerald.

55

Mercyful Fate, October 30, 1984.
Photo by Patricia Fitzgerald.

GUS RIZOS* REMEMBERS...

I played at Mississippi Nights a lot back in the early '80s. It was a time when the demand for cover bands was huge, probably at its peak, and clubs had to have live music.

One night, something funny happened when I was performing with Ammaretto [at Mississippi Nights]. I noticed the crowd in front of me was joyously smiling at me while I was playing. I thought, "Cool. I must be sounding good tonight," until I felt a draft hitting my butt and realized my pants were ripped right up the seam. I wasn't wearing any underwear.

*Guitarist of Ammaretto

MISSISSIPPI NIGHTS WELCOMES

MON. JAN 23

REGGAE

LIVE !! from Austin

KILLER BEES

W/THE RYTHM ROCKERS
AND
THE MIGHTY STRIKER

DOORS OPEN 8 P.M.

$3.00 COVER

YOU MUST BE 21 YEARS OLD.

MISSISSIPPI NIGHTS   914 N. FIRST St.
LACLEDE'S LANDING   421-3853

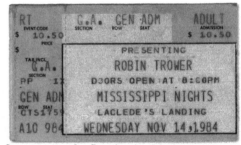

Courtesy of Randy Avellone.

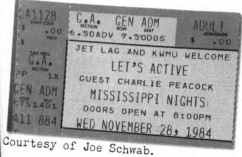

Courtesy of Joe Schwab.

56

(above) Diane Reichert and Lyla Turner and (right) Jane Bain of Girl Talk, November 3, 1984. Photos courtesy of Diane Reichert.

ROB WAGONER* REMEMBERS...

JFA (Jodie Foster's Army) performed on June 27, 1984. This was the first concert I attended at Mississippi Nights. In 1984, if you were under 21, you were forced to sit in the underage section known as the "kiddie corral." Sun City Girls opened the concert. Since the dance floor was empty, the band turned their instruments to face the underage section and played for them. By the time JFA came to play, there were around 60 people in attendance, and 50 of them were sitting in the small underage section. Only two or three people were in front of the stage during their set.

*Guitarist of White Suburban Youth, Ultraman, Snake Ranch, Bent, Adoring Heirs, and bassist of Spacetrucker

JOYOUSLY FUN ACTION

Jody Foster's Army/Sun City Girls
June 27
Mississippi Nights

wasn't expecting another Bernard Pub incid...
when JFA

Jody Foster's Army played next. To me, they
are a small bright spot in the music world.
These guys know how to have fun. Th...
that th...

EXCITER

Courtesy of Rich Frame.

John Ricci of Exciter, November 20, 1984.
Photo by Patricia Fitzgerald.

(right) Jeff Hanneman and (below) Kerry King of Slayer, November 27, 1984. Photos by Bill Siegler and Tim Goggins.

KCFV·FM 89
METAL MANIA
SUNDAYS NOON–5 pm

MONDAYS 10 PM–1 AM
METAL ATTACK
THE HEAVIEST HOUR OF HEAVY METAL
ROCK 120

AND

WELCOMES

"HAUNTING THE CHAPEL" /TOUR/ '84

SLAYER

SLAYER IN CONCERT
Nov-27-84
Be There!

UNKNOWN HEADBANGER

Doors Open 7 -pm

TUES - NOV. 27

—TO—

Mississippi Nights
ON THE LANDING

ALL AGES ADMITTED

SUPPORT HEAVY METAL ROCK 'N' ROLL !!!!

Mississippi Nights
914 1st Street
Laclede's Landing

Courtesy of Tim Goggins.

58

1985

Brad   Graham   Rob

THE ELVIS BROTHERS

8504

The Elvis Brothers

Many local and regional bands that made it big returned to Mississippi Nights again and again: Uncle Tupelo, The Urge, Anacrusis, to name just a few. Also among the regional bands to make Mississippi Nights their St. Louis outpost was the Champaign, Illinois, trio (and sometimes quartet) The Elvis Brothers.

For drummer and Pekin, Illinois, native Brad Steakley, the Mississippi Nights stage was a home for more than two decades. Since he was a young teen, Steakley kept a logbook of every concert he'd performed since 1970. As of 2020, he has performed 4,371 shows, many at Mississippi Nights.

In 1979, Steakley played for the Illinois band Screams, who had just released their first album on the MCA subsidiary Infinity Records. In April 1979, the band prepared to start their tour, including a show at Mississippi Nights. The group arrived in St. Louis two weeks early to see Roxy Music; the show moved to Mississippi Nights at the last moment for underwhelming ticket sales. Being only 20 and not inclined to sue, lead vocalist David Adams sat by the back door and listened to the concert. Although that night was a success, the age restriction posed a dilemma for the band. Two weeks later, the night of the Screams gig, the band neglected to mention the singer's age to venue management and performed their set as planned.

Screams toured opening for Van Halen for four months, including a sold-out show at the LA Forum. The band learned that MCA had dissolved Infinity Records during their headlining tour of the UK. They were left without a label. The band continued throughout 1980 before playing their final show on New Year's Eve in Pekin.

KWMU FM 91 welcomes
Polydor Recording Artist, from England...
**THE
RICHARD
THOMPSON
BAND**
with **DAVID SURKAMP**
(SOLO)
Thurs. March 21
Newly Remodeled
Mississippi Nights*
doors open 8 p.m.

Mississippi Nights
914 N. First St.
St. Louis, Mo. 63102

A FACELIFT

Mississippi Nights added three-tier seating and removed any décor alluding to the club's *Urban Cowboy* past.

59

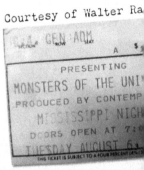

Before long, Brad Steakley returned to Mississippi Nights as Brad Elvis of the Elvis Brothers. Formed in 1981, the band consisted of Brad Elvis (Brad Steakley) on drums, Rob Elvis (Rob Newhouse) on guitar and vocals, and Graham Elvis (Graham Walker) on bass and vocals. The Elvis Brothers played Mississippi Nights for the first time on November 2, 1982, opening a four-date tour for Paul Carrack's Noise to Go featuring Nick Lowe. They also opened for Scottish band Big Country on their North American tour in 1983, including at Mississippi Nights on November 21. Many in attendance claim the show was the loudest concert ever at the club. The Elvis Brothers made their way to St. Louis often and played their favorite venue, Mississippi Nights, twenty-six times.

The band released two albums with Portrait Records (a sister label of Epic Records): *Movin' Up* and *Adventure Time*.

The Elvis Brothers' poster hung on the wall alongside many other great bands that played Mississippi Nights throughout the years. "We were so honored to have our six-foot poster framed on the wall of Mississippi Nights along with many other bands that we respected...We felt like we had made it!" Steakley exclaims.

Musicians were drawn to the club. Lots of touring bands spent their downtime at Mississippi Nights. Steakley remembers one such memorable night. "One evening at the club [December 3, 1985], we were playing our set, and we were surprised to see Anthony Kiedis and Flea of the Red Hot Chili Peppers standing right in front of us, digging the band and smiling. They were in town to play Mississippi Nights the next evening," he says. "Anthony had a glass beer mug clipped on each shoulder of his black motorcycle jacket. Afterward, they were just hanging at the club playing pinball, and no one was bothering them."

The Elvis Brothers played their last Mississippi Nights show in 1994 and broke up in 2002. Brad Steakley went on to join The Romantics and play on their album *61/49* in 2003. The Handcuffs, another band of Steakley's, has released four albums and continues to play concerts. But Mississippi Nights was one of his favorite spots to play. "Pat Lacey [office manager] from the club loved us, and we loved her. We were her favorite band until she discovered The Alarm!" he notes. But when the club closed for good, it wasn't The Alarm poster that Pat Lacey took home and hung in her living room; it was The Elvis Brothers.

Courtesy of Walter Ra

Ticket stubs courtesy of Daniel Durchholz.

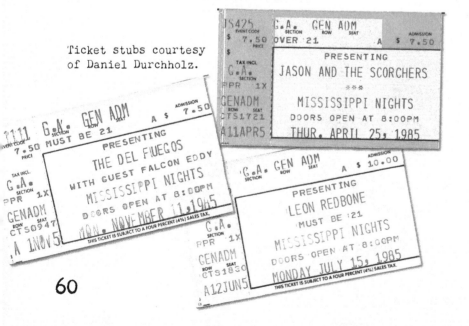

Annie Haslam of Renaissance, November 14, 1985. Photo by Randy Avellone.

60

J.C. KIRKWOOD* REMEMBERS...

After his concert, I sat at the bar and talked to Jeff Lorber [jazz fusion keyboardist-composer-producer]. He was one of my musical idols. We talked and drank a beer as woman after woman came up to him. They kept giving him a rose, then, he, in turn, gave it to the next woman that walked up to him. He said he felt like a horny flower shop delivery man. [April 24, 1985]

*Mississippi Nights patron

LISA McMICHAEL* REMEMBERS...

On November 6, 1985, we [Girl Next Door] opened for Minutemen at Mississippi Nights. That show was crazy! Our band was managed by Jay Barry, and he booked us for that show at the last minute. The bill had a punk band Minuteman, an all-girl band called Broken English, a '70s rock cover band named Relayer, and us. We should have never been on that bill. Our music was so different.

One of the best bar fights I've ever seen happened that night. Once the Minutemen started playing, the Relayer fans started going crazy, jumping in the pit, and being dicks. Chairs were being thrown across the bar. It was insane! I dragged my amp out the back door to get out of the way. Then, I checked on some guy that was lying out in the alley. Even with all the chaos, Minutemen still played their entire set.

*Bass player of Girl Next Door, Delilah, Livid, and Book Of Lies and guitarist of Final Prophecy, Billy Coma, and Bitch Slap Barbie

Girl Next Door (clockwise from left): Laura Hansen, Michelle Dalton, Tammy Gibson, Lisa McMichael, and Sonya Parker. Courtesy of Lisa McMichael.

photo: Naomi Petersen

MINUTEMEN

SST
P.O. BOX 1 LAWNDALE, CA 90260 U.S.A.
OFFICE: (213) 676-0110
BOOKING: (213) 372-5536

Concert November 6, 1985. Courtesy of Greg Kessler.

61

on the Riverfront

Laclede's Landing is situated on the historic St. Louis riverfront, where riverboats housing fine restaurants, lively theatre, and both day and evening downriver excursions dot the Mississippi. The famous Gateway Arch, Jefferson National Expansion Memorial, Busch Stadium, Cervantes Convention Center, and downtown St. Louis border the Landing, enhancing the "riverfront experience." For up-to-date information on riverfront activities and free tours of Laclede's Landing, contact the St. Louis Visitors Center, (314) 241-1764.

For more information, contact the Laclede's Landing Merchants' Association, (314) 241-5875.

DIRECTIONS:
1. Highways I-70, I-44, I-40, I-64, and I-55 all lead to downtown St. Louis. Follow signs to the "Arch" and "the Riverfront."
2. Once in the area, Laclede's Landing is just north of the Arch parking garage, beyond the Eads Bridge.
3. You will find entry to the Landing from Washington Avenue, Laclede's Landing Boulevard, Third Street and L.K. Sullivan Boulevard.
4. Refer to the map below for convenient parking in and around Laclede's Landing.

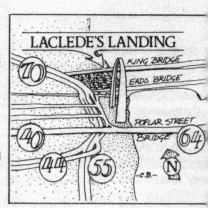

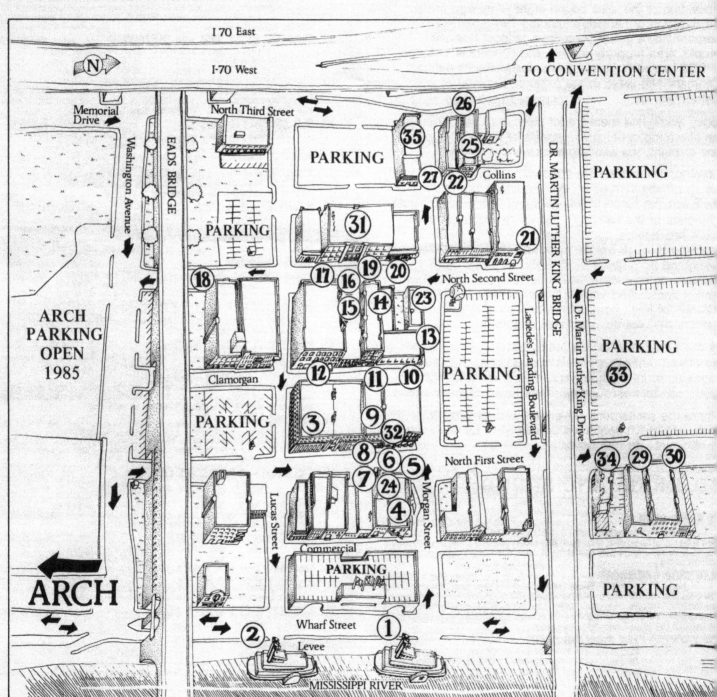

Courtesy of Tracey Rayfield.

Courtesy of Greg Kessler.

A SUITE RELATIONSHIP

In May 1985, the Embassy Suites hotel opened across the street from Mississippi Nights (also a part of the redevelopment area). The neighbors got along and had a symbiotic relationship for the most part. Since bands and patrons of Mississippi Nights needed a place to stay, many stayed at the hotel. However, Embassy Suites did complain about the noise from time to time.

KEN KRUEGER* REMEMBERS...

Supertramp was playing at the Kiel Auditorium on November 8, 1985. They called Mississippi Nights during the day and said, "Hey, we want to play a jam session. Can you get a band together?"

Big Fun was already set up to play that night, so we said, "Yeah, come on down."

The sax player that was with them had played at Mississippi Nights a couple of times before. I played harmonica and sang backing vocals for them that night.

*Singer of Ferrari, Big Fun, and Heads Above Water, and Mississippi Nights crew

From the collection of Garrett Enloe.

NOBODY, REALLY PRESENTS
METAL CHURCH
DOORS OPEN AT 8:00PM
MISSISSIPPI NIGHTS
LACLEDE'S LANDING
MON. NOVEMBER 18,1985

Courtesy of Tracey Rayfield.

K-SHE 95 WELCOMES
THE OUTFIELD
DOORS OPEN AT 8:00PM
MISSISSIPPI NIGHTS
MON DECEMBER

THE BLASTERS

Concert April 18, 1985. Courtesy of Rich Frame.

The Robert Cray Band

the rosebud agency
P.O. Box 20905
San Francisco, CA 94102
415-386-3456
Telex: 340813
ROSEBUD SFO

Concert June 27, 1985. Courtesy of Rich Frame.

64

Ken Hensley, July 1, 1985. Photo by Pat Fitzgerald.

tesy of Rich Frame.

EEG36 GEN 25CT3
EG.A. ROW GEN ADM
ADULT
EVENT CODE
7.00AD
DOORS OPEN AT 8:00PM
EUROGLIDERS
WITH GUEST BLIND DATES
MISSISSIPPI NIGHTS
MUST SHOW ID
WED MARCH 6,1985
G.A. GEN ADM
7.00ADV 8.00DOS

ADMISSION .00
G.A. GEN ADM
PRESENTING
RORY GALLAGHER
$8.50ADV $10.00DOOR
MUST BE 21
MISSISSIPPI NIGHTS
DOORS OPEN AT 8:00PM
WEDNESDAY MAY 29, 1985
RG5379
PRINT CODE
G.A.
PPR GENADM
CTS1815
A25APR5

Courtesy of Robert Hill.

JET LAG MAGAZINE P
SST Recording Artists
Hüsker Dü
—AND—
Fever Recording Artists
Get Smart!
$5
297

Mississippi Nights - 914

Hüsker Dü and fans behind
Mississippi Nights,
June 20, 1985. Photo by
Rick Buenaventura.

⚓ REGGAE ⚓
From the north coast of JAMICA
together Since 1962
The TWINKLE BROTHERS
MON. MAR.18
DOORS OPEN 8PM $5⁰⁰ cover
no under 21
REGGAE at its BEST!
MISSISSIPPI NIGHTS
LACLEDE'S LANDING

TUE.MAR.19
KWMU WECOMES
the **Del-Lords**
& Steve, BoB & Rich
$5⁰⁰ cover
DOORS
OPEN 8PM
LIMITED
UNDER 21
Seating
**914 N.1st.
421-3853**

Courtesy of Rich Ruth.

MAYNARD FERGUSON

ENTERTAINMENT MANAGEMENT
P.O. Box 716
Ojai, California 93023
(805) 646-8156

Concert June 3, 1985. Courtesy of Rich Frame.

G.A. GEN ADM ADULT
SECTION ROW SEAT ADMISSION
08 EVENT CODE 6.00ADV 7.00DOS
G.A.
GEN ADM
CTS1721
A 21185
DOORS OPEN AT 8:00PM
THE D B'S
WITH SPECIAL GUEST
MISSISSIPPI NIGHTS
MUST SHOW ID
TUE FEBRUARY 26,1985

Courtesy of Joe Schwab.

65

Todd Rundgren, October 28, 1985. Photo by Jack Twesten.

PRESENTING
THE ALARM
WITH SPECIAL GUEST
MISSISSIPPI NIGHTS
DOORS OPEN AT 8:00PM
WED. NOVEMBER 20,1985
THIS TICKET IS SUBJECT TO A FOUR PERCENT (4%) SALES TAX.

Ticket stub courtesy
of Daniel Durchholz.

Laurie Richardson, Zak, Arlene Almeyer,
Debbie (Guiffrida) Bannerman, Kurt Sodergren, and
Christine Rosvall waiting for the Alarm concert in
November. Courtesy of Laurie Richardson.

ST. LOUIS GETS BLUE!
WEDNESDAY, AUGUST 21
when **MISSISSIPPI NIGHTS**
proudly presents an evening with
RECORDING ARTIST

LUTHER "GUITAR JR." JOHNSON

Doors Open
At 8 p.m.

$5.00 Cover

Courtesy of Andy Mayberry.

The Music Club In St. Louis
914 N. FIRST
LACLEDE'S LANDING
421-3853

Courtesy of Gian Vianello.

MISSISSIPPI NIGHTS
presents
The FABULOUS THUNDERBIRDS
MONDAY, OCT. 7
$7.50 COVER
DOORS OPEN AT 8

Special Guest
BLUE CITY BAND
421-3853

HOT FUN in the SUMMERTIME

blank SPACE

THURS., JULY 23

SPECIAL GUEST **painkillers**

MISSISSIPPI NIGHTS
$3 Cover FOR MORE INFO ALL AGES
421-3853

Courtesy of
Greg Kessler.

PRESENTING
SUZANNE VEGA
PLUS DAVID SURKAMP
MISSISSIPPI NIGHTS
DOORS OPEN AT 8:00PM
MON. NOVEMBER 25,1985
THIS TICKET IS SUBJECT TO A FOUR PERCENT (4%) SALES TAX.

PRESENTING
THE FABULOUS THUNDERBIRDS
PLUS SPECIAL GUEST
MISSISSIPPI NIGHTS
DOORS OPEN AT 8:00PM
MON. OCTOBER 7,1985
THIS TICKET IS SUBJECT TO A FOUR PERCENT (4%) SALES TAX.

Ticket stubs courtesy of
Daniel Durchholz.

1986

Singing the Blues by the Mighty Mississippi

The Soulard Blues Band was formed in 1978 by bassist Art Dwyer and harmonica player Jim McClaren. The band has been through many incarnations throughout their forty-three-year career, varying the players and the brass instruments. One vocalist, Thurston Lawrence, left the band, rejoined several years later, and left again. Art Dwyer remains the constant in the Soulard Blues Band.

Mississippi Nights' records indicate that the band played the club seven times. However, Dwyer remembers a summer when The Soulard Blues Band stood in as the club's house band, playing every Wednesday night. They opened for artists such as Oliver Sain and Johnnie Johnson and backed many national acts that rolled through town. So, as with many bands, their time on the Mississippi Nights stage was much higher than recorded. "They treated us right, man," recalls Dwyer.

On March 22, 1986, The Soulard Blues Band played the first Blues Heritage Festival sponsored by the St. Louis Blues Society at Mississippi Nights. The event featured seventeen performers, including Henry Townsend, Billy Peek, Ron Edwards, Doc Terry, James Crutchfield, and Rondo's Blues Deluxe. "It was jam-packed at noon, and it was that way until 3 a.m. Everybody was fired up to play," remembers Dwyer. "Just for grins [Tommy Bankhead] got up and played a polka. The crowd went crazy." Robbie Montgomery, an ex-background singer for Ike and Tina Turner, hosted the event that brought 1,000 people through the doors at Mississippi Nights.

The Soulard Blues Band has released eight CDs and one cassette. They continue playing around town several times a week, including most Monday nights at the Broadway Oyster Bar.

1st ANNUAL ST. LOUIS BLUES FESTIVAL

"A classic afternoon and evening of Blues"

Featuring
Tommy Bankhead and the Blues Eldoradoes, Blue City Band, James Crutchfield, David Dee, James DeShay, Big George and the House Rockers, Tom Hall, Clayton Love, Billy Peek, Piano Slim, Leroy Pierson Band, Rondos Blues Deluxe, Oliver Sain Revue, Soulard Blues Band, Silvercloud and the St. Louis Blues Band, Doc Terry, Henry and Vernell Townsend with Ron Edwards
Master of Ceremonies—Lou "Fatha" Thimes

Saturday March 22
1 til 1 $10 Admission

Mississippi Nights
914 1st St. 421-3853

Produced by the St. Louis Blues Club

Courtesy of John Wegrzyn.

Eric Johnson, July 15, 1986. Photo by Harry Pilkerton.

EVENTS IN 1986

Benefit for Abused Children
Hands Across America Benefit
Yes Video Viewing
Jet Lag Party

Courtesy of Joe Schwab.

Wednesday - April 2
JOHNNY THUNDERS
JUNGLE RECORDS Recording Artist
Also featuring: The Primitives, Times
Beach and Dread Finks. Doors open 8PM

$5.75 Advance
$8.50 At The Door

JOHNNY THUNDERS

APRIL 2

EX: **New York Dolls** MEMBER: **JOHNNY THUNDERS**

For More Information,
Call **421-3853**

**MISSISSIPPI
NIGHTS** THE MUSIC CLUB IN ST. LOUIS

914 NORTH FIRST STREET   OPEN UNTIL 3:00 A.M.

Tickets available now for:
$5.75 In Advance
$8.50 At The Door

ALSO FEATURING
DREAD FINKS &
PRIMITIVES

Courtesy of Sheri Beezley.

KMMU & SLCAA WELCOMES
GIL SCOTT-HERON
BY A.M.K. & ASSOC.
MISSISSIPPI NIGHTS
DOORS OPEN 8PM · SHOW 9PM
FEBRUARY 25, 1986

GSZ25 ticket code
$ 12.00
TAX INCL.
G.A.
PPR 1M
A S 12.00
GENADM
07-51543

SEAT   ROW   SEC.
G.A.
PPCTS601   GEN
12.00   GEN
ADM   ADM

NO REFUND
NO EXCHANGE
2279497

From the collection
of Garrett Enloe.

00041
SEC   ROW   SEAT
GEN. ADM.
APR. 10-8 PM
ADMIT ONE THIS DATE ONLY
KYMC 89.7 FM
WELCOMES
THE VICTIMS
WITH
SPECIAL GUEST
STATE
OF SHOCK
IN CONCERT AT
MISS. NIGHTS
LACLEDES
LANDING
A RELAX
PRODUCTION
PRICE NO EXCHANGE
NO REFUND
COMPLIMENTARY

Courtesy of Jim Jablonski.

68

Lee Rocker (left),
Earl Slick (right),
Slim Jim Phantom (drums)
of Phantom Rocker & Slick,
Feburary 26, 1986. Photo by
Harry Pilkerton.

Mississippi Nights
LACLEDE'S LANDING · ST. LOUIS

**Presenting the
Finest in Live Music**
914 N. FIRST ST.
LACLEDE'S LANDING
421-3853

WED. FEB. 12
CONDITION 90

THURS. FEB 13
STEVE BOB & RICH

FRI. FEB. 14
Riverfront Times
presents
**CUPID
ATTACKS**
THE ULTIMATE VALENTINE'S DAY PARTY
Featuring
Street Corner Symphony
SOULARD BLUES BAND
& BIG FUN

SAT. FEB. 15
BIG:FUN

WED. FEB. 19
**ROBERT
CRAY**
"...Contemporary blues at its best,
Strongest, and most fulfilling." ★★★★½
Pete Welding, Downbeat

THURS. FEB. 20
HÜSKER DÜ

FRI. & SAT. FEB. 21 & 22
NOT ON FILE

MON. FEB. 24
COMMANDER CODY

TUES. FEB. 25 A.M.K. & ASSOCIATES
presents
KWMU 90.7 FM welcomes
GIL SCOTT-HERON
AN EVENING OF MUSIC & POETRY

WED. FEB. 26
Welcomes
Phantom, Rocker & Slick

THURS. FEB. 27
PAINKILLERS

MON. MARCH 3
**CURTIS
MAYFIELD**

SAT. MARCH 1
MURDER CITY PLAYERS

TUES. MARCH 4
THE ELVIS BROTHERS

THURS. MARCH 6
Welcomes
MONTROSE

WED. MARCH 5
SAXON

WED. MARCH 12
BIG TWIST
and the mellow fellows

NANCY WUJCIK HAGIN REMEMBERS...

My friends and I went to Mississippi Nights almost every Friday and Saturday night to see Big Fun in the mid-'80s. The first time I talked to [manager] Pat Hagin was at an after-closing hotel party at the Sheraton. [Sometimes, after closing, the party continued at a local hotel]. I knew Mark Shalgolski from high school, and he invited my friends and me to the party.

After that night, Pat would stop by our table at Mississippi Nights and bring my friends and me free T-shirts and shots. He eventually asked me for my phone number. A couple of months later, Pat called and asked me if I wanted to go out. He apologized for not calling sooner. For some reason, I forgave him and accepted his offer. Our first date was at Broadway Oyster Bar. In 1989, Johnnie Johnson played at our wedding reception at The Whittemore House, and afterward, he went down to the stadium to play with The Rolling Stones. The rest is history!

* Wife of Mississippi Nights manager Pat Hagin

BRAD ELVIS* REMEMBERS...

We were getting ready to play a show at Mississippi Nights on April 24, 1986, when Gregg Allman's road manager or handler approached us in the makeshift dressing room. He introduced himself and said Gregg Allman wanted to sit in with us. He filled us in and said, "I ask one thing of you. Don't bring up his ex-wife, Cher!" That was almost an invitation for us to say something, but we didn't.

I believe it was during our encore that Gregg came up onstage. Gregg was mainly a keyboardist, and we were a trio with guitar, bass, and drums. So, Gregg strapped on one of Rob Elvis' guitars and asked us what we wanted to do.

Rob asked, "How about "Whipping Post?" (Which we didn't even know).

Gregg said, "Shit, man. I'm an organ player, not a guitarist!"

So, we followed Gregg and played a blues song with him singing. We know a bit about playing the blues, but mainly from Zeppelin, Yardbirds, Johnny Winter — stuff from our generation. It went okay, but the fun-time Elvis Brothers weren't known for playing the blues. Our crowd wasn't really into it, and it seemed like a weird vibe to be playing blues songs at the end of our energetic set of originals.

*Drummer of The Elvis Brothers

Albert King, April 19, 1986.
Photo by Mark Gilliland.

From the collection of Garrett Enloe.

Tickets courtesy of Daniel Durchholz, Jamie Welky, and Garrett Enloe.

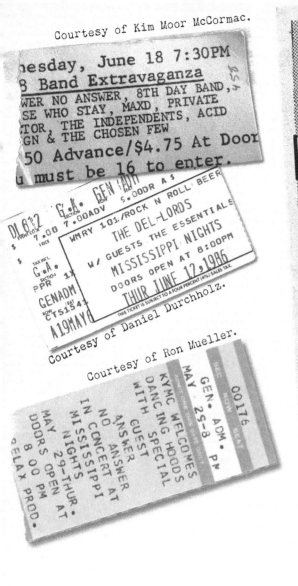

Courtesy of Kim Moor McCormac.

...esday, June 18 7:30PM
...8 Band Extravaganza
...WER NO ANSWER, 8TH DAY BAND,
...SE WHO STAY, MAXD, PRIVATE
...TOR, THE INDEPENDENTS, ACID
...GN & THE CHOSEN FEW
...50 Advance/$4.75 At Door
...u must be 16 to enter.

THE DEL-LORDS
w/ GUESTS THE ESSENTIALS
MISSISSIPPI NIGHTS
DOORS OPEN AT 8:00PM
THUR JUNE 12 1986
THIS TICKET IS SUBJECT TO A FOUR PERCENT (4%) SALES TAX.

Courtesy of Daniel Durchholz.

Courtesy of Ron Mueller.

KYMC WELCOMES
DANCING HOODS
WITH SPECIAL
GUEST
NO ANSWER
IN CONCERT AT
MISSISSIPPI
NIGHTS
MAY 29-THUR.
DOORS OPEN AT
8:00 PM
RELAX PROD.

Courtesy of Greg Kessler.

KEN KRUEGER* REMEMBERS...

One of my best memories was the John Lee Hooker concert in 1986. The hair on my arms still stands up when I think about it. I was doing lights. The club still had that big picture window in the back. In the middle of the set, Hooker sat by himself on the stage. First, I had a light that hit his face, just enough to barely see him. Then, I used a color called congo blue: dark, almost like a black light. Then, I hit an intense red light that came across the chair. He started chugging on his guitar, and right at that moment, I looked out the picture window to see a freight train coming down the track.

I don't know if anyone appreciated it as much as I did, but it was one of those perfect moments. I made the lights the way the music sounded. I was never able to capture that feeling again. [June 25, 1986]

70   *Singer of Ferrari, Big Fun, and Heads Above Water, and Mississippi Nights crew

PAT LACEY* REMEMBERS...

I ate dinner with Kenny G when he played in '86. It was his first tour. He wasn't as well-known as he is now. Patrick [Pat Hagin] was the manager, and he said, "Lacey, can you take Kenny G and his band out for dinner?"

I said, "Yeah, why?"

He said, "Well, they are vegetarians, and you know where the good vegetarian restaurant is."

I said, "Yeah, I do. Sunshine Inn over in the Central West End."

He said, "Will you take them?"

I said, "Sure."

They were so nice, really down to earth. We sat and talked, and Kenny G said, "If I don't make it in music, my girlfriend and I have a bakery. We bake cakes and sell them." And after they made it big, I thought to myself, 'Well, I guess they're not baking cakes anymore.' He wound up playing the Fox [Theatre] many times and always put Mississippi Nights people on the guest list. [December 16, 1986]

*Mississippi Nights office manager

Courtesy of Daniel Durchholz.

MIKE SCHRAND* REMEMBERS...

My first Mississippi Nights show was Albert Collins in 1986. He had a 100-ft guitar cable, so he could wander around the club with his horn section in tow. He soloed around the club for a few minutes. Then, Albert laid across the handrails of a wheelchair. The lady in the wheelchair got so Pentecostal that I swore she was going to get up and walk again! [August 25, 1986]

*Vocalist/guitarist of Salt of the Earth

Albert Collins. Photo by Mark Gilliland.

Albert Collins and fan Tony Cabanellas, August 25, 1986. Courtesy of Tony Cabanellas.

71

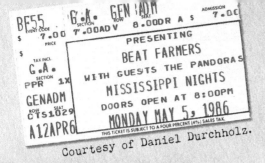

Courtesy of Daniel Durchholz.

(left to right) Rolle Love, Jerry Raney, and Joey Harris of The Beat Farmers, May 5, 1986. Photo by Kelly Hoener.

KEN KRUEGER* REMEMBERS...

Country Dick, the singer of Beat Farmers, stood up on the waitress station at the end of the bar by the bathrooms. The ceiling fan came around and knocked his hat off, almost knocking him out. [May 5, 1986]

*Singer of Ferrari, Big Fun, and Heads Above Water, and Mississippi Nights crew

Courtesy of Joe Schwab.

FROM MINNEAPOLIS, MN via THE TWILIGHT ZONE

MISSISSIPPI NIGHTS PRESENTS

THE WALLETS
AN EVENING OF "FUNKROCKSTOMPARTGROOVEOUT"
WED., AUG. 27
with their special guest from BOULDER, COLORADO
little women
REGGAE DANCE PARTY BAND

AT MISSISSIPPI NIGHTS
914 N. FIRST STREET   LACLEDE'S LANDING
DOORS OPEN AT 8 P.M.   SHOWTIME 9 P.M.
$5.00 Cover at the door
ALL AGES WELCOME
for more info, call 421-3853

Ticket stub courtesy of Doug Jeffries.

METAL MANIA PRESENTS
ANTHRAX
* * *
MISSISSIPPI NIGHTS
ALL AGES•DOORS OPEN 8PM
MON APRIL 14, 1986

Scott Ian (left) and Dan Spitz of Anthrax at the bar, April 14, 1986. Photo by Doug Jeffries.

Doug Jeffries, Jody Timmerman, and Mike Conway goof off behind Mississippi Nights before Anthrax, April 14, 1986. Courtesy of Jody Timmerman.

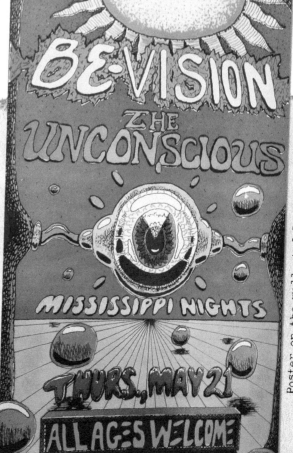

Poster and ticket stub from the collection of Garrett Enloe.

Ticket stubs from the collection of Garrett Enloe.

Rock & Roll Beer presents
"GOOD ROCKIN', HOT LICKS HOUSE PARTY IV"

starring

Queen of the Blues

KOKO TAYLOR
and The Blues Machine

Thursday May 8

"GOOD ROCKIN', HOT LICKS HOUSE PARTY III"
an evening with "The Originator"

BO DIDDLEY
with BILLY PEEK

Saturday May 10
at
Mississippi Nights
914 N.1st Street
advance general admission tickets available at all TICKETMASTER locations, Mississippi Nights, by phone through DIALTIX 421-1400
FOR TICKET INFO CALL 421-1701

PRODUCED BY A.M.K. and Associates

BH1025 G.A. · GEN ADM
EVENT CODE SECTION ROW SEAT
$ 5.00 MUST BE 21 A $ 5.00 ADMISSION
PRICE ADULT
TAX INCL.
G.A.
SECTION
PPR 1X
GENADM
ROW
CTS1529 SEAT
A240CT6

ROCK & ROLL BEER & WMRY101
BUGS HENDERSON
BY A.M.K. & ASSOCIATES
MISSISSIPPI NIGHTS
DOORS OPEN AT 8:00 PM
SATURDAY OCTOBER 25, 1986
THIS TICKET IS SUBJECT TO A 4.225% STATE SALES TAX.

EBH1025
EVENT CODE
CN 1014
ADULT
G.A.
PPCTS60
GEN
5.0
ADM

DL179 G.A. · GEN ADM
EVENT CODE SECTION ROW SEAT
$ 9.00 A $ 9.00 ADMISSION
PRICE ADULT
TAX INCL.
G.A.
SECTION
PPR 1X
GENADM
ROW
CTS1400 SEAT
A16JUN6

ROCK & ROLL BEER & WMRY101
DAVID LINDLEY & EL RAYO-X
BY A.M.K. & ASSOCIATES
MISSISSIPPI NIGHTS
DOORS OPEN AT 8:00PM
WEDNESDAY JULY 9, 1986
THIS TICKET IS SUBJECT TO A FOUR PERCENT SALES TAX.

EDIL79
EVENT CODE
CN 2530
ADULT
G.A.
PPCTS60
GEN
9.0
ADM

BG423 G.A. · GEN ADM
EVENT CODE SECTION ROW SEAT
$ 10.00 A $ 10.00 ADMISSION
PRICE
TAX INCL.
G.A.
SECTION
PPR 1X
GENADM
ROW
CTS1604 SEAT
A19MAR6

ROCK & ROLL BEER WELCOMES
BUDDY GUY / JUNIOR WELLS
BY A.M.K. & ASSOCIATES
MISSISSIPPI NIGHTS
LACLEDE'S LANDING
WED APRIL 23, 1986 8:00PM
THIS TICKET IS SUBJECT TO A FOUR PERCENT (4%) SALES TAX.

BG423
EVENT CODE
G.A.
PPCTS601
GEN
10.00
ADM

ADMISSION $ 8.50
ADULT

ROCK & ROLL BEER WELCOMES
KOKO TAYLOR
& THE BLUES MACHINE
MISSISSIPPI NIGHTS
BY A.M.K. & ASSOCIATES
THUR MAY 8, 1986 8:00PM
THIS TICKET IS SUBJECT TO A FOUR PERCENT (4%) SALES TAX.

EVENT CODE
CN 409
ADULT
G.A.
PPCTS6
GEN
8.
ADM

ADMISSION $ 12.50
ADULT
$
TAX INCL.
G.A.
SECTION
PPR 1X
GENADM
ROW
CTS1609 SEAT
A10MAY6

ROCK & ROLL BEER WELCOMES
BO DIDDLEY
WITH BILLY PEEK
MISSISSIPPI NIGHTS
BY A.M.K. & ASSOCIATES
SAT MAY 10, 1986 8:00PM
THIS TICKET IS SUBJECT TO A FOUR PERCENT (4%) SALES TAX.

EVENT CODE
CN 25988
ADULT
G.A.
PPCTS601
GEN
12.50
ADM

Courtesy of Rich Hartman.

Poster on the wall at J Gravity Strings.

73

YO MISS.
KNIGHTS of
SouL RocK
NRocK till
YOU WHORE!
MOJO
NIXON

Forever
and
then
some...

Skid Roper

RBI
records
Marketed Worldwide by Enigma Records

MOJO NIXON
AND
Skid Roper

ENIGMA
ENIGMA RECORDS
P O BOX 2428
EL SEGUNDO CA 90245
213-640-6869

The Smithereens
TO Mississippi Nights
All the Best!
Jim Babjak
Mike Mesaros
Pat DiNizio

thanks
for the
cookies!
Dennis
Diken

The
SMITHEREENS

L-R: JIM BABJAK
DENNIS DIKEN
MICHAEL MESAROS
PAT DINIZIO

(above)
Grant Fleming,
Stiv Bators,
Nick Turner,
and Brian
James of
Lords Of The
New Church,
May 14, 1986.
Photo by
Kelly Hoener.

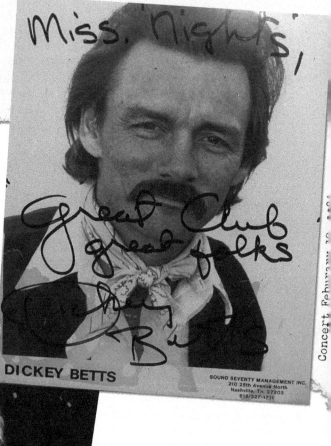

Miss. Nights,
great club
great folks

DICKEY BETTS

SOUND SEVENTY MANAGEMENT INC.
210 25th Avenue North
Nashville, Tn. 37203
615/327-1711

Melanie Vammen (left)
and Paula Pierce of
The Pandoras, May 5, 1986.
Photo by Kelly Hoener.

74

Off Beat Band

In 1983, after their band The Felons broke up, Jeff Schneider (keyboards), Mark Condellire (vocals), and Pete Sikich (bass) decided to form a reggae band and created Murder City Players. Over the next five years, the guitar, brass, and drum positions were filled by a parade of other musicians. During this time, the band accidentally acquired a second vocalist while playing at Cicero's: they asked a fan from the audience to join them onstage, Jamaican native Phillip McKenzie, who Schneider would later dub "Prince Phillip."

From 1984 to 2000, Murder City Players played Mississippi Nights thirty-seven times, including opening for national acts like U-Roy, Skatalites, Toots and the Maytals, and Itals. Not only did the band open for the Itals, but they were also their backing band.

Murder City Players was a regular band at The Elvis Room in the Blueberry Hill restaurant, owned by businessman Joe Edwards. Interested in helping St. Louis bands, Edwards formed Blueberry Hill records, and Murder City Players was the second artist on the label after Be-Vision. The band released a 12-inch single with "Big City Life" and "Mr. Brown" on the label. Then, on December 17, 1986, Blueberry Hill Records sponsored a concert at Mississippi Nights with bands from its roster: Murder City Players, Be-Vision, and Rondo's Blues Deluxe.

Later, Murder City Players released two CDs on Night Hawks Records — *Power Struggle* (1996), including guest performances by Oliver Sain and Leonard "The Ethiopian" Dillion, followed by *Speak No Evil* (1999). In 2005, the band self-released the EP *Big City Life* under their label.

Concert April 11, 1987. Courtesy of John Wegrzyn.

Concert cancellations can happen for many reasons, most often because of an illness of a band member or poor ticket sales. Once, Jeff Schneider witnessed an unusual concert cancellation at Mississippi Nights. On April 21, 1989, the Bunny Wailer concert had been moved from the Fox Theatre to Mississippi Nights due to poor ticket sales. Manager Pat Hagin booked Murder City Players to open the show. Jeff Schneider remembers Wailer's impression of Mississippi Nights, "Bunny Wailer walked in and said, 'I don't play no drunkin' house' and turned around and walked out." (Being a Rasta, Wailer adhered strictly to the dietary laws of Rastafari, which hold the belief that alcohol is unnatural and dirty.) Since the cancellation was on short notice, Pat Hagin decided to continue the show with just Murder City Players and without an admission charge.

Murder City Players continues to play around St. Louis with Jeff Schneider, Mark Condellire, Bryan Coughlan (Trombone), and Reggie Morrow (Trumpet).

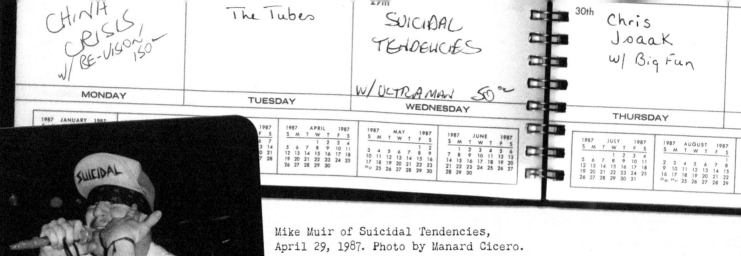

CHINA CRISIS, w/ RE-VISON 150

MONDAY

The Tubes

TUESDAY

29th

SUICIDAL TENDENCIES

w/ ULTRAMAN 50°°

WEDNESDAY

30th Chris Isaak w/ Big Fun

THURSDAY

Mike Muir of Suicidal Tendencies,
April 29, 1987. Photo by Manard Cicero.

A SPECIAL EARLY SHOW
SUICIDAL TENDENCIES
ALL AGES WELCOME
MISSISSIPPI NIGHTS
DOORS OPEN 6PM★SHOW 7PM
MONDAY SEPTEMBER 7,1987

Courtesy of Tracey Rayfield.

MICHAEL DOSKOCIL* REMEMBERS...

I wouldn't necessarily use the phrase 'thrown out' to describe my evening in question, but it'll do. Mississippi Nights had a double entryway. In this vestibule were dozens of black and white photos of bands that played at the club over the years, and one, in particular, made me green with envy every time I passed it. It was Angus Young of AC/DC. I was 16 when they played in 1977, and my mom wouldn't let me go.

Fast forward to me at the club in 1987: standing in that vestibule, it just came to me that I needed that photo, and I needed to haul ass to make it so. At the time, all the photos were tacked up using finishing nails. I was milling about during the headliner when I saw my moment, and with both hands, I leaned into that night's plan. I was surprised wire braid nails could hold so firm. In the second it took me to pull, turn, and boogie, the door person and one very large security guy saw my whole scheme unfold. In no time, the tubby one was off and running in hot pursuit.

Too many beers and a few shots can have a detrimental effect on the choice in crime and the ability to make for a clean getaway. That night, I only made it as far as the south parking lot before tripping all over myself in foolish laughter, tumbling down with the security guard rolling on top of me. B & D Security was always kind to me, even when I was leaping off speaker towers boots first, and this night was no exception. I think he didn't much care how it played out, as long as he got the photo back. After our asphalt dance, I made no effort to keep my ill-gotten goods and promptly handed over the cherished talisman. He got up, held out a hand to help me up, and asked me just what the fuck I was thinking doing that right in front of the staff. He had a point. I should've waited 'til they walked away or created a diversion.

A week later, Ultraman, the band I was gigging with, played Mississippi Nights opening up for Suicidal Tendencies. None of the staff brought up the incident, but I noticed they had bolted all the photos down in the entryway with half-inch flat head bolts. On my next visit, I was gonna need a pry bar.

*Vocalist/songwriter of Drunks with Guns and drummer of Ultraman and Antimation

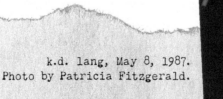

k.d. lang, May 8, 1987.
Photo by Patricia Fitzgerald.

I LOVE U SO MUCH I NEVER LEAVE ME!

Chris Isaak

RIS ISAAK

MONTEREY
PENINSULA
ARTISTS
Carmel California 93921

Photo Credit: Rio Lopez

Concert April 30, 1987.
Courtesy of Rich Frame.

DOUGLAS SCRONCE* REMEMBERS...

For some reason, my friend, Donald Williams, had loaned his sister his car. So, she dropped us off at the door at Mississippi Nights to see the Red Hot Chili Peppers. We knew we would know enough people there to find a ride home to North County.

Upon entering, we realized the show was sold out. This sucked since we didn't have tickets or a ride home. A couple of other tiny dudes (like our height) walked in. We were surprised when we recognized them as Jack Irons and Anthony Kiedis of the Red Hot Chili Peppers.

Donald, brazenly, said to Jack, "The show is sold out. Is there any way you can get us in?"

He asked our names, and that's the last I thought we'd see of them that night. Suddenly, the guy that always sat on the stool to stamp hands pointed at us with his jumbo sausage finger. Then, he used that same girthy finger to give us the *come here* signal. I was sure he was going to tell us to beat it since we didn't have tickets. Without a word spoken, he stamped our hands, and we were in. To a pair of teenage kids, it was pretty epic. I took the money I had for my ticket and bought a RHCP mad cow shirt, which I eventually wore out. While it wasn't the best show I've seen at Mississippi Nights, it is my favorite memory.

Mississippi Nights patron

Ticket stubs
courtesy of
Greg Kessler.

Courtesy of Greg Kessler.

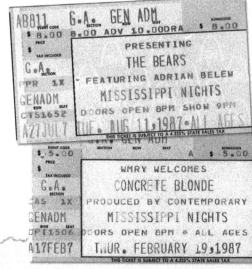

Ticket stubs courtesy
of Lonnie Payeur.

77

ERIC MARTIN

Photo: Randy Bachman / 1987

Capitol RECORDS

CHUCK MCPHERSON* REMEMBERS...

I saw the Eric Martin Band, pre-Mr. Big, in spring of 1987. Wade Monnig and I went down early with a couple of our friends. Eric came walking out, stopped to talk to us, and thanked us for coming to the show. We mentioned that we were fans of his song "Sucker for a Pretty Face." He said he had a new band, and the song wasn't on the list. So, he proceeded to sing an abbreviated acapella version, asking us to join in. I just listened because it was an awesome, private one-song show just for us. Martin and his band played like 5,000 people were in the audience that night instead of fifty -- a consummate professional and entertainer with a fantastic voice. [April 21, 1987]

*Mississippi Nights patron

Tommy Skeoch of Tesla, June 22, 1987. Photo by Scott Gates. Ticket stub courtesy of Joe Vickery.

(left) Martin Eric Ain, (middle) Reed St. Mark, and (right) Thomas Gabriel Fischer of Celtic Frost, December 3, 1987. Photos by Harry Pilkerton. Ticket stub courtesy of Tracey Rayfield.

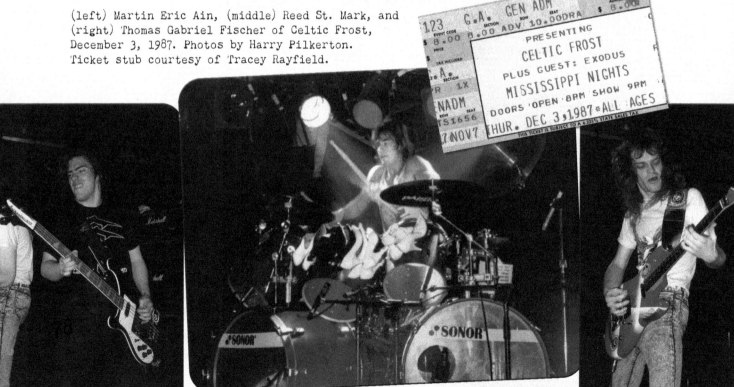

Roy Buchanan, November 1, 1987. Photo by Jack Twesten.

Anacrusis, March 19, 1987. Courtesy of Ken Nardi.

Concert August 31, 1987. Courtesy of Gian Vianello.

MEAT PUPPETS

Left to right: Curt Kirkwood
Derrick Bostrom
Cris Kirkwood

Photo by Joseph Cultice

P.O. BOX 1, LAWNDALE, CA 90260 USA
(213) 835-8977

79

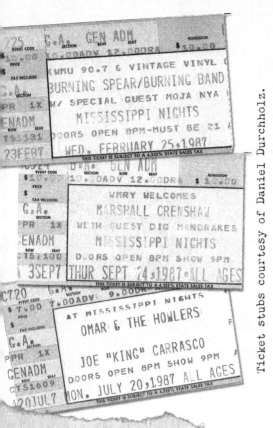

SCOTT WRIGHT* REMEMBERS...

I saw a Bad Brains show before Mississippi Nights expanded. The pit seemed to be the entire crowd, but everyone was having a blast. Amps and equipment eventually fell over, and HR [the singer] was completely into it. I've always compared all other shows to this one. Nothing has ever matched the time I had that night! [March 2, 1987]

*Mississippi Nights patron

ROB WAGONER REMEMBERS...

Flaming Lips opened for Soul Asylum and used a bubble machine during their set, causing the soap to cover the stage. When they finished, I noticed a roadie for Soul Asylum slip and slide completely across the stage. All night, Soul Asylum had trouble keeping balance during their performance. [June 24, 1987]

*Guitarist of White Suburban Youth, Ultraman, Snake Ranch, Bent, Adoring Heirs, and bassist of Spacetrucker

80

NOBODY REALLY PRESENTS
HELIX
AND GUEST: AXE MINISTER
MISSISSIPPI NIGHTS
DOORS OPEN 8PM SHOW 9PM
TUES. OCT 20 1987 *ALL AGES

WSIE WELCOMES
FISHBONE
W/ GUEST NICHOLAS TRE
MISSISSIPPI NIGHT
DOORS OPEN 9PM SHOW
TUE OCT 27, 1987 *ALL

DOUG WICK* REMEMBERS...

I remember the Fishbone show on October 27, 1987. [Singer] Angelo Moore crowd surfed to the back of the house and went out the back exit. Security tried to block him from entering when he came in through the front door because he didn't have a ticket. He was standing there with a mic in his hand and no shirt on, with everyone around screaming that he was the lead singer.

*Drummer of Sstik and Monsewer Rat.

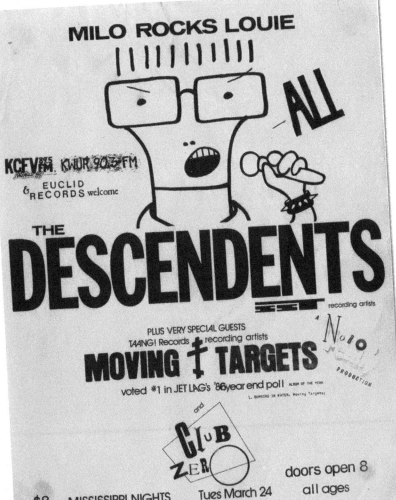

MILO ROCKS LOUIE

ALL

KCFV FM. KWUR 90.3 FM
& EUCLID
RECORDS welcome

THE
DESCENDENTS

recording artists

PLUS VERY SPECIAL GUESTS
TAANG! Records recording artists
MOVING † TARGETS
voted #1 in JET LAG's '86 year end poll

NoBo
PRODUCTION

CLUB ZERO

$8   MISSISSIPPI NIGHTS   Tues March 24   doors open 8   all ages

Brian Canham of Pseudo
Echo, May 12, 1987. Photo
by Patricia Fitzgerald.

81

John Lee Hooker,
August 6, 1987. Photo
by Mark Gilliland.

Ticket stub
courtesy of
Joe Vickery.

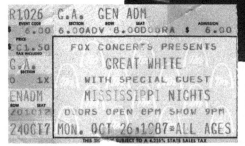

Jack Russell of Great White,
October 26, 1987. Photo by
Harry Pilkerton.

Mason Ruffner,
July 22, 1987. Photo
by Mark Gilliland.

THE LEMP MANSION IS ALIVE WITH THE SPIRIT OF MUSIC
PAGE 4

FREE!   June 25–July 8, 1987   Issue No. 10

SPOTLIGHT
The St. Louis Music and Entertainment Newspaper

OH WHEN THE SAINTS . . .

After 10 years these Australian rockers
still march to the beat of a
different drummer

Story on Page 5

82

Plus SATYRE, star search auditions, Sri Chinmoy,
Judas Priest and the sixty-second interview

Heart Like
A Rabbit

1988

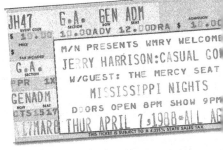

The New and Improved Mississippi Nights

In 1988, Mississippi Nights was nearly the same as when Rich Frame bought it almost a decade earlier. The club had a 600-seat capacity and a storage area with dirt floors next door. Frame and Pat Hagin recognized an opportunity to expand Mississippi Nights to draw in more people for local shows and bring in more national acts. Frame jokes, "We had this warehouse next door that wasn't being used, except for the rats. So we decided to evict them and expand."

Frame was developing some apartment buildings simultaneously and hired those subcontractors to work on the Mississippi Nights expansion. He had used these guys on other projects, and Frame trusted them to handle the challenges of fixing the structural problems with the old building next door, combining the two spaces into one larger, more functional space.

Ticket stubs courtesy of Daniel Durchholz and Greg Kessler.

The wall between the venue and the storage area was removed to nearly double the space. The stage was redesigned. The original small, half-stop sign-shaped stage tucked into the back corner became larger, about a foot taller, rectangular, and centered along the back wall. Another bar and set of restrooms were added. The existing restrooms were retrofitted with quick flush toilets, saving countless work hours for maintenance man Cliff Schmitz. The occupancy capacity grew to 1,000. The expansion took three or four months to complete and cost $300,000.

Besides doubling the size of the venue, the remodel ushered in two other significant changes to Mississippi Nights. Before the expansion, the business license referred to Mississippi Nights as a "bar." After the expansion, the new label, "place of entertainment," allowed the venue to operate on Sundays. (Sunday liquor sales in bars were not made legal until 1990). Also, they were able to host more underage concerts since the underage patrons no longer had to go through the over-21 section to use the restrooms.

Frame explained that Mississippi Nights had a lot of competition before the expansion as many venues had a capacity of around 500. "When we expanded, we took our competition away." Mississippi Nights was now able to book shows for up to 1,000 people. Bands could be booked at the venue when they had smaller audiences, and they didn't have to find a new place to play when their fan base doubled.

Anthony Kiedis, Jack Irons, and Hillel Slovak of Red Hot Chili Peppers, April 14, 1988. Photo by Jenny Polk.

Courtesy of Greg Kessler.

83

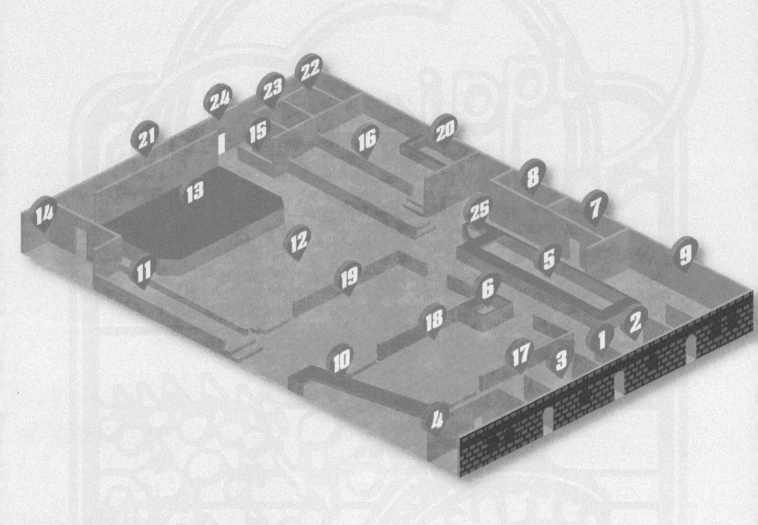

LEGEND

1. MAIN ENTRANCE
2. TICKET OFFICES
3. ARCADE
4. BATHROOM
5. BAR
6. SOUNDBOARD
7. WOMEN'S BATHROOM
8. MEN'S BATHROOM
9. OFFICES
10. BAR TWO
11. SEATING
12. DANCE FLOOR
13. STAGE
14. BACKSTAGE
15. MONITOR
16. UNDERAGE (TWO TIERS)
17. SEATING TIER ONE
18. SEATING TIER TWO
19. SEATING TIER THREE
20. BAND MERCH
21. WALKWAY
22. STORAGE
23. OPENING ACT BACKSTAGE
24. BACK DOOR
25. WAITRESS STATION

Lita Ford, April 21, 1988.
Photo by Scott Gates.

After the remodel was complete, the venue had a soft re-opening on April 2, 1988, with The Radiators and Fortunetellers performing on the virgin stage. The sold-out show had a $5 cover charge.

The Grand Re-Opening Party was a KSHE-95-sponsored, sold-out, free show on April 12, 1988, with The Rhythm Method opening for The Rainmakers. Some of the other artists that played the new stage that month were The Alarm, Big Fun, Red Hot Chili Peppers, Lita Ford, Jake's Leg, and Rosanne Cash.

From Rising Star to Sold-out Show to Multi-Platinum

Melissa Etheridge's self-titled debut album had been released less than four months before she rolled into Mississippi Nights on August 24, 1988. Her third show on her first American tour, they were shooting a video for her first single, "Bring Me Some Water," at and around Mississippi Nights. The video begins with shots of the St. Louis Arch and the train behind the venue, cuts to a roadie unloading gear at the front of the club, and another roadie carrying

Concert August 24, 1988. Courtesy of Rich Frame.

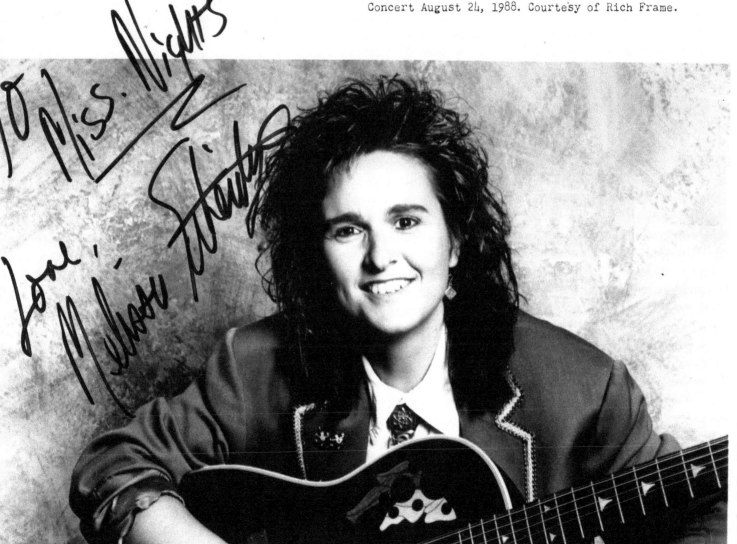

To Miss. Nights
Love, Melissa Etheridge

Photo Credit: Gary Nichamin

Unconscious backstage at Mississippi Nights, January 14, 1988. Photo by Mark Gilliland.

John Bush of Armored Saint, Febuary 23, 1988. Photo by Harry Pilkerton.

Robb Flynn of Vio-lence, July 27, 1988. Photo by Harry Pilkerton.

Wattie Buchan of The Exploited, September 9, 1988. Photo by Mitch Hall.

86

guitars down the walkway towards the stage. Etheridge's performance in the video was filmed after her hour-long set when she lip-synced to the studio version of "Bring Me Some Water." The video ends with her exiting down the back steps of Mississippi Nights and entering her tour bus.

The bus left the iconic St. Louis venue and headed for another iconic place in St. Louis. "After the show, we went to Ted Drewes [Frozen Custard]," recalls Etheridge.

Etheridge's aunt, from St. Louis, videotaped the entire concert. You can download it on a subscription-based streaming platform, Etheridge TV, hosted by Etheridge.

Along with shooting her first video, Etheridge had another first that day. "Mississippi Nights was the first time a fan came backstage," she remembers. "I had no security at the time. Nobody knew who I was."

Etheridge returned for another concert at Mississippi Nights on March 16, 1989. This show, which sold out in two hours, was a KSHE-95 Listener Appreciation Concert with a $4.95 ticket price. Etheridge contrasted her two shows at Mississippi Nights: "The first time everybody stayed at their tables. The second time everybody was right down front." She remembers the venue as "a special place."

Her debut album, *Melissa Etheridge,* became certified double platinum. To date, she has made sixteen albums, selling 25 million, and has won two Grammy Awards (with fifteen nominations) and an Oscar.

Courtesy of Paul Ebenreck.

The singer-songwriter champions many causes, such as LGBTQ rights, breast cancer research, medical cannabis, reducing food insecurity, ending the cycle of domestic violence, and fighting opioid addiction. Also, Etheridge and her wife Linda Wallem support women-owned businesses by seeking out women-owned restaurants to dine in. In 2021, Etheridge even hosted the Grand Re-opening of Cathy's Kitchen in Ferguson, Missouri, after befriending owner Cathy Jenkins.

Courtesy of Daniel Durchholz.

Tim Coles, Mike Mesey, blues artist James Cotton, and Mark Gilliland, October 15, 1988. Courtesy of Mark Gilliland.

From the collection of Garrett Enloe.

WMRY WELCOMES
PRODUCED BY CONTEMPORARY
* * *
OINGO BOINGO
MISSISSIPPI NIGHTS
MON NOV 7,1988 7:30PM

222 927
2776   1
GA ADULT
CAS   0.00
GEN   15.00
38A
ADM ADM/GO GA

Sam Phipps
Leon Schneiderman
Dale Turner

Steve Bartek
Danny Elfman
Johnny "Vatos" Hernandez

Carl Graves
John Avila

OINGO BOINGO   BOINGO ALIVE   .MCA RECORDS

TIM BREWER* REMEMBERS...

My favorite memory of Mississippi Nights was getting all the guys from Oingo Boingo (even the horns) on the *Boingo Alive* tour to sign a concert poster for me. I also got a setlist. [A setlist is a typed or handwritten list of the songs played live that night taped to the stage so the band members can keep in sync.] I met them all except Danny Elfman [lead vocals, guitar], who stayed in the back. However, Steve Bartek [guitar] took the poster back to him and had him sign it. They were all really cool. I met John "Vatos" Hernandez [drums] and John Avila [bass] there again when they returned on the *Food for Feet* tour. [November 7, 1988]

*Mississippi Nights patron

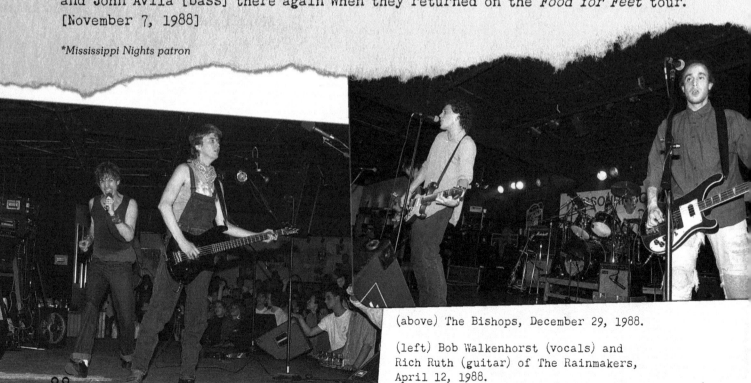

(above) The Bishops, December 29, 1988.

(left) Bob Walkenhorst (vocals) and Rich Ruth (guitar) of The Rainmakers, April 12, 1988.

Photos by Mark Gilliland.

88

10,000 Maniacs vs. Tracy Chapman

On April 20, 1988, Mississippi Nights presented 10,000 Maniacs and Tracy Chapman. On the day of the show, the club was informed by 10,000 Maniacs' management that the opener, Tracy Chapman, was no longer on the tour. But, confusingly, just before the doors opened to the public, Chapman arrived with her manager. The concert had been promoted as "10,000 Maniacs with Tracy Chapman," so Mississippi Nights set up a spot for her on the stage to play her acoustic set.

Owner Rich Frame remembers, "Tracy Chapman was amazing. A lot better than 10,000 Maniacs that night. After her set, she was called out for an encore. In all my years at Mississippi Nights, I'd never seen an opening act come out for an encore." *St. Louis Post-Dispatch's* concert critic and Pavlov's Dog frontman, David Surkamp, was so impressed that he listed her as one of his "Top 5 Concerts of 1988." He wrote, "...Chapman floored me with her voice, songs, and natural charisma. With only her acoustic guitar for accompaniment, she made it quite obvious to everyone that her performance was something very special."[b]

After the concert, Rich Frame found out that 10,000 Maniacs management had lied about Chapman because she didn't just warm up audiences, she upstaged the headliner, and they wanted her gone.

Courtesy of Michael Kathriner.

(b) Surkamp, David (1989, January 1; St. Louis Post-Dispatch; p. 7D.) Retrieved from www.newspapers.com.

TRACY CHAPMAN

Concert April 20, 1988. Courtesy of Rich Frame.

Joe Satriani, Joe Vickery, and Andy Mayberry behind Mississippi Nights, June 3, 1988. Courtesy of Joe Vickery.

89

Vinnie Vincent Invasion, July 13, 1988. (above left) Vinnie Vincent. (above right) Mark Slaughter on the shoulders of Dana Strum. Photos by Harry Pilkerton and Scott Buettmann.

JOE VICKERY* REMEMBERS...

L.A. Guns were supposed to open for Vinnie Vincent Invasion. Earlier in the day, Tracii Guns [guitar] got into an argument with Vinnie Vincent [guitar]. Vincent ended up with a black eye, and L.A. Guns left the tour. The show did not start until 9:30 since there was no opener that night. [July 13, 1988]

*Mississippi Nights patron

IID622 G.A. GEN ADM
EVENT CODE SECTION ROW SEAT
10.00 10.00ADV 12.00DRA $10.00
PRICE ADMISSION
$ TAX INCLUDED
G.A. SECTION ROW SEAT
APR 1X
ENADM
TS1703 ROW SEAT
11MAY8 WED JUNE 22, 1988 ALL AGES
THIS TICKET IS SUBJECT TO A 4.225% STATE SALES TAX

WMRY FM 101 WELCOMES
MIDNIGHT OIL
GUEST: HOUSE OF FREAKS
MISSISSIPPI NIGHTS
DOORS OPEN 8PM SHOW 9PM

Courtesy of Jeff Herschel.

WMRY WELCOMES
AT MISSISSIPPI NIGHTS
WITH GUEST
THE RAMONES
OPEN 8:PM SHOW 9:PM
THUR SEPT 29, 1988
$15 DAY OF
SEP GA GA-463 ADULT 14.25

90

From the collection of Garrett Enloe.

Courtesy of Greg and Tom Kricho.

KQV-FM 89 METAL MANIA welcome
DEATH ANGEL

Wed.
SEPT 21
all ages
doors open 8pm

SUPPO
HEAVY ME

Tickets $8 in Advance $10 Day of Show
Tickets on sale at all Tickets Now Outlets
Dial-Tix at 434-6600
Vintage Vinyl Euclid Records West End Wax
Gravity Strings Mississippi Nights Box Office

PLUS VERY SPECIAL GUESTS
RIGOR MORTIS

MISSISSIPPI NIGHTS
914 N 1st
Laclede's Landing

JOE SCHWAB* REMEMBERS...

Here at Euclid Records, we've always had a soft spot for The Pogues. Aside from being a unique sound in the 1980s and '90s, mixing traditional Irish music and punk rock, we have fond memories of their only appearance in St. Louis at our beloved Mississippi Nights.

We had sold tickets for the show. (Remember when record stores sold concert tix?) We had to return the unsold tickets and pay the venue the day of the show. So, we always had a good excuse to come when the band was doing soundcheck and get a sneak preview. (Dinner, next door at Sundecker's, was the other incentive of the ticket selling ritual.)

We watched The Pogues do their soundcheck, and while we were hanging out, having a smoke out front, lead singer Shane McGowen came outside. Before we could tell him how much we admired the band, he told us how much he admired our Euclid Records T-shirts! A holy shit moment, to be sure. But hey, it gets better. We told him we'd snag one for him, so we dashed back to the Central West End and grabbed shirts for everyone in the band.

The Pogues tore the f'ing roof off the joint. And the glory of glories, they came out for their encore wearing their new Euclid T-shirts!

The next day, every kid at that show came in to buy a shirt. They were sold out late that afternoon. [June 15, 1988]

*Owner of Euclid Records

Courtesy of Daniel Durchholz.

Courtesy of Gian Vianello.

Flyer on the wall at J Gravity Strings.

91

KEN KRUEGER* REMEMBERS...

King Diamond almost did not play. [The stage prop] The Gates of Hell didn't fit through the front door, and he wasn't going to play if he couldn't use The Gates of Hell. We talked him into performing without it. [Things like that] happened there a lot because Mississippi Nights was getting bands that played larger venues in other cities. They came to St. Louis and couldn't use their light, sound, or stage props. [October 26, 1988]

*Singer of Ferrari, Big Fun, and Heads Above Water, and Mississippi Nights crew

92 FRANK GAMBALE   DAVE WECKL   CHICK COREA   ERIC MARIENTHAL   JOHN PATITUCCI

CHICK COREA ELEKTRIC BAND

Concert September 12, 1988. Courtesy of Rich Frame.

RANDY RALEY* REMEMBERS...

My band, Randy Raley and the Traffic Jam, opened for Jeff Healey. He was such a doll. As we left the stage, he grabbed my arm and said, "You guys kicked ass. Go get an encore."

I said, "Opening bands don't get encores."

He said, "Mine do," and we hit the crowd with a very slowed-down version of "Crossroads."

We all loved Jeff. He was incredibly cool.

Later, John Ulett [fellow DJ at KSHE-95] and I were talking, and he told me how much he had liked the band that opened for Jeff Healey. He was wondering who they were. (I didn't tell him it was me behind the drum kit.) [December 21, 1988]

*DJ on KSHE-95 from 1985-1993, DJ on KFTK 97.1, KLOU 103.3, as well as radio stations in Kansas City, Iowa, and Illinois, and broadcasting teacher. In 2022, Raley can be heard as the morning show host on KBDZ 93.1.

Randy Raley, December 21, 1988. Photo by Mark Gilliland.

Management:
Forte Records & Productions
326½ Howland
Toronto, Ontario
Canada M5 R3 B9

THE JEFF HEALEY BAND   ARISTA

Ronnie Montrose, July 28, 1988. Photo by Scott Buettmann.

Courtesy of Tony Vitale.

MIS950
1937 ALL
1 AGES
GA DAYOS
CAS 1.00
GEN 12.00
3D
ADM 03UNOV GA

MINISTRY
WITH GUEST
CONCERT ONE PRESENTS
MISSISSIPPI NIGHTS
OPEN 8:PM SHOW 9:PM
WED NOV 30,1988
$12 DAY OF
GA-853   13.00

Courtesy of Paul Ebenreck.

MIS789   BILL BRUFORDS EARTHWORKS
1001 ALL   WITH GUEST
20 AGES   ** **
GA ADULT   MISSISSIPPI NIGHTS
0.00   OPEN 8:PM SHOW 9:PM
2.00   WED JUNE 29,1988
JUN GA $14 DAY OF   ADULT
GA-175   12.00

93

WED., SEPT. 21

EATH ANGEL

us **RIGOR MORTIS**   ALL AGES
ADV/$10⁰⁰ DAY OF SHOW

THURS., SEPT. 22

EGGAE FALL FEST

EATURING

ENNIS BROWN

AND

NI KAMOZE

W/ONE-
WO CREW

& SPECIAL GUEST
EDUBE
FOOD BOOTH BY
HOUSE OF JAMAICA

12/ADV/$14 DAY OF SHOW   ALL AGES

FRI. & SAT., SEPT. 23 & 24

BIG FUN

$2⁰⁰ COVER

WED., SEPT. 28

KDHX WELLCOMES
NRBQ

w/**THE WAGONEERS**
$8⁰⁰ ADV/$10⁰⁰ Day of Show   ALL AGES

THURS., SEPT. 29

WELCOMES   ~~SOLD OUT~~
THE RAMON

W/**THE DICKIES**

FRI., SEPT. 30

WMRY
WELCOMES

THE CHURCH

plus **TOM VERLAINE**
$13⁰⁰ ADV/$15⁰⁰ Day of Show   ALL AGES

SAT., OCT. 1

BIG FUN

WED. OCT. 5

WMRY
WELCOMES

CAMPER VAN BEETH
with **ROYAL CRESCENT MCB**
$13⁰⁰ ADV/$15⁰⁰ Day of Show

MON., O

FISHBONE

W/**SPECIAL GUEST**
$12⁰⁰ ADV/$1⁷ Day of Show — ALL AGES

TUES., OCT. 11

SUICIDAL TENDENCIES

Courtesy of Scott Buettmann.

Marc Storace of Krokus, June 27, 1988. Photo by Scott Gates.

Sally Cato of Smashed Gladys. Courtesy of Scott Buettmann.

Courtesy of Gian Vianello.

© Bob Kreher.

KROKUS

ROCK N ROLL
MON JUNE 27

PLUS

all ages   doors open 8 p.m.

MISSISSIPPI NIGHTS

MISSISSIPPI NIGHTS PRESENTS & KDHX 88.1 FM WELCOMES

A JAM PACKED EVENING OF
GOOD MUSIC ☆ GOOD FOOD ☆ GOOD TIMES

CAJUN & ZYDECO REVUE

Featuring

"The Toot-Toot Man" **ROCKIN' SIDNEY**

"The Master of the Button Accordion" **AL RAPONE**
and the Zydeco Express

"The King of the Cajun Fiddle" **ALLEN FONTENOT**
and the Country Cajuns

EACH OF THESE LOUISIANA SUPERSTAR BANDS PERFORM THEIR
OWN SET—THEN ALL 14 MUSICIANS JOIN ON STAGE FOR
A FINAL SET THAT WILL KNOCK YOUR SOCKS OFF!

MONDAY, AUGUST 15
MISSISSIPPI NIGHTS
914 N. FIRST STREET .... LACLEDE'S LANDING
DOORS OPEN AT 8:00 P.M.   SHOWTIME 9:00 P.M. ALL AGES!
TICKETS ARE $10.00 IN ADVANCE AND $12.00 DAY OF THE SHOW
ON SALE NOW AT ALL TICKETS NOW OUTLETS, VINTAGE VINYL,
EUCLID RECORDS, WEST END WAX, MISSISSIPPI NIGHTS & DIAL-TIX 434-6600

FOOD BOOTH BY BROADWAY OYSTER BAR

CAJUN ZYDECO REVIEW
ROCKIN SIDNEY, AL RAPONE
ALLAN FONTENOT
MISSISSIPPI NIGHTS
OPEN 8:PM   SHOW 9:PM
MON AUG 15, 1988
$12 DAY OF   PREP
GA-61   10.00

#S839
19 KDHX
9WELCM
PREP
0.00
N 10.00
1P
M 022JUL GA

1989

Case of the Missing Mic

Bang Tango from Los Angeles had a Spinal Tap moment at Mississippi Nights. It happened while headlining on September 21, 1989. After exiting the stage at the show's end, they ran back out for their encore. When singer Joe Lesté tried to grab the mic, it wasn't there. After a moment of confusion, an employee barked into the PA, "We got the mic." Someone had grabbed the cordless mic from the stage and attempted to run out the door with it. Thanks to security, the show continued.

Courtesy of Tony Willingham.

KELLY HOENER* REMEMBERS...

I met Kathy Enloe at an Elvis Brothers show at Mississippi Nights in 1983, and we became great friends.

We went to Mississippi Nights in 1989 to see the Stray Cats with our friends "Country" Larry, who was blind, and Kathy O'Brian. After the show, we went out back to wait by the bus for the band. As we were waiting, the bus started backing up slowly, so we followed the bus, dragging poor Larry along with us. Then, the bus came back, and we came back with it. I think the bus driver was just messing with us. We looked like total morons. When the band finally came out of the club, they went straight onto the bus, but that didn't deter Kathy Enloe, who started screaming at them. The crazy fan approach worked because the band came out to sign autographs.

I had a Brian Setzer 12-inch [record] for him to sign. When he saw it, he said, "Wow! Where'd you get this? I don't even have this."

When the bus headed out, we got in the car and followed it to the Embassy Suites. But we gave up on our half-baked plan when we saw the police. [May 4, 1989]

*Mississippi Nights patron

Courtesy of Kathy Enloe.

Stray Cats, May 4, 1989. Photo by Kelly Hoener.

PAT HAGIN* REMEMBERS...

The local scene was so strong with bands like Big Fun, The Unconscious, and The Eyes. We would not book national talent on Fridays and Saturdays if we could avoid it.

*Mississippi Nights manager

THE EYES
"FREEDOM IN A CAGE"
Body Fall · Way Strange · One Of A Kind
Freedom In A Cage · Flow My Tears

DOLBY SYSTEM   Side 1

PRODUCED BY DAVID PROBST AND THE EYES
ALL SONGS WRITTEN BY THE EYES

From the collection of Garrett Enloe.

Ticket stubs courtesy of Daniel Durchholz, Paul Ebenreck, Kathy Enloe, Stacy Enloe, Eric Eyster, Jeff Frelich, Greg Kessler, Mark Lewis, Lonnie Payeur, and Gian Vianello.

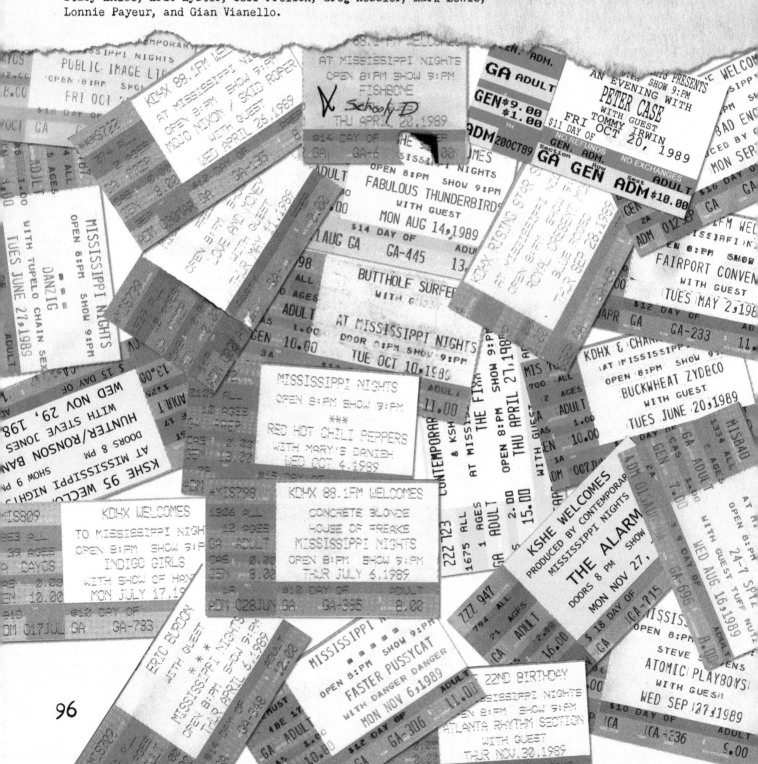

96

PRAISES FROM TESTAMENT

Arron Blow of *Fox Senior High Fox Fax* interviewed Alex Skolnick of Testament after the band's hour and a half headlining set at Mississippi Nights on December 6, 1989. When asked about his favorite clubs to play, Skolnick said, "Believe it or not, I really like Mississippi Nights. I like this place because the staff is very hospitable, everyone is on time, the crowd is really good, and the food is really good which makes a big difference... Mississippi Nights is in the top ten."[a]

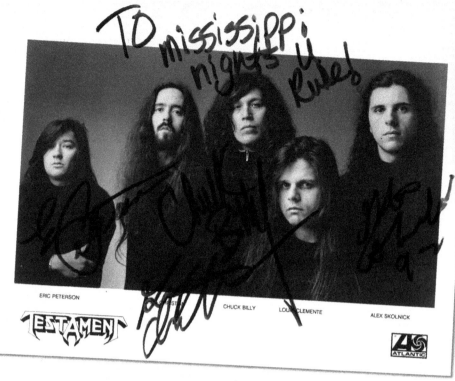

ERIC PETERSON   CHUCK BILLY   LOUIE CLEMENTE   ALEX SKOLNICK

TESTAMENT

ATLANTIC

_____

(a) Blow, Aaron, *"Testament Plays at Mississippi Nights."* Fox Senior High Fox Fax, *vol. 35, 5 no. (1989, December 22) p.5*

MISSISSIPPI NIGHTS
#1 MUSIC CLUB IN ST. LOUIS
ANNOUNCES...

THE CLUB CARD

FOR LIVE MUSIC FANS
WHO CAN'T GET ENOUGH
OF A GOOD THING

THIS MEMBERSHIP CARD ENTITLES YOU TO:
* $1.00 discount each for you and a guest to every event at Mississippi Nights
* 12 FREE shows each year (our choice) for you and a guest
* Placement on our *Exclusive Mailing List*
* Preferential treatment by our *Adoring Staff*
-MEMBERSHIP FEE: $25.00 ANNUALLY-

-CLUB CARD APPLICATION-
PLEASE PRINT CLEARLY

TODAY'S DATE

NAME

ADDRESS

CITY, STATE, ZIP

PHONE#(

SIMPLY FILL OUT THIS FORM AND GIVE IT (WITH $25) TO THE MANAGER ON DUTY AND YOU'RE ALL SET!

RULES
YOU MUST BE 21 YEARS OF AGE OR OLDER

CARD IS NOT TRANSFERRABLE

DISCOUNT ON CONCERT TICKETS APPLIES AT MISSISSIPPI NIGHTS ONLY.

Club Card Promotion. Courtesy of Mark Goldman.

—MISSISSIPPI NIGHTS—
THE MUSIC CLUB IN ST. LOUIS
PRESENTS

SOCIAL DISTORTION

TUESDAY
AUGUST
8

AND

DEAD PLANET

TICKETS
ON SALE NOW

for more info. call 421-3853 ALL AGES ADMITTED

Courtesy of Greg Kessler.

New Year's Eve party with Big Fun. Photo by Mike O'Neil.

ANDY LITTLE* REMEMBERS...

I met my wife on New Year's Eve in 1989 at Mississippi Nights during a Big Fun show. I was with my friends from [Washington University's] Olin School of Business. One of the women in our group, Lexie, ran into a friend. She asked her to join us. Vicki and I hit it off and started dating. The following spring, we took a trip to London and Paris. We loved Paris so much that we stayed there longer than we planned. I had the Big Fun cassette with the song "I Want to Go to Paris," which I played a lot. The next New Year's Eve, we got engaged. We were married the following year.

*Mississippi Nights patron

Kreator behind Mississippi Nights, September 19, 1989.
Photo by Harry Pilkerton.

98

Courtesy of Mark VonDrasek.

SUPPORT HEAVY METAL

MISSISSIPPI NIGHTS

Tickets on sale at all Tickets Now Outlets
Dial-Tix at 434-6600
Vintage Vinyl Euclid Records West End Wax
Gravity Strings Mississippi Nights Box Office

FROM ENGLAND LOUD AND PROUD

MANOWAR

Thursday
JAN 26

SPECIAL GUESTS:
CONQUEST

From the collection of Stacy Enloe.

Courtesy of Greg Kessler.

JET LAG MAGAZINE ®

9TH ANNIVERSARY CELEBRATION

with Jane's Addiction

TUES. MAR. 14

Gary Holt of Exodus, June 22, 1989.
Photo by Harry Pilkerton.

MIS 782
131 ALL
2 AGES
GA ADULT
CAS   1.00
GEN 10.00
1A
ADM 017JUN GA

MISSISSIPPI NIGHTS
* * *
OPEN 8:PM SHOW 9:PM
EXODUS
WITH FORBIDDEN
THUR JUNE 22,1989
$ DAY OF   ADULT
GA-375   11.00

Courtesy of Sam Reeves.

MIS678
1594 ALL
3 AGES
GA ADULT
CAS   1.00
GEN   6.00
1A
ADM 021FEB GA

JANE'S ADDICTION
WITH GUEST
JET LAG'S 9TH ANNIV.
MISSISSIPPI NIGHTS
OPEN 8:PM SHOW 9:PM
TUE MAR 14,1989
$ 8 DAY OF   ADULT
GA-506   7.00

Courtesy of Lonnie Payeur.

*MIS817
1572 ALL
13 AGES
GA DAYOS
CAS   2.00
GEN 12.00
44D
ADM 025JUL GA

STAN RIDGWAY
WITH GUEST
OPEN 8:PM SHOW 9:PM
AT MISSISSIPPI NIGHTS
LACLEDE'S LANDING
TUES JULY 25,1989
$12 DAY OF   DAYOS
GA-542   10.00

Courtesy of Daniel Durchholz.

MIS71b
1403 ALL
1 AGES
GA ADULT
CAS   1.00
GEN 12.00
3A
ADM 020MAR GA

KDHX 88.1 FM WELCOME
AT MISSISSIPPI NIGHT
OPEN 8:PM SHOW 9:P
FISHBONE
WITH GUEST
THU APRIL 20,198
$14 DAY OF   ADU
GA-295   13.

Courtesy of Lonnie Payeur.

TIM URSCH* REMEMBERS...

I worked for the Embassy Suites hotel just across the
street from Mississippi Nights. I was in my early twenties, working as a
bellman, and in college at SIUE [Southern Illinois University Edwardsville].
The bands stayed at the hotel and comped me and three or four of my
friends tickets to the show. I saw Jane's Addiction's first tour, Dada,
Stan Ridgeway, Red Hot Chili Peppers, The Ramones, Fishbone, Rollins, and
more -- all for free.

*Mississippi Nights patron

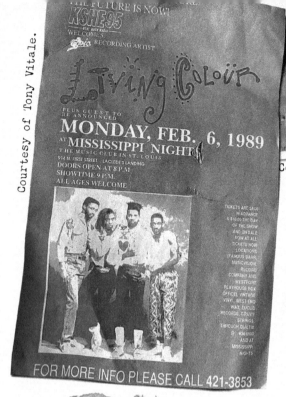

THE FUTURE IS NOW!
KSHE95
WELCOMES
Epic RECORDING ARTIST
Living Colour
PLUS GUEST TO BE ANNOUNCED
MONDAY, FEB. 6, 1989
AT MISSISSIPPI NIGHTS
THE MUSIC CLUB IN ST. LOUIS
914 N. FIRST STREET · LACLEDE'S LANDING
DOORS OPEN AT 8 P.M.
SHOWTIME 9 P.M.
ALL AGES WELCOME

FOR MORE INFO PLEASE CALL 421-3853

KSHE WELCOMES
AT MISSISSIPPI NIGHT
OPEN 8:PM SHOW 9:PM
LIVING COLOUR
WITH GUEST T.B.A.
MON FEB 6, 1989

MISSISSIPPI NIGHTS
PRODUCED BY CONTEMPO
* * *
MR. BIG
DOORS 8:PM SHOW 9:PM
MON NOV 20,1989

Mr. Big, November 20, 1989. Photo by Harry Pilkerton. Ticket stub from the collection of Garrett Enloe.

MIKE SCHRAND* REMEMBERS...

I saw Red Hot Chili Peppers during the 1989 *Mother's Milk* tour at Mississippi Nights. I happened to be standing in the under-21 section when [guitarist] John Frusciante started "Backwoods." I looked out over the crowd, and as the full band launched into the song, everybody on the floor leaped in perfect rhythm to the song. It was amazing to watch. [October 4 or 5, 1989]

*Guitarist/vocalist of Salt of the Earth

MISSISSIPPI NIGHTS
OPEN 8:PM SHOW 9:PM
RED HOT CHILI PEPPERS
WITH GUEST
THU OCT 5 1989

Ticket stub courtesy of Paul Ebenreck.

KSHE 95 WELCOMES
AT MISSISSIPPI NIGHTS
OPEN 8:PM SHOW 9:PM
MEAT LOAF
& THE NEVERLAND EXPRESS
WED JUNE 7,1989

Heuy Lewis of Huey Lewis and the News, performing as Sports Section, September 30, 1989. Photo by Terry Lewis.

1990

The Eyes/Pale Divine

Opening an exciting new decade for St. Louis music, Richard Fortus was the guitar player of arguably the most popular local band in St. Louis, The Eyes. Fortus founded the band six years earlier when he was merely fifteen with vocalist Michael Schaerer, bassist Steve Hanock, and drummer Greg Miller (later in Radio Iodine and Suave Octopus). Hanock left the band before 1990 and was replaced with Dan Angenend. The Eyes rose through the ranks of local bands in St. Louis, constantly playing at the under-21 club Animal House, Kennedy's 2nd Street Company (that would come to be known simply as Kennedy's) on Laclede's Landing, and Mississippi Nights.

One night in 1990, record executive Jason Flom saw a line of people waiting in the rain to get into 1227, a club on Washington Avenue in Downtown St. Louis, to see The Eyes. Flom was famous for signing hard rock bands like Skid Row and Twisted Sister. So he decided to send his assistant to Mississippi Nights to judge the musical merits of this band that weren't his forte but had a large fan base. Fortus says, "I'll never forget her calling [Flom] from the dressing room on the payphone at one in the morning and saying, 'If you don't sign this band, I'm going to quit.'" The band was soon signed to Atlantic Records.

The Eyes changed their name to Pale Divine to avoid confusion with the '60s band of the same name and released the prophetically titled *Straight to Goodbye*.

Troubles began for Pale Divine in 1992 as the band tried to prepare for their sophomore record. Fortus says, "We couldn't get our singer to do anything. It was really frustrating, and he was becoming more and more estranged from us." He continues, "We had a meeting, and Michael came in and said, 'I want to do a solo acoustic album.'" At that point, the band realized they couldn't continue. "I put everything into [Pale Divine], and to have to say, 'Alright, I'm going to walk away from this,' was very difficult," recalls Fortus.

However, the dissolution of Pale Divine prompted Fortus to move to New York, which led him down the path to an incredible career. Fortus wrote, recorded two albums, and toured with Love Spit Love featuring Richard Butler of the Psychedelic Furs. He kept busy as a first-call session musician. Fortus also provided music for TV commercials, TV shows, films, and video games. He, also, toured with electronic artist BT, Julio Iglesias, and others.

Mississippi Nights shirt and patio bricks salvaged from the Mississippi Nights building. Model Merril Barden. Courtesy of Andy Mayberry.

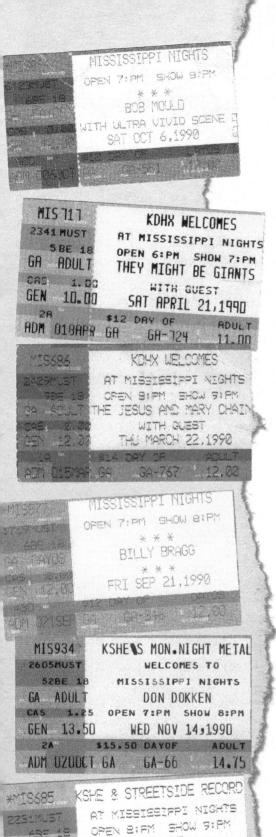

MISSISSIPPI NIGHTS
OPEN 7:PM   SHOW 8:PM
* * *
BOB MOULD
WITH ULTRA VIVID SCENE
SAT OCT 6,1990

MIS 717
2341 MUST
5BE 18
GA ADULT
CAS   1.00
GEN 10.00
2A
ADM 018APR GA

KDHX WELCOMES
AT MISSISSIPPI NIGHTS
OPEN 6:PM   SHOW 7:PM
THEY MIGHT BE GIANTS
WITH GUEST
SAT APRIL 21,1990
$12 DAY OF   ADULT
GA-724   11.00

MIS686
2429 MUST
5BE 18
GA ADULT
CAS   2.00
GEN 12.00
1A
ADM 015MAR GA

KDHX WELCOMES
AT MISSISSIPPI NIGHTS
OPEN 8:PM   SHOW 9:PM
THE JESUS AND MARY CHAIN
WITH GUEST
THU MARCH 22,1990
DAY OF   ADULT
GA-762 $ 12.00

MISSISSIPPI NIGHTS
OPEN 7:PM   SHOW 8:PM
* * *
BILLY BRAGG
* * *
FRI SEP 21,1990
$12 DAY OF   DAYOS
GA-348 $ 12.00

MIS934
2605 MUST
52BE 18
GA ADULT
CAS   1.25
GEN 13.50
2A
ADM 02OCT GA

KSHE'S MON.NIGHT METAL
WELCOMES TO
MISSISSIPPI NIGHTS
DON DOKKEN
OPEN 7:PM   SHOW 8:PM
WED NOV 14,1990
$15.50 DAYOF   ADULT
GA-66   14.75

*MIS685
2251 MUST
6BE 18
GA DAYOS
CAS   2.00
GEN 2.00
12A
ADM 06MAR GA

KSHE & STREETSIDE RECORD
AT MISSISSIPPI NIGHTS
OPEN 8:PM   SHOW 9:PM
X Y Z
WITH GUEST
WED MARCH 21,1990
DAYOS
GA-998 $ 2.00

Ticket stubs from the
collection of Garrett Enloe.

102

During a three-day break from the 2001 tour with Julio Iglesias, Fortus auditioned to join Guns N' Roses. He's been a member ever since, playing sold-out stadiums. While doing session work, he had forged a friendship with Josh Freese (drummer of Guns N' Roses) and Tommy Stinson (bassist of Guns N' Roses), which helped Fortus land the position. During downtime with Guns N' Roses, Fortus stays busy performing and recording with artists of various genres and recording songs for movie soundtracks. In the fall of 2020, Guns N' Roses released the *Not in This Lifetime* pinball machine, making Fortus and Chuck Berry the only St. Louis musicians ever to be cast as characters in a pinball game. So, where did this accomplished musician catch his big break? It was in a club in St. Louis down by the Mississippi River — Mississippi Nights.

Concert August 4, 1990. Gold Award presented to Mississippi Nights. Courtesy of Rich Frame.

The Master of Sound

From 1990 until 2001, Jamie Welky was the sound engineer at Mississippi Nights. He trained at The Recording Workshop in Ohio before he got his foot in the door running sound for Big Fun, the club's house band, from 1986 to 1989. Front-of-house engineer and production manager Larry Gronemeyer recognized his talent and brought him in as crew for some national acts.

After his stint with Big Fun ended, Welky left to work independently with the St. Louis band The Unconscious.

"About 1990, Larry [Gronemeyer] left for the Fox [Theatre], and they asked me to take over as front-of-house," states Welky. His official title was the front-of-house engineer and production manager, and besides running the sound, his duties included coordinating everything for the stage production. He communicated with band's production engineers and tour managers in advance of the show by fax and telephone until the show's end, ensuring everyone worked together for the best production. "If there was an issue, I was there to make sure it got resolved as quickly as possible," he asserts. Welky also maintained a small staff (monitor engineer and lighting technician) and hired up to thirteen additional stagehands for many national bands. He says, "Often, the additional crew I hired were musicians who already had a good understanding of the basics, and I would just level them up to work well in a setting with more moving parts, people, and structure than they were probably used to. Through the years, I worked to maintain an evolving core of people I could rely on."

Welky took pride in being efficient, so things ran smoothly from the stage. He recalls one example, "Over time, I created a system that would help change over from band to band. First, I'd create a master sheet for each show of where all the mics and cables should be. Then, I'd give a copy to each person on my stage crew to minimize the movement of mics, stands, and cables while accommodating each band's specific stage setup."

Jamie Welky 1998. Courtesy of Jamie Welky.

Welky stressed the importance of "knowing the room" to get the sound right, and he knew Mississippi Nights. "In a way, it was a tough building because it has such a low metallic roof on it. But the fact that it was not a complete box helped to disperse the sound," he remembers.

Randy Noldge
and Jamie Welky.
Photo by
Brian Nolan.

Welky upgraded the sound system while in charge as the front-of-house engineer. First, the Soundcraft mixing console was upgraded to a Crest. Eventually, Rich Frame told Welky he could spend some money on a new sound system. "We had this old JBL system, and I'd have to go get a speaker re-coned every few months because people would drive it. It just didn't quite do it for some types of bands," remembers Welky. "I trialed a few different systems and settled on the Electro-Voice X-Array. *That* was a huge improvement in the sound."

Welky had a few go-to songs that he played over the system to get a feel for the sound in the room before soundcheck. First, he chose Bob Mould's "Sunspots" and "Heartbreak a Stranger" because of the tonality of the guitars. "It's not the slickest sounding, but it's an honest sound…and it also has some deep kick and bass guitar on it," he says. "And the other one is Rage Against the Machine's *Bombtrack*, which is considered one of the best sounding rock albums of all time, because that will excite a room acoustically, and you'll hear all the reflections."

The calm, reserved, professional Welky felt starstuck only once. Bob Mould, the singer and guitarist of Husker Dü, was scheduled to play a stripped-down solo show at Mississippi Nights on May 13, 1997. Unlike most pre-production telephone conferences where Welky talked with a tour manager, he spoke with Mould. When Mould arrived at the venue, Welky let his no-nonsense, work attitude slip for just a moment to ask him to sign his CD insert. "It might be the only autograph I ever got," states Welky.

"Mississippi Nights was such a special place," says Welky. He believes the professionalism of the staff, the intimacy of the venue, and the fact that Mississippi Nights wasn't defined by a single genre of music were the characteristics that made the club rise above other venues. However, perhaps out of modesty, he left out one thing repeatedly mentioned about the club: the kick-ass sound.

EVENTS IN 1990

Vintage Vinyl 10th
Anniversary Party

Rock for
Reproductive Rights

Hard Rock Benefit
for the Homeless

Jake's Leg Gets a Surprise

Jake's Leg has been one of St. Louis' most sought-after jam bands for more than four decades. They played Mississippi Nights thirty-three times beginning in 1986. "We loved to play there," says lead guitarist Dave Casper. "I mean *loved* to play there. The staff, managers, and bartenders were awesome. But, most importantly, the venue was almost always packed. It created such great energy."

One of their most memorable moments was during their second set at a packed Mississippi Nights on June 16, 1990. Casper remembers, "I'm guessing it was a tour manager that came up to the stage while we were in between songs and asked me if some members of Fleetwood Mac could sit in with us on a couple of songs." Shocked, Casper responded that the band would be honored. Fleetwood Mac was playing the next night at The Arena [known as the Checkerdome from 1977 to 1983], and apparently, their idea of a fun night on the town the day before a show was jamming at Mississippi Nights.

Mick Fleetwood (drums), Billy Burnette (guitar), and Rick Vito (guitar) made their way from the back of the club to the stage. The excitement in the room increased as people started recognizing them. "They came on stage with smiles, and we played two songs. I wish I could remember the songs we played, but I don't," says Casper. "I do remember it was a whole lot of fun."

Dan Casper adds, "I'm sure a big reason we did so well [at Mississippi Nights] is the fact that they handled their business so well. They advertised heavily and made it such a great place to go and listen to music."

BEN RICKER* REMEMBERS...

I have seen hundreds of shows at Mississippi Nights. I saw Sonic Youth there three times. Once, it was so crowded [the staff] moved the soundboard to the side of the stage and had bouncers lined up to push the pit away from it. It was so packed that I had trouble staying on my feet. I remember [guitarist] Thurston Moore praising the venue, saying it was the best venue in the U.S. [November 10, 1990]

*Mississippi Nights patron

SEAN HALEY* REMEMBERS...

Sonic Youth was sold out, so my friend, Tim, and I just sat out front fucking around. After my fifth beer, I decided to go on a recon mission around back, up the back stairs, to find nobody at the backstage door. I went back around the front, told Tim, and we went in through the back door. It was our only free show at The Nights. [November 10, 1990]

*Mississippi Nights patron

MIS930
4382MUST
340E 18
GA ADULT
CAS 1.00
GEN 12.00
IA
ADM 002NOV GA

MISSISSIPPI NIGHTS
OPEN 7:PM   SHOW 7:45P
- - -
SONIC YOUTH
WITH GUEST
SAT NOV 10,1990
314 DAY OF
GA-422   ADULT
$ 13.00

From the collection of Garrett Enloe.

November 1990

SUNDAY	MONDAY	TUESDAY	WEDNESDAY	THURSDAY	FRIDAY	SATURDAY
				✓1 Babes in Toyland SKINNY PUPPY 8 & 9 at show #1500 17:00 005 305/060	2 Big 306/059 #3	3 Fun 307/058
4	✓5 Energy Orchard	6 ELECTION DAY J. J. Lee + Jumpin Pavlov's	7 The Geardaddys + Big Fun	8 RANDY'S B-DAY Showcase Mama's Pride Duya Duya Rando's Blues Deluxe (Shaking Family) 313/052	9 Finn Bros 3 00	10 Doors at 7 Music is Good w/ Jesus Lizards SONIC YOUTH #12 #14.00 314/051 Jordan

105

MEET
RATT
at
MV
MUSIC·VISION

CYPRESS VILLAGE (on the Rock Road)

Friday, December 7th
4:00 p.m.

Register to Win
An Autographed Guitar
(ROCK ROAD STORE ONLY)

DRAWING WILL BE HELD AT 5:00 p.m.

RATT appears LIVE at MISSISSIPPI NIGHTS
Friday, December 7th

Pick up RATT's DETONATOR

for only $6.93 (tape)   or $12.93 (CD)

Prices good thru December 9th.

From the collection of Stacy Enloe.

AN ANONYMOUS CONCERTGOER REMEMBERS...

When I was sixteen, my two friends and I drove an hour from our hometown to see the sold-out Ratt show at Mississippi Nights. In the middle of Ratt's set, I noticed the girls having trouble breathing or looking like they were going to pass out were getting pulled up onto the stage by security and going backstage. I wanted to go backstage, so without warning my friends, I pretended to swoon. I was pulled on stage and led to the back. I was so excited.

Then, the door opened, and I was outside... behind the building. I was so mad and even more upset when they wouldn't let me back in. Eventually, my friends came out the front, looking for me. A guy sitting out front told us that he was the band's manager, and if we would like to meet the band, they were going to PT's [a strip club in Centerville, Illinois] after the concert. We decided to cross the river and try to meet them. We waited in PT's parking lot for two hours, but neither one of the bands showed up. We didn't make it home until 4 a.m.

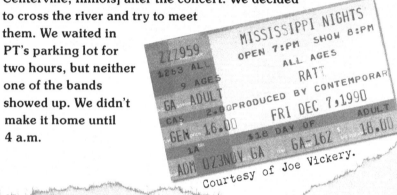

Courtesy of Joe Vickery.

Alannah Myles, May 16, 1990.
Photo by Scott Buettmann.

Doro Pesch October 12, 1990.
Photo by Harry Pilkerton.

106

JOE VICKERY* REMEMBERS...

Now that everybody seems to own a cell phone, taking videos and photos at concerts is common. Things were different back in the days of Mississippi Nights. Most bands didn't allow photos, most likely due to the amateur photographers that sold the photos. Venues had strict policies about no photography, but that didn't stop people from sneaking in cameras and video equipment. When security caught someone with a camera, they took the film and sometimes ejected the offender.

I snuck in my 110 camera into the Ratt show in 1990. I had taken two photos when the security Mississippi Nights had hired caught me. They grabbed me by my neck and dragged me to the back of the club. They asked me for the camera. Right before they grabbed me, I had shoved the camera down my pants, so they could not find it. I told them that I dropped the camera during the scuffle. They both walked away to find it. I quickly headed back to the dance floor. I ended up with one good photo of Stephen Pearcy, the singer of Ratt. [December 7, 1990]

*Mississippi Nights patron

JUAN CROUCIER   STEPHEN PEARCY   BOBBY BLOTZER   ROBBIN CROSBY   WARREN DeMARTI

RATT

Courtesy of Joe Vickery.

MANAGEMENT SHAKE-UP

Manager Pat Hagin left Mississippi Nights to start a management company in 1990. A couple of months later, he received a call from office manager, Pat Lacey, urging him to return. Hagin agreed to return, but only to book bands. He booked shows for Mississippi Nights until 1999, and he also managed The Urge, Stir, and Blue Dixie.

Al Jourgensen of Ministry, December 15, 1990. Photo by Michael Wood, *surFACE* magazine.

METAL BLADE RECORDS
18653 Ventura Blvd. #311
Tarzana, CA. 91356
818-981-9050

LIZZY BORDEN

To Rich:
Thanks for
everything,
Kiss, Lizzy

Master C
Disguise

Concert December 17, 1990. Courtesy of Rich Frame.

Courtesy of Kathy Enloe.

MIS955
981MUST
18E 18
GA ADULT
CAS 0.00
EN 12.00
86
M 006NOV GA
GA-274

MISSISSIPPI NIGH
OPEN   SHOW 8
* * *
ERIC JOHNSON
WITH GUEST
MON DEC 3.1990
914 DAY OF
ADUL
12.00

From the collection of Stacy Enloe.

MIS965
23867 AL
3 AGES
GA ADULT
CAS 1.00
GEN 10.00
1A
ADM 010DEC GA
GA-60

MISSIS IPPI NIGH
OPEN 7 PM SHOW 8
* * *
EVERY MOTHERS NIGH
WITH CHILDS PLA
THUR DEC 13,199
$12 DAY OF
ADL
11.

107

MIS692
6130MUST
74BE 18
GA ADULT
CAS 1.00
GEN 8.00

KDHX WELCOMES
AT MISSISSIPPI NIGHTS
OPEN 8:PM SHOW 9:PM
FAITH NO MORE
WITH GUEST
WED MARCH 28, 1990
$10 DAY OF
ADULT

nickaby
now
0635253
NO REFUNDS
NO EXCHAN

***
CULTURE
WITH GUEST
WEDNESDAY JAN 24, 1990
GA GA-248
12.00

Courtesy of Daniel Durchholz.

NC. NCA18 ROCK FOR REPRODUCTIVE
A18 EVENT RIGHTS *3 MERRY WIDOWS*
PRT VALID FOR THE BISHOPS*3 FOOT THICK
GA ADV. SINISTER DANE*B HENNEMAN
CAS ADMISSION MISSISSIPPI NIGHTS
IF ATTACHED
ROW PRICE $5.00 THUR OCT 18, 1990 9PM
SEAT 10/05 GA DOOR PRT P ADV
SEC/BOX ROW SEAT $5.00
TAX INCLUDED

MIS751
240MUST
2BE 18
GA ADULT
CAS 1.25
GEN 13.00
2A tax

KSHE 95 WELCOMES
AT MISSISSIPPI NIGHTS
OPEN 8:PM SHOW 9:PM
J. J. CALE BAND
WITH GUEST
WED MAY 23, 1990
$15 DAY OF
M 00MAY GA GA-1 2 14.25

Courtesy of Kathy Enloe.

MISSISSIPPI NIGHTS
PRODUCED BY CONTEMPORARY
OPEN 8:PM SHOW 9:PM
BRITNY FOX
WITH GUEST
THUR MARCH 15, 1990
$15 DAY OF
ADM 015MAR GA GA-351 15.00

MISSISSIPPI NIGHTS
OPEN 8:PM SHOW 9:PM
***
DENNIS QUAID
AND THE MYSTICS
MON APRIL 30, 1990

Courtesy of
Tony Willingham.

KDHX WELCOMES
AT MISSISSIPPI NIGHTS
OPEN 8:PM SHOW 9:PM
ROBYN HITCHCOCK
WITH GUEST
THUR JULY 19, 1990
$14 DAY OF
ADULT
JL GA GA-132 13.25

Courtesy of
Tony Vitale.

LUIS MENESES* REMEMBERS...

My favorite memory at The Nights was my first big show at age thirteen. I went to see Danzig, Soundgarden, and Corrosion of Conformity. I dove into the brutal pit during COC. I chilled out for a heavy dose of love rock from Soundgarden. Then, the crowd went crazy for Danzig. My friend Micah and I got right up against the stage and stood on crates.

Security snatched up my buddy Chris while he tried to get to us. They dragged him to the front door, only to look at him and say, "Damn, wrong guy." They thought he was another guy that was fighting. Chris never made it back to the front with Micah and me.

After the show, we went over the wall [at the end of the parking lot] and met John Christ and Eerie Von from Danzig. They were awesome and chatted with us for quite a while. We caught Glenn Danzig for his autograph. Christ and Von told us to go up the fire escape to the dressing room and get Chuck [Biscuits] to complete our autograph collection. As we got to the top, Chuck came out with a woman under his arm and one over his shoulder.

Being young and enthusiastic, we immediately asked for his autograph. He said, "Sure, just let me get down the stairs."

After adding Chuck to our collection, we noticed Micah's mom yelling for us at the top of the wall. She had been lost in East St. Louis while we were meeting the band.
[August 7, 1990]

*Mississippi Nights patron

108

ROCK

Danzig And Soundgarden Are Musical Powerhouses

By David Surkamp

ONE of the hottest tickets in town was for a musical slug-

to a musical blast furnace as anyone I've ever witnessed. Contrasting vocalist Chris Cornell's shriek-back style, with down and dirty harmonic drones,

THE 2 LIVE CREW

OPENING GUEST **POISON CLAN**

AT MISSISSIPPI NIGHTS

Thursday, October 25

2 SHOWS Doors - 6:30; Show - 7; Under 21 Allowed
Doors - 9:30; Show - 10; MUST BE 21

TICKETS - $17.50 ADV.; $19.50 D.O.S.

TICKETS AVAILABLE AT ALL TICKETS NOW OUTLETS
INCLUDING ALL FAMOUS-BARR, ALL MUSIC VISIONS,
WESTPORT PLAYHOUSE, DIALTIX (434-6600), OR AT
THE MISSISSIPPI NIGHTS BOX OFFICE (421-3853).

```
*MIS913              MISSISSIPPI NIGHTS
                   OPEN 6:30PM.SHOW 7:PM
202MUST                    * * *
   1BE 21             2 LIVE CREW
GA  ADULT              WITH GUEST
CAS   0.00          THUR OCTOBER 25.1990
GEN  17.50
            $19.50 DAYOF       ADULT
92A  TAX                         $ 17.50
ADM 021AUG GA    GA-92
```

```
MIS899        MISSISSIPPI NIGHTS
16DAMUST      OPEN 8:PM  SHOW 9:PM
   2BE 18              * * *
GA  DAY05          EXTREME
CAS   1.00      W/ ALICE IN CHAINS
GEN   9.00      THUR OCT 11,1990
   2D          $ 9 DAY OF        DAY05
ADM 0110CT GA      GA-446        10.00
```

CHUCK HESTAND* REMEMBERS...

I saw Alice in Chains on the *Facelift* tour opening for Extreme. It was packed, and the vast majority of the audience had no idea who AIC was since *Facelift* had recently been released. They opened with "It Ain't Like That," and Layne Staley wore overalls and a straw hat. They were incredible, and the entire audience was losing their collective shit. The guys next to me, who were Extreme fans and had never heard of AIC, said, "Fuck Extreme. These guys rule!" It was like watching the death of hair bands happening right in front of my eyes. [October 11, 1990]

*Mississippi Nights patron

Michael Owen of Anacrusis with his parents, Jim and Jackie Owen, October 3, 1990. Courtesy of Jim Owen.

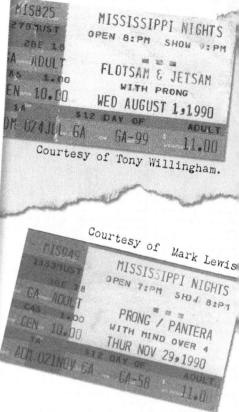

Tommy Victor of Prong, August 1, 1990. Photo by Harry Pilkerton.

MIS825
278MUST
2BE 18
GA ADULT
CAS   1.00
EN 10.00
1A
DM 024JUL GA

MISSISSIPPI NIGHTS
OPEN 8:PM SHOW 9:PM

FLOTSAM & JETSAM
WITH PRONG
WED AUGUST 1,1990
$12 DAY OF
GA-99   ADULT
              11.00

Courtesy of Tony Willingham.

Courtesy of Mark Lewis

MIS949
1153MUST
3BE 18
GA ADULT
CAS   1.00
GEN 10.00
1A
ACM 021NOV GA

MISSISSIPPI NIGHTS
OPEN 7:PM SHOW 8:PM

PRONG / PANTERA
WITH MIND OVER 4
THUR NOV 29,1990
$12 DAY OF
GA-58   ADULT
              11.00

Dimebag Darrell of Pantera, November 29, 1990. Photo by Mike Shupe.

Phil Anselmo of Pantera, November 29, 1990. Photo by Mike Shupe.

1991

Nirvana's First and Last Concert in St. Louis

On Wednesday, October 16, 1991, Nirvana played their only concert in St. Louis, and it was at Mississippi Nights. The show took place only twenty-three days after *Nevermind* was released, and Mississippi Nights was the nineteenth stop on the small tour with Urge Overkill.

Richard Fortus, the guitarist of Pale Divine and Guns N' Roses, recalls the first time he heard "Smells Like Teen Spirit." "I remember just thinking, this is the future of music. This is going to change everything," he says. "I couldn't get my ticket fast enough."

Since the show was booked before the breakout album was released, Mississippi Nights had low expectations for the Nirvana concert. Tickets were only $8. Management was surprised when the show sold out, and they hired extra security to manage the sell-out crowd.

From the first note, the crowd went wild. The entire club was a mosh pit. The first few songs went down without a hitch. Gradually, the security got more and more aggressive with fans.

Concertgoer Barry Kuhlmann recalls, "The bouncers were getting rough with the stage divers," which didn't sit well with singer Kurt Cobain. Kuhlmann continues, "In between songs, he said something along the line of, 'These people are totally respectful, and you bouncers are stepping all over our shit.' He was beginning to get aggravated but managed to stay calm."

Riverfront Times ad for Mississippi Nights.

JESUS
ANEURYSM
DRAIN J.
SCHOOL
FLOYD
TEEN
ABOUT A GIRL
BREED
POLLY
SLIVER
LOVE BUZZ
COME AS YOU R
BEEN A SON
CREPE
ON A PLAIN
BLEW

"Shortly after Cobain's announcement, security violently threw a kid off the stage, and in the process, he unplugged one of Cobain's pedals," says Richard Fortus. That was the last straw.

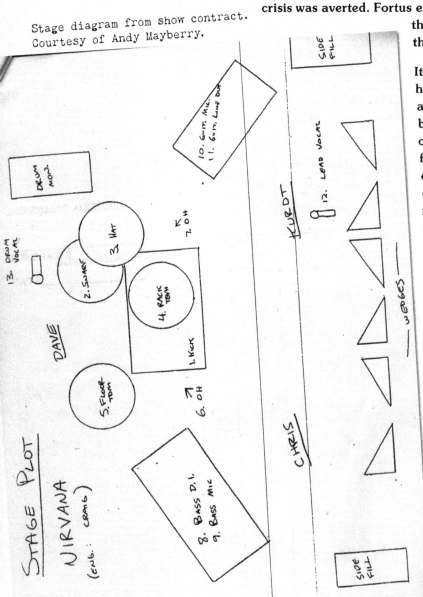

Courtesy of Jim Bielicke.

Stage diagram from show contract.
Courtesy of Andy Mayberry.

"[Cobain] threw down his guitar and very briefly walked off the stage with the rest of the band," recalls Fortus. "He came back to the stage, walked up to the microphone, and said, 'Everybody on the stage now.'"

Over a hundred people climbed up on the stage. "I even saw somebody standing on Dave Grohl's drum kit [on loan from Urge Overkill]," says Fortus.

Security was concerned about a riot breaking out, considering the recent Guns N' Roses riot at Riverport Amphitheatre in St. Louis. When the staff informed owner Rich Frame of the situation, he locked himself in the office "to protect the money," he laughs. However, the crisis was averted. Fortus explains, "[Bassist] Krist Novoselic persuaded the crowd to leave the stage, and they finished their set."

It easily could have been a riot. Many articles have been written about the Nirvana show at Mississippi Nights that exaggerate events by using the word 'riot.' If the band hadn't come back... if Novoselic hadn't acted... if a fan had become unruly... mayhem may have ensued. However, the tipping point never came. Calling it a near-riot doesn't sell as many magazines, and that's what it was: a near riot.

As of 2021, *Nevermind* has sold over 30 million copies worldwide, making the album one of the best-selling of all time. In 2014, Nirvana was inducted into the Rock and Roll Hall of Fame. The Nirvana show is one of the best examples of Mississippi Nights getting a band on their way up.

EVENTS IN 1991

John Lennon Benefit

Route 66: The Road West
(film making)

Kimberly Witthaus and Bret Michaels, October 19, 1991. Courtesy of Kimberly Witthaus.

```
MIS 19OCT     MISSISSIPPI NIGHTS
0258 ALL         WELCOMES
      AGES    OPEN 8:PM SHOW 9:PM
GA ADULT        BRET MICHAELS
CAS $1.25    AND THE GUTTERCATS
GEN $18.00      SAT OCT 19,1991
  3A $0.00  GEN ADM         ADULT
ADM K255EP  GA    GEN ADM $19.25
```

Courtesy of Cyndi Bauman.

Anacrusis

St. Louis' Anacrusis is well respected worldwide and one of the first bands to mix thrash with progressive metal. Their albums *Manic Impressions* and *Screams and Whispers* are thrash-metal and prog-metal classics.

Before joining Anacrusis, guitarist Ken Nardi was in the three-piece band Heaven's Flame. Heaven's Flame had hints of Black Sabbath, Trouble, Venom, and Motorhead with Judas Priest-style vocals. They played Mississippi Nights twice, once opening for Metal Church. Right before Nardi graduated high school in 1986, Heaven's Flame broke up.

Anacrusis began with a classic rock style. They had one performance under their belt when guitarist Kevin Heidbreder chose to shift to heavier music. Drummer Mike Owen and bassist John Emery heard Ken Nardi was available, and the four joined together in 1986.

"Anacrusis was just starting, and we had set up our self-financed first performance at the Bridgeton Community Center," John Emery remembers. "Then, we had the opportunity to play The Nights opening for The Killer Dwarfs in March 1987. Playing Mississippi Nights was like Madison Square Garden for us. Not a lot of folks there, but it was cool to get our feet wet at such a prestigious and heralded facility."

KENN NARDI
GUITAR / VOCALS

JOHN EMERY
BASS

MIKE OWEN
DRUMS

KEVIN HEIDBREDER
GUITAR

MN! RULES!! ANACRUSIS

METAL BLADE
18653 VENTURA BLVD.
SUITE 311 TARZANA
CA 91356 818 981 9050

TCI TALENT CONSUL. INTERN. Ltd.
200 WEST 57TH STR
SUITE 910
NEW YORK, N.Y. 1
212 582 9661
FAX 212 974 9163

Management:
Kathy Kohler
415-332-8716

113

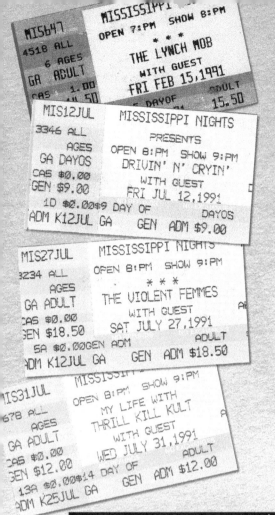

MIS647
4518 ALL
6 AGES
GA ADULT
CAS 1.00
15.50

MISSISSIPPI
OPEN 7:PM   SHOW 8:PM
* * *
THE LYNCH MOB
WITH GUEST
FRI FEB 15,1991
DAYOF   ADULT
15.50

MIS12JUL
3346 ALL
AGES
GA DAYOS
CAS $0.00
GEN $9.00
1D $0.00$9 DAY OF
ADM K12JUL GA

MISSISSIPPI NIGHTS
PRESENTS
OPEN 8:PM   SHOW 9:PM
DRIVIN' N' CRYIN'
WITH GUEST
FRI JUL 12,1991
DAYOS
GEN ADM $9.00

MIS27JUL
3234 ALL
AGES
GA ADULT
CAS $0.00
GEN $18.50
5A $0.00GEN ADM
ADM K12JUL GA

MISSISSIPPI NIGHTS
OPEN 8:PM   SHOW 9:PM
* * *
THE VIOLENT FEMMES
WITH GUEST
SAT JULY 27,1991
ADULT
GEN ADM $18.50

MIS31JUL
678 ALL
AGES
GA ADULT
CAS $0.00
GEN $12.00
13A $0.00$14 DAY OF
ADM K25JUL GA

MISSISSIPPI
OPEN 8:PM   SHOW 9:PM
MY LIFE WITH
THRILL KILL KULT
WITH GUEST
WED JULY 31,1991
ADULT
GEN ADM $12.00

CYNDI WEINMANN BAUMAN* REMEMBERS...

I often sat outside the club for hours to (1) meet the bands and (2) be in the front row. Once, I escorted Butch Walker (at the time, he was with Southgang) to Barnes Hospital because he had problems hearing. The intake coordinator giggled at the irony of a rock musician having hearing problems. [August 12, 1991]

Mississippi Nights patron

MIS10DEC
1511 ALL
AGES
GA DAYOS
CAS $1.00
GEN $12.00
2D $0.00$12 DAY OF
ADM K10DEC GA

MISSISSIPPI NIGHTS
PRESENTS
OPEN 8:PM   SHOW 9:PM
SCATTERBRAIN
WITH GUEST
TUE DEC 10,1991
DAYOS
GEN ADM $13.00

114   Ticket stubs courtesy of Cyndi Bauman.

"We went on to open for several other national acts over the coming years and also did a couple of record release shows there as well," notes Emery.

Kevin Heidbreder adds, "[We were] blessed indeed to have played there and to have seen so many shows there."

Anacrusis' first full-length album, *Suffering Hour,* was self-financed and released in 1988 on the UK label Axis Records. They recorded a music video for the song "A World to Gain" at Mississippi Nights but never released it. Nardi explains, "The song is doomy and dark, but the video looks like the Van Halen 'Jump' video." He continues, "We did not dress for the part. My hair looks like the singer of The Alarm, not heavy metal at all." Since the band was young and new to the video-making experience, silly antics ended up in the video, like Mike Owen using his shoes as drumsticks. Nardi remembers, "Thankfully, the video had no budget. Mississippi Nights had let us shoot the video in a couple of hours for free."

The band toured with DRI in 1990 to support their second release, *Reason.* Following that tour, Anacrusis signed to Metal Blade Records, which re-released their back catalog. The band released Manic Impressions in 1991 and did an eight-date tour with Megadeth, followed by a thirty-eight-city tour with Overkill.

On June 19, 1993, KSHE-95 sponsored a record-release show at Mississippi Nights for their fourth studio album, *Screams and Whispers.* Admission was 95¢, playing off of KSHE's 94.7 FM channel frequency. Around 750 people attended, including Ross Valory and Gregg Rolie from Journey, who were in town working on a side project called The Storm. The entire concert was filmed for the Double Helix cable access show *Critical Mass.*

In September 1993, Anacrusis did an eighteen-date tour of Europe with Death. Unfortunately, when the band returned to the United States, they broke up.

After a seventeen-year hiatus, they played at T Billy Buffett's on April 18, 2010, and released a DVD of their reunion. After that, Anacrusis occasionally played over the next few years. Then, they took another six years off. Finally, on December 7, 2019, they played a reunion concert at Delmar Hall, which included every member of Anacrusis. The reunion coincided with the re-release of their four albums remastered by Metal Blade Records.

MN! RULES!!

Kingofthehill

The band that would eventually become Kingofthehill began in 1985 with "Frankie" slapped on their demo tapes. They hadn't come up with a name yet, so they used the singer's first name on their demo tape, and the name stuck. With Frankie Muriel (vocals), Rich Goodman (guitar), Cubby Smith (bass), and Vito Bono (drums), Frankie won a "Battle of Bands" at Mississippi Nights in 1986.

Muriel says, "Rich [Frame] and Pat [Hagin] put us on the slot, and we started opening up for all the bands we fit with." He notes, "Out of high school parties, I went right to Mississippi Nights."

After Rich Goodman accidentally put his hand through a glass door in 1987, Jimmy Griffin joined on guitar, and the band changed their name to Broken Toyz. Later, George Potsos took over on bass to cement the lineup.

Broken Toyz was signed in 1990 to a subsidiary of EMI. Muriel says, "There was a brand-new label [SBK]." SBK's roster included Vanilla Ice, Wilson Phillips, Jesus Jones, and Technotronic. "They had their rap, their pop, their alternative, and they had their electronica, and they wanted a rock band...these guys approached us and said, 'you'll be our priority because you'll be our only rock band.'"

"But it bit us," Muriel explains, "because they didn't have any experience with promoting a rock band."

"We had to give up the name Broken Toyz because the management company had a band called Dangerous Toys," George Potsos notes. So, pressed for time as they wrapped up recording their debut, self-titled album, their song, "Kingofthehill," became their new name.

On March 3, 1991, Kingofthehill played a free showcase at Mississippi Nights sponsored by KSHE-95. SBK rented a floor at the Embassy Suites across the street for the band to conduct interviews and press events.

Concert March 14, 1991. Courtesy of Rich Frame.

VITO BONO   JIMMY GRIFFIN   FRANKIE   GEORGE POTSOS

KINGOFTHEHILL   SBK Records

After extensive touring, including opening for Extreme on the European leg of their *Pornograffitti* tour, Kingofthehill was ready to do a second record when their A&R guy was fired. "The new guy came in, and we were just something else on his desk," Muriel says. "We sat in limbo forever." Next, Muriel attempted a solo record but eventually concentrated on producing other regional bands.

Then in 1996, Muriel was approached by former bandmate Cubby Smith. "Cubby said, 'Hey, we're doing that disco band that you always wanted to do but never had time to do.'" Muriel asserts, "I literally was going to do it for a week."

Disco, dance, and rock cover band Dr. Zhivegas sold out multiple nights at Mississippi Nights, playing twenty-five shows in four years. During the Mississippi Nights era, the band was Frankie Muriel (vocals), Paul Chickey (drums), Cubby Smith (bass), Dee Dee James (guitar), Steven Button (guitar), Chris Krieger (keyboards vocals), Kasimu Taylor (trumpet), and Eric Rhodes (sax). Twenty-five years after its inception, and a few member changes later, Dr. Zhivegas continues touring and playing to sold-out crowds.

Muriel remembers Mississippi Nights fondly. "There were so many great shows there. For every one of my incarnations, I've had such great success in that room," he says. "That's the fabric of my career."

The eleven employees identified in this 1991 photo are listed in alphabetical order: John Cavanaugh, Robin Duncan, Greg Kenney, Mike Kleb, Tim Mullen, Steve "Pac-Man" Pack, Janet Roberts, Mitch Shelton, Donna, Janice, and Ross. Photo courtesy of Greg Kenney.

Fugazi was the hottest show I ever played. My band Ultraman opened. Fugazi brought their own halogen lights, which were used for both bands. The stage was easily 125 degrees. We played for forty minutes. During the set, I drank three pitchers of water. Afterward, I wrung a puddle of sweat out of my shirt. [June 4, 1991]

*Guitarist of White Suburban Youth, Ultraman, Snake Ranch, Bent, Adoring Heirs, and bassist of Spacetrucker

Ticket stubs courtesy of Mark Lewis.

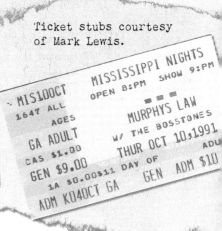

The Career of a St. Louis Punk

Rob Wagoner, guitarist for White Suburban Youth, Ultraman, Snake Ranch, Bent, Adoring Heirs, and bassist for Spacetrucker, has been part of the St. Louis punk music scene since 1982.

Wagoner and Tim Jamison formed White Suburban Youth in 1982. Before dissolving in 1986, the band played everywhere in St. Louis, including twice at Mississippi Nights: once with MIA, and once with Battalion of Saints and Drunks with Guns. Before long, Michael Doskocil from Drunks with Guns (who once tried to steal the AC/DC photo from the Mississippi Nights lobby) was playing drums with Wagoner and Jamison. Two weeks after White Suburban Youth broke up, Wagoner and Jamison formed Ultraman with John Corcoran (bass), Bob Zuellig (guitar), and Mike Doskocil (drums).

Ultraman made its Mississippi Nights debut on April 29, 1987, opening for Suicidal Tendencies.

Mark Deniszczuk replaced Doskocil on drums in 1987.

Between 1986 and 1988, Ultraman released a demo cassette, two 7-inch singles, and in 1988, they toured the East Coast. In 1989, Nicky Garratt, former guitar player for UK Subs, was looking for a Midwest band with name recognition and tour experience to join his New Red Archives record label. When he heard Ultraman's second single, "Destroys All Monsters," Garratt signed the band and invited them to New York to record their first album, *Freezing Inside,* released in 1989. To promote *Freezing Inside,* Ultraman toured the West Coast with St. Louis foodcore/beer metal band Whoppers Taste Good. Later that year, Ultraman toured the East Coast and Canada with UK Subs.

The band's second album, *Non-Existence,* was recorded in San Francisco and released in 1990. Shortly after, they embarked on the "European in Your Pants" tour with labelmates Samiam. On their first swing through Europe, they played, among others, Germany, Austria, Switzerland, England, and France.

117

Ultraman returned to the US to support the album with a short tour and then headed back to Europe in the middle of 1991, playing in the Netherlands, Belgium, Germany, and Austria. Later that year, Ultraman announced its dissolution. The grueling tour, the departure of John Corcoran, and changes in musical direction had all helped hasten the demise of Ultraman. On December 30, 1991, the band's final concert was at Mississippi Nights.

Rob Wagoner claims that night remains his proudest moment as a musician, and when he heard the show was sold out, he cried. Ultraman arrived at the venue to see the line wrapped around the block. The final Ultraman show happened two months after the legendary Nirvana performance. It was the beginning of a new direction in music. Wagoner recalls, "That Ultraman show marked the end of the underground scene [in St. Louis]. Bands either fizzled away or were signed in the early days of the alternative scene. That concert showed other bands in St. Louis that an underground band could sell out Mississippi Nights."

Concert May 11, 1991. Courtesy of Gian Vianel[

THE SKELETONS

ESD
EAST SIDE DIGITA[

Rik Emmett, May 22, 1991.
Photo by Terry Lewis.

From the collection of Stacy Enloe.

LISADE DONOVAN* REMEMBERS...

I was pulled on stage by the scary blonde guy in Firehouse and forced to sing along. Thinking back, it was pretty cool, but then, I thought, 'No, this isn't happening.' I probably looked like a deer in the headlights. I think he did it because we had matching hair. [April 24, 1991]

*Mississippi Nights patron

Courtesy of
Cyndi Bauman.

Shortly after Wagoner left Ultraman, he formed Bent with former members of Whoppers Taste Good (Rich Ulrich), Snake Ranch (Marc Sova), and Ultraman (Mark Deniszczuk). Between 1993 and 1997, Bent played Mississippi Nights eleven times, including one night when REO Speedwagon keyboardist Neal Doughty, in the audience as a guest of his niece, sat in on a tiny Casio keyboard for a performance of REO Speedwagon's "Riding the Storm Out." A recording exists but remains unreleased.

In 1994, *Nothing Grows Here Anymore* was released on Grass Records. After a concert in 1996, Bent was temporarily banned from playing Mississippi Nights for handing out free paper stickers to everyone. On nearly every surface of the club, the resulting mess took maintenance hours to remove.

Over the years, Ultraman played several reunions, some with Wagoner and some without him, but Tim Jamison has remained the constant in the band. The current Ultraman lineup includes Jamison, Tim O'Saben (Fragile Porcelain Mice), Bob Fancher (For the Last Time), Ryan Meszaros (Cuban Missiles), and Gabe Usery (The Disappeared).

Aldo Nova, August 26, 1991.
Photo by Scott Buettmann.

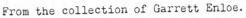

From the collection of Garrett Enloe.

Joe Thebeau of The Finns, January 24, 1991.
Photo by Dave Probst.

SONNY ROLLINS

Photo: Phil Bray

Photo © 1991, Fantasy, Inc.
Permission to reproduce this photograph is
limited to editorial uses in regular issues of
newspapers and other regularly published
periodicals and television news programming.

Milestone

Concert October 1, 1991. Courtesy of Rich Frame.

UNCLE TUPELO

AND

The **MAGNOLIAS**

WED.

MARCH 20

All Ages

MISSISSIPPI NIG

Courtesy of John Wegrzyn.

MIS29JUN KSHE WELCOMES
0136 ALL TO MISSISSIPPI NIGHTS
AGES OPEN 8:PM SHOW 9:PM
GA ADULT KANSAS
CAS $1.25 WITH GUEST
GEN $16.50 SAT JUNE 29,1991
2A $0.00 $18.50 DAYOF ADULT
ADM K07JUN GA GEN ADM $17.75

Courtesy of
Rick Comello.

MIS9NOV KSHE 95 WELCOMES
3101 ALL MISSISSIPPI NIGHTS
AGES OPEN 8:PM SHOW 9:PM
GA ADULT RTZ
CAS $1.00 WITH GUEST
GEN $10.00 SAT NOV 9,1991
2A $0.00 $12 DAY OF ADULT
ADM K06NOV GA GEN ADM $11.00

MIS12NOV MISSISSIPPI NIGHTS
1070 ALL OPEN 8:PM SHOW 9:PM
AGES * * *
GA ADULT BUZZCOCKS
CAS $0.00 WITH GUEST
GEN $14.00 TUE NOV 12,1991
6A $0.00 $16 DAY OF ADULT
ADM K21OCT GA GEN ADM $14.00

From the collection of Garrett Enloe.

MIS18SEP MISSISSIPPI NIGHTS
1792 ALL OPEN 9:PM SHOW 10:30PM
AGES AN EVENING WITH
GA ADULT FRONT 242
CAS $0.00 ONE SET
GEN $16.00 WED SEP 18,1991
5A $0.00 $ DAY OF ADULT
ADM K13SEP GA GEN ADM $16.00

Courtesy of Tricia Zelazny.

MIS22AUG MISSISSIPPI NIGHTS
2350 ALL OPEN 8:PM SHOW 9:PM
AGES - - -
GA ADULT BULLET BOYS
CAS $1.00 WITH GUEST
GEN $12.00 THUR AUG 22,1991
2A $0.00 $14 DAY OF ADULT
ADM K27JUL GA GEN ADM $13.00

Courtesy of Joe Vickery.

Courtesy of Mike Bellew.

WARNING:

COMBAT THRASH

THE GRINDCRUSHER TOUR

FEATURING:

 **GODFLESH**

WILL DEVASTATE ST. LOUIS

MISSISSIPPI NIGHTS
THE MUSIC CLUB IN ST. LOUIS
LACLEDE'S LANDING

IN CONCERT MAY 1, 1991

Mississippi Nights advertisement in the *Riverfront Times*.

THANKS TO MISS. NIGHTS

Courtesy of Mark VonDrasek.

THE URGE

VALENTINE'S DAY MASSACRE – THURS. 2/14
at Mississippi Nights → ALL AGES
w/ THE Jungle Dogs and Life w/out Wayne

2/15 THE REGENCY (Springfield)

2/16 Kennedys

2/22-23 THE Hangar (carbondale)

2/28 Ciceros

3/1 Mississippi Nights

3/2 THE Hi Pointe

***S675   KSHE & MUSIC VISION
1571 ALL   PRESENTS
   31 AGES   ***
GA ADULT   CRY WOLF
CAS   0.00   OPEN 8:PM SHOW 9:PM
GEN   0.00   MON MARCH 11,1991
 29A   FREE SHOW   ADULT
ADM 020FEB GA   GA-1329   0.00

From the collection
of Garrett Enloe.

KSHE WELCOMES
MUSIC VISION PRESENTS
DOORS 8:PM SHOW 9:PM
SPIRIT
AT MISSISSIPPI NIGHTS
THURS FEB 7, 1991

Courtesy of
Randy Avellone.

Jayce Fincher of Southgang and
Stacy Enloe. August 12, 1991.

Play that Mother F***ing Urge S***!

One of St. Louis' most popular bands, The Urge, called Mississippi Nights their home away from home. Mississippi Nights' calendars show that The Urge played the venue ninety-three times from 1989 to 2007. However, that figure is most likely short by a dozen or so since lead singer Steve Ewing remembers the night manager Tim Weber announced The Urge were playing their 100th show at Mississippi Nights.

The Urge combine many styles: ska, reggae, hardcore punk, heavy metal, funk, rock, and rhythm and blues. They are an energetic live band with a talent for getting everyone dancing or moshing.

The band was formed in 1987 by Pat Malecek (guitar) of Saint Louis University High School and Webster Groves High School classmates Jeff Herschel (drums) and Karl Grable (bass). They went through two different singers before Steve Ewing joined in 1988. The band added a saxophonist, Jordan Chalden, in 1990. Saxophonist/keyboardist Bill Reiter replaced Chalden in 1992, and the horn section was rounded out with trombonists Matt Kwiatkowski and Todd Painter.

The Urge's first performance at Mississippi Nights was on September 27, 1990, with Sinister Dane and Tuff Nutz opening the show. Tickets were $4.

On April 29, 1994, at Mississippi Nights, founding member Jeff Herschel played his last Urge concert. He wanted to go out with a bang, so he concocted a surprise. Audience member Rob Wagoner recalls,

Flyer courtesy of Jeff Herschel.

STEVEN "ROCK" BLACK* REMEMBERS THE URGE...

The Urge shows were always fun because they were just chaos. Everyone went nuts. Everyone had a good time. There was a good vibe in the room. Everyone really looked out for each other. The mosh pit was active, but people were helping each other up.

*Mississippi Nights doorman/assistant manager

"After the last song, he got out a circular saw and proceeded to cut his drums in half on the stage, cutting through metal, sparks flying everywhere. The bass drum was in two pieces. Then, he proceeded to throw all the cut-up drums into the crowd."

"Right after he tossed the drums," Bill Reiter says, "I remember seeing somebody run out of the club with his hi-hat. [Herschel] forgot we still had to do an encore, which was twenty-five minutes of music. Luckily, a friend of ours had a drum set in his car. He quickly set it up, and we were able to finish the set."

Before being signed to a major record label in 1996, The Urge released four independent albums: *Bust Me Dat Forty* (1989 on cassette), *Puttin' the Backbone Back* (1990), *Magically Delicious* (1992), and *Fat Babies in the Mix* (1993). The latter was recorded live by Mississippi Nights' sound engineer, Jamie Welky, from the closet-sized

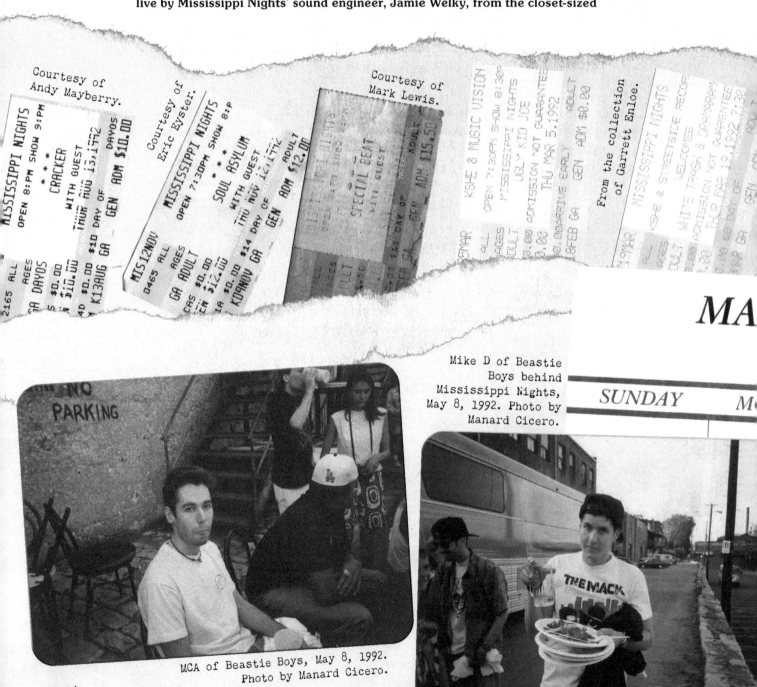

Mike D of Beastie Boys behind Mississippi Nights, May 8, 1992. Photo by Manard Cicero.

MCA of Beastie Boys, May 8, 1992. Photo by Manard Cicero.

124

second dressing room. Urge shows are known for getting hectic and crazy, and the band was concerned that the audience's enthusiasm might adversely affect the live recording. So, Saxophonist Bill Reiter recalls, "The night of the recording, we made an announcement to tell our fans to chill out a little bit, so we wouldn't have any problems."

However, the announcement was in vain. The crowd managed to knock over microphones and make enough noise to be picked up on the recording. Reiter continues, "Nevertheless, the concert was going as planned and sounding great. We had two songs left in the set, and we ran out of tape. The last two songs [on *Fat Babies in the Mix*] were [recorded] from the night before."

On the strength of their independent releases, The Urge toured with 311 in 1994. After the tour, founding member Pat Malecek left the band about six months after Herschel's departure.

In 1995, the band released *Receiving the Gift of Flavor* on their own Neat Guy record label. Successful album sales led to attention from Epic Records. The Urge signed to Immortal (an imprint of Epic Records), and the label re-released *Receiving the Gift of Flavor* in 1996. *Master of Styles,* which contains the hit "Jump Right In," was released in 1998. Following the release of *Too Much Stereo* in 2000, the band toured for nine months.

"When we got off the road, we were pretty physically exhausted," emphasized singer Steve Ewing. "We were going through a weird period where we weren't agreeing on what we wanted to do musically."

Spencer Riggle with King Ad-Rock of Beastie Boys behind Mississippi Nights, May 8, 1992. Courtesy of Spencer Riggle.

Courtesy of Mark Lewis.

MISSISSIPPI NIGHTS
OPEN 8:PM SHOW 9:PM
* * *
BEASTIE BOYS
WITH GUEST
FRI MAY 8, 1992

125

The band's label, Immortal, was going under in the United States during this time. Additionally, the band was unhappy with their new management company. So, with the cards seemingly stacked against their success, the band decided to split up in late December 2001. However, they still played shows occasionally.

The Urge became synonymous with Thanksgiving and Christmas at Mississippi Nights. The tradition began on Thanksgiving in 1992 and had a $5 ticket price. "That was my idea," declares Pat Hagin, who managed the band at the time, as well as booked shows for Mississippi Nights. "Because I knew The Urge's crowd... on Thanksgiving night they were sick to death of being with their parents and wanted something to do."

"Those were some rough nights," Ewing remembers. "We'd do a sold-out underage show. Then, Hagin would kick all the kids out, and we would play from midnight until 3 a.m." The last Thanksgiving show was in 1995, and the Christmas shows were expanded to multiple sold-out nights.

In the last three years of The Urge holiday spirit, 1998, 1999, and 2000, the band played four Christmas shows each year for $15 a ticket.

"Mississippi Nights was like the varsity club as far as St. Louis goes," states Ewing. "You feel like all the other clubs are feeding into the moment when you start playing Mississippi Nights. It got to the point where it became home."

Thirteen years after the release of *Too Much Stereo*, the band came together to record their seventh studio album, *Galvanized,* in 2013. In addition, The Urge has revived the annual holiday tradition by playing at The Pageant the day after Thanksgiving. Now, perhaps The Urge's crowd is too busy driving their kids crazy on Thanksgiving.

JAMIN HURT*
REMEMBERS THE URGE...

One show that stands out was my first time seeing The Urge at Mississippi Nights. When they took the stage, Steve [Ewing] yelled, "Heyyy!" The place immediately went nuts: stage diving, crowd surfing, guys crawling on the rafters and falling into the crowd. A big shirtless dude with a tattoo of a black hand on his shoulder was in the center of the pit, just laughing and shoving everybody, almost as if he was directing the pit. Awesome times -- none of which you can do anymore without getting kicked out by security.

*Mississippi Nights patron

Ticket stubs from the collection of Garrett Enloe.

126

Public Enemy

On September 14, 1992, Public Enemy played at Mississippi Nights with The Urge in support. The Urge singer Steve Ewing remembers the crowd was divided between The Urge fans and Public Enemy fans, the latter who seemed confused by the moshing and crazy antics of the former. "By the end of our set, everyone was totally into it, though," remembers Steve Ewing. The band always enjoyed the challenge of winning over people.

Public Enemy's intro began about 45 minutes after the band was scheduled to start. Then, it stopped. *St. Louis Post Dispatch* music critic Steve Pick reported, "A few minutes later, the familiar voice of Public Enemy's leader, Chuck D, could be heard testing his microphone. The theme came up again, and the show actually started."[c] However, someone was missing: rapper Flavor Flav.

_____

(c) Pick, Steve, "Show Goes On, Finally, For Public Enemy." St. Louis Post Dispatch, *Wednesday, September 16, 1992, P. 6F*

Concert September 14, 1992. Courtesy of Rich Frame.

L-R	BROTHER ROGER	BROTHER JAMES I	TERMINATOR X	CHUCK D	FLAVOR FLAV	JAMES BOMB	BROTHER MICHAEL	THE DREW

PUBLIC ENEMY

Columbia
9003

Pick recounted, "It didn't take long for Chuck D to announce that Flavor Flav was late and that [he] wasn't too happy about it."

Flav arrived 30 minutes later, and "Chuck D asked him to apologize to the audience for being late," wrote Pick. "Flavor refused. Instead, the latecomer insisted he be allowed to perform one of his songs and started naming different ones on which he had been lead rapper." Many concertgoers reported that at this point, Chuck D fired Flavor Flav. "Chuck D led the rest of the group offstage, leaving Flav to rant and rave all by himself," Pick reported.

Eventually, the rest of the group returned to the stage. "From there, we were treated to about 20 minutes of prime Public Enemy," wrote Pick.

"Still, the late start meant the show had to end before it had run its course," noted Pick, "and the encore, a song from a new album, *Greatest Misses,* released this week, did not include Flavor Flav." Pick concluded his review with, "It was a strange way to end a strange, and sometimes brilliant, concert."

One of the great legends of Mississippi Nights is the whereabouts of Flav that night, causing him to be so late to the concert. Ask around, and you may get some opinions.

Albert Collins, May 6, 1992. Photo by Kevin Belli.

Joe Walsh
pyramid records
MONTEREY PENINSULA ARTISTS
epic 9206

Concert October 12, 1992.
Courtesy of Rich Frame.

Clockwise from top: Tom Dumont   Eric Stefani   Adrian Young   Gwen Stefani   Tony Kanal

Concert September 26, 1992.
Courtesy of Rich Frame.

Gwar

Brutal heavy metal, gore, sacrifices, chaos, elaborate costumes that spray blood, humor, monsters, and mutilation of infamous or political figures: this all adds up to Gwar!

Gwar, the brainchild of vocalist Dave Brockie, formed in 1984 in Richmond, Virginia. What was first called "Gwaaarrrgghhlllgh" started as a side project joke band, often opening for Brockie's other band, Death Piggy. After several refinements, including shortening the band's name to just "Gwar," Death Piggy was phased out. Dave Brockie, known as "Oderus Urungus from planet Scumdoggia," was the singer from the band's inception in 1984 until he died in 2014.

Gwar's first appearance in St. Louis was at Mississippi Nights on June 13, 1992. The club was aware of the elaborate stage show but not fully prepared. There was no plastic protecting equipment, lights, or monitors. It took several days to clean up the mess the band left behind, but Gwar returned to play Mississippi Nights five more times.

In the 1870s, the Mississippi Nights building was a slaughterhouse, so the floors were slanted to drain blood from animal carcasses. One hundred twenty years later, the fake blood from Gwar's show flowed down those slanted floors and out the back door. During their concerts, band members sprayed the audience with two types of fluids. The thinner liquid, made of water and powdered food coloring, washes off easily. The thicker liquid was made from carrageenan, a red seaweed extract used as a thickening agent in foods. Unfortunately, the thicker stuff sticks to and stains everything, causing most people leaving a Gwar show to look like they were in a bloody battle.

Server Angela Prada remembers, "These shows were fantastic! Newbies that worked their first Gwar show were initiated by being thrown in the after-goo. [It left] stains for days on your skin. It never came out of clothing... *ever.*"

The band and their crew were very organized in juxtaposition to their live show. The production ran like a well-oiled machine, and the Mississippi Nights management had no problems with them. Angela Prada says, "After the show, a few of them would always

PHOTO BY: JOSEPH CULTICE

2345 ERRINGER RD.
SUITE 108
SIMI VALLEY, CA 93065

(805)522-9111

walk down to Kennedy's [2nd Street Company] with me to get their French onion soup. It was a ritual. They were a super great group of people!" She says, "Gwar shows were some of my favorites to work."

From 1988 to 2022, Gwar released fifteen studio albums, two live albums, and two extended play albums. The band was nominated for a Grammy for Best Long Form Music Video for their 1993 film, *Phallus in Wonderland*. In 1995, Gwar was nominated for a Grammy for Best Metal Performance for the song "SFW." Gwar continues to perform without any original members.

MISSISSIPPI NIGHTS' PERSONAL TOUCH

Christopher Ellis was a runner (a person that shuttles the band or does errands for them) for a few years at Mississippi Nights. He says, "I remember taking Gwar's laundry to the coin laundromat in Soulard. They were shocked that I cleaned and folded it all instead of just dropping it off to have the laundromat worker take care of it. I saved them some bucks!"

Jamming with Blue Dixie

Blue Dixie was formed in the fall of 1988 at the University of Missouri, Columbia. They played a mixture of originals, Grateful Dead covers, and rock 'n' roll standards. Two weeks before they played their first gig, they used sidewalk chalk all over the university to promote themselves. As a result, their first show at a backyard barbeque (complete with a stage, lights, and a PA system) drew a crowd of about 1,000 people. After that, the band began playing around town and the Midwest, eventually landing gigs at Mississippi Nights in 1990. By the time Blue Dixie arrived on Laclede's Landing, the band had consisted of Andy Barnes (bass), David "Chopper" Campbell (guitar & vocals), Larry Lund (keyboards & vocals), David Nichols (drums & vocals), Brad Sarno (guitar & vocals) and Michael "Smitty" Smith (drums).

In 1990, Blue Dixie moved to Charlottesville, Virginia, to establish an East Coast presence in the centrally-located college town. When the band toured, eventually hitting thirty-seven states, they always made their way back to Mississippi Nights. Andy Barnes says, "Mississippi Nights became our home away from home at that point. It was kind of like playing from your living room, really comfortable." The band cites the professional crew, excellent monitor mix, great lighting that didn't impede the band's view of the crowd, nice site lines, and ease of load-in and setup as the reasons for the homey feel.

Michael "Smitty" Smith recalls, "Because of the low ceiling, it was loud so when people were responding, you could feel it. The sound had nowhere to go but right at the stage. It was an exciting place to play..." Smith says, "We learned a lot of the sonic aspect of performances from Mississippi Nights."

Blue Dixie, February 7, 1992. Photo by Terry Lewis.

The Mississippi Nights show that stands out the most in the band's collective memory is the one where they played a practical joke on lead guitarist Brad Sarno in the early '90s. "He was prettier than the rest of us, or at least the ladies seemed to think so," Andy Barnes acknowledges. "We [had] superimposed Brad's head with David Lee Roth's [lead singer of Van Halen] body on the *Women and Children First* album [sleeve] where he's chained to the fence, shirtless in black leather pants." The posters announced a "Win a Dream Date with Brad" contest. Andy continues, "We sent him to get dinner for us at the Old Spaghetti Factory. While he was gone, we postered the club." Despite having a new girlfriend, Brad was a sport and took the contest winner on a date.

Blue Dixie played their farewell show at Mississippi Nights on December 31, 1994, marking the end of touring for the band. However, they continue to play reunion shows. Blue Dixie's first reunion show was on November 21, 1997, back at Mississippi Nights. The show was recorded and released on the CD titled *Welcome Back*. David "Chopper" Campbell notes, "Part of the proceeds went to the Terrapin Station Project [an interactive museum documenting the Grateful Dead]." Between 1990 and 2005, Blue Dixie played forty-eight shows at Mississippi Nights.

EVENTS IN 1992

Benefit for Haiti • AIDS Benefit • Rock the Vote

St. Louis Blues Society's Billy Williams Benefit

Keith Richards CD Listening Party

STACY ENLOE* REMEMBERS...

KSHE sponsored a free concert by Tora Tora on July 28, 1992, but I would have gladly paid because I love Tora Tora.

My friend and I arrived early, around 1 or 2 p.m., as we usually did for shows at Mississippi Nights. We had two goals in mind that required an early arrival: meet the band and get the spot front and center of the stage. We usually brought CD inserts, markers, and a camera, as well as a deck of cards to pass the time. We'd run across the street to the Embassy Suites when we needed a restroom. I don't remember ever bringing food with us or buying food on Laclede's Landing, so I guess the music was our sustenance.

We often had conversations with the people waiting around us, swapping music-related stories as rock fans usually do. That day, we met fellow music fans Cyndi Weinmann (Bauman) and Brian Schleifer.

When the tour bus pulled up, we jumped from our concrete seats and greeted them as they emerged. The four of us had our CD inserts signed and our pictures taken with each band member. The boys from Memphis, Tennessee, had that sweet Southern friendliness. Goal one was accomplished.

When the band went inside the venue, we went back to chatting on the sidewalk until it was door time. Then, with hands stamped and tickets torn, we hurried down the ramp to the front of the stage. Goal two was accomplished, and we lost ourselves in the music of Tora Tora.

Cyndi Bauman and Keith Douglas of Tora Tora July 28, 1992. Courtesy of Cyndi Bauman.

Over the next year, we ran into Cyndi and Brian several times while waiting on the sidewalk at Mississippi Nights. Then, in August 1993, we were hanging out on the sidewalk waiting to get into the American Theater to see Jackyl when Cyndi asked us if we wanted to join her and Brian on a trip the following year to attend the Woodstock '94 festival in New York. Of course, being young and impulsive, we jumped at the idea (and finally exchanged phone numbers). Cyndi made all the travel arrangements, and with her forethought to bring her sturdy Doc Martins and a roll of toilet paper, she helped me wade through ankle-deep mud on the treacherous journey from the tent to the port-a-potties. We have been great friends ever since.

*Author

From the collection of Garrett Enloe.

SHAE HILEMAN* REMEMBERS...

My best story of Mississippi Nights was the time I hung out at the after-show party for Alice in Chains, Screaming Trees, and Gruntruck. I went around back (like I did a lot) to try and slip into the green room through the back door. While I was waiting, I started talking to some guy. Small talk led to firing up a joint with him, and he told me he was friends with the guys in AIC. He was in town running sound for another show and dropped by to hang out with the band. He talked about his brother Tommy's band. As he continued, I found out his older brother "Tommy" was Tom Araya of Slayer. When he went inside, I tried to stroll in with him, but security kicked me out.

Since that failed, I waited until after the show to try a different approach. I got my attractive female friend, took her to AIC's bus, and knocked on the door. Someone came to the door, and I said we had some green to smoke if anyone in the band was interested. He said to wait a minute. I knew [Singer Lane] Staley was already passed out. I had seen two guys drag him out of the club and onto the bus. [Bassist] Mike Starr came to the door, took us inside the club, and we smoked a joint in the green room. [Guitarist Jerry] Cantrell was an arrogant dick, so I spent the whole time hanging with Mark Lanegan [singer of Screaming Trees], who was super cool.

It was a very memorable night. I had quite a few memorable nights at The Nights. [December 7, 1992]

*Mississippi Nights patron

Courtesy of Sarah Baue.

DECEMBER SHOWS

4	PHISH (1 show, 2 sets) **SOLD OUT**
5	SOUP DRAGONS w/Thousand Yard Stare
7	ALICE IN CHAINS w/Screaming Trees/Gruntruck **SOLD OUT**
9	VOICE OF GOD w/Fragile Porcelain Mice (Bring a Bible, any version)
**10	NEW POTATO CABOOSE w/Guest
**11	TRIP SHAKESPEARE w/27 Various
12	PALE DIVINE w/Guest
15	MUDHONEY w/Supersuckers
18	UNCLE TUPELO w/Guest
25	THE URGE w/Guest
26	LONDON CALLING w/Eric Anthony
31	MISSISSIPPI NIGHTS NEW YEAR'S EVE PARTY w/BLUE DIX Open Bar, Free Champagne, $30 per ticket

For questions/info, call 421-3853.
REMEMBER—A Club Card makes a _PERFECT_ holiday Gift!
**Designates Club Card Shows

JAMIE WELKY* REMEMBERS...

Tori Amos toured on *Little Earthquakes*. Her performance was one of the most sensual things I've ever seen in my life: just her, a piano, and a piano bench. (October 6, 1992)

*Mississippi Nights front-of-house engineer and production manager

Courtesy of Greg Kessler.

Concert October 6, 1992. Courtesy of Rich Fisk

TORI AMOS

MISSISSIPPI NIGHTS
OPEN 8:PM SHOW 9:PM
* * *
J.D. BLACKFOOT
WITH GUEST
FRI NOV 6 1992
$14 DAY OF
GEN ADM $14.00

Courtesy of Mark Lewis.

MISSISSIPPI NIGHTS
OPEN 7:30PM SHOW 8:00PM
* * *
MIGHTY MIGHTY BOSSTONES
WITH GUESTS
THU JULY 16 1992

133

BEN RICKER* REMEMBERS...

One thing I think is seldom mentioned about Mississippi Nights is the sound system. It's the best sound system I have ever heard. It gets freaking loud. Skinny Puppy's bass shook your chest cage like a vibrating cell phone, but with no distortion. I have seen shows in Chicago, San Francisco, NYC, and Portland, and no club has come close to Mississippi Nights' sound system. It truly was one of the best clubs in the US, if not the world. [June 29, 1992]

*Mississippi Nights patron

MIS29JUN
0393 ALL
AGES
GA ADULT
CAS $0.00
GEN $14.00
4A $0.00 $16
ADM K05JUN GA

MISSISSIPPI NIGHTS
PRESENTS
DOORS 8:PM SHOW 9:PM
SKINNY PUPPY
WITH GODFLESH
MON JUNE 29,1992
DAY OF ADULT
GEN ADM $14.00

From the collection of Garrett Enloe.

MIS9JUL
0582 ALL
AGES
GA ADULT
CHQ $1.25
GEN $12.00
2A $0.00 $12
ADM K24JUN GA

MISSISSIPPI NIGHTS
OPEN 8:PM SHOW 9:PM
■ ■ ■
RICHARD THOMPSON
WITH GUEST
THUR JULY 9,1992
DAY OF ADULT
GEN ADM $13.25

MIS23SEP
1532 ALL
AGES
GA ADULT
CAS $1.25
GEN $10.00
1A $0.0 $12
ADM K22SEP GA

MISSISSIPPI NIGHTS
DOORS 8:PM SHOW 9:PM
■ ■ ■
POI DOG PONDERING
WITH GUEST
WED SEP 23,1992
DAY OF ADULT
GEN ADM $11.25

Tickets courtesy of Paul Ebenreck.

Courtesy of Sheri Beezley.

MISSISSIPPI NIGHTS
UPCOMING SHOWS

JULY 1 — STREETSIDE RECORDS presents **ROLLINS BAND** w/ TOOL — $10 ADV — $12 DAY OF SHOW — DOORS OPEN 8:00 — SHOW AT 9:00 — NEW ALBUM "THE END OF SILENCE" IN STORES NOW

JULY 14 — the **charlatans UK** w/ THE WOLFGANG PRESS — $10 ADV — $12 DAY OF SHOW — DOORS OPEN 8:00 — SHOW AT 9:00

JULY 20 — **SIR MIX A LOT** w/ Guest TBA — $13 ADV — $15 DAY OF SHOW — DOORS OPEN 8:00 — SHOW AT 9:00

JULY 31 — **THE DEAD MILKMEN** w/ Guest TBA — $10 ADV — $12 DAY OF SHOW — DOORS OPEN 8:00 — SHOW AT 9:00

AUG 7 — **ALL** w/ JAWBOX, JUDGE NOTHING, BY NAME — $10 ADV — $12 DAY OF SHOW — DOORS OPEN 7:00 — SHOW AT 7:30

TICKETS AT ALL TICKETS NOW OUTLETS, INCLUDING FAMOUS BARR, STREETSIDE RECORDS, BLUE NOTE SPORTS, DIALTIX, MISSISSIPPI NIGHTS.

914 N. FIRST ST. LACLEDE'S LANDING 421-3853

PHISH

PHISH

MARCH 30th

Courtesy of Ashley B.

APRIL 8TH

MERL SAUNDERS
(Jerry's friend)
AND THE
RAIN FOREST BAND

THE MUSIC CLUB IN ST. LOUIS

MIS17MAR
224B ALL
AGES
GA ADULT
CAS $0.00
GEN $7.00
2A $0.00 $9
ADM K25FEB GA

MISSISSIPPI NIGHTS
OPEN 7:30PM SHOW 8:30PM
■ ■ ■
MATTHEW SWEET
WITH GUEST
TUE MAR 17,1992
DAY OF ADULT
GEN ADM $7.00

Courtesy of Daniel Durchholz.

Taime Downe of Faster Pussycat and Cyndi Bauman,
September 2, 1992. Courtesy of Cyndi Bauman.

MIS 15DEC	MISSISSIPPI NIGHTS
0002 ALL	OPEN 7:30PM SHOW 8:30
AGES	* * *
GA ADULT	MUDHONEY
CAS $0.00	WITH GUEST
GEN $10.00	TUE DEC 15,1992
16A $0.00	GEN. ADM. ADULT
ADM K29NOV GA	GEN ADM $10.00

Courtesy of Eric Eyster.

EMIS 17NOV	MISSISSIPPI NIGHTS
1344	OPEN 7:30PM SHOW 8:PM
ALL AGES	* * *
GA	TESTAMENT
$1.50	WITH GUESTS
GA $14.00	TUE NOV 17, 1992
ADULT	$16 DAY OF ADULT $15.50
CAS	
AAL 921022 GA	GA AAL

Courtesy of Steve Buschart.

From the collection of Garrett Enloe.

George Lynch of Lynch Mob,
September 1, 1992. Photo by
Cyndi Bauman.

Budweiser Presents

1ST Saturday

Saturday, September 5

BUDWEISER BATTLE OF THE BANDS
12-6 P.M.

Six Bands Battling Outside in the Landing

Q106.5

Mississippi Nights Stage
12:00 Bowery Boys
1:30 Sammy & The Snow Monkeys
2:30 Off Centre

Alley Stage
12:45 Mixxed Company
2:15 Sable
3:45 The Boorays
5:00 Winner's Announced

Grand Prize: $1000,
Booking at Boomer's,
Q106.5 "Unplugged"

Also Check Out . . .

The great sounds on the Progressive Stage near Kennedy's, Roger From
The Dark (2:00 pm), Burnt Nervends (3:30 pm), The Choice (5:00 pm).
Enjoy outside food booths sponsored by Landing Merchants.
Take a ride in the Gyro Space Ball or put your kids in.
Bring a lawnchair & stay awhile!

First Saturday
Sponsored By:

Riverfront Times

Courtesy of Bob Kreher.

MIS 16NOV	MISSISSIPPI NIGHTS
1395 ALL	OPEN 7:30PM SHOW 8:30
AGES	* * *
GA ADULT	ARC ANGELS
CAS $0.00	WITH GUEST
GEN $10.00	MON NOV 16, 1992
25A $0.00	$12 DAY OF ADULT
GA	GEN ADM $10.00

MIS 7OCT	MISSISSIPPI NIGHTS
0630 ALL	OPEN 7:30PM SHOW 8:30P
AGES	* * *
GA ADULT	STEELHEART
CAS $1.25	WITH GUEST
GEN $7.00	WED OCT 7,1992
3A $0.00	$9 DAY OF ADULT
ADM KU6OCT GA	GEN ADM $8.25

Courtesy of Kimberly Witthaus.

135

Chris McLernon of Saigon Kick and
Stacy Enloe, October 26, 1992.

"Let's Party!," we'll say
on the 18th of May
as Walt and Kim, his wife,
celebrate their new life
and frolic the night away
it's bound to be fun
from 7 till 1
so R.S.V.P. today!

**Mississippi Nights
914 N. First Street**

Regrets only   Snacks & Soda provided
428-2155   Cash Bar Available

KYLE KEITH* REMEMBERS...

I saw Tool [opening for Rollins Band]
at Mississippi Nights. *Opiate* had just
been released. There were about five
people on the floor. Elisa Leon from
BMG [music publishing and recording
company] put Mike Baker and me on
the list because we were obsessed
with [Tool's] promo cassette.

The band played as if the place was
packed. I didn't want to get too
close to the stage because [singer]
Maynard [James Keenan] scared the
shit out of me. [July 1, 1992].

Mississippi Nights patron

From the collection
of Stacy Enloe.

MISSISSIPPI NIGHTS
Presents

SPECIAL
GUESTS

 Skin flick

LACLEDE'S LANDING
ALL AGES WELCOME

914 N.1ˢᵗ   **$3**   **THUR.**
421-3853   cover   **May**
                  Doors open at 8 p.m.   **21ˢᵗ**

1993

The Mississippi River Meets Mississippi Nights

The Great Flood of 1993, which lasted from April to October, caused the Mississippi River to overflow its banks up to the steps by Mississippi Nights' back door, forcing bands to load out through the front door. The health department came by regularly to make sure the flood didn't cause the sewers to back up.

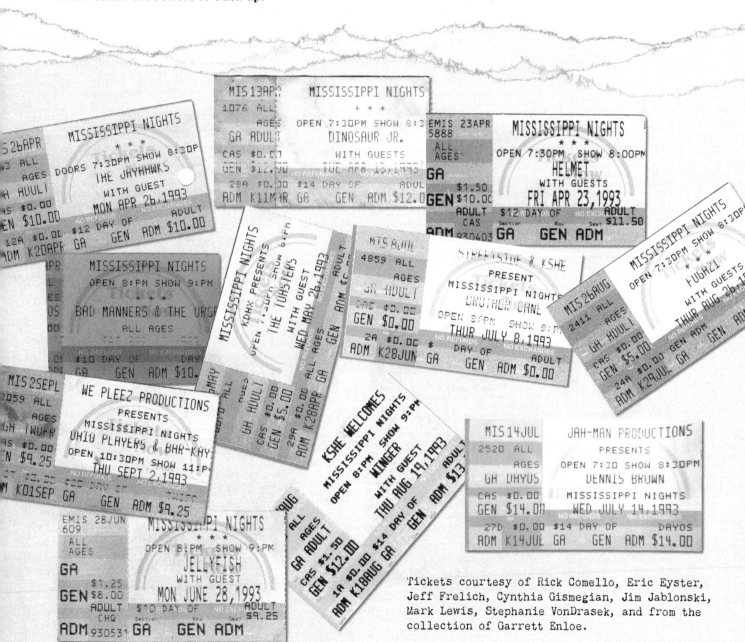

Tickets courtesy of Rick Comello, Eric Eyster, Jeff Frelich, Cynthia Gismegian, Jim Jablonski, Mark Lewis, Stephanie VonDrasek, and from the collection of Garrett Enloe.

STEVE "DOC" DACHROEDEN* REMEMBERS...

I moved from Australia to St. Louis in 1988 and immediately found a home at Mississippi Nights. I was a full-fledged punk rocker, already an aging punk at twenty-two years old, and was so excited to have a venue where I could see all of my favorite bands. That year, I joined DeDe Schofield and her cable access TV show, *Critical Mass,* as a cameraman and editor. We filmed countless bands at The Nights. That got me access to my favorite venue before shows for interviews and during shows for videos.

In 1990, I started working at St. Louis Music. Being a musician my whole life, I was so proud to work at the factory where we built Ampeg bass guitar amplifiers (the best bass amp in the world, hands down), Ampeg guitars, Crate guitar amps, Audio Centron PA gear, and Alvarez and Electra guitars. A few years in, I moved from factory grunt to a position working for Ken Hensley of Uriah Heep fame and Mary Ann Dill in the Artist Relations division — a dream job for sure!

We worked with nearly every one of the biggest bands in the world. My job was to acquire new endorsements, get bands the gear they needed, do repairs on the fly in the dressing room at Mississippi Nights, and get photos of the musicians and their gear for promotional advertising (see pictures in 2003 and 2006 sections). Our amazing photographer Mark Gilliland and I would meet up at Mississippi Nights, get the gear sorted, do a photoshoot, shoot some live stuff, and hang out afterward. Without the amazing and helpful Mississippi Nights staff, this would have been a daunting task.

On a more personal note, my wife Shelly and I had our first date at Mississippi Nights on November 6, 1997, at a Veruca Salt show.

I was out on tour the day The Nights closed down. I shed a tear and regret to this day not flying home to be there.

Owner of Silver Ballroom and The Waiting Room

Blues musician Hubert Sumlin, October 8, 1993. Photo by Mark Gilliland.

David Vincent of Morbid Angel, August 17, 1993. Photo by Michael F. Coles.

Calendar (March 1993, handwritten notes):

21	22	23	24	25	26	27
$3 cover		$3 cover	w/ Bent $5 ST. PATRICK'S DAY	505 Project $20 ROW $17.50 A $20 DOS	London Calling $3 cover	Reggae At will Niyah Worthy $5 cover SPRING BEGINS
			KDHX The Subdudes $5 cover	Doors 7:00 Chan 7:30 A Night on the Town Chaka Khan Geoffrey Album High Mastela Dan Seigal Phillip Bailey $20 Flr $15 cd	Doors 7:00 Chan 7:30 Joan Baez w/ John Wesley Harding $17 dos	Back Doors w/ Tongue in Groove $6 cover
28	29	30	31			

FEBRUARY 1993
S M T W T F S
1 2 3 4 5 6
7 8 9 10 11 12 13
14 15 16 17 18 19 20
21 22 23 24 25 26 27
28

APRIL 1993
S M T W T F S
1 2 3
4 5 6 7 8 9 10
11 12 13 14 15 16 17
18 19 20 21 22 23 24
25 26 27 28 29 30

FIRST QUARTER 1-31
FULL MOON 8
LAST QUARTER 15
NEW MOON 23

ROY DRIPPS* REMEMBERS...

Joan Baez stepped in front of the mic to the very edge of the stage to sing "Swing Low, Sweet Chariot" unamplified and a cappella. Gorgeous does not begin to describe it. [March 26, 1993]

*Mississippi Nights patron

EVENTS IN 1993

Dramarama CD
Listening Party

Farm Aid

Concert February 3, 1993. Courtesy of Rich Frame.

Photo © DAN MURO

JAMES LaBRIE   MIKE PORTNOY   JOHN PETRUCCI   JOHN MYUNG
KEVIN MOORE

DREAM·THEATER   Mississippi Nights — THANKS!!   ATCO

THE ST. LOUIS BLUES SOCIETY

Guitar 93 MASTERS

10 Showcase Performances

Max Baker
Buffalo Bob
Larry Griffin
Alvin Jett
Jimmy Lee
Tam Milano
Q.T. Macon
Steve Waldman
Jelly Jaw Johnson

Very Special Guest - Bullseye Recording Artist
LARRY DAVIS
McMurray Music provides all support and new Fender Stratocaster to be given away at show!

SATURDAY · MAY 8
MISSISSIPPI NIGHTS
8 PM-2 AM / TICKETS $10

Courtesy of Gian Vianello.

MISSISSIPPI NIGHTS
OPEN 7:30PM SHOW 8:30PM
THE SUNDAYS
WITH GUEST
MON MAR 8 1993
GEN ADM $14.00 $16 DAY OF
ADM K24FEB GA

MISSISSIPPI NIGHTS
7:PM SHOW 7:30PM
BIG COUNTRY
WITH 700 MILES
SUN NOV 28 1993

MISSISSIPPI NIGHTS
OPEN 7:30PM SHOW 8:30
POI DOG PONDERING
WITH GUEST
WED NOV 10, 1993
GEN ADM $12 DAY OF

Ticket stubs courtesy of Paul Ebenreck.

139

MIX 97.1 WELCOMES
WE PLEEZ PRODUCTIONS PRESENTS

OHIO PLAYERS & BAR-KAYS

Thursday, September 2, 1993
MISSISSIPPI NIGHTS
Tix: $18.50 Adv. $20.00 Day of Show

TWO SHOWS   TWO SHOWS

DOORS OPEN 7:00 & 10:3

Limited amount of reserved tickets available at
REGAL SPORTS and MISSISSIPPI NIGHTS

mix 97.1—

Advance tickets available at all TICKETS NOW Outlets:
Famous Barr, Streetside Records, Scott Air Force Base,
All 13 Schnucks/Video Locations and Tuckers Department Store

244-2466 or 421-3853

...ers discounted Tickets by calling 994-6685

Terry Richardson, Matt Harris, Aaron Aedy
(from Paradise Lost), and Michael F. Coles
behind Mississippi Nights, August 17, 1993.
Courtesy of Michael F. Coles.

140

DUE TO INSURANCE COMPANY RESTRICTIONS, WE ARE FORCED TO REMOVE ANYONE SLAM DANCING, STAGE DIVING OR OTHERWISE DISPLAYING DISRUPTIVE BEHAVIOR FROM THE PREMISES. PLEASE COOPERATE WITH US TO ENABLE US TO CONTINUE PROVIDING MUSIC FOR ALL ST. LOUISANS.

Steve Vai, October 6, 1993.
Photo by Terry Lewis.

BRIAN SULLIVAN* REMEMBERS...

I had unexpectedly fallen in love with Steve Vai's *Sex and Religion* album, so I was not going to miss his show.

Burnt Nervends was the opener. I recognized the great Cubby Smith on bass from one of my favorite local bands ever, T.H.U.G.S. [Smith is currently in Dr. Zhivegas]. I worried the whole set that T.H.U.G.S. had broken up. When I said hello to Smith in between sets, I found out they didn't.

Vai had a whole new live band, including [Frank] Zappa veteran Scott Thunes on bass, Will Riley on keyboards, and Abe Laboriel Jr., who would later work with Paul McCartney and Seal, on drums. The unknown 20-year-old Vancouver singer Devin Townsend (later in Strapping Young Lad) walked on stage shirtless with black sweatpants, black high-tops, and a short blonde mohawk. He acted very goofy, but he was one of the most passionate singers I've ever seen, with a voice spanning the range of hellish screaming, dripping melody, and everything in between. He strapped on a guitar around the fourth or fifth song and started playing very well, lick for lick with Vai.

At some point, they whipped right into White Zombie's "Thunder Kiss '65." That one got things fired up. I was surprised Steve would be into such a basic groove. Also, there were multicultural elements in the show, like the sitar in "State of Grace."

I doubted whether the touring band could pull off what players like Terry Bozzio did on the album, but they did. The sound quality was great. My personal favorites were the beautiful guitar ballad "Touching Tongues" (with Devin singing an operatic, Freddie Mercury-esque vocal ad-lib), "Still My Bleeding Heart" (the finale of the song was a climactic drum-vocal duel), and one of the most painful songs about loving someone from afar: "In My Dreams with You." That lineup had magic chemistry that never happened again for Steve Vai. The show was phenomenal. [October 6, 1993]

Drummer of Chaos Collective, Brian Sullivan Quartet, Uncle Terrible, My Posse in Effect, and Warhorse.

MIS6OCT
1145 ALL
AGES
GA ADULT
CAS $1.50
GEN $14.00
1A $0.00 $16 DAY OF
ADM KO8SEP GA

MISSISSIPPI NIGHTS
WELCOMES
OPEN 7:30 SHOW 8:PM
STEVE VAI
WITH GUESTS
WED OCT 6,1993
ADULT
GEN ADM $15.50

Courtesy of Cyndi Bauman.

MIS29OCT
1529 ALL
AGES
GA ADULT
CAS $1.25
GEN $10.00
2A $0.00 $12 DAY OF
ADM K15OCT GA

MISSISSIPPI NIGHTS
OPEN 8:PM SHOW 9:PM
* * *
SAIGON KICK
WITH GUEST
FRI OCT 29,1993
ADULT
GEN ADM $11.25

MISSISSIPPI NIGHTS
WELCOMES
0305 ALL
AGES OPEN 7:30PM SHOW 8:30
GA ADULT
CAS $1.25
GEN $10.00
1A $0.00 $12 DAY OF
ADM K13JAN GA
TORA TORA
WITH GUEST
MON FEB 1,1993
ADULT
GEN ADM $11.25

MIS14OCT
1594 ALL
AGES
GA DAYOF
CAS $0.00
GEN $16.00
ADM K14OCT GA

MISSISSIPPI NIGHTS
OPEN 7:30PM SHOW 8:30P
Ticketm
THE THRILL KILL KULT
* * * L.O.
THU OCT 14 1993
NO REFUNDS   NO EXCHANGES
GEN ADM $16.00

Tickets from the collections of Garrett and Stacy Enloe.

Concert July 22, 1993.
Courtesy of Rich Frame.

L-R : BILLY ZOOM, D.J. BONEBRAKE, EXENE CERVENKA, JOHN DOE

PHOTO CREDIT : KEN MARCUS 1993

Elektra Entertainment

Concert April 14, 1993.
Courtesy of Rich Frame.

AMY RAY   EMILY SALIERS

i n d i g o   g i r l s

Epic

142

The Genuine Draft Festival Light
Stage was in the Mississippi Nights'
parking lot. Advertisement from
The *Riverfront Times*.

1994

Andy Mayberry in the Mississippi Nights' office.

Andy Mayberry Takes the Helm

Andy Mayberry's fiancée left him. He realized his job working on towboats, which kept him away from home for long stretches, was not conducive to meeting women. He decided the best way to accomplish his goal of meeting ladies would be working in a bar. He began working at Mississippi Nights in 1981 as a doorman and eventually moved up to bartender and assistant manager.

In 1985, Mayberry left Mississippi Nights and started working for Contemporary Productions, managing Westport Playhouse and the American Theater and doing promotions. After leaving Contemporary in 1992, he managed several other clubs around St. Louis.

In 1994, Rich Frame sought to replace manager Mark Andrews and brought Mayberry back into the Mississippi Nights fold as general manager.

Mississippi Nights are cool. Thankyou Dave Matthews

DAVE MATTHEWS BAND

BOOKING / MANAGEMENT BY
CORAN CAPSHAW
804-979-9695

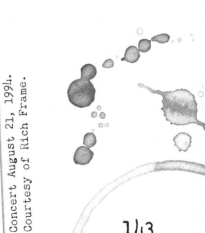

MIS 21 OCT   MISSISSIPPI NIGHTS
0268 ALL   OPEN 8 PM. SHOW 9 PM.
AGES
GA ADULT   DAVE MATTHEWS BAND
CAS $1.25   WITH RUSTED ROOT
GEN $5.00   FRI OCT 21, 1994

Courtesy of Angela Prada.

Concert August 21, 1994.
Courtesy of Rich Frame.

143

KM EGBERT* REMEMBERS...

My first live show was Gwar. I was in high school, on curfew, and worried because of the late start. Plus, X-Cops opened, which was Gwar in different costumes, so the gap between bands was long. They performed an insane stage show of beheading Nazis, pulling the insides out of child-molesting priests, and [singer] Oderus Urungus "pissing" (and more) all over the audience with the Cuttlefish of Cthulhu [part of Urungus' costume].

It was an absolutely insane mosh pit, the first of my metal life. Multiple moshers were tossed out.

After the show, I stopped by an IHOP to wash the fake blood off my face and arms and change my shirt. Luckily, I had no trouble at home, but I did have a bit of trouble with my hearing for the next week. [May 26, 1994]

*Mississippi Nights patron

From the collection of Garrett Enloe.

Video Shoo

Wednesday, July 27th

Mississippi Nights

Columbia Records

Courtesy of Mark Lewis.

Courtesy of Mark Lewis.

MISSISSIPPI NIGHTS

Laclede's Landing

SATURDAY

July 9th

Sinister Dane Shoots a Video

From their first show, local heroes Sinister Dane developed a reputation around the Midwest for being one of the highest energy bands to hit the stage. They shared the spotlight with notable bands such as Living Color and Fishbone. After recording their self-titled album for Columbia Records, Sinister Dane shot their first video at Mississippi Nights on Wednesday, July 27, 1994, at 2 p.m.

Sinister Dane arrived to see a long line of fans waiting to get into the building. A large crowd turned out to support the band: family, friends, the band's A&R representative Pablo Mathiason, manager Casey Sutton, and extended family from Altered Skates in the University City Loop. As nervous as the video shoot made him, guitarist Jay Summers relaxed seeing those familiar faces, as well as the trusted co-workers and friends in the Mississippi Nights staff who kept the venue running.

Skateboarders were mixed in the crowd, many performing tricks for the cameras, hoping to be a part of the production. The video concept was conceived in an attempt to get Sinister Dane "on video screens in skate and snowboard shops, and local and college video shows," recalls Pablo Mathiason. "Back then, those shops had videos on loops all day, so while you were shopping, you couldn't ignore the in-store play. So the concept of seeing Sinister Dane live and having the skaters in it was a one-two marketing punch."

Columbia chose "48 Months" for the band's first single. Mathiason recalls, "The budget was around $20,000, which was a small budget." The completed video shows off Mississippi Nights in all its chaotic glory with a giant mosh pit on the floor and stage divers uncharacteristically unimpeded by security.

"As far as the filming process," says bassist Donald Williams, "I remember playing the song what seemed like 100 times." Drummer Matt Martin reflects, "Making that video gave me a whole new perspective on being in the limelight. Granted, it wasn't the big time, but it certainly was looking behind the curtain." He says proudly, "I could not have chosen better brothers to go through it with."

Singer Joe Sears had one regret about filming the video: "The part of the shoot where I took off my shirt was sexy. I thought. Until around the tenth take when I had to put on the sogging, sweaty, ice-cold shirt over and over again," Sears laughs. "Also, during the stage dive, someone grabbed my balls during one take."

"When we were finished with the video shoot," says Williams, "we went home, kicked back for a few hours, and then returned later that evening to headline a show with the majority of the crowd from the video shoot in attendance. When it was time to play '48 Months' in our set, I can remember the band collectively groaning before counting it off and watching parts of the crowd reacting the same way."

When questioned why the video was shot at Mississippi Nights, guitarist Jay Summers reflects, "There was no other venue that the band would have chosen! Mississippi Nights was home to us and so many other St. Louis bands."

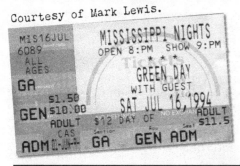

MISSISSIPPI NIGHTS
OPEN 8:PM SHOW 9:PM
★ ★ ★
GREEN DAY
WITH GUEST
SAT JUL 16, 1994
ADULT $12 DAY OF ADULT $11.5
GA GEN ADM

Billy Joe   Tré Cool   Mike Dirnt

GREEN DAY

© 1994 Reprise Records/ Permission to reproduce limited
pers and other regularly published periodicals and tele

CHRIS GIBBONS* REMEMBERS...

Billie Joe, the singer of Green Day, invited a fan onstage to sing any song he wanted, and he chose "Rock You Like a Hurricane." Then, Billie Joe took a doobie from the fan and smoked it. [July 16, 1994]

*Mississippi Nights patron

EVENTS IN 1994

Terry Bozzio's Drum Clinic • Kennedy's Benefit (to help the struggling club) • MRMF (Midwest Regional Music Festival) • St. Louis Blues Society's 10th Anniversary • Riverfront Times Music Awards: The Slammies

MISSISSIPPI NIGHTS
OPEN 7:30PM SHOW 8:30PM
GREAT WHITE
WITH GUEST
WED OCT 12, 1994
$17 DAY OF ADULT $16.50
GA GEN ADM

MISSISSIPPI NIGHTS
OPEN 7:30PM SHOW 8:30P

MISSISSIPPI NIGHTS
OPEN 7:30PM SHOW 8:30PM
★ ★ ★
SLAYER
WITH BIO HAZARD
MON AUG 8, 1994
$17 DAY OF ADULT $16.75
GA GEN ADM

Ticket stubs courtesy of Sarah Baue, Paul Ebenreck, Scott Gates, Mark Lewis, Gian Vianello, Joe Vickery, and the collection of Garrett and Stacy Enloe.

KSHE & MUSIC VISION
MISSISSIPPI NIGHTS
OPEN 7:PM
CRY LOVE
WITH GUEST
SUN FEB 20 1994

MIS4JAN
1414 ALL AGES
GA ADULT
CAS $1.25
GEN $6.00
MISSISSIPPI NIGHTS
OPEN 7:30PM SHOW 8:30PM
★ ★ ★
BROTHER CANE
WITH GUEST
TUE JAN 4, 1994
$8 DAY OF ADULT $7.25
GA GEN ADM

MISSISSIPPI NIGHTS
OPEN 7:30PM SHOW 8:30PM
★ ★ ★
SLAYER
WITH BIO HAZARD
MON AUG 8, 1994
$17 DAY OF ADULT $16.50
GA GEN ADM

MISSISSIPPI NIGHTS
OPEN 7:30PM SHOW 8:30PM
FISHBONE
WITH GUEST
WED NOV 16, 1994
$14 DAY OF ADULT $15.50
GA GEN ADM

MISSISSIPPI NIGHTS
OPEN 7:30PM SHOW 8:30P
AN EVENING WITH
RICHARD THOMPSON
WED MAR 30, 1994

MISSISSIPPI NIGHTS
OPEN 7:30PM SHOW 8:30P
KINGS X
WITH GUEST
MON MAY 2, 1994

MISSISSIPPI NIGHTS
OPEN 8:PM SHOW 9:PM
BAD BRAINS
WITH GUEST

MISSISSIPPI NIGHTS
OPEN 8:PM SHOW 9:PM
★ ★ ★
AMERICA
WITH GUEST
SAT JUL 30, 1994

146

A Hole Mess

The Courtney Love-fronted band, Hole, played at Mississippi Nights on October 26, 1994, with Chicago's popular Veruca Salt (featuring St. Louis native Louise Post) and New York City-based Madder Rose opening the sold-out show. According to club manager Andy Mayberry, Love was in quite a state that evening. Before the show started, club runner Cindy Mikulait was sent out to find baby powder for Love to mask the greasiness of her hair. Mayberry remembers, "[Love] wanted to cancel the show. She wanted morphine. Eventually, 'Dr. Rock' [a licensed medical doctor that made calls to hotels or clubs for bands] came to Love's room at the Embassy Hotel and gave her a shot of something."

Sioux Loncaric wrote in her short-lived fanzine, *Wildflower Unleashed*:

> *[Courtney Love] staggered onto the stage, all greasy, looking like she hadn't showered in a couple of days. She wore a shiny white dress and vintage white shoes with torn-up black pantyhose. Her daughter, Frances Bean Cobain, watched from the side of the stage with yellow headphones. The first thing Love did was spit on the audience. [Hole] opened their set with "Best Sunday Dress," and it was magical....*

> *Then things started to go downhill. Love started complaining that she was sick with a 103-degree fever. She needed someone to put her guitar on her. She stumbled all over the stage. For being sick, she could scream pretty well. I noticed she let Eric Erlandson do most of the guitar playing. She played some more songs and then stopped to complain again, this time about the audience....*

> *As the show went on, Love kept putting baby powder in her hair.... She came back out [for the encore] and started horsing around with Erlandson. There was a bunch of crap on the floor. Love and Erlandson were pushing each other around. Then, Love slipped and fell right on her ass.... She laid there until Erlandson and a stagehand helped her up, and when she got up, everyone could see her skinny butt....*

Waitress Angela Prada says, "I can almost guarantee that show is on the 'Top Five Worst Shows To Work' list for anyone who worked at Mississippi Nights. It was awful, and we all felt bad for the state she was in."

Courtney Love of Hole, October 26, 1994. Photo by Sioux Loncaric.

147

Fragile Porcelain Mice

Singer Scott Randall was in the short-lived band Disco Zombies before Fragile Porcelain Mice. Randall explains, "Disco Zombies were what we called weirdo rock. We were all over the place but rooted in punk rock. We did covers like Black Sabbath's 'War Pigs,' but with the lyrics of REO Speedwagon's 'Golden Country.'" The band performed in leisure suits, and Randall's unique dance moves formed during his Disco Zombies era.

At the same time, drummer Mark Heinz was in Dementia 13 with his Belleville, Illinois, classmates, bassist Dave Winkeler, guitarist Tim O'Saben, and Tim's brother Dan on vocals. The band, with a distinct Soundgarden sound, was formed in 1989. In 1991, the band wanted to do more touring, but Dan O'Saben had a family and other responsibilities, so he stepped down.

The rest of the group decided to carry on and asked Randall to join. Their music changed from rock to hard alternative with Randall on board, so they needed a new name. The band's first show was at Kennedy's 2nd Street Co. on Laclede's Landing in early 1992, and they had yet to come up with something to call themselves. Randall remembers, "The band Suede Chain wanted to know our name. At that moment, without even asking the other guys, I said, 'Fragile Porcelain Mice.' I never even asked the other three guys about it," Scott declares. The name had stuck in Randall's head from a David Letterman list of Top 10 Rejected NFL Names. "It was one of the worst decisions I ever made," Randall laments. "Since that night, the name stuck, and I still feel bad about it." (Years later, they found out from a fan that "Fragile Porcelain Mice" was a nerd gang in the book *The Wanderers*.)

From 1992 to 1998, the band self-released three full-length CDs and an EP, and they toured with The Urge, HUM, and NIL8. They were most successful in the college circuit in the Midwest. Fragile Porcelain Mice even opened for System of a Down in Wichita, Kansas. During 1996, the band played 200 shows all over the country.

From 1992 to 2007, Fragile Porcelain Mice performed at Mississippi Nights forty-seven times and shared the bill with other local bands like The Urge, Sinister Dane, Judge Nothing, and Voice of God. Among their most memorable shows was opening for The Urge on

David Jack Peverett of Foghat, November 22, 1994. Photo by Terry Lewis

George Thorogood, December 2, 1994. Photo by Brian Baybo.

Fragile Porcelin Mice, September 15, 1994. Photo by Julia Bramer.

Thanksgiving night in 1994. Winkler remembers, "The Urge bought five or six butterball turkeys. Then, they chained them to the rafters in the ceiling right above the stage." Between the heat from the packed crowd and the Mississippi Nights lights, the ornamental poultry became a problem. "It was easily 100 degrees in the building that night," he explains. "During our set, the turkeys began to thaw and drip onto the stage. The stage began to get slippery." For Winkler, the turkey slime posed a particular problem. He continues, "That night, I played bass barefoot. I was probably getting salmonella poisoning. After we played, The Urge took them down." The following year, with The Urge signed and touring more, Fragile Porcelain Mice headlined the Thanksgiving night shows.

"Mississippi Nights was *the* club in St. Louis to truly make a lasting name for yourself," Tim O'Saben asserts. "To me, as a musician, Mississippi Nights was more than just a great concert venue; it was a challenge and a goal. The challenge was to be able to land a gig at Mississippi Nights and then do well enough at that gig to be asked back. The goal, for me personally at least, was then to be able to sell out a headlining show there," says O'Saben. "The first time Fragile Porcelain Mice sold out Mississippi Nights was a very special moment for me. One I am proud of, and one I will never forget."

JASON NICO REMEMBERS*...

I remember playing pinball with Joey Ramone before soundcheck. I loved that cyclone machine. It took all my quarters. [March 23, 1994]

* Mississippi Nights security, barback, and merch

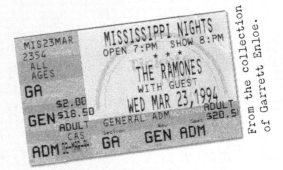

Left to right: Sharyn Altam, Bob Gooldy, David Lee Roth, Stephanie VonDrasek, Lorie Matter, and Cathy Swain. April 2, 1994. Courtesy of Bob Gooldy.

MIS2APR
234
ALL
AGES

MISSISSIPPI NIGHTS
OPEN 8:PM   SHOW 9:PM
* * *
AN EVENING WITH
DAVID LEE ROTH
* * *
SAT APR 2, 1994

GA
$1.50
GEN $15.00
ADULT $17 DAY OF   ADULT $16.5
BUY
ADM   GA   GEN ADM

Courtesy of Joe Vickery.

WAYNE JUDGE* REMEMBERS...

I was there at Mississippi Nights to see Dio on the *Strange Highways* tour. There was a delay in letting the crowd in. Ronnie James Dio came out and walked down the entire line, shaking hands, signing autographs, and apologizing for the hold-up. I had him sign my copy of the first Elf album. Great show. The place was packed. [July 6, 1994]

*Mississippi Nights patron

MIS6JUL
2129
ALL
AGES

MISSISSIPPI NIGHTS
OPEN 7:30PM SHOW 8:30PM
* * *
DIO
WITH GODSPEED
WED JULY 6, 1994

GA
$1.50
GEN $14.00
ADULT $16 DAY OF   ADULT $15.50
CHQ
ADM   GA   GEN ADM

From the collection of Garrett Enloe.

Ronnie James Dio (left) entering Mississippi Nights, July 6, 1994. Photo by Steven Buschart.

MIKE MUELLER* REMEMBERS...

My friend Brad Goodnight and I were
elated when we scored tickets to see Fight
[with Judas Priest's singer Rob Halford
and drummer Scott Travis] at Mississippi
Nights. We had never seen Judas Priest,
and we figured seeing Fight may be as close
to seeing Judas Priest as we would ever
get. But, unfortunately, a week before the
show, I woke up with a painful, swollen jaw.
I ended up scheduling an appointment to get
my wisdom teeth removed the day before the
concert, but I wasn't going to miss that show
for anything, or so I thought.

Brad picked me up, and we headed over to
meet my friend Elizabeth and her group of
friends who would follow us to the show.
On the ride, Brad and I shared a pint of
Jack Daniels. When we arrived, I pulled out my bottle
of Vicodin, and although it clearly stated on the label

Rob Halford of Fight, January 28, 1994.
Photo by Jim Stewart.

"DO NOT MIX WITH ALCOHOL," I popped a few pills in my mouth and offered the bottle to
Brad. He took one. When we got inside, Fight was about to take the stage.

The place was packed. Brad went to the bar, and the rest of us worked our way through the
crowd in the back section. When the band came on, the place went nuts. Brad made it to
where we were and handed me a beer. We slammed them down quickly, and just when it
seemed like we were in for the time of our lives, things got very strange. Brad headed back
to the bar to get more beer, and I pulled out a joint. I fired it up right where I stood, and
everyone around me stepped away from me. After a couple of hits, I got tremendously dizzy
and confused. I was on the verge of passing out and having trouble breathing. I headed out
the door, focusing on not passing out. The air outside was good. The street lights were bright,
but they were not taunting me, just like the stage lights inside. I could still hear the music, but
it was comfortably distant. I staggered across the street into the parking lot and made it to
the truck.

I sat down against the back wheel with my arms and head on my knees. Soon, everything
started spinning, and I started puking. I slid down a bit to avoid the mess and realized I was
on an incline. The mess was following me. I slid down several more times until I ran out of
truck. I took a deep breath, stood up, took four of five steps, spun around, and landed flat
on my back behind the truck. I lay there in a state of paralysis. No matter how hard I tried,
I couldn't open my eyes. I heard voices heading my way, and soon they were right above me.
I could hear everything the girls were saying.

I heard, "Oh my God, is he breathing?

"Hey, dude, are you okay?"

They seemed legitimately concerned. I finally managed to open my eyes, and I heard, "Okay,
he's not dead," and "Hey! He's looking up our skirts!" (I was, accidentally, looking right up
their skirts.)

151

Then, one of them kicked me in the ribs and said, "Pervert!" as they all laughed and walked away. I somehow managed to crawl around to the driver's side and roll under the truck, so I wouldn't encounter any more people. I passed out.

I woke up with Elizabeth shaking me. After I had disappeared, Brad went looking for me. They found him sitting on a fire hydrant, refusing to budge. Brad and I just sat there for hours until he felt normal enough to drive home. To this day, neither of us has ever mixed alcohol with any pill that warns against it. Neither of us will ever forget the time we tried to see Fight at Mississippi Nights. [January 28, 1994]

Mississippi Nights patron

MIDWEST REGIONAL MUSIC FESTIVAL

The MRMF was an annual, three-day event held every September from 1994 to 1998. The *Riverfront Times* sponsored event showcased 200 to 250 bands playing in about twenty venues around downtown St. Louis, with Mississippi Nights showcasing the bands with the biggest buzz. In addition, panels and workshops were held at a downtown hotel to help the musicians hone various skills they needed off stage.

CHAD TAYLOR   PAT DAHLHEIMER   ED KOWALCZYK   CHAD GRACEY

LIVE

radioactive   3/9

Concert May 25, 1994.
Courtesy of Rich Frame.

Zakk Wylde of Pride and Glory, November 25, 1994.
Photo by Andy Mayberry.

152

1995

Night Times

"I started *Night Times* to meet Matthew Sweet," recalls editor and publisher Julia Gordon-Bramer. She met and interviewed Sweet, and the magazine was off and running. The first two issues of *Night Times* were intended to be a newsletter exclusively for Mississippi Nights (hence, the name) interviewing bands and promoting upcoming concerts for the club. Later issues had a strong focus on Mississippi Nights and highlighted other venues in St. Louis.

With 105.7 FM The Point dominating the St. Louis radio airwaves in the alternative music genre, 1995 was the perfect year to introduce a new alternative music magazine. *Night Times'* tagline was "The True Alternative."

Night Times was the first St. Louis magazine to interview and feature bands like Radiohead, Bush, No Doubt, Local H, Squirrel Nut Zippers, and many other national and international acts. They also covered the local scene extensively. So if you happened to be in a band in St. Louis during the three years of the magazine's existence, your group was likely mentioned. Gordon-Bramer reflected about her years running *Night Times,* "I was fortunate to be in St. Louis music at a time when the entire nation knew about our

Mattew Sweet and Julia Bramer, Febuary 18, 1995. Courtesy of Julia Bramer.

153

local scene. Many major label bands come from this town: The Urge, Radio Iodine, Kristeen Young, Gravity Kills, Pale Divine, Sinister Dane, and more. *Night Times* brought me a musical family, friends for life, and a husband! I'll never forget the fun we had."

By 1998, the alternative scene had changed. The bubble had burst on the post-Nirvana period when labels were signing local alternative acts left and right. Venues closed their doors because people stopped going downtown. *Night Times* was yet another casualty of the scene's downfall. The final issue was published in March 1998.

Courtesy of Mark Goldman.

WILL COKER* REMEMBERS...

For my first Mississippi Nights show, I had the pleasure of seeing the Circle Jerks killing it on stage. Out of nowhere (apparently surprising the band as well), Chuck Berry joined them for a top-shelf rendition of "Roll Over Beethoven." I saw a lot of great shows there over the next eleven years, but nothing matched that moment. [August 14, 1995]

*Mississippi Nights patron

Oliver Sain, June 24, 1995.
Photo by John Wegrzyn.

Courtesy of
John Wegrzyn.

Courtesy of Andy Mayberry.

V88 KDHX Welcomes Z108 katz AM 1600

OLIVER SAIN'S SOUL REUNION '95

FEATURING
RUFUS THOMAS
CLAYTON LOVE
MARSHA EVANS
VERNON GUY
OM "PAPA" RAY
LADY DEE

SAT, JUNE 24, 8 PM
MISSISSIPPI NIGHTS
Advance Tickets • $15 Day of Show
ble at Mississippi Nights & Tickets Now Locations

KMJZ 100.3 FM & WSIE presents

A NIGHT on the TOWN

HERBIE HANCOCK   VAIL JOHNSON
TERRI LYNN CARRINGTON   GIL SCOTT-HERO
DAN SIEGEL   LALAH HATHAW
GERALD ALBRIGHT   DOC POWE

TWO SHOWS:
DOORS 7:00 / SHOW 7:30
DOORS 10:00 / SHOW 10:30

$22.50 Flat at all Tickets Now locations including: Famous Barr, Streetside Records, Blue Note Sports Shops, 13 Schnucks Video Clubs, Dialtix at 291-7600, the Mississippi Nights Box Office and Regal Sports

THURSDAY, JULY 27TH
Limited capacity / guaranteed seating

MISSISSIPPI NIGHTS

914 N. FIRST STREET ON LACLEDE'S LANDING
421-3853

"The Music Club of St. Lou

Ellen Perysn and Tom Bramer of Radio Iodine, December 5, 1995. Photo by Julia Bramer.

Radio Iodine

The female-fronted St. Louis techno-alternative band Radio Iodine rocked the region hard with incredible vocals and songwriting by Ellen Persyn and music and production by her husband, Tony. "Radio Iodine played most of the venues in St. Louis, but Mississippi Nights was one of our favorites," says lead guitarist Tom Bramer.

Bramer joined Radio Iodine after leaving his band Spiny Norman, named after a Monty Python sketch about a giant and possibly imaginary hedgehog. Spiny Norman's sound was "...a sort of experimental sound, combining '70s and '80s progressive rock undertones and the popular grunge sounds of the day," says Bramer. Spiny Norman played most of their shows from 1992 to 1993 in the Delmar Loop. During this time, he met Tony Persyn.

Tony Persyn was the bassist of 9 Days Wonder, and his wife Ellen was the singer and co-songwriter. 9 Days Wonder had a mellow alternative-pop sound. The band needed a new guitar player. After auditioning over twenty people, they picked Bramer. The fact that Bramer and the Persyns were already acquainted made the decision a little easier.

Bramer had only played a few shows with the band when another band threatened to sue 9 Days Wonder over rights to the name. Persyn had already been thinking about taking the band in a new musical direction with a more industrial sound, so it was a good time for a name change. As a result, 9 Days Wonder became Radio Iodine in the summer of 1994. The original lineup was Tony Persyn (bass), Ellen Persyn (lead vocals), Tom Bramer (lead guitar), Steve Held (drums), and Anna Berry (keyboard, backing vocals). After only a few weeks, Held was replaced with drummer Greg Miller from the recently disbanded Pale Divine.

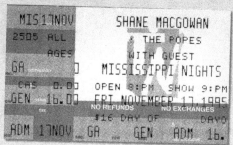

THURS., NOV. 23, 1995 - THANKSGIVING NIGHT

The Point welcomes

the urge

w/guests

MISSISSIPPI NIGHTS • 914 N. FIRST • ST. LOUIS, MO
DOORS 7:30 PM • SHOW 8:00 PM • ALL AGES
$5 ADVANCE / $6 DAY OF SHOW

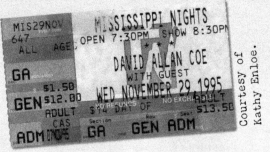

Radio Iodine soon began to attract attention. KPNT 105.7 The Point included them on the *Pointessential Vol. 2* compilation in 1995, playing "Never Meant to Lie" on heavy rotation. After the band was featured in *Billboard* magazine's "Continental Drift" section, reps from major labels scouted their concerts.

Radio Iodine signed to Universal/Radioactive in late 1995 and released their self-titled EP in 1996. A full-length CD, *Tiny Warnings,* was released in 1997.

The band concentrated their touring in the Midwest, with small two- or three-day tours. The longest excursion was a seven-week run with My Life with the Thrill Kill Kult in the summer of 1997. After that tour, internal issues caused the band to release Anna Berry (keyboards, backing vocals). Shortly after, in October 1997, Bramer left the band. Bramer was replaced with Mike Speckhard from local band Bellyfeel, and Linda Gaal from the Ultraviolets briefly replaced Berry. Radio Iodine continued another year, playing their final show at Mississippi Nights on December 12, 1998.

Although the Radio Iodine only played at Mississippi Nights ten times, Bramer's most stressful concert happened when the band played The Point's Ho Ho Show with Poe, Tonic, Tracy Bonham, and Failure on December 7, 1996. "Because a few bands were playing that night, we needed to change over fast," Bramer recalls. "As soon as I set up my rig, I noticed that some of my gear wasn't turning on. I spent way too much time trying to fix it — even the guys from Failure tried to help — and ran out of time before we had to start playing." He continues, "Usually guitarists use foot pedals to control [their] gear, but that night I had to manually control some of my gear with my hands. It meant that I had to spend the whole show pretty much glued to my amp and rack, trying to figure out several measures ahead of time the sequence of hand-foot actions I would need to make in order to make it through each song. A friend said I looked like I was doing calculus." (Bramer married St. Louis *Night Times* publisher Julia Gordon on May 1, 1999.)

Concert July 20, 1995. Courtesy of Julia Bramer.

From the collection of Garrett Enloe.

JOE STULCE* REMEMBERS...

As soon as we were old enough to drive, we borrowed our parents' cars to go see live music. Mississippi Nights was a favorite spot. It was an all ages venue, and we went to as many shows as we could... local favorites like The Urge, Fragile Porcelain Mice, MU330, NIL8... plus any touring bands that we liked and could afford to see. We saw a ton of memorable shows there, but one that really stands out is Pennywise in 1995, and they didn't even play.

My best bud, Tim Wilkinson, drove us in his mom's minivan. At first, it was like any other punk show we'd seen, but the mood quickly soured. The club was packed, and security seemed extra aggressive. We always steered clear of security as we had often witnessed the way that they treated kids who would stage dive or get a little too rambunctious while dancing or moshing. Sometimes it was necessary to remove someone causing trouble, fighting, or being an asshole, but the bouncers at Mississippi Nights were notorious for being overly violent bullies. We avoided them at all costs.

During the opening set by The Joykiller, security was hammering kids, more so than usual, and the band picked up on that. The band made a few comments about security, but that only seemed to fuel the fire. At some point, the band, clearly frustrated at watching fans get hit, thrown around, and knocked to the ground by people bigger than them, said something along the lines of, "Ya know, there are a lot more of *you* [fans] than there are of *them* [security]...."

That was the turning point. The band continued playing, and fights broke out all around us. Kids were fighting back and ganging up on security. It was crazy, and I should have known right then that the night would not end well.

157

After The Joykiller's set, there was a feeling of unease in the room. Later, we heard a rumor that management had removed the staff from the building for safety concerns. [Authors' note: The rumor was true.] After a while, a member of Pennywise came onstage and said that they were not allowed to play and everyone should leave. The announcement was met with profanities and airborne missiles. The next thing I knew, police marched into the club and lined the walls, looking dead serious. An officer took the stage and said everyone had to leave the vicinity; the show was over. This was met with more profanities and a few more airborne missiles.

Angry, fired-up people started slowly filing out of the club. We saw a couple of unruly punks get taken down by the cops. When we got outside, the crowd was not dispersing despite the police demands. A wise choice would have been to leave, but we were young, dumb teenagers, and our plans had just been ruined. Our new plan was to watch this new, scary, strangely exciting scene unfold.

The police in riot gear formed a line from one side of the street to the other and marched toward the crowd. That got everyone moving, but not quick enough for police. Out of nowhere, I was grabbed by the back of my shirt collar and yanked out of the crowd. Before I could comprehend what was happening, my head was shoved onto the hood of a parked car, and I was handcuffed. Tim asked, "What's going on?" They told him to keep moving.

He said, "No, that's my friend, and I'm his ride." They told him to keep moving, or they're cuffing him, too.

Tim said, "No, I'm not leaving without him!" This is one of many reasons he remains one of my closest friends to this day. We have been on many adventures together, and this wasn't the first or last time that Tim would stick his neck out for me. The police officer cuffed him and threw both of us into the back of a paddy wagon with six to eight other handcuffed people. Before the cop slammed the doors, he sprayed the interior with a big cloud of pepper spray.

Marilyn Manson,
November 15, 1995.
Photo by Mike Glader.

MIS30JAN   MISSISSIPPI NIGHTS
2116 ALL   OPEN 7:30PM SHOW 8:30PM
AGES   * * *
GA ADULT   MARILYN MANSON
CAS $1.25   WITH GUEST
GEN $8.00   MON JAN 30,1995
2A $0.00 $10 DAY OF   ADULT
ADM K11JAN GA   GEN ADM $9.25

MISSISSIPPI NIGHTS
OPEN 7:30PM   SHOW 8:30PM
    * * *
MARILYN MANSON
WITH CLUTCH
12.00 WED NOV 15,1995 8:30PM
$14 DAY OF
GA   GEN ADM 13.5

Ticket stubs from the
collection of Garrett Enloe.

Ian MacKaye (singer of Fugazi) and
Rob Dunnett behind Mississippi Nights,
October 8, 1995. Courtesy of Rob Dunnet

Being pepper-sprayed is a pretty horrible experience: you can't see, you can't breathe. Your eyes, nose, and throat are on fire, and if your hands are cuffed behind your back, you can't do anything about the snot and tears oozing out of your face. It seemed like it was 100 degrees in that wagon, and everyone was coughing, hacking up snot, and moaning in agony. I heard the sound of at least one guy vomiting.

When we were finally able to gain our composure, we started asking each other how we ended up in the paddy wagon from hell. Everyone had the same story: we were walking with the crowd and were suddenly grabbed by an officer and cuffed. One guy said, "Yeah, I've seen this kind of thing before. They're just using us as examples to get the crowd to leave. Once everyone is gone, they'll let us go." His explanation made sense, and everyone felt relieved. We were just pawns, and soon, we would get to go home. We sat cuffed and covered in snot and tears in that wagon for what seemed like hours. And then, it started moving.

They brought us to the station, marched us in, and handcuffed us to a big horizontal pole attached to a wall. By the time they got to Tim, they had run out of pole, so they un-handcuffed him and put him in a chair across the room. Tim gave us a smirk as if to say, "Haha, suckers!" Hours went by as they took our belongings, IDs, and personal information while filling out paperwork. Eventually, they put us into holding cells. One-by-one, people arrived to bail out their loved ones.

We had to take a day off school to go to court. The judge called me up, and they read the charges. They said that I had led the crowd in a chant of "Fuck the police," and I was charged with inciting a riot. I plead not guilty. I don't even recall there being any organized chants. None of the police officers showed up for the proceedings. Our cases were thrown out, and the charges were dropped.

Long live Mississippi Nights. [July 20, 1995]

*Co-owner of Planet Score Records

Juliana Hatfield, July 8, 1995. Photo by Mike Glader.

John Rzeznik of Goo Goo Dolls, July 31, 1995. Photo by Julia Bramer.

Jade 4U of Lords of Acid, July 18, 1995. Photo by Mike Glader.

Andy Mayberry (4th from left) with UFO, August 20, 1995. Courtesy of Andy Mayberry.

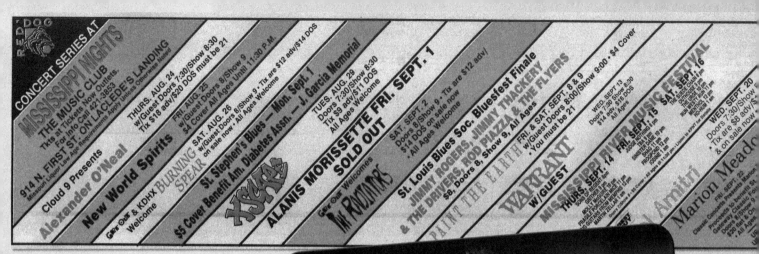

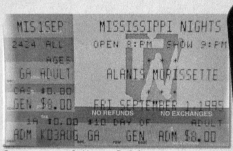

Courtesy of Mark Goldman.

Alanis Morissette, September 1, 1995.
Photo by Sean Derrick.

Courtesy of Sarah Baue.

From the collection of
Stacy Enloe.

Courtesy of Mark Lewis.

160

JASON & THE SCORCHERS

Concert March 25, 1995. Courtesy of Rich Frame.

MIKE LATOUR* REMEMBERS...

I was at Foo Fighters' first show in St. Louis with Hovercraft and Mike Watt. Eddie Vedder [singer of Pearl Jam] played drums for Hovercraft and joined Watt for a few songs on guitar. Vedder was in disguise while playing drums for Hovercraft. Grohl watched part of the show from the crowd. When Foo Fighters were playing, Vedder filmed us in the front row as we rocked out to this new band.

When Vedder came out to play with Watt, I was crushed against the stage for the rest of their set. Somehow, my contact fell out, so that was fun. The photographer from *Rolling Stone* was next to me in the front row. Amazing show! [April 18, 1995]

[The instrumental experimental industrial group Hovercraft opened the show, followed by Foo Fighters and Mike Watt. The bassist of Hovercraft, Beth Liebling, was Eddie Vedder's wife.]

*Mississippi Nights patron

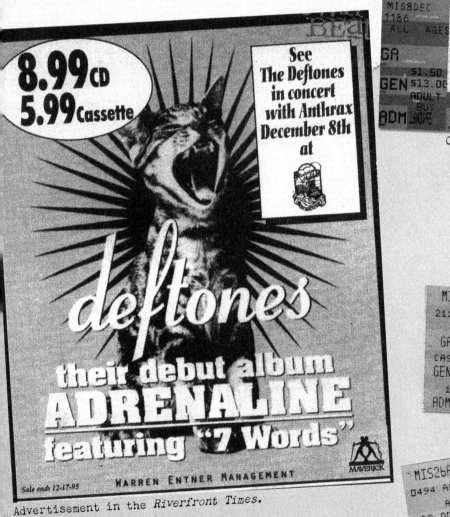

8.99 CD
5.99 Cassette

See
The Deftones
in concert
with Anthrax
December 8th
at

deftones

their debut album
ADRENALINE
featuring "7 Words"

WARREN ENTNER MANAGEMENT

MAVERICK

Sale ends 12-17-95

Advertisement in the *Riverfront Times*.

MISSISSIPPI NIGHTS
MIS8DEC
1186
ALL AGES   OPEN 7:30PM   SHOW 8:00PM
GA
GEN $1.50
$13.00
ADULT
ADM
ANTHRAX
WITH GUESTS
FRI DEC 8, 1995 8:00PM
NO REFUNDS   NO EXCHANGE
GA   GEN ADM
ADULT
$14.50

Courtesy of Scott Gates.

MISSISSIPPI NIGHTS
MIS7MAY
1633
ALL AGES   OPEN 7PM   SHOW 8PM
GA
GEN $1.50
$16.00
ADULT
EXTREME
WITH GUEST
SUN MAY 7, 1995
ADULT
$17.50
GA   GEN ADM

MISSISSIPPI NIGHTS
MIS21FEB
2117 ALL
AGES   OPEN 7:30PM   SHOW 8:30PM
GA ADULT
CAS $1.50
GEN $12.00
1A $0.00 $14 DAY OF
ADM K03FEB GA
CINDERELLA
WITH GUEST
TUE FEB 21, 1995
ADULT
GEN ADM $13.50

From the collection of Garrett Enloe.

MISSISSIPPI NIGHTS
MIS26APR
0494 ALL
AGES   OPEN 7:30PM   SHOW 8:30PM
GA ADULT
CAS $1.50
GEN $10.00
1A $0.00 GENERAL ADM
ADM K14APR GA
THE REVEREND HORTON HEAT
WITH GUEST
WED APR 26, 1995
ADULT
GEN ADM $11.50

Courtesy of Mark Lewis.

161

Retro Dance Party

Mayor's Party

St. Louis Regional
Showcase Normal Benefit

Jerry Garcia Tribute
for the Diabetes
Association

MRMF (Midwest Regional
Music Festival)

Talent Search

Rock for Choice

Riverfront Times Music
Awards: The Slammies

NEW YEAR'S EVE '96
MISSISSIPPI NIGHTS
CHAMPAGNE & PARTY FAVORS
TASTES LIKE CHICKEN
MUST BE 21 / OPEN BAR
TUE DECEMBER 31, 1996 8PM

Courtesy of Gary Embry.

Courtesy of Joe Vickery.

MISSISSIPPI NIGHTS
ALL AGES   OPEN 7:30PM   SHOW 8:30PM
SLASH'S SNAKEPIT
WITH GUEST
MON MAY 1, 1995

Slash of Slash's Snakepit,
May 1, 1995. Photo by
Brian Baybo.

THE MUSIC CLUB
914 N. FIRST ST.
ON LACLEDE'S LANDING
Missouri Liquor Law Age Requirements Apply
Unless Otherwise Noted

WELFARE MUSIC WED. APRIL 12
SUN SAWED IN 1/2 SKILLET SISTERS
HIGHWAY MATRONS ELEANOR
Proceeds to benefit R.O.W.L.
Doors 7:30/Show 8 • $4 Cover • You must be 21

Louis Blues Society WELCOMES **THUR. APRIL 13**
Roomful of Blues
ne Show - 2 Sets
7:30/Show 8:30 • Tix are $10 adv/$12 DOS • All Ages Welcome

WELCOMES **FRI. APRIL 14**
Material Issue
w/ THE LUPINS
Doors 8/Show 9 • Tix are $8 adv/$10 DOS
& on sale now • All Ages Welcome

SAT. APRIL 15
Tastes Like Chicken
w/Guest
rs 8/Show 9:30 • $3 Cover • All Ages until 11:30 pm

TUE. APRIL 18
MIKE WATT
FOO FIGHTERS & HOVERCRAFT
Doors 7:30/Show 8 • Tix are $7 adv/$9 DOS
& on sale now • All Ages Welcome

WED. APRIL 19
Melvins
GODHEAD SILO
Doors 7:30/Show 8
Tix are $7 adv/
$9 DOS on sale now
All Ages Welcome

WELCOMES **THURS. APRIL 20**
VERUCA SALT w/ THE MUFFS
and FIGDISH
Doors 7:30/Show 8 • Tix are $12 adv/

162

1996

The Evolution of Pit Management

To the outsider, the mosh pits and crowd-surfing of heavy metal and punk rock shows probably seem like dangerous, violent, and crazy acts that should be banned from music venues. A mosh pit is a circular space formed in a crowd where fans stomp to the tempo of the music, slamming into each other. Crowd-surfing is when an audience member is hoisted or jumps on top of the crowd, often from the stage, and is propelled by the hands underneath towards the stage or the back of the venue. People choose to participate in these activities because they like the adrenaline rush or release of aggression. But mostly, they want to be one with the music.

Outsiders do not know the unwritten rules for the pit that heavy metal and punk rock fans know and usually follow. Some of the rules are for safety, such as 'Pick someone up if they're down,' 'Catch surfers,' and 'No fighting.' Other rules are about respect and kindness, such as 'No groping,' 'Respect those who choose not to join in,' and 'Hold lost items over your head until claimed.' Doing something like purposely hurting someone in the pit or groping a female surfer will likely be met with punishment from a fellow audience member.

Tim Weber was the head of security and eventually manager of Mississippi Nights from 1998-2007. The security staff's relations with kids in the pit were often strained. Some punk rockers and heavy metal fans outright refused to attend concerts at Mississippi Nights due to security issues. Weber says, "We used to circle the mosh pit with security, a half dozen or so in a half-moon around the edge of the pit. We'd push people back in. If someone went surfing, you'd go get them. We were starting more fights than we were stopping, and we were hurting more people than we were protecting."

Many attendees have stories about extremely excited fans and overly eager security that ended in violence or injury. Mississippi Nights was not alone in struggling with the play violence breaking out in front of the stage. Venues all over the country also had difficulties managing aggressive audiences. Many bands, such as

Tim Weber. Photo by Meshia Barton.

163

Concert March 5, 1996. Courtesy of Rich Frame.

PHOTOGRAPHER: SIMON FOWLER
©1995 IRON MAIDEN HOLDINGS LTD

IRON MAIDEN

Kelli Scott of Failure with Mississippi
Nights' popcorn machine. Extra popcorn
was kept in a large plastic trash can.
December 7, 1996. Photo by Meshia Barton.

FAILURE

164

Anthrax, Megadeth, Nine Inch Nails, Alice in Chains, and Slayer, turned to security adviser Jerry Mele for help. Mele, a 6-foot-1, 170-pound Vietnam veteran and martial arts expert, was "in demand in the rock world because of his friendly, not combative, view of moshers."[d]

Mele recognized security wouldn't be able to stop the moshing and stage diving. Instead of being reactive, they needed to be proactive in creating a safe environment, so the audience could enjoy themselves. "Caring, not demanding, will give you a better end result. And the bottom line is to stop accidents before they happen," Mele told the *Boston Globe* in 1995.

"It was not at The Nights that we first met Mele and his partner, Jerry Meltzer," say B&D Security supervisor Walter Wright. "It was at the American Theater with Slayer in 1995." B&D Security was trained in Mele's approach. Since B&D Security also had a contract to provide security at Mississippi Nights, Mele's methods made their way to Laclede's Landing. "We pulled security off the floor entirely when there was a pit, and it made all the difference," says Tim Weber. "We ended up with an incredibly safe environment. People self-policed. We had people with flashlights up on the speaker racks to keep an eye on them." Also, security pointed at the incoming crowd-surfers, warning audience members in that area to protect themselves. The security behind the stage barricade helped surfers over the barricade and ushered them to the side of the stage, back into the audience.

Security also implemented a "timeout." "It was right outside of the front door," recalls Wright. "If we were escorting someone out that just needed to calm down, we'd tell the guy at the front door to make them stand outside for a song or two and then let them back in. It was a better alternative than having to throw somebody out and wasting their money for the show," he asserts.

Jerry Mele's security techniques continue to be used in venues around St. Louis today.

(d) Source: Morse, Steve. "For Jerry Mele, security is not the pits." Newspapers.com by Ancestry, The Boston Globe (Boston, Massachusetts), 15 February 1995, http://www.newspapers.com/image/441081263. Accessed 12 October 2020.

From the collection of Stacy Enloe.

From the collection of Garrett Enloe.

From the collection of Garrett Enloe.

Courtesy of Mark Lewis.

MATEO DUCKWORTH* REMEMBERS...

Sepultura played at Mississippi Nights in 1996. Some guy from the audience hung on a ceiling beam toward the back of the pit. Then, he "crawled" upside-down toward the stage while the band was playing. He let go, landed on the stage, and security rushed in to grab him. Max Cavalera [singer and guitarist] pushed back security. The guy stood there on stage with his arms up like he was king of the city. The crowd went nuts, and the band kept playing. After he had his brief triumphant moment, he jumped into the crowd, and the show went on. Things really could have gone bad if security didn't back off. [August 14, 1996]

Mississippi Nights patron

Mississippi Nights advertisement in Night Times.

FRI OCT 11 **JOHN CALE** Doors 8/Show 9
Red House Painters $10 ADV/$12 DOS
All ages

SAT OCT 12 **Dirty Dozen** Doors 8/Show 9
Squirrel Nut Zippers $8 ADV/$10 DOS
All ages

FRI OCT 18 Wired Women Present Doors 8/Show 9
Ani DiFranco TIX $15
All ages

SAT OCT 19 **The Specials** Doors 8/Show 9
Schleprock $12 Adv/$14 DOS
All ages

TUE OCT 22 **KORN** Doors 7:30/Show 8:30
Delinquent Habits **Limp Biscuit** TIX $10
All ages

THU OCT 24 **PORNO FOR PYROS** Doors 7:30/Show 8:30
Fun Loving Criminals TIX $20
All ages

WED OCT 20 **GWAR** Doors 7:30/Show 8:30
w/ Guest $13 Adv/$15 DOS
All ages

FRI NOV 1 **Better Than Ezra** Doors 7:30/Show 8
Satchel **James Hall** $12 Adv/$14 DOS
All ages

SAT NOV 2 **The Connells** Doors 8/Show 9
w/ Guest $12 Adv/$14 DOS
All ages

Tickets available at all Tickets Now outlets
For More Information Call 421-3853

Mississippi Nights advertisement in the Riverfront Times.

LOS LOBOS
w/WILD COLONIALS
Doors 7:30/Show 8:30•Tickets are $15 adv/$17 DOS•All Ages Welcor

POINT Welcomes THURS. NOV.
THE LEMONHEADS
w/Imperial Teen & froSTed
Doors 7:30/Show 8:00 • Tickets are $12 Flat • All Ages Welcome

FRI. NOV.
w/HEPCAT & SENSE FIELD
Doors 8/Show 8:30 • Tickets are
$12 adv/$14 DOS • All Ages Welcome

SAT. NOV.
the Back Doors
The Shocking Reincarnation of
Jim Morrison & The Doors w/guest
Doors 8/Show 9 • $6 Cover • All Ages Until 11:30 p.m.

SUN. NOV. 10
MEDESKI, MARTIN & WOOD
Doors 7 • Tickets are $10 Flat • All Ages Welcome

TUES. NOV. 12
god street wine
w/Robert Bradley's Blackwater Surprise
Doors 7:30/Show 8:30 • Tickets are $6 adv/$8 DOS •
All Ages Welcome

POINT Welcomes WED. NOV. 13
WEEZER
w/SUPERDRAG Doors 7:30/Show 8:30 • Tickets are
$15 Flat • All Ages Welcome

THURS. NOV. 14
JACKOPIERCE
w/COLONY Doors 7:30/Show 8:30 • Tix are
$8 adv/$10 DOS • All Ages Welcome

FRI. NOV. 15
Sugardaddy • Calery
Java • 247 Spyz
Soul Function
Doors 7 • $5 Cover • All ages til 11:30 pm

POINT Welcomes SAT. NOV. 16
radio iodine w/Pave
The Rocket
Doors 8/Show 9 • Tix are $5 adv/$7 DOS
All Ages Welcome

THURS. NOV. 21
MONTELL JORDAN
WITH GUEST
Doors 7:30/Show 8:30 • Tix are $18.50 flat
All Ages Welcome

THE WHY STORE FRI. NOV. 22
W/JOE D'URSO & STONE CARAVAN
Doors 8/Show 9 • $5 Cover • All Ages Welcome

SAT. NOV. 23 & SUN. NOV. 24
SON VOLT
W/BIG SANDY & HIS FLY-RITE BOYS
Sat: Doors 8/Show 9 • Sun: Doors 7/Show 8
Tickets are $10 adv/$12 DOS • All Ages Welcome

MON. NOV. 25
Everything But The Girl
W/FRENTE & BEN WATT
Doors 7:30/Show 8:30 • Tickets are
$14adv/$16 DOS • All Ages Welcome

STIR WED. NOV. 27
w/19 WHEELS

166

Sioux Loncaric from Her *Wildflower Unleashed* Fanzine...

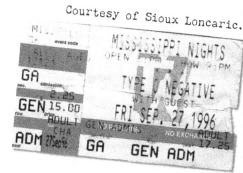

On September 27, 1996, I went to see Type O Negative. They were appearing at Mississippi Nights. So I thought I'd have a chance to meet the band.

We got there in the middle of the first band's set. Manhole is a hardcore band from Los Angles, with a screaming female lead singer. They were cool. Then, Life of Agony played. They were okay. While the opening bands played, I scoped out the bar and the crowd. To my dismay, I didn't see Peter Steele [singer and bassist of Type O Negative]....

After that, I decided to get closer to the stage. I forced my way up through all the sweaty bodies. I had a great view with only a few people between me and the stage.... Peter looked tall and godly, dressed in all black, his hair blowing in the breeze, with a chain as a strap to hold his bass. He must work out everyday.... When they played a song from the *Bloody Kisses* album called "Too Late: Frozen," fake snow blew on everyone. That was cool. They played "Gravity," "My Girlfriend's Girlfriend," and The Doors' song "Light My Fire...." Then, they played "Black No. 1," and Peter let the audience sing it. He ended the show stating, "Just remember. If it wasn't for you guys, we wouldn't be here tonight." Then, they walked off the stage and didn't do an encore.

Concert November 21, 1996. Courtesy of Rich Frame.

167

Courtesy of Julia Bramer.

you & a guest are invited to the POINTESSENTIAL vol.3 cd release party at mississippi nights friday, may 3rd, 1996

doors open at 8:00p.... first band starts at 8:30p please rsvp to amanda @ 259.5777 by 5/1/96

THE POINT 105.7 FM

POINTESSENTIAL VOLUME 3

From the collection of Stacy Enloe.

MISSISSIPPI NIGHTS
OPEN 8:PM SHOW 8:30PM
POINT ESSENTIAL VOL. 3
RELEASE PARTY
SAT MAY 1996

Night Times' Bash for Cash

Pointessential Vol. 3 Release Party

Riverfront Times Music Awards: The Slammies

EVENTS IN 1996

Courtesy of Randy Avellone.

POINT CHRISTMAS PARTY
POE, TONIC, RADIO IODINE
TRACY BONHAM & FAILURE
MISSISSIPPI NIGHTS
DOORS OPEN 7:PM
SAT DECEMBER 7 1996

MISSISSIPPI NIGHTS
OPEN 7:30PM SHOW 8:30PM
ME'SHELL NDEGE'OCELLO
MON OCTOBER 28 1996

MISSISSIPPI NIGHTS
OPEN 8:PM SHOW 9:PM
THE SPECIALS
WITH GUEST
SAT OCTOBER 19,1996 9:P

Courtesy of Mark Lewis.

TOM HENKEY* REMEMBERS...

Porno for Pyros in October of 1996 was my most memorable show. The temperature had to be at least 90 degrees, and as the set went on, one overheated kid after another was physically carried out of the mosh pit, at least six or eight during the set. Did the band stop playing? Hell, no. Did kids stop dancing? Hell, no. And that was a perfect snapshot of The Nights. [October 24, 1996]

*Mississippi Nights patron

Page Hamilton of Helmet, December 3, 1996.
Photo by Mike Glader.

Chris Duarte,
June 21, 1996.
Photo by Terry Lewis.

Danny Drabb, Mike Kociela (holding their *Riverfront Times* Slammie Award), and Steve Hunt (sitting on the pony wall by the bar) of New World Spirits, and Brandi Welti. December 3, 1996. Photo by Andy Mayberry.

Members of Frosted hanging out with a fan, Sam Gordon, Jenifer Patterson, and Julia Bramer, December 7, 1996. Photo by Julia Bramer.

Doyle Wolfgang von Frankenstein
of The Misfits, June 8, 1996.
Photo by Mike Glader.

Bent, November 29, 1996. Photo by Mike Glader.

CHUCK HESTAND REMEMBERS...

I wrote for *Night Times* magazine, and one of my assignments was to interview Jonathan Davis from Korn when they played at Mississippi Nights at the start of their *Life is Peachy* Tour about a week before the album came out. We were sitting on the bus talking, and he had just finished telling me how his biggest wish was for his band to be successful enough that he could make sure his kid wouldn't have to endure a shitty childhood as he did. Right at that moment, the band's manager came on board to inform him that *Life is Peachy* was going to debut at #1 on the *Billboard* charts. Jonathan was crying. Everyone was freaking out, and I didn't get to finish my interview. [October 22, 1996]

170

Mississippi Nights Advertisement in the Riverfront Times

RED DOG

CONCERT   SERIES AT

MISSISSIPPI NIGHTS
THE MUSIC CLUB
914 N. FIRST ST.   ON LACLEDE'S LANDING
Missouri Liquor Law Age Requirements Apply Unless Otherwise Noted

OUR BEST BETS OF THE WEEK
WEDNESDAY SEPTEMBER 18

MY LIFE WITH THE
THRILL KILL KULT

THE INFERNO
X★PRESS TOUR
1996
W/DEATH RIDE 69

Doors 7:30/Show 8:30 • Tickets are

mrMf
MIDWEST REGIONAL MUSIC FESTIVAL

Tin RIVERFRONT TIMES PRESENTS

MIDWEST REGIONAL MUSIC FESTIVAL

Wristbands on sale at Mississippi Nights
$8 Cover based on availability

THURS. SEPT. 19
Crushed 8 p.m.
Bellyfeel 9 p.m.
Kill Hannah 10 p.m.
New World Spirits 11 p.m.
Tin Horn Midnight
Robert Bradley's
Blackwater Surprise

FRI. SEPT. 20
Farmer 8 p.m.
Colony 9 p.m.   } Aware Records
19 Wheeels 10 p.m.   Showcase
STIR 11 p.m.
Waco Bros. Midnight
The Bottle Rockets 1 a.m.

SAT. SEPT. 21
United States Three 8 p.m.
12 Rods 9 p.m.
Frogpond 10 p.m.
Fragile Porcelain Mice 11 p.m.
Shiner

The Most Important Lesson

Emmylou Harris played a sold-out show on July 18, 1997. During the tour, Harris was stalked by a guy in a station wagon covered with stickers. In St. Louis, the stalker repeatedly drove up and down North 1st Street the day of the show. Manager Tim Weber remembers, "We had five people go across the street to the Embassy Suites to surround her like they do the president and walk her across. She didn't want to call the cops."

Harris' performance was beautiful, and the atmosphere was quiet that night. Rich Frame sat in the lighting booth, his usual spot to watch a show. From where he sat, he motioned Weber over and said, "What in the hell are you doing? I can hear the cash registers running."

Weber thought this was a good thing, as the money was pouring in.

"Turn those fucking things off," said Frame.

Weber argued they would miss out on sales if they turned the registers off.

"Fuck that! Some things are more important than money. This is a special show."

"So, I went around and opened all the cash drawers, and we 100-percent guessed at what we were selling that night," remembers Weber.

That interaction taught Weber the most important business lesson he has ever learned from Rich Frame: "Businesses are built on more than money, and when you get a special moment like that, you better take advantage of it," asserts Weber.

Courtesy of Sarah Baue.

Emmylou Harris, July 18, 1997. Photo by Sarah Baue.

MISSISSIPPI NIGHTS
914 N. 1ST ST.
ERIC JOHNSON
$14 ADV * $16 DAY OF
DOORS OPEN 7:30PM
TUE. AUG 19, 1997 8:30PM
MIS19AUG
2766 ALL
GA
GEN $16.00
ALL AGES
GEN ADM $16.00
ADM 19AUG

MISSISSIPPI NIGHTS
914 N. FIRST STREET
TONIC
W/GUEST * DOORS 8PM
$10 ADV/$12 DOS*ALL AGES
SAT. NOV 1, 1997 9PM
MIS1NOV
3126
GEN $10.00
GA GEN ADM $10

MISSISSIPPI NIGHTS
FOR DAMATO
$12 ADV * $14 DAY
WED. OCT 29, 1997

MISSISSIPPI NIGHTS
914 N. 1ST ST.
BOTTLE ROCKETS
$8 ADV * $10 DAY OF
DOORS OPEN 8PM
SAT. AUG 2, 1997 9PM
MIS2AUG
3808 ALL
GA
GEN $10.00
ALL AGES
GEN ADM $10.00
ADM 02AUG

MISSISSIPPI NIGHTS
914 N. 1ST ST.
POWER STATION
$15 FLAT * ALL AGES WELCOME
MON. SEP 8, 1997 8:30PM
MIS8SEP
940
GA
GEN $15.00
GA

MISSISSIPPI NIGHTS
3031 806
GEN $14.00
GA

MISSISSIPPI NIGHTS
914 N.
ROBIN TROWER
W/GUEST * DOORS 7:30PM
$14 ADV * $16 DAY OF
WED. JULY 2, 1997 8:30PM
MIS2JUL
1080 ALL
GA
GEN $16.00
ALL AGES
GEN ADM $16.00

MISSISSIPPI NIGHTS
KPNT*ANOTHER POINT
SEVEN MARY THREE
W/GUEST * DOORS 7:30PM
$10 ADV * $12 DAY OF
THU. JUL 17, 1997 8:30PM
MIS17JUL
5291 ALL
GA
GEN $12.00
ALL AGES
GEN ADM
ADM 17JUL

MISSISSIPPI NIGHTS
OPEN 7:30PM
L7
GEN ADM
GA

MISSISSIPPI NIGHTS
PRESENTS
MATTHEW SWEET
ALL AGES * DOORS 7:30PM
$10 ADV * $12 DAY OF
WED. JUL 16, 1997 8:30PM
GEN $12.00
ALL AGES
GA GEN ADM $12.00
ADM 16

MISSISSIPPI NIGHTS
914 N. FIRST ST.
HELMET
W/GUESTS
8PM DOOR*ALL AGES
SAT. SEP 13, 1997 8:3
EMIS13SEP
2832 SN470
GA
BUY 2.00
GEN $14.04
OA 0.96
GA GEN ADM
ADM 9SEP

MISSISSIPPI NIGHTS
914 N. FIRST STREET
COWBOY MOUTH
W/GUEST 7:30 DOORS
$10 ADV *$12 DAY OF SHO
WED. OCT 8, 1997 8:3
MIS8OCT
2303
GA
GEN $12.00
GA GEN ADM $12.00
ADM 08OCT

MISSISSIPPI NIGHTS
914 N. 1ST ST.
SONIA DADA
$10 ADV *$12 DAY OF
MUST BE 21 * DOORS 7:30
WED. AUG 20, 1997 8:30PM
MIS20AUG
3234
GA
GEN $12.00
GEN ADM $12.00
ADM 20AUG

MISSISSIPPI NIGHTS
914 N. FIRST STREET
CLUTCH
W/GUEST*7:30 DOORS
$8 ADV * $10 DAY OF SHOW
THU. OCT 2, 1997 8:30PM
MIS2
2808
GA
GEN $10.00
GEN ADM $10.00

MISSISSIPPI NIGHTS
OPEN 7:30PM SHOW 8:30PM
L7
THU. APRIL 17 1997
MIS17APR
GA
GEN $16.00
GA GEN ADM
ADM

MISSISSIPPI NIGHTS
914 N. 1ST
K'S CHOICE
WITH PROTEIN
ALL AGES*DOORS 7:30PM
WED. SEP 10, 1997 8:30PM
MIS10SEP
2658
GA
GEN $10.00
GA GEN ADM $10.00
ADM 10SEP

Andy Mayberry

172

Ticket stubs courtesy
of Andy Mayberry.

Guitarist vs. Mississippi Nights' Steps

Free Dirt opened for Stillwater at Mississippi Nights on July 18, 1997, and Free Dirt's bassist Dave Harris remembers, "We had lots to drink, as usual. During the load-out, one of our guitarists, Tom, was carrying his amp out the back and took a tumble down the metal stairs."

Tom Buescher recounts, "I was carrying my heavy 100W all-tube amp head down the back steps. They were steep. My heel slipped off the front of a step halfway down, and I twisted my ankle." Buescher sacrificed the amp to save himself, and the amp tumbled down the metal steps.

"I couldn't push the clutch pedal down on my truck, so my girlfriend drove me to the hospital. I broke my leg, but the amp worked," says Buescher. "I still have the amp and the girl, so it all worked out."

"The next weekend, we played the Hi-Pointe Theatre," says Harris. "Tommy played the entire show lying on his back [due to mandatory leg elevation], with his vocal mic positioned right above his head."

Courtesy of Michael Rose.

Concert August 16, 1997. Courtesy of Rich Frame.

BRYAN BASLER* REMEMBERS...

I was at the Demolition Doll Rods/Guitar Wolf/The Cramps show. It was packed. During the show, I thought I saw Lux, the singer of The Cramps, kill a dude by yanking him up onto the stage and throwing him off the opposite side walkway that led backstage. The song stopped, and everyone was dead silent. Lux just picked up something white, threw it at the dude, and said, "He forgot his diaper." Then, the band started up again. Since I was in the middle seating section, I didn't see anything leading up to the incident. However, I found out many years later that the dude was in the pit throwing elbows and hit a 14-year-old girl in the face, so Lux just took him out. [November 26, 1997]

*Mississippi Nights patron

Concert November 26, 1997. Courtesy of Julia Bramer.

THE CRAMPS

2798 SUNSET BLVD., L.A., CA 90026
PH:213.413.7353   FX:213.413.9678

Courtesy of Joe Vickery.

Bob Kevoian, Katy Kruze (D.J. on KSHE 95), and Tom Griswold during the Bob & Tom Show, June 13, 1997.

The Bob & Tom Show was a syndicated morning show which aired on KSHE 95 from 1996-2012.

174

Battle of The Bands
Sugar sticky Girl
Uncle Albert
Johnny Magnet
The Mighty Big Band
$3.00 cover   ↑ 21
Doors 6:30
show 7:30

23 PALM SUNDAY
24
25
26
27 10 adv $12 DOS
28 GOOD FRIDAY ↑ 21
29 $3.00 cover

Oakes w/ Diesel head
CC Thrash Hermet w/
Martha Byrne w/
Chicken

John Prine
$23.50 Tix

30 EASTER SUNDAY
31

Fiona Apple w/ morcheeba
Duncan Sheik Jill Sobule
Stir w/ Darla hood

$15 flat $10 adv $12 DOS $8 adv $10 DOS

Fiona Apple, March 27, 1997. Photo by Mike Glader.

Skye Edwards of Morcheeba, March 27, 1997. Photo by Mike Glader.

Thank You
John Prine

MISSISSIPPI NIGHTS
ALL AGES OPEN 6:30PM SHOW 7:30P
* * *
JOHN PRINE
ALL AGES WELCOME
SUN MARCH 23, 1997

Courtesy of Mark Goldman.

CHUCK YEAGER REMEMBERS...

My band, Ultrafink, opened for W.A.S.P. in the late '90s, and we had to perform with their "mechanical bull" made out of a motorcycle on the stage. Then, we stole W.A.S.P.'s beer from the dressing room. [June 28, 1997]

GEOFF LAVEINE* REMEMBERS...

Silverchair played at Mississippi Nights on Labor Day, September 1, 1997. That show was a 105.7 The Point promotion where you had to win tickets to attend the show, so I couldn't buy them. I remember dragging my dad and a friend to some bar/restaurant where The Point was blowing out tickets every 15 minutes, and my dad won a pair that he gave to me.

*Mississippi Nights patron

Courtesy of Andy Mayberry.

Kay Hanley of Letters To Cleo,
October 31, 1997.
Photo by Mike Glader.

THE URGE
VS.
THE POINT
2 THE REMATCH

In recognition of your outstanding support
of the Make-A-Wish Foundation
for The Urge/Point Hockey Game

Mississippi Nights
December 1997

Make-A-Wish Foundation®
of Metro St. Louis, Inc.

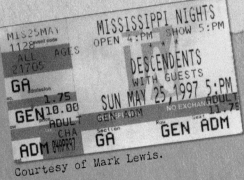

Courtesy of Mark Lewis.

Courtesy of Sioux Loncaric.

Robert Palmer of Power Station with
Carl The Intern and Katy Kruze
(KSHE D.J.s), and a fan, September 8, 1997.
Courtesy of Katy Kruze.

EVENTS IN 1997

Angie's [Prada] Graduation Party

Disco Ball

Big '80s Dance Night

Riverfront Times Music Awards:
The Slammies

River of Toys (Toys for Tots)

'80s Dance Party

Hairball '97 (benefit for
the Miriam Cancer Center)

Pointessential Vol. 4
CD Release Party

Juneteenth Heritage and
Jazz Festival

MRMF (Midwest Regional
Music Festival)

Tribute to Oliver Sain

Jakob Dylan [of the Wallflowers] threatened to "kick the shit" out of a photographer during the first song. I could hear the photographer yelling, "I'm with *Rolling Stone!*" Someone offstage pulled Dylan over and said something. Then, Dylan apologized from the stage. [March 15, 1997]

*DJ at 105.7 The Point and 106.5 The Arch

THE WALLFLOWERS

Everclear holding a *Night Times* magazine, October 31, 1997. Photo by Julia Bramer.

Concert October 17, 1997. Courtesy of Julia Bramer.

1998

The Baton Passes to Tim Weber for the Final Stretch

Tim Weber started working at Mississippi Nights in 1996, but his relationship with Rich Frame and Mississippi Nights went way back. Weber and Frame's son, Brad, were best friends as kids. One time, the boys had problems with kids picking on them as they walked to school, so Rich found a creative solution. He gave the boys Mississippi Nights baseball jackets to wear. The bullies thought the jackets were cool and decided to leave Tim and Brad alone. "I'm a hero. I saved them with a jacket," Frame boasts.

Tim Weber. Photo by Brian Nolan.

In 1996, Tim Weber came home from Southeast Missouri State University, where he played baseball and studied English. But somehow, he found himself working at Mississippi Nights. "I screwed my life all up and stayed there," Weber jokes. And he stayed until the end. Weber began as a doorman and moved up the ranks: head of security, marketing director, manager, and talent buyer. "My favorite part of The Nights was the people that worked there," he emphasizes.

Weber's first two days on the job illustrate the diversity of bands and audiences that came through Mississippi Nights. His first show was Slayer on August 18, 1996. Slayer is a thrash metal band with an enthusiastic audience and an expected mosh pit. Weber's job was to stand at the elevated waitress station and shine a flashlight on people causing trouble, instructing security to throw them out. The second show was a blues show, where the audience dressed up and stayed seated. Weber recalls, "We used to sell VIP seating on the dance floor for those, and my job was to wristband people."

Weber reflects on the lasting impact of Mississippi Nights, "There's probably not a month that goes by that somebody doesn't come up to me and say, 'Man, that show at The Nights... and that thing that happened... That was awesome!'"

Since 2009, Weber has been a partner in the Old Rock House in downtown St. Louis, where he facilitated the club's change from a "bro bar" to a classy rock club. Unfortunately, as of 2022, his current project, a 1,200-seat venue in downtown St. Louis, is sidelined due to the COVID-19 pandemic.

STEVEN "ROCK" BLACK* REMEMBERS...

My first time coming to Mississippi Nights was for Fragile Porcelain Mice in 1998. I was in the mosh pit. That's kind of the reason I ended up working there. I was having a real good time and started talking with one of the security guys working down in the pit. He dragged me up front at the end of the show. I thought I was getting kicked out, but he gave me an application. [November 26, 1998]

Mississippi Nights assistant manager

From the collection of Garrett Enloe.

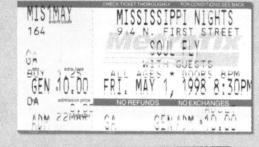

Courtesy of Tony Vitale.

MISSISSIPPI NIGHTS
914 N. FIRST STREET
THE CRYSTAL METHOD
$2 SURCHG MINORS AT DOO
ALL AGES * DOORS 7:30
TUE. SEP 1, 1998 8:00
NO REFUNDS   NO EXCHANGES
GA   GEN ADM 10.00

MIS1MAY
164
MISSISSIPPI NIGHTS
914 N. FIRST STREET
SOUL FLY
WITH GUESTS
ALL AGES * DOORS 8PM
GEN 10.00
FRI. MAY 1, 1998 8:30PM
NO REFUNDS   NO EXCHANGES
ADM 22MAY   GA   GEN ADM 10.00

MISSISSIPPI NIGHTS
914 N. FIRST STREET
MARTENS PRESENTS
HENRY ROLLINS
ALL AGES * DOORS 7PM
SUN. OCT 25, 1998 8:00P
NO REFUNDS   NO EXCHANGES
GA   GEN ADM 12.00

Courtesy of Daniel Durchholz.

MIS21MAY
4019 MUST
MISSISSIPPI NIGHTS
914 N. 1ST ST * PRESENTS
RUN DMC
w/GUEST
DOORS 7PM * MUST BE 21
GEN 12.00
THU. MAY 21, 1998 8:00PM
NO REFUNDS   NO EXCHANGES
MUST BE 21   DAYOS
ADM 21MAY   GA   GEN ADM $12.00

Courtesy of Tony Vitale.

MIS9MAR
921 ALL
MISSISSIPPI NIGHTS
PRESENTS
CHUMBAWAMBA
WITH GUEST A 3
DOORS 7:30PM/SHOW 8:30P
GEN 15.00
MONDAY, MAR 9, 1998
NO REFUNDS   NO EXCHANGES
ALL AGES
ADM 06FEB   GA   GEN ADM 5.00

Courtesy of Andy Mayberry.

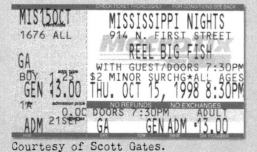

MIS15OCT
1676 ALL
MISSISSIPPI NIGHTS
914 N. FIRST STREET
REEL BIG FISH
WITH GUEST/DOORS 7:30PM
$2 MINOR SURCHG*ALL AGES
GEN 13.00
THU. OCT 15, 1998 8:30PM
NO REFUNDS   NO EXCHANGES
DOORS 7:30PM   ADULT
ADM 21SEP   GA   GEN ADM $13.00

Courtesy of Scott Gates.

180

Mississippi Nights advertisement in the *Riverfront Times*.

GARRETT ENLOE* REMEMBERS...

On June 7, 1998, James Harvey and I went down to Laclede's Landing. Not only was Slayer in town, but thousands of bikers had stopped in St. Louis to party on their way to the 95th Harley Davidson birthday celebration in Milwaukee.

First, we went behind Mississippi Nights to try to meet Slayer. While we listened to the sound check from outside, the opening band, System of a Down, hung out with us. Since their first CD wouldn't be released for another two weeks, we had never heard of them. However, they were very friendly guys. Next, we watched as our friend Tim Howard, who had a radio show called The Scream on KCFV from the Florissant Valley location of St. Louis Community College, interviewed guitarist Daron Malakian.

After Slayer's soundcheck, guitarist Kerry King and drummer Paul Bostaph came down the stairs. We managed to get autographs and photos before they headed to the Harley convention. After that, we hung out for another hour. Then, we left to explore, too.

Thousands of Bikers were in St. Louis that day, and streets surrounding Mississippi Nights were filled with motorcycles and food vendors. The restaurants and bars were filled with people. In the streets, bands played all different genres of music: rock, jazz, blues, you name it. Of course, we were pleased with the cheap beer.

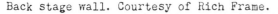

SUN. JUNE 7
Slayer
w/System of a Dawn & Clutch
Doors 7/Show 7:30 • Tickets are $20 flat • All ages concert

The Riverfront Times welcomes **TUES. JUNE 30**
Brian Setzer Orchestra **Featuring**
Brian Setzer & His 17-Piece Rockin' Big Band
Doors 7:30/Show 8:30 • Tickets are $20 Flat
All ages concert • $2 surcharge for minors

Mississippi Nights advertisement in the *Riverfront Times* with misspelling of System of a Down.

Back stage wall. Courtesy of Rich Frame.

181

With all the activity, James and I lost track of time. We rushed to get back to Mississippi Nights when we realized how late it was. At that point, the line was extremely long. When we finally stepped into the club, we heard, "Thank you! We are System of a Down." We had missed their entire set!

Clutch was second on the bill. They were good, but the crowd was primed for Slayer.

This mid-summer show was sold-out, so I knew it would be a hot one, a 'sweatfest concert,' as I used to call them. I never experienced that kind of heat at any venue other than Mississippi Nights. You'd buy a drink and see water vapor coming off the ice.

Slayer was incredible! The energy was amazing! I was in the pit during the set and noticed something in my hair. One of Jeff Hanneman's guitar picks had landed and stuck in my sweaty, curly hair. Out of all my guitar picks in my collection, the one I caught in my hair is my most cherished. (R.I.P. Jeff Hanneman.)

About thirty of us gathered behind the building after the show, hoping to have a moment with the band. We all looked like we had survived a battle. We were bonded by sweat, adrenaline, and our love for the almighty Slayer. This was the fourth and last time Slayer played Mississippi Nights. Later, they opted to play The Pageant, Riverport Amphitheatre, and Pops (once) before retiring in 2019. Of the fourteen times I've seen Slayer, this one at Mississippi Nights was the best.

*Author

Courtesy of Michael Rose.

Advertisement in the *Riverfront Times*.

What's The Point?

On February 17, 1993, a new radio station hit the
airwaves, 105.7 KPNT The Point, focusing on modern
and alternative music. The station was an exciting new
format for St. Louis. Before The Point, the only place to hear artists
like Red Hot Chili Peppers, The Cure, or Pixies was smaller bandwidth
college radio. The Point became successful almost immediately.

During their first year, KPNT sponsored the first Pointfest, an all-day, outside concert
showcasing the most popular national and international touring bands on the station and
some local bands. The first few Pointfests at Riverport Amphitheatre featured They Might
Be Giants, Midnight Oil, MC 900 Ft. Jesus, The Ramones, Big Audio Dynamite, and Love and
Rockets.

In 1994, The Point released its first *Pointessential* CD featuring local bands. All of the bands
on the first CD had played at Mississippi Nights. Among the bands on *Pointessential Vol. 1*
were Wilco, Judge Nothing, The Finns, MU330, Suede Chain, and Bellyfeel. The seventh and
final volume of *Pointessential* was released in 2002, and sixteen of the nineteen bands on the
disc were Mississippi Nights alums.

On December 10, 1995, The Point held their first Ho Ho Show at Mississippi Nights.
The sold-out show featured Lisa Loeb, The Toadies, Deep Blue, and The Nixons. Later, the
event moved to The Pageant.

Even though KPNT The Point was a younger station than KSHE-95, they sponsored more
shows at Mississippi Nights. Some of The Point sponsored shows were Violent Femmes,
Matthew Sweet, Juliana Hatfield, Fishbone, Jellyfish, Lemonheads, Goo Goo Dolls, Concrete
Blonde, The Proclaimers, and Wilco.

In the early years, The Point focused solely on alternative bands. As times changed, so did
the station. On any given day, listeners can still hear a wide variety of music from Tool to
Korn to Mumford and Sons. 105.7 KPNT The Point continues to influence the St. Louis
music scene.

KY KATZMAN* REMEMBERS...

Los Lobos was playing Mississippi Nights on October 18, 1998, and my friend and I ran down to buy tickets. When we got there, we found out that the only way in was with 500 Marlboro Miles. (In 1998, Marlboro put on secret shows in random cities. They told you where to show up, gave you 24-hours' notice, but didn't tell you the artist.)

Neither of us smoked, so we stood outside begging for miles from passers-by. We eventually got in, along with about fifty other folks. Half of them had no idea who Los Lobos was. They were Marlboro smokers who were just there for the free drinks and buffet. The atmosphere was non-existent that evening, but the band put on a rip-roaring concert and had a long meet-and-greet afterward. It was probably my most unusual concert experience at The Nights.

Mississippi Nights patron

Courtesy of Scott Gates.

From the collection of Garrett Enloe.

Toni Halliday of Curve, June 23, 1998. Photo by Mike Glader.

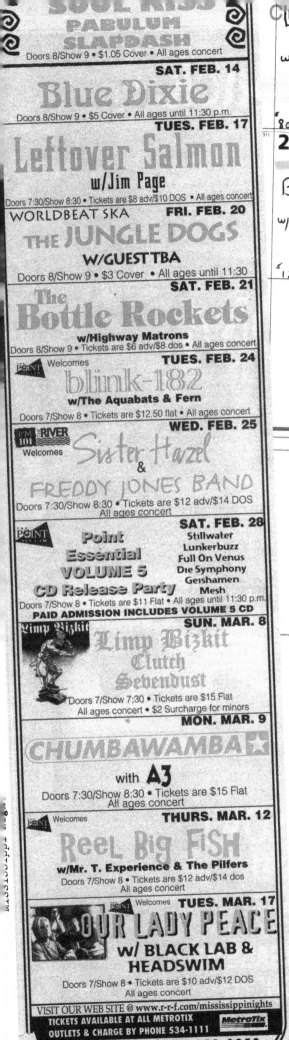

SOUL KISS
PABULUM
SLAPDASH
Doors 8/Show 9 • $1.05 Cover • All ages concert

SAT. FEB. 14

Blue Dixie
Doors 8/Show 9 • $5 Cover • All ages until 11:30 p.m.

TUES. FEB. 17

Leftover Salmon
w/Jim Page
Doors 7:30/Show 8:30 • Tickets are $8 adv/$10 DOS • All ages concert

WORLDBEAT SKA   **FRI. FEB. 20**

THE JUNGLE DOGS
W/GUEST TBA
Doors 8/Show 9 • $3 Cover • All ages until 11:30

SAT. FEB. 21

The Bottle Rockets
w/Highway Matrons
Doors 8/Show 9 • Tickets are $6 adv/$8 dos • All ages concert

POINT Welcomes   **TUES. FEB. 24**

blink-182
w/The Aquabats & Fern
Doors 7/Show 8 • Tickets are $12.50 flat • All ages concert

FM RIVER 101   **WED. FEB. 25**
Welcomes

Sister Hazel
&
FREDDY JONES BAND
Doors 7:30/Show 8:30 • Tickets are $12 adv/$14 DOS
All ages concert

POINT   **SAT. FEB. 28**
Point   Stillwater
Essential   Lunkerbuzz
VOLUME 5   Full On Venus
                     Die Symphony
CD Release Party   Geishamen
                     Mesh
Doors 7/Show 8 • Tickets are $11 Flat • All ages until 11:30 p.m.
PAID ADMISSION INCLUDES VOLUME 5 CD

SUN. MAR. 8

Limp Bizkit
Clutch
Sevendust
Doors 7/Show 7:30 • Tickets are $15 Flat
All ages concert • $2 Surcharge for minors

MON. MAR. 9

CHUMBAWAMBA ☆
with **A3**
Doors 7:30/Show 8:30 • Tickets are $15 Flat
All ages concert

POINT Welcomes   **THURS. MAR. 12**

Reel Big Fish
w/Mr. T. Experience & The Pilfers
Doors 7/Show 8 • Tickets are $12 adv/$14 dos
All ages concert

POINT Welcomes   **TUES. MAR. 17**

OUR LADY PEACE
W/ BLACK LAB & HEADSWIM
Doors 7/Show 8 • Tickets are $10 adv/$12 DOS
All ages concert

VISIT OUR WEB SITE @ www.r-r-f.com/mississippinights
TICKETS AVAILABLE AT ALL METROTIX
OUTLETS & CHARGE BY PHONE 534-1111   **MetroTix**
FOR MORE INFORMATION CALL 421-3853

Club Card

Leftover
Salmon
w/ Jim
Page

$8 adv $10 DOS

The
Jungle Dogs
w/
Boro City
Rollers

$3.00 cover

Club Card

Bottle
Rockets
w/ Highway
Matrons

$6 adv $8 DOS

24 Door 7 Show 8   **25** Rich Back   **26**   **27** Doors 7 Show 8   **28**

BlinK-182
w/ The Aquabats
+ Fern

$12.50 flat

Sister Hazel
+
Freddy Jones
Band.

$12 adv $14 DOS

Tibet Freedom Benefit
w/
Full on Venus
Ghoul 5
Nunqu Girl
Galaxia
Collaborateur
£5.00 cover

Point Essential
Vol 5
C.D. Release
Party

$11. Tix

2/28
St Louis City
Drinking Place
License

Brian Teal walking in front of Mississippi Nights.
Photo by Paul Hilcoff.

EVENTS IN 1998

Tibet Freedom Benefit

Pointessential Vol. 5 CD Release Party

MRMF (Midwest Regional Music Festival)

The Point Platinum CD Release Party

185

Vanilla Ice and Andy Mayberry,
March 27, 1998. Courtesy of
Andy Mayberry.

MISSISSIPPI NIGHTS
914 N. FIRST STREET
VANILLA ICE
ALL AGES ★ DOORS 8PM
$12 ADV ★ $14 DAY OF
FRI. MAR 27, 1998

EMIS27MAR
2997
SN241
GA
BUY
GEN 11.23
OA 0.77
ADM 6MAR

NO REFUNDS   NO EXCHANGES

GA   GEN ADM 12.00

Courtesy of Andy Mayberry.

Dilbert McClinton Band
and Andy Mayberry
(red staff shirt)
in the Mississippi
Nights dressing room,
December 11, 1998.
Courtesy of
Andy Mayberry.

186

1999

GARRETT ENLOE* REMEMBERS...

When Charles Coffell and I learned that Fantomas was coming to Mississippi Nights on December 18, 1999, we couldn't get our tickets quick enough. The band was a musical supergroup featuring vocalist Mike Patton (Faith No More, Mr. Bungle), drummer Dave Lombardo (Slayer, Suicidal Tendencies), guitarist Buzz Osborne (Melvins), and bassist Trevor Dunn (Mr. Bungle). I am a rabid Lombardo-era Slayer fan, and Coffell is a huge Patton fan. So we were beyond excited about the concert.

Neither of us knew what to expect of Fantomas, even after hearing the CD. Mike Patton makes weird noises, sings, screams, and moans on it. Dave Lombardo plays drums faster than when he was in Slayer on some songs. Yet, sometimes the music is slow and beautiful. Fantomas has been labeled as avant-garde metal, alternative metal, and experimental rock.

Coffell and I arrived at the show at 5:30 p.m. Since doors didn't open until 8 p.m., I thought we would stand in line early to get a good spot right by the stage. However, Coffell had another plan. When we walked up to the front door, he said, "Let's just go inside!" Before I could even respond, he walked right in. I followed.

From the collection of Garrett Enloe.

The managers were busy meeting with the security. Although they saw us, no one said a word. Right when we made it to the stage, Fantomas began soundcheck. They played a couple of great original songs. At the end of soundcheck, they played one of the greatest heavy metal songs of all time, and one of my favorites, Slayer's 1986 "Angel of Death." Lombardo's drum kit faced sideways, so you could watch him perform. Being at Mississippi Nights with only a handful of other people watching them play that song so perfectly was an incredible moment for me.

EXIT PAT HAGIN

Pat Hagin had started to notice Laclede's Landing was in a state of decline. So in April 1999, he left Mississippi Nights for a new endeavor. Teaming up with Joe Edwards, they opened The Pageant, a 2,300-seat venue in University City, in October 2000.

CHRISTOPHER ELLIS* REMEMBERS...

The lead singer of Buckcherry tried to get me to sit in for his mandatory, court-ordered Narcotics Anonymous class. I'm 6'3" and 325 pounds, not to mention black, so I didn't think I'd be able to pull off filling in for a skinny, tattooed, white guy. We both laughed about it, and he wrote "Buckcherry" on the frosty, passenger side back window. I dropped him off, wasted, at a place on Lindell for three hours. I laughed about it the whole night. [December 9, 1999]

*Mississippi Nights runner

Concert July 20, 1999.
Courtesy of Rich Frame.

Courtesy of Rich Frame.
Photo by Matt Albers.

Gypsy, July 9, 1999. Photo by Terry Lewis.

Tickets courtesy of Scott Gates.

188

Mike Patton of Fantomas (right) and Charles Coffell.
December 18, 1999. Photo by Garrett Enloe.

As soon as the soundcheck was over, Patton and Lombardo came over to us. We talked and took photos with them. Patton even agreed to let Coffell take pictures of his odd microphone setup. Lombardo spoke with me for about fifteen minutes, even introducing me to some of his family who lived in St. Louis. We also met guitarist Osborne and drummer Dunn. You can find a LepersTV cable access interview of Fantomas at Mississippi Nights on YouTube.

After the security opened the doors, someone in a staff shirt asked us if we had tickets. We handed them over. The staff member tore them and walked away.

We still got those spots right in front of the stage I wanted. Then, during the encore, we heard them play "Angel of Death" for the second time that day. It's a night I'll never forget!

*Author

Ticket stubs courtesy of Daniel Durchholz, Kathy Enloe, John Gierse, Tony Vitale, and from the collection of Garrett Enloe.

FANTôMAS
BUZZ OSBORNE / TREVOR DUNN / MIKE PATTON / DAVE LOMBARDO

189

EVENTS IN 1999

LAAW Benefit

Pointessential Vol. 6 CD Release Party

Marlboro Miles Parties: 6/30, 8/5, 10/13

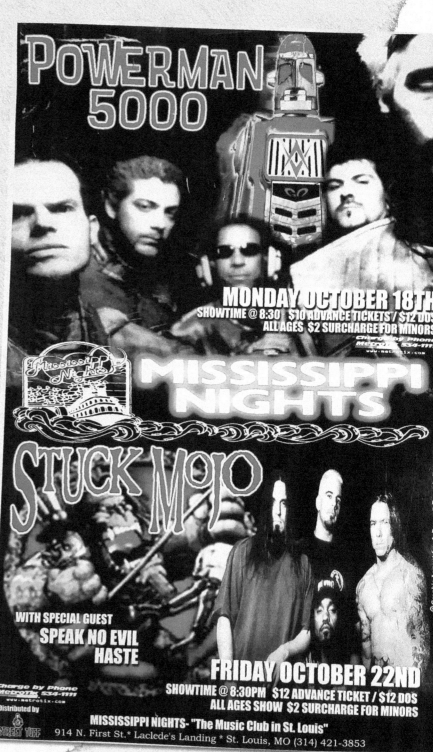

MIS12JUN
2870
MISSISSIPPI NIGHTS
914 N. FIRST STREET
POINT ESSENTIAL*VOL. VI
GA   DOORS 8:00PM * $15 FLAT
BUY 1.75   ALL AGES UNTIL 11:30PM
GEN 15.00   SAT. JUN 12, 1999 8:30PM
            NO REFUNDS   NO EXCHANGES
1D   0.00   DAYOS
ADM 12JUN   GA   GEN ADM 15.00

From the collection
of Garrett Enloe.

Courtesy of Scott Foster.

SLACKERS CDS & GAMES
AND MISSISSIPPI NIGHTS
presents:

ELI STONE

(CD Release Show)
SATURDAY JUNE 26, 1999
7:30PM Door - 8:00 Show
All Ages
special guests:
PLAYGROUND KING, BROKE, DJ B-CZAR
ADV: $8.00 D.O.S.: $10.00

$1.00 OFF
Any Purchase
of $5.00 or more
at all

ELI STONE
Positive
in
stores
JUNE 28TH

slackers
CD's & Games

POWERMAN 5000

MONDAY OCTOBER 18TH
SHOWTIME @ 8:30 $10 ADVANCE TICKETS / $12 DOS
ALL AGES $2 SURCHARGE FOR MINORS
Charge by Phone
MetroTix 534-1111
www.metrotix.com

MISSISSIPPI NIGHTS

STUCK MOJO

WITH SPECIAL GUEST
SPEAK NO EVIL HASTE

FRIDAY OCTOBER 22ND
SHOWTIME @ 8:30PM $12 ADVANCE TICKET / $12 DOS
ALL AGES SHOW $2 SURCHARGE FOR MINORS

Charge by Phone
MetroTix 534-1111
www.metrotix.com

Distributed by
STREET TUFF

MISSISSIPPI NIGHTS- "The Music Club in St. Louis"
914 N. First St.* Laclede's Landing * St. Louis, MO (314) 421-3853

EMINEM

TUESDAY, MAY 18

w/ BEATNUTS

MISSISSIPPI NIGHTS
914 N. FIRST STREET

EMINEM

MIS18MAY 1569

GA BITY GEN 25.00 WITH GUESTS 7:30PM DOOR
ALL AGES TUE. MAY 18, 1999 8:00PM
NO REFUNDS NO EXCHANGES
0.00
ADM 15MAY GA GEN ADM $25.00 ADULT

@ MISSISSIPPI NIGHTS

ALL AGES 914 N 1ST, ST LOUIS, MO (314)421-3853

	Sat
	1 WEEK 17 Mesh Simple m Dian Slapda $5. cover
6 126-239 Jibe Broke Triple Clamp $5 coun 21 7 coun 21	**7** 127/238 Belle Star Rock House Ramblers Stubblefield @ 12 mn $5 cover	**8** CC Moe "an Evenin $2. mino S $10 adv $12
13 7:30 133/232 Bruce Hornsby $2. Surcharge $20 flat	**14** 134/231 Country Hoedown Spectacular Reverend Horton Heat Junior Brown BR5-49 18+ over $20 adv $25. DOS	**15** Armed Force Najee w/ Brian Quar ↑ 21 $15.
16 WEEK 20	**17**	**18** S8 EMINEM w/ The Beatnuts + Pacewon $85 flat	**19**	**20** Dental 140/225 8:30 Creature Comforts Exit 159 Shudderbug moaninghisa 4.00 21 6.↓21	**21** 141/224 CC Michael Schenker w/ Vinnie Moore ↑21 $12 adv $14 DOS	**22** The Ohio Playe w/ Friend $12 adv $15
23 0 6:30 143/222 WEEK 21 Morris Day + The Time + w/ Boogie Chyld 21 15.00	**24** 144/221 Victoria Day (Canada)	**25** 145/220 CC Flotsam + Jetsam w/ Cong	**26** 146/219	**27** D 7 148/217 S 8 Groundationi	**28** 148/217 1 Pm Benne Vargas Swing w/ Jive Turkey $5 cover	**29** Fragile Porcelain mice w/ Nil8 + clever $6. cover
30 D 7 S 8 160/215 WEEK 22	**31** 151/2 Memorial Day Observed (US) Spring Bank Holiday (United Kingdom)	$8 adv				

QuickNotes®

★ 5/31 Dance Hall Food + Beverage

REVEREND HORTON HEAT
JUNIOR BROWN & BR5-49
MISSISSIPPI NIGHTS
DOORS 8:00PM/SHOW 8:30PM
MUST BE 18 OR OLDER
FRIDAY, MAY 14, 1999
NO REFUNDS NO EXCHANGES

MIS14MAY 5190 734
GA BUY GEN 25.00
OD 0.00 DAYOS
ADM 14MAY GA GEN ADM $25.00

16

KID ROCK

w/LIT
adv/$14 dos • All ages concert

GATEWAY SHOWCASE **THURS. APRIL 15**

Earl Bros. • Stillwater
My Two Planets

Doors 7:30/Show 8 • $4 Cover • All ages until 11:30 p.m.

BETTERTHANEZRA **FRI. APRIL 16**

w/JUDE

Doors 8/Show 9 • $12.25 Adv/$14.25 DOS • All ages concert

The Devil Without a Cause Tour **SAT. APRIL 17**

KID ROCK

w/STAIND & DISTURBING THE PEACE

Doors 8/Show 8:30 •Tickets are $10 Adv/$12 DOS
•All ages concert • $2 surcharge for minors

SAT. APRIL 24

NEW WORLD SPIRITS

w/Ram Jet Engine

Doors 8/Show 9 • $5 Cover • All ages until 11:30 p.m.

An evening with **TUES. APRIL 27**

Charlie Hunter

Doors 7:30/Show 8:30 • Tickets are $10 Adv/$12 DOS
All ages concert

GATEWAY SHOWCASE **FRI. APRIL 30**

Pepperland • The Outsiders
Mind Over Soul

Doors 7:30/Show 8 • $4 Cover • All ages until 11:30 p.m.

moe. **SAT. MAY 8**

w/Guest

Doors 8/Show 9 • Tickets are $10 adv/$12 dos
All ages Concert • $2 Surcharge for minors

Bruce Hornsby **THURS. MAY 13**

Doors 7:30/Show 8:30
Tickets are $20 Flat on sale
3/24 • Must be 21 over

Mississippi Nights advertisement in
the *Riverfront Times.*

MIS17SEP
4857

MISSISSIPPI NIGHTS
914 N. FIRST STREET
CIBO MATTO
ALL AGES * 8PM DOOR
$2 SURCH MINORS AT DOOR
FRI. SEP 17, 1999 9PM

GA
BUY 0.00
GEN 12.00
ODD
0.00
admission price
ADM 17SEP
GA GEN ADM 12.00
NO REFUNDS NO EXCHANGES
DAYOS

Tickets courtesy of Mark Lewis.

EMIS10NOV
2748
SN227

MISSISSIPPI NIGHTS
914 N. FIRST STREET
MEDESKI MARTIN & WOOD
ALL AGES * 7:00PM DOOR
$2 MINOR SURCHG AT DOOR
WED. NOV 10, 1999 7:30PM

GA
BUY 2.00
GEN 18.50
7A 0.00
ADM 16SEP GA GEN ADM 18.50
NO REFUNDS NO EXCHANGES
ADULT

MIS5NOV
4476

MISSISSIPPI NIGHTS
914 N. FIRST STREET
JUNIOR BROWN
ALL AGES * DOORS 8PM
$2 MINOR SURCHG AT DOOR
FRI. NOV 5, 1999 9PM

GA
BUY 0.00
GEN 17.00
23D 0.00
ADM 05NOV GA GEN ADM 17.00
NO REFUNDS NO EXCHANGES
DAYOS

Courtesy of John Wegrzyn.

Junior Brown, November 5, 1999. Photo by John Wegrzyn.

2000

Big Blue Monkey: The Story of the Year

The band 67 North was formed in 1995 by guitarist Ryan Phillips, drummer Dan Marsala, vocalist John Taylor, and bassist Perry West. They changed their name in 1998 to Big Blue Monkey and released their first EP, *Three Days Broken,* that same year. In 1999, they released their second EP, *Truth in Separation.*

West and Taylor left the group in 2000, and Marsala moved to vocals. Josh Wills filled Marsala's spot on drums, and Adam Russell joined on bass. "I was originally a guitar player and a singer," says Marsala. "My goal never was to be a drummer. I was just doing it because I thought it was kind of fun, and we couldn't find a drummer." Marsala wanted to be a singer since the '80s when he pretended to be a rock star singing along with Skid Row and Motley Crüe in his bedroom mirror. Marsala and Phillips shared a passion and commitment to make it as a band and decided that solidifying their songwriting partnership would be the way to make this happen.

The band released an EP titled *Story of the Year* on Criterion Records in 2002.

Later that year, Big Blue Monkey added Greg Haupt on rhythm guitar and relocated to Los Angeles. Before they left, they played a farewell concert at Mississippi Nights on May 24 with the bands 84-40 and Swift Kixx opening. When Big Blue Monkey arrived at 2 p.m., the line of concertgoers already stretched down the street for the sold-out show. The band was thrilled they had become big enough to sell out Mississippi Nights.

"That was the standard if you were a local band: to sell out Mississippi Nights," says Marsala.

Patti Smith, July 13, 2000.
Photo by John Wegrzyn.

KOTTONMOUTH KINGS
w/CORPORATE AVENGERS • LINKIN PARK • REHAB
Doors 7 / Show 7:30 / Tickets are $13.50 ADV/$15 DOS
All Ages concert / $2 Minor Surcharge

SAT. OCT. 7 JENSENERGY Presents
BT
with HOOVERPHONIC
Doors 8 / Show 8:30 /Tickets are $17.50 ADV/$20 DOS
All Ages concert / $2 Minor Surcharge

TUES. OCT. 10
CULTURE CLUB
Featuring all original members
including BOY GEORGE • w/THE OUTSIDERS
Doors 7:30 / Show 8:30 /Tickets are $33.50 ADV/$35 DOS
All Ages concert / $2 Minor Surcharge

FRI. OCT. 13 WIL92FM WELCOMES
An Evening with the Legendary
MERLE HAGGARD
Doors 8 / Show 9 /Tickets are $40 Flat /
Must be 21 or over / *Limited Capacity*

SAT. OCT. 14
SGM Records Agressive Rock Showcase
FEATURING
UNCHAINED
SELF RESTRAINT
DRAWPOINT
ORAL DEFACATION
Doors 7 / Show 8 / $5 Cover / All Ages until 11:30 pm

WED. OCT. 18
Better Than Ezra
W/GUEST
Doors 7:30 / Show 8:30 / Tickets are $15 Flat /
All Ages Concert / $2 Minor Surcharge

FRI. OCT. 20
NEUTER THE STUPID
W/GUEST
Doors 9 / Show 10 / $3 Cover / Must be 21 or over

SAT. OCT. 21 "An evening with"
maceo parker
Doors 8 / Show 9 / Tickets are $18.50 adv/ $20 DOS
All Ages Concert / $2 Minor Surcharge

TUES. OCT. 24 An evening with
BLUE FLOYD
Blues Explorations into the Music of Pink Floyd
Featuring MARC FORD (of the Black Crowes)
MATT ABST (of Gov't Mule) • JOHNNY NEEL
(of the Allman Brothers) • BARRY OAKLEY
(of the Robby Krieger Band)
Doors 7 / Show 8 / Tickets are $15 Flat /
All Ages Concert /$2 Minor Surcharge

WED. OCT. 25
SR-71 (10:20 pm)
HARVEY DANGER (9 pm)
WHEATUS (8 pm)
Doors 7 / Show 8 /Tickets are $13 adv/$15 DOS
All Ages concert / $2 Minor Surcharge

THURS. OCT. 26
THE FIXX
w/Guest/ Doors 7:30 / Show 8:30 /Tickets are $15 Flat
All Ages Concert / $2 Minor Surcharge

FRI. OCT. 27
GALACTIC
w/LAKE TROUT
Doors 7 / Show 8:15/Tickets are $12 ADV/$14 DOS
All Ages Concert / $2 Minor Surcharge

SAT. OCT. 28
The Samples
w/Guest
Doors 8 / Show 8:30/Tickets are $12 ADV/$14 DOS
All Ages Concert / $2 Minor Surcharge

SAT. NOV. 4
LOS LOBOS
w/Guest
Doors 8 / Show 9 /Tickets are $20 ADV/$22 DOS Must be 21 or over

FRI. NOV. 17

194

Mississippi Nights advertisement in the Riverfront Times.

Ampeg promotional photo shoot
with Conrad Lozano of Los Lobos,
November 4, 2000. Photo by
Mark Gilliland.

An acoustic evening with
medeski
martin
& wood

wednesday may 10
8:30pm $20adv/$22dos
all ages $2 surcharge for minors

MISSISSIPPI NIGHTS
THE MUSIC CLUB OF ST. LOUIS 914 N. 1ST IN LACLEDES LANDING (314) 421-3853
TO CHARGE BY PHONE (314) 534-1111 VISIT OUR WEBSITE: r-r-f.com/mississippinights

Courtesy of Brian Nolan.

"A couple of months later [in LA], we ended up getting the Goldfinger tour," recalls Marsala. Big Blue Monkey had played the local stage at Pointfest 14, five days before their farewell show at Mississippi Nights, and the band had attracted the attention of Goldfinger, who headlined the second stage that evening.

After the tour, the band signed a record deal with Maverick Records, a subsidiary of Warner Bros., and changed their name to Story of the Year. "We got signed to Maverick Records as Big Blue Monkey, and the label hated [the name]. We hated it at that point," Marsala confesses. "So, we made up a story that another band had the name, but that was a lie. We just didn't like the name anymore."

Goldfinger's guitarist, John Feldmann, produced the band's first full-length album, *Page Avenue,* released in September 2003. Haupt was kicked out of the band during the recording due to personality clashes and replaced with Philip Sneed. To date, *Page Avenue* has sold over a million copies. In addition, Story of the Year released six more CDs, including *Live in the Lou,* recorded at The Pageant in St. Louis. The band also released two DVDs.

The band played Mississippi Nights five times as Big Blue Monkey and returned to the venue as Story of the Year on December 21, 2002.

"It was the epitome of what local bands wanted to play," says Marsala. "You knew that it was going to be a different caliber of show there. Something about it was a little more upscale."

EVENT IN 2000

Benefit for Muffy

TIM HAAR* REMEMBERS...

There was an Urge show with a $16 ticket price way back when I was young and broke. I only had eight dollars in my pocket, so I tried to negotiate with the door guy. Since I had half the amount for a ticket, I promised him I'd only stay for half the show. The door guy laughed, waved me through, and let me keep my eight bucks.

*Guitarist of ELI-STONE

Courtesy of Daniel Durchholz.

- Too much
- Don't ask
- Gene Machine
- Violent
- Straight Hell
- Flintstone
- Bark
- All wash
- Divide C.
- Closer
- Gunville
- Killing easy
- She don't care
- 4 letters
- one love
- Jump in
- Liquor

MIS20JUL
2438
MISSISSIPPI NIGHTS
TOO MUCH STEREO TOUR
THE URGE
GA
DOORS 7PM * ALL AGES
$2 SURCHG FOR MINORS
GEN 15.00 THU. JUL 20, 2000
0.00
NO REFUNDS   NO EXCHANGES

195

PHOTO BY STEVE PACK

421-3853

Call for further information or to reserve a date. Lighting and stage plots are available upon request. If the event you are planning has special needs, please let us know so we can work with you.

Anybody can have a party or a business meeting. You can have an *event* at Mississippi Nights.

Location

Mississippi Nights is conveniently located on the St. Louis riverfront at Laclede's Landing. We are approximately three blocks north of the Arch, and easily accessible by Highways 40 and 70.

There are two nearby parking lots. One is next to the club, and the other is just across the street next to the Embassy Suites Hotel.

Mississippi Nights
914 N. First Street
St. Louis, MO 63102

The Stars come out at the Nights, so should you.

CYNDI BAUMAN* REMEMBERS...

I attended so many concerts that I knew many of the concertgoers and usually knew who to expect at each show. However, when iconic British band Culture Club played Mississippi Nights on their reunion tour, one friend that I certainly did not expect arrived: Garrett Enloe with his son, Kyle. They didn't have tickets but hoped to meet the band, a regular occurrence at Mississippi Nights.

Most bands that played at Mississippi Nights stayed at the [Embassy Suites] hotel right across the street. If an eager fan showed up before soundcheck, that fan usually got their wish: an autograph and a photo with their favorite artist. Sometimes bands added ticketless fans to their guest list.

We saw a tour bus pull up in front of the club at about 4 p.m. [Culture Club's] Roy Hay (guitarist), Mikey Craig (bassist), and Jon Moss (drummer) exited the bus for soundcheck. I had a 1980s MTV flashback seeing all the original members of Culture Club except Boy George. They looked great and were very friendly to us. Garrett asked Jon for a drumstick, and he was kind enough to oblige. He retrieved a set from the bus and gave them to Kyle.

The bus drove to the back of the building, and Boy George came out. He signed plenty of autographs and took lots of photos before joining the rest of the band for soundcheck.

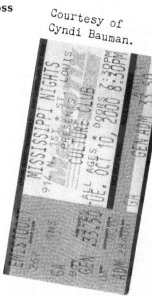

Courtesy of Cyndi Bauman.

196

Mississippi Nights is available for:

☆ **Private Parties**

☆ **Business Meetings**

☆ **Video Taping**

☆ **Award Banquets**

☆ **Charity Events**

Mississippi Nights has all the facilities you need for a successful party. We have continually won awards as the best St. Louis nightclub from the *Riverfront Times* and *SurFACE* magazine. We have been equally successful with parties and meetings for national and local organizations including KTVI TV and Ralston Purina. Stage, lights, sound system, and bars are available complete with bartenders, sound men, and any other assistance you need.

Call: 421-3853

Contact: Cindy Fehmel or Pat Lacey for further assistance.

Food and Drink

Flexibility is the key and you are the boss. For business meetings, we can provide coffee, tea, soft drinks, and juice. If there is a specific product you need, let us know so we can arrange for it.

For parties, Mississippi Nights has two fully stocked bars with everything you would need for a big dance to an intimate reception. Flexibility is the key again. The bar can be open or cash bar, and we can just open one if you are expecting a smaller crowd. We will work with you to find what best suits your needs.

Catering at a reasonable rate can be arranged through Mississippi Nights, or you can secure your own. We can help with everything from coffee and doughnuts for an early seminar, to a full buffet for a big celebration.

Facilities

We are a full facility nightclub in an 1880's warehouse in the entertainment district on St. Louis' riverfront. You can easily seat 650 people at tables or auditorium style. There is an elevated 26½×21 stage, and a huge dance floor for dancing at your party or product displays for your business meeting. Microphones and lights can be arranged pertaining to your needs.

Sound System

As *the* music club in St. Louis, Mississippi Nights has an excellent sound system for live or recorded performances. Whether for a speech of encouragement, kudos for an award winning effort, music to set a mood, or a live band to keep the party going, Mississippi Nights' sound system has everything you need to be successful. A sound crew is available through Mississippi Nights.

Lights

We have an 18 channel house board with bump, solo, and chase. We also have house dimming. We can supply the light technician if needed. For video taping, let us know how our lighting system could be best used for your project.

Boy George of Culture Club behind Mississippi Nights, October 10, 2000. Photo by Garrett Enloe.

Since I could not attend their last concert in St. Louis in 1984, I had waited for this reunion tour for many years. Culture Club was one of the first pop bands I discovered as a tween, and I still sing their songs at karaoke night.

The setlist didn't disappoint, and neither did the band. Culture Club played the songs I expected to hear, like "Do You Really Want to Hurt Me" and "The War Song." Boy George's extrovert personality kept the crowd engaged throughout the entire show. As expected, his outfit was outrageous. At one point, George asked the crowd, "Are there any homosexuals in the crowd tonight?" which garnered an extremely rousing response. The band was tight and gave an incredible performance. Culture Club exceeded my expectations, and I'll never forget that show. [November 3, 2000]

*Mississippi Nights patron

197

YOU GUYS KICK ASS!!
MISSISSIPPI NIGHTS RULEZ!!

Vaughan Kyle Enloe, and Mike Shinoda
of Linkin Park, November 24, 2000.
Photo by Garrett Enloe.

King's X and Vaughan Kyle Enloe, August 18, 2000.
Photo by Garrett Enloe.

198

Steve Ewing of The Urge
and Vaughan Kyle Enloe,
December 25, 2000.
Photo by Garrett Enloe.

EARL TROUT* REMEMBERS...

One day, I left work early so I could have some fun with my good friend and roommate, Kevin Wesley. His favorite band, The Mighty Mighty Bosstones, was playing a sold-out show at Mississippi Nights. When I arrived home, I said, "Grab a shower. We're going to see The Bosstones!"

He asked, "Do you have tickets, or are you on the list?" The latter usually happened because I worked for Music Vision.

I said, "No, but we're getting in!"

We were the first people to arrive at Mississippi Nights. After a while, the radio station The Point showed up and asked if we were the contest winners. Kevin said, "No, but we can be."

I told one of them it was Kevin's birthday, The Mighty Mighty Bosstones were his favorite band, and the show was sold out. They told us that we would be named the winners if the contest winners did not show up. Very cool!

Then, the band showed up. One member approached us and asked if we were the contest winners. We repeated our story. He put us on the guest list. Score! The contest winners showed up, and we congratulated them. The Point came back out a short while later and told us we were also contest winners. We got to see The Bosstones do a soundcheck while having pizza and sodas. After the soundcheck, the band hung out with us, signed some CDs, and took photos. Kevin told me that was the best birthday he ever had. I told him it was the best birthday I never had. [May 6, 2000]

*Mississippi Nights patron

From the collection
of Garrett Enloe.

Vaughan Kyle Enloe and
Henry Rollins, May 16, 2000.
Photo by Garrett Enloe.

199

MIS25APR
1790
event code

CHECK TICKET THOROUGHLY   FOR CONDITIONS SEE BACK
MISSISSIPPI NIGHTS
914 N. 1ST ★ ST. LOUIS

STATIC-X

GA
BUY 2 ₅ᵐ
GEN 15.00
DA   admission price
         0.00
ADM UTMAX

ALL AGES ★ DOORS 7:30PM
$2 SURCHG FOR MINORS
TUE. APR 25, 2000 8:00PM

NO REFUNDS   NO EXCHANGES
GA   GEN ADM $15.00
sec   row   seat   tax included

The Bobby Roberts
Company, Inc.
SE BOX 1547
E, TN 37070-1547
(615) 859-2200

MERLE HAGGARD   RCA

MIS13OCT
1929
event code

CHECK TICKET THOROUGHLY   FOR CONDITIONS SEE BACK
MISSISSIPPI NIGHTS
914 N. 1ST ★ ST. LOUIS

MERLE HAGGARD

GA
BUY
GEN 40.00
         admission price

DOORS 8:00PM
MUST BE 21+ TO ENTER
FRI. OCT 13 2000 9:00PM
NO REFUNDS   NO EXCHANGES

ADULT
GA   GEN ADM   40.00

NOISY FEST

a one year anniversary showcase

SATURDAY AUGUST 12
at
MISSISSIPPI NIGHTS
featuring

ROCKET PARK

SIMPLE MARY'S DIARY

THE BLASTOIDS

TERRI LANGERAK

BRANDY JOHNSON
FROM DRIFT

CHRIS DECKARD

JULIA SETS

CHILDREN'S AUDIO

hosted by

JEFF SHAW

2001

ELI-STONE

In December 1997, singer Scott Stoltz was ready to hang up his microphone when he caved in to the pressure to goof around with a group of musicians. "The first night that we got together and jammed, we wrote three songs, and I thought my heart was going to fly out of my chest," remembers Stoltz. The chemistry was undeniable, and Stoltz joined the group. Drummer Justin Schmitt, rhythm guitarist Tim Harr, lead guitarist Mark Willaredt, and bassist Tony Cappello made up ELI-STONE.

For their third show, the band opened for Full On Venus and Drain STH at the EXTREME 104.1's Low-Dough Show at Mississippi Nights on September 2, 1998. The radio station used KSHE-95's marketing tactic of using the station frequency as the ticket price, charging $1.04 for the show. (Later, the event name was shortened to "Lo-Do Show.")

ELI-STONE played thirteen more shows at Mississippi Nights over the next few years with local bands such as Purge, Die Symphony, and Broke, and they landed the opening slot for Gwar and Redrum on July 14, 1999. "[Mississippi Nights manager] Tim Weber was quoted in our press release," recounts Stoltz. "He said that he's never seen a band win over one of the toughest audiences in the market, and that was Gwar's audience. The band that played after us [Redrum] was nearly booed off the stage."

For ELI-STONE, 1999 was a year of changes and firsts. First, Lonnie Dunham replaced Tony Cappello on bass. Next, the band held a record release show at Mississippi Nights for their debut CD, *Positive,* on June 26. They also became the first artists to have a sponsorship contract from Slackers, a regional CD and video game store. Lastly, they won a battle of the bands to open Extreme 104.1's Hoe Down show on the main stage at Riverport Amphitheatre supporting Slipknot, Coal Chamber, Kid Rock, and more on August 21.

Advertisement in the *Riverfront Times*.

202

Bob Weir of Ratdog, March 27, 2001.
Photo by Ron Odenthal.

Benefit for Backstoppers

Les Claypool of Les Claypool's Frog Brigade,
July 9, 2001. Photo by Mark Gilliland.

In 2000, Loren Bruns replaced Tim Harr on rhythm guitar, and Scott Pingel officially joined the band, adding samples and backing vocals. The band toured extensively and was picked up by radio stations nationwide.

ELI-STONE released *Driven* in 2001. Later that year, they flew out to California to play a sold-out showcase (with an opening band) for seventeen record companies at the Whiskey a Go-Go on Hollywood's Sunset Strip. To make sure they sounded their best, they also flew out Mississippi Nights' lead sound engineer Jamie Welky. The band ended the event with four record companies interested in signing them. Meetings with those four companies were scheduled for the next day.

The band returned to their suite at the Hyatt West Hollywood. The hotel, formerly called The Continental Hyatt House, had received the nickname "The Riot House" in the '70s because of the antics of touring musicians that frequented the establishment, including Led Zeppelin and The Who. ELI-STONE partied the night away at The Rainbow Bar and Grill and on that three-suite floor of the Hyatt.

"About 6 a.m. the next morning — I think we had all been in bed an hour — the phone started ringing like crazy," says Stoltz. His wife was on the other end, imploring him to turn on the TV. The day was September 11, and the planes had just hit the twin towers of the World Trade Center.

All four record companies canceled the meetings, and all shows booked for the return trip home were also canceled. Along with everything else that was happening, "We lost $135,000 right there [on the showcase and the many expenses that went with it]," laments Stoltz. With their golden opportunity lost and a city-wide shut down pending, the band quickly packed and drove for thirty-eight hours straight home to St. Louis. Welky stayed at a friend's house until flights resumed.

The band did not stay idle long. ELI-STONE returned to touring regionally and geared up for a national tour in the spring of 2002. Since Mississippi Nights was the band's home base, they often chose to kick off a tour or play a homecoming show at the venue.

Over the next two years, ELI-STONE lost its agent, manager, and bass player. However, they put all their energy into writing a new record. Chris Grieves joined for a brief stint on bass but was replaced when founding member Tim Haar returned in 2006. The band worked with Grammy Award-winning producer Malcolm Springer to self-release their third full-length CD in 2006, aptly titled *Hard Times*.

After more member changes and a shift in musical direction, ELI-STONE disbanded in 2008.

Singer Scott Stoltz reminisced about both the good and the bad of Mississippi Nights. "I enjoyed the load-in in the front much more than the load-out out the back," he chuckles, recalling the steep metal stairs in the back. "[Manager] Tim [Weber] was really good to us. He was tough on us. He was blunt with us. He was hard on us. But I wouldn't trade any of those moments with him," asserts Stoltz. "Mississippi Nights always had a feel of home to it that we appreciated," he remembers. "We loved the openness of the space. It was sheerly focused on the music. There was an intimacy within Mississippi Nights I just don't think can be replaced in the market. Playing on that stage gave us chills!"

THE STROKES

Photo Credit: COLIN LANE   07/01

Concert November 21, 2001. Courtesy of Rich Frame.

Concert June 27, 2001. Courtesy of Rich Frame.

John Mayer

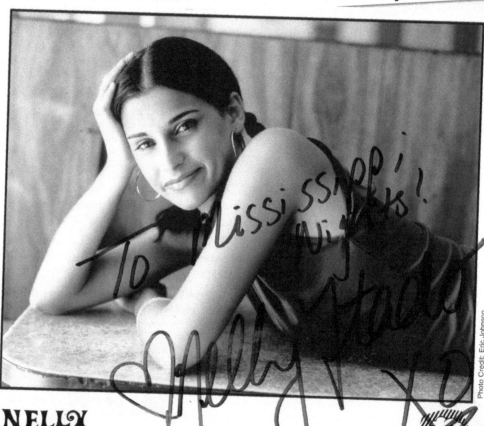

Concert March 23, 2001. Courtesy of Rich Frame.

204

NELLY FURTADO
WWW.WHOANELLY.COM

Photo Credit: Eric Johnson

JOEL LOVINS REMEMBERS...

Night Gallery was a short-lived Goth and Industrial music night at Mississippi Nights. The evening of July 18, 2001, featured DJ Mystress Lily, a DJ on college station KWUR, and a local synthpop band called SCSI. The event was simulcast on KWUR as well. The evening of August 15, 2001, had DJ Skeletal (myself) and DJ Annabel Evil, a Kansas City resident who now spins in New York, and The Skabs, an electro-punk band from New York City. The event was promoted by Wolfspirit Productions.

Courtesy of John Wegrzyn.

Due to a temporary shutdown of Laclede's Landing, our last event in September 2001 was relocated to the now-defunct South Grand Coffee Co. The venue cited a lack of advertisement as the reason for the event's demise. Attendance varied from twenty-seven to around sixty people.

205

Gob with Vaughan Kyle Enloe,
October 31, 2001. Photo by
Garrett Enloe.

2002

Sandra Bernhard Gets a Bit Weird

A reduction is an agreement between the artist and the venue where the artist accepts a lower payment than initially agreed upon, often to compensate for low ticket sales. "In the rock 'n' roll world, this happens ahead of time. It happens through agents," says manager Tim Weber. "In the comedy world, it gets a bit weird."

On June 7, 2002, comedian Sandra Bernhard was booked to do one of the few comedy shows booked at Mississippi Nights. Unfortunately, the show did not sell well. When Bernhard and her entourage arrived, Weber told the tour agent about the situation, stressing that they needed a reduction or the show would have to be canceled. The agent told Weber that Bernhard must approve this. As show time got closer, the agent delayed Weber's meeting with Bernhard.

Finally, Weber had had enough. He took the agent to the front door, locked it, and pocketed the key. "That's not getting unlocked until we have this conversation," he asserts. The reduction was accepted. Weber says, "And the first 20 minutes of the concert was her standing up on stage ripping me to shreds."

Five Feeler, August 31, 2002.
Photo by Mike Hadley.

From the collection of Garrett Enloe.

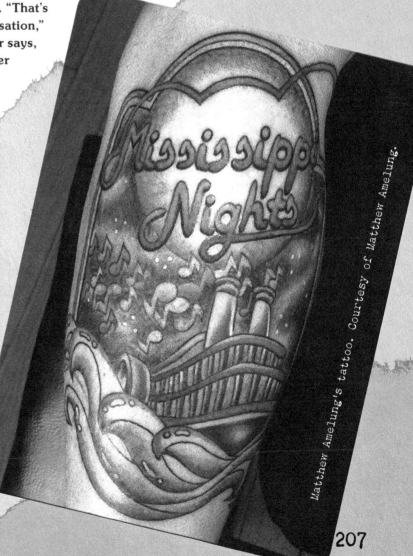

Matthew Amelung's tattoo. Courtesy of Matthew Amelung.

207

THUR. 10/24/02
Doors 7:00pm
Show 8:00pm
88¢ Cover
All Ages

KDHX LO-DO SHOW FEATURING
SPOOKIE DALY PRIDE

FRI. 10/25/02
Doors 7:00pm
Show 8:00pm
$15 Flat
All Ages

YOHIMBE BROTHERS
FEATURING: DJ LOGIC AND VERNON REI

SAT. 10/26/02
Doors 7:00pm
Show 8:00pm
$15 Flat
All Ages

GOOD CHARLOTTE
SOLD OUT
W/ AU... OFF & SIMPLE PLAN

SUN. 10/27/02
Doors 7:00pm
Show 8:00pm
$18 Adv
$20 DOS
All Ages

JOHNNY WINTER
W/ T-MODEL FORD

MON. 10/28/02
Doors 7:00pm
Show 8:00pm
$15 Flat
All Ages

VANESSA CARLTON
W/ BEN LEE

WED. 10/30/02
Doors 7:00pm
Show 8:00pm
$15 Adv
$17 DOS
All Ages

KOTTONMOUTH KINGS
W/ THE MIXMOB

FRI. 11/1/02
Doors 6:30pm
Show 7:00pm
$5 Cover
All Ages

5TH ELEMENT
& ELI STONE
W/ CALICO SYSTEM & SUGAR COATED

SUN. 11/3/02
Doors 8:00pm
Show 9:00pm
$16 Adv
$18 DOS
All Ages

GOV'T MULE

THUR. 11/7/02
Doors 7:00pm
Show 8:00pm
$12 Flat
All Ages

THE ATARIS
W/ SUGARCULT,
RUFIO & AUTOPILOT OFF

FRI. 11/8/02
Doors 7:00pm
Show 7:30pm
$15 Flat
Over 21 Only
NEW DATE!

THE JAYHAWKS
W/ TIM EASTON

SAT. 11/9/02
Doors 7:00pm
Show 7:30pm
$6 Cover
All Ages
NEW DATE!

SUPERVILLAIN ZERO
W/ THE BREWS, K.T.M.A. & FLINCH

SUN. 11/10/02
Show 8:00pm
$18 Adv
$20 DOS
All Ages

JIM BREUER
THE "LIGHTEN UP" TOUR

TUES. 11/12/02
Doors 7:00pm
Show 8:00pm
$13 Adv
$15 DOS
All Ages

CIRCLE JERKS
W/ GUEST

WED. 11/13/02
Doors 7:00pm
Show 8:00pm
$8 Adv
$10 DOS
All Ages
NEW DATE!

BOB SCHNEIDER
W/ GUEST

FRI. 11/15/02
Show 8:00pm
$18 Adv
$20 DOS
All Ages

LEO KOTTKE AND
MIKE GORDON

SAT. 11/16/02
Doors 8:00pm
Show 8:30pm
$10 Flat
All Ages
NEW DATE!

UNCHAINED
CD RELEASE PARTY!

MON. 11/18/02
Doors 7:00pm
Show 8:00 pm
$17.50 Flat
All Ages

LORDS OF ACID
W/ DJ REDBOY

THUR. 11/28/02
Doors 7:00pm
Show 8:00pm
$6 Flat
All Ages

POMEROY
W/ GUEST

FRI. 11/29/02
Doors 7:00pm
Show 8:00pm
$5 Cover
All Ages

CORE PROJECT
W/ D.T.P.

SAT. 11/30/02
Show 9:00pm
$17.50 Adv
$20 DOS

JAY FARRAR
W/ THE ROCKHOUSE TRIO

Mississippi Nights advertisement in the *Riverfront Times*.

Vaughan Kyle Enloe and Joey McIntyre, June 8, 2002. Photo by Garrett Enloe.

Courtesy of Bob Kreher.

MISSISSIPPI NIGHTS
presents
GOOD CHARLOTTE
ALL AGES * DOORS 7:00
$2 SURCHG FOR MINORS
SAT. OCT 26, 2002 8:00P

Courtesy of John Wegrzyn.

MISSISSIPPI NIGHTS
AN EVENING WITH
RATDOG
ALL AGES * DOORS 8PM
$2 SURCHG FOR MINORS
FRI. MAR 22, 2002 9:00P

From the collection of Garrett Enloe.

MISSISSIPPI NIGHTS
914 N. 1ST * ST. LOU
KING'S X
ALL AGES * DOORS 7:00
$2 SURCHG FOR MINORS
SUN. JUL 14, 2002 8:00PM

MISSISSIPPI NIGHTS
914 N. 1ST * ST. LOUIS
LE TIGRE
ALL AGES * DOORS 7:00P
$2 SURCHG FOR MINORS
WED. MAR 20, 2002 8:00P

Courtesy of Lisa McMichael.

EVENTS IN 2002

Benefit for MSD Workers

Benefit for Children's Miracle Network

Benefit for Open Door Animal Shelter

Ralston Private Party

NIKKI VOSS* REMEMBERS...

My great memories of Mississippi Nights started with the day I was the underage kid that [manager] Tim Weber wouldn't let in. (I stood out front the entire night for a few years). The day I hit eighteen, he kicked me out for not having a ticket. Staff members became friends. Most still are. Sadly, some have passed. I met so many people, rock stars, wannabe rock stars, and unique concertgoers. I saw so many mind-blowing shows.

I was pregnant with [staff member] Nate Hill's baby when I had to miss the sold-out John Mayer concert [April 20, 2002]. John gave Nate an autographed 8x10 for me that said, "Nikki, I guess a girl!" During the Sandra Bernhard show [June 7, 2002], Weber called Nate away from tending the bar to tell him our son was being born. John Mayer was wrong.

I had many fun times hanging out at Sundecker's [the restaurant a couple of doors down] after sold-out shows with my best friends Derek Kehl and Eric Holshouser, "Web" [Tim Weber], and many others. On my twenty-first birthday, [Bartender Tim] Mullen made me twenty-one shots, and I barfed on the last one. I went to the last show ever played at Mississippi Nights.

I don't have just one great memory. The first, the hundreds in between, to the very last show, and all the people involved made my years at Mississippi Nights the greatest time in my life that I will forever cherish.

Mississippi Nights runner/door

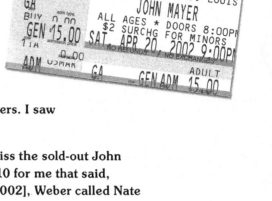

Courtesy of Daniel Durchholz.

TONIGHT'S PERFORMANCE

You are at: Mississippi Nights in St. Louis, Missouri

NOVEMBER 12, 2002

Doors Open: 7:00 pm
Show Starts: 7:30 pm

The Forgotten	From: 7:30	To: 8:00
Set Change	From: 8:00	To: 8:20
The Casualties	From: 8:20	To: 9:00
Set Change	From: 9:00	To: 9:30
CIRCLE JERKS	From: 9:30	To: 10:45

House Mgr.:	**Tim Weber**	Stage Mgr.:	**Animal**
Lighting:	**Tony**	Monitors:	**Brian**
Security:	**Rock**		

All ages. Midnight curfew.

Courtesy of Brian Nolan.

Unchained

CD Release Party
Mississippi Nights
November 16, 2002

Courtesy of Shane Brown.

209

HAPPY BIRTHDAY TO RICH

Willie Nelson played sold-out shows on August 19 and 20, 2002. The setlist was the same each night, except for one change the second night. Nelson sang "Happy Birthday" to Rich Frame, a surprise Tim Weber had arranged for Frame's sixtieth birthday. Frame and his wife Mary spent some time hanging out with Nelson and his family on Nelson's tour bus.

Courtesy of Rich Frame.
Photo by Matt Albers.

2003

Just Add Water

Just Add Water's singer, Steve Waller, admired his guitar teacher who played in local Illinois cover bands as a kid. So, Waller assumed playing other people's songs and working one or two originals into the set was the way to succeed in music. But his eyes were opened to other possibilities when he attended a concert at Mississippi Nights.

"My brother and I got tickets because I was a fan of Pale Divine," says Waller. "I looked at the pictures [on the walls] of the artists that had played there, and I thought, 'I've been doing this all wrong,'" remembers Waller. "When I listened to Pale Divine and watched them play on stage, I thought, 'Okay, this is where I need to be.'"

In 1997, Waller met guitarist Brian Nicoloff, and they formed the pop-rock band Just Add Water the following year. Twelve other musicians filled out the band on rhythm guitar, bass, and drums across their six-year career.

The band released a three-song EP in 2000, followed by the full-length CDs *The Other Side of You* in 2001 and *Holiday* in 2002. The band's title-track single "Holiday" was featured on *Pointessential Vol. 7* in 2002.

When Nicoloff graduated college, he decided to leave the band and was replaced with lead guitarist Clint Wilson. That lineup continued with Waller, Wilson, drummer Peter Lang, bass player Dan Martin, and guitarist Mike Steimel.

"Once that final lineup formed in early 2003, we recorded our self-titled album in my home studio in the basement of my house in Maplewood, the JAW house," remembers Steimel. "The goal during the recording sessions was to move away a bit from the more Rob Thomas sound [Matchbox Twenty] and more towards Foo Fighters type of rock while keeping Steve's very hooky, melodic vocal style," says Steimel. Unfortunately, Waller didn't have the same enthusiasm for changing musical direction, explaining, "I didn't have Dave Grohl's voice."

Just Add Water landed a Budweiser True Music sponsorship, receiving the perks and one challenge. They opened for Staind at The Pageant in St. Louis and the VH1 End of Summer Concert featuring Goo Goo Dolls and The Donnas at the Paris Hotel and Casino in Las Vegas,

Tickets courtesy of Chris Sutton.

211

which aired in part on VH1. "We felt like rock stars," says Steimel. "It was nice," notes Waller, "but it was also dangerous at the same time. Cases of beer were being delivered to the band house. That's not a recipe for productivity."

Just Add Water played Mississippi Nights twenty-four times between 2001 and 2004, including the release party for their self-titled CD on May 31, 2003. "We focused on playing in St. Louis once a month and played the other weeks regionally throughout the month to bring in the largest crowd possible in each market," recounts Brian Nicoloff.

Guitarist Mike Steimel remembers, "Tim Weber and all of his staff always treated us with such professionalism and respect." He adds, "We knew that we were going to be able to get to the venue in the late afternoon, wheel in our gear, have a professional soundcheck, set up our shirts and CDs in that iconic merch booth, and then walk over to Show Me's for pre-show dinner."

Along with their street team captain Burt McClimmins and manager Mike LaMartina, the band would hand out promo CDs and flyers after almost every major show at Mississippi Nights to promote their upcoming shows.

"My favorite memory [of Mississippi Nights] was probably playing after Lucky Boys Confusion and Colony one evening when Stubhy from LBC invited the entire crowd back to the Sheraton Hotel downtown where they were staying," recalls Nicoloff. "We had half the club show, taking up over an entire floor, before finally getting shut down. They were always a fun group of guys to play with on and off stage."

"I felt like we had made it every time we played [Mississippi Nights] because I remember seeing all my favorite bands there throughout high school and seeing the signatures backstage from The Police, Nirvana, and the likes," remembers Brian Nicoloff.

The band decided to call it quits in 2004, citing the difficulties of juggling work, family, and a music career, along with different musical directions. They played their farewell show at Mississippi Nights on August 21, 2004.

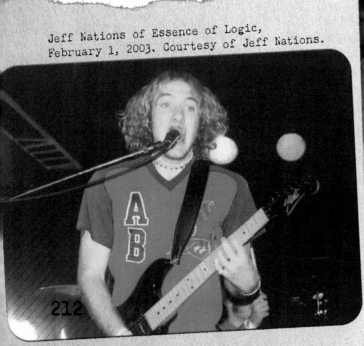

Jeff Nations of Essence of Logic, February 1, 2003. Courtesy of Jeff Nations.

Heather Baker Beerman, Heather Schneider Roberts, Mike Smith, Jeana Irene, and Stephanie Welch at the Broken Shadow concert on June 28, 2003. Courtesy of Jeana Irene.

Mike Kennerty   Tyson Ritter   Nick Wheeler   Chris Gaylor

Concert May 14, 2003. Courtesy of Rich Frame.

THE ALL-
AMERICAN
REJECTS

Photo Credit: Marina Chavez

dreamworks
RECORDS

JOHN JARVIS* REMEMBERS...

On May 12, 2003, I saw An Evening with the Deftones (no opening act) at Mississippi Nights. During the show, [singer] Chino [Moreno] jokingly said, "Hello, Cleveland." He got some boos from the crowd, so to make up for it, he said something like, "I'm sorry. I'll buy everyone a beer. Just go to the bar." Sure enough, the next beer I ordered was free!

*Mississippi Nights patron

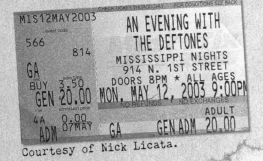

MIS 12 MAY 2003
566
814
GA
BUY 3.50
GEN 20.00
4A 0.00
ADM 07MAY   GA

CHECK TICKET THOROUGHLY   FOR CONDITIONS SEE BACK

AN EVENING WITH
THE DEFTONES
MISSISSIPPI NIGHTS
914 N. 1ST STREET
DOORS 8PM * ALL AGES
MON. MAY 12, 2003 9:00PM
NO REFUNDS   NO EXCHANGES

ADULT
GEN ADM 20.00

Courtesy of Nick Licata.

Courtesy of Brian Nolan.

TONIGHT'S PERFORMANCE

You are at: Mississippi Nights in St. Louis, Missouri

February 20, 2003

Doors Open: 7:00 p.m.
Show Starts: 8:00 p.m.

My Chemical Romance	From: 8:00 To: 8:30
Set Change	From: 8:30 To: 8:55
The Movie Life	From: 8:55 To: 9:25
Set Change	From: 9:25 To: 9:50
THE USED	From: 9:50 To:10:35
Set Change	From:10:35 To:11:00
FINCH	From:11:00 To:11:45

213

House Mgr.:	**Tim Weber**	Stage Mgr.:	**Animal**
LD:	**Tony**	Monitors:	**Brian**
Security:	**Rock**		

JESS JENNINGS* REMEMBERS...

I was a band runner for Dickey Betts once, and his drummer and I went to several music stores all over the city looking for a certain type of guitar pick. We also had to get him Bic lighters -- any color but green. Apparently, green ones were "unlucky." I had to drop something at his hotel room. He wasn't there, but I noticed he had a bow and arrow target set up in the room, so he could practice on tour. [August 7, 2003]

*Mississippi Nights server

Courtesy of Angela Prada.

Courtesy of Brian Nolan.

CLB28FEB2003 CHECK TICKET THOROUGHLY   FOR CONDITIONS SEE BACK
1560 MUST
GA   24
BUY
GEN 25.00
23A
ADM 23JAN
MYSTIC KNIGHTS
OF THE PURPLE HAZE
15TH MARDI GRAS BALL
W/DIRTY DOZEN BRASS BAN
CASA LOMA BALLROOM
FRI. FEB 28, 2003 8:00P
NO REFUNDS   NO EXCHANGES
9.00 MUST BE 21
GA   GEN ADM ADULT
25.00

Courtesy of Daniel Durchholz.

Phat Tuesday
the **Phat Buddha Ball** presented by phat buddha productions

the **Codetalkers** featuring
Col. Bruce Hampton

plus guest NAKED GROOVE

Tuesday, March 4
@ Mississippi Nights

Courtesy of Brian Nolan.

Advertisement in the Riverfront ~.

SAT. 5/3/03
Doors 7:00pm
Show 8:00pm
$8 Includes CD
All Ages

TUE. 5/6/03
Doors 7:00pm
$10 flat
All Ages

FRI. 5/9/03
Doors 8:00pm
Show 9:00pm
$42.50 adv
$45 dos
Over 21 Only
Limited Capacity
Concert

SAT. 5/10/03
Doors 8:00pm
Show 9:00pm
$12 adv
$14 dos
All Ages

WED. 5/14/03
Doors 7:00pm
Show 8:00pm
$10 adv
$12 dos
All Ages

THUR. 5/15/03
Doors 7:00pm
Show 8:00pm
$8 adv
$10 dos
All Ages

FRI. 5/16/03
Doors 7:00pm
Show 8:00pm
$12 flat
All Ages

SAT. 5/17/03
Doors 8:00pm
Show 8:30pm
$6 cover
All Ages

FRI. 5/23/03
Doors 7:00pm
Show 8:00pm
$6 cover
All Ages

SAT. 5/24/03
Doors 8:00pm
Show 8:30pm
$6 cover
All Ages

FRI. 5/30/03
Doors 7:00pm
Show 9:00pm
$6 cover
All Ages

W/ FLYNOVA & SPENT

AMP STL PRESENTS
SOFACHROME CD RELEASE
W/ DIONYSIA, TRIPLE CLAMP & UNUNBIU

THE BIG WU
W/ PERPETUAL GROOVE

92.3 WIL PRESENTS
DWIGHT YOAKAM

THE SAMPLES
W/ FICTION PLANE

105.7 PRESENTS
ALL AMERICAN REJECTS
W/ WAKEFIELD & LIMBACK

ZUVUYA
FEATURING MICHAEL TRAVIS of THE STRING CHEESE INCIDENT

ROBERT RANDOLPH
& THE FAMILY BAND

UNCHAINED
W/ GUEST

THE REACTIONS
W/ THE JULIA SETS, SULLEN
& GOOD NIGHT GHOST

CORE PROJECT
W/ KNOW BOUNDARIES & ART THUGS

THE BREWS

214

NATHAN HILL* REMEMBERS...

Chris Robinson from the Black Crowes was playing with his side project, New Earth Mud. His wife, actress Kate Hudson, walked in: sweatpants rolled up to the knee, a tiny, thin T-shirt cut off at the belly, so damn hot she nearly stopped the soundcheck. Instead, she gave way to Chris Robinson, who did just that. With one swing of the guitar, he launched the drum kit clean off stage right. Some of it even carried into the dressing room. Then, he flipped a lit cigarette into the face of the drummer and called him a "whiny...rock star...bitch." The irony of the words he chose was not lost on me, especially after what happened next.

He wanted to go to the hotel but wouldn't get in my Oldsmobile Cutlass. So I had to call [manager] Tim Weber, advise him that I had a whiny, rock star bitch, and ask if he could please bring his Durango down to drive him. Weber replied, "Does this dude know we only have 200 tickets sold in advance? He's aware this is New Earth Mud, not the Black Crowes playing tonight, right?" Weber is bar-none, the funniest, no-nonsense, call a duck a duck, human I have ever met.

It turned out that Randy "Animal" Martin, the front-of-house engineer, had recorded the soundcheck. From then on, we had a running joke that anytime anyone was acting like a "whiny, rock star bitch" during load-in or soundcheck, "Animal" played Chris Robinson's words back over the PA. [March 1, 2003]

*Mississippi Nights assistant bartender/manager/promotions director, writer for the Riverfront Times, and singer of Cross Examination

Dick Dale, June 4, 2003.
Photo by Garrett Enloe.

MISSISSIPPI NIGHTS
914 N. 1ST * ST LOUIS
DICK DALE
ALL AGES * DOORS 7:00
$2 SURCHG FOR MINORS
WED, JUN 4, 2003 8:0
NO REFUNDS   NO EXCHANGES
GA   GEN ADM 18.0
DAYO

Warren Haynes of Gov't Mule, October 29, 2003.
Photo by Mark Gilliland.

LANCE®

Notes™

March 2003

Mon	Tue	Wed	Thu	Fri	Sat
					1 60/305 WEEK 9 — Chris Robinson and The New Earth Mud ... $20 flat ✓
3 61/304	**4** 62/303 — Phat Buddha's Phat Tuesday:	**5** First of Muharram 63/302	**6** Ash Wednesday 64/301 — Snocore w/ Glassjaw Hot water music Sparta	**7** 65/300 Amp Stl. Presents 13 Lokci, switch sophomore and Last Flight Home 66/299	**8** Matts Dad's Basement w/ Sonic Reduction 67/298

215

Promotional photo shoot for Ampeg with Roger Miret, singer of Roger Miret and The Disasters, before concert on September 16, 2003. Photo by Mark Gilliland.

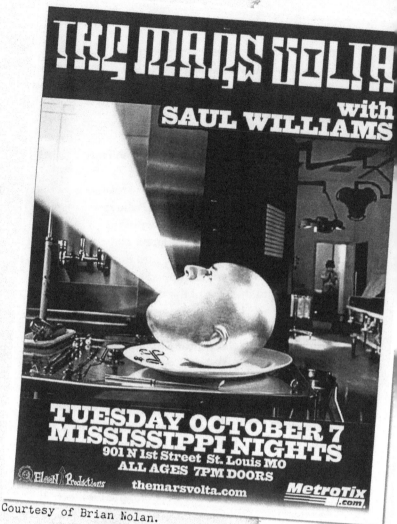

Courtesy of Brian Nolan.

EVENTS IN 2003

Lil' Buster's Rhythm and Blues Expo benefit for the National Federation of the Blind

VH1 Save the Music Foundation Concert

Courtesy of Brian Nolan.

216

2004

Neptune Crush

Full On Venus and Radio Iodine both dissolved in 1999, leaving Full On Venus guitarists Eric Lysaght (L.O.V.E. and Neuter the Stupid) and Jimmy Griffin (Kingofthehill), and Radio Iodine bassist Tony Persyn at loose ends. Griffin and Persyn decided to form a band and asked Lysaght to join on vocals. They started Neptune Crush with Griffin on guitar, Lysaght on vocals and guitar, Persyn on bass, and Ed Spinaio on drums.

Griffin and Lysaght moved into Persyn's home, nicknamed "Disgraceland," off Grand Avenue in St. Louis City. "It was a huge, castle-like place, like a mansion," says Lysaght. "We all lived upstairs, and downstairs had all these big band rooms with huge high ceilings. It was perfect for guys in bands."

Neptune Crush's self-titled debut was recorded in Persyn's in-home recording studio in 2001. Shortly after, Persyn had some personal problems and decided to move home to Indiana. Wil Pelly replaced Persyn on bass.

Neptune Crush played Mississippi Nights sixteen times, including a CD release party on June 16, 2001, with Instar and The Brews. "Lenny Lindsay was our light guy," says Wil Pelly. "We had placed ten or so disco balls all across the stage. When we played our song 'Emeralds,' [Lindsay] turned some smart lights towards the disco balls and made millions of green beams of light through the entire room!"

The band continued to make their home at "Disgraceland" and upgraded the studio. The addition of Pro Tools assisted in recording their next EP, *Blinky,* released in 2002.

Griffin left the band to join the group, Nadine. Lysaght blamed the departure on musical differences. After trying out some guitarists, the band decided to continue as a three-piece rather than replace Griffin.

Shortly after Griffin's departure, the band's single "Dead Air" appeared on *Pointessential Vol. 7.* The song received airplay on KPNT The Point and KSHE-95, and drew attention from Epic Records. Unfortunately, although the band played a showcase for Epic in New York City, the record deal they had hoped for didn't materialize.

Persevering, Neptune Crush released *Evening at the Starlight* in 2004.

Hoodies from the collection of Walter Wright. Models Alivia and Sara Mayer. Photo by Garrett Enloe.

Tickets courtesy of Hal Greens.

217

National Poetry Slam

Alzheimer Benefit

CD from the collection of Garrett Enloe.

Courtesy of Brian Nolan.

Calendar

	OCTOBER 2004		DECEMBER 2004

Fri	Sat
5 310/56	**6** 311/55
PAPA ROACH	THE DRESDEN DOLLS
D 7:00 / SH 8:00 $15 FLAT ALL AGES	D 7:00 / SH 8:00 $8 ADV / $10 DOS ALL AGES
12 317/49	**13** 318/48 (Eid) al Fitr
ROBERT SCHIMMEL	JAY FARRAR
D 7:00 / SH 8:00 $25 FLAT ALL AGES	D 7:00 / SH 8:00 $17 ADV / $20 DOS ALL AGES
19 323/43 324/42	**20** 325/41 Revolution Anniversary (M)
Pomeroy	Alzheimers Benefit
	D 7:00 / SH 8:00 $8 FLAT ALL AGES
26 330/36 Thanksgiving (US)	**27** 331/35 332/34
Bockmans Euphio	THE HELPING FRIENDLY BAND
D 7:00 / SH 8:00 COVER ALL AGES 218	D 7:00 / SH 8:00 $6 COVER ALL AGES

TONIGHT'S PERFORMANCE

You are at: Mississippi Nights in St. Louis, Missouri

February 17, 2004

Doors Open: 7:00 p.m.
Show Starts: 7:30 p.m.

	From	To
Dynamite Boy	7:30	8:00
Set Change	8:00	8:15
Matchbook Romance	8:15	8:45
Set Change	8:45	9:00
Fall Out Boy	9:00	9:40
Set Change	9:40	10:00
Mest	10:00	11:00

House Mgr.:	**Tim Weber**	Stage Mgr.:	**Animal**
LD:		Monitors:	**Brian**
Security:	**Tony**		
	Rock		

All ages. Midnight curfew. SET TIMES ARE...

Mississippi Nights advertisement in the Riverfront Times.

Trading shows, or bands arranging shows in each other's hometowns, is typical for up-and-coming bands. Under the best circumstances, clubs are in on the arrangement. Mississippi Nights recognized the benefit of increasing the diversity of bands that came through town. "We'd always be swapping out shows at Mississippi Nights because people wanted to get into Mississippi Nights. It was hard to get in that room if you're not from St. Louis because it was the premier place to play," remembers Lysaght. This arrangement saved venues time booking opening bands. "Tim [Weber] would always trust our judgment," Lysaght says. "The shows that we swapped out with Kill Hannah from Chicago were a lot of fun. They were probably the biggest band in Chicago," he explains, "They would trade with us just to expand their reach. We would go up there and play at the Metro opening up for them, and they'd come down here and open for us at Mississippi Nights." Lysaght says, "We made some good friends that are still friends, and it gave us a chance to play some cool places in Chicago."

The band continued as Neptune Crush until 2007, when a shift in musical direction prompted a name change to Salisbury. Since Spinaio and Pelly left, Lysaght kept the band going by bringing in other musicians for recording and live shows. He's currently working on Salisbury's third album.

Tony Campos of Static X, Vaughan Kyle Enloe, Zach Moiser (drummer of Inimical Drive), and Wayne Static of Static X, August 1, 2004. Photo by Garrett Enloe. Ticket stub from the collection of Garrett Enloe.

219

DIE SYMPHONY
with Celldweller

Friday, January 23

Mississippi Nights

All Ages • $8 advance/$10 day of show • Tickets on sale now at all MetroTix outlets

Die Symphony's new album THE EVERLASTING SHAME available in stores and online NOW at www.diesymphony.com

Advertisement in *Playback: stl.*

Courtesy of Julia Bramer.

Jethro (Jett) Dirt   J.D. Dirt   Johnny Dirt   Joey Dirt

Joe Dirt and the Dirty Boys Band

www.joedirt.net

Booking: Dave Kalz, American Bands
(314)724-5152

JESS JENNINGS REMEMBERS...

I waitressed at Mississippi Nights. On New Year's Eve of 2004, North Mississippi Allstars didn't want to do the actual countdown, so when our shift [manager], Tim Weber, asked if anyone wanted to do it. I said, "Hell, yes! I Do!"

I was also working at The City Museum at the time, and I got a box full of old hats from there, decorated them all funky, gave them to the band, and threw them out in the crowd after my countdown. There were so many great nights, but this one has got to top my list. I'm proud and privileged to have worked at Mississippi Nights for a few years with some of the best people and great music!

Fans waiting for the Gavin Degraw and Sevenstar concert, July 18, 2004. Photos by Dustin Keller.

Sevenstar with Gavin Degraw (2nd from left) July 18, 2004. Courtesy of Dustin Keller.

221

Concert November 12, 2004. Courtesy of Rich Frame.

THE WAILERS

fmp stl.com

presents

The
ULTIMATE
S H O W C A S E
Volume I

Two Nights of St. Louis Music
plus everyone in attendance will receive a free compilation CD
including tracks from these artists as well as
RANDOMDYAD (former members of SLAPDASH)

FRIDAY DECEMBER 17TH

3JC
LOCO 88
FIELD OF GREY
MORPHEATE
UNDER RATED X

SATURDAY DECEMBER 18TH

Final Drive
COLLINSVILLE ALL STARS
LOUIS-C
Reigning Heir

Both Shows
Doors at 7 Show at 7:30
$8 ADV $10 Day of show
ALL AGES

Watch St.Louis Locals
Final Drive
battle it out on MTV

STL scene
Support The Scene
www.stlscene.com

THE MUSIC CLUB OF ST. LOUIS

222

From the collection
of Garrett Enloe.

the KILLERS

Monday September 13
Early Show 6 - 9pm

with special guest:
Ambulance LTD

www.metrotix.com
ON SALE SAT. AUGUST 7 - 10AM

Brought to you by
THE POINT

MISSISSIPPI NIGHTS
914 N. 1ST AVE. St. Louis, MO - 314.421.3852

2005

LAURA HAMLETT SCHLATER* REMEMBERS...

I was the proverbial maker of mixtapes in high school. I loved absolutely nothing more than sharing my musical discoveries with friends, often obscure findings from used record stores and mail-order catalogs. [My magazine] *PLAYBACK:stl* was like a mixtape for St. Louis and beyond through words, photographs, letters, colors, and, yes, music, but streaming on the web.

Jim Dunn and I were music lovers, writers, and graphic designers, energies we put into creating a monthly music and entertainment magazine. *PLAYBACK:stl* ran for over 15 years, debuting in April 2002 and bowing in July 2017. The magazine was on the web for its entire run and in print from April 2002 to October 2006.

In April 2002, we were at Mississippi Nights to see Elbow open for Pete Yorn, and we were mesmerized. We approached one of the boys from Manchester, England, and asked for an interview. Elbow ended up being on our second cover, and we couldn't have been prouder.

Courtesy of Laura Hamlett Schlater.

Ticket stubs courtesy of
Daniel Durchholz, John
Lamwersiek, Nick Licata,
and from the collections of
Garrett and Stacy Enloe.

TOP TEN REASONS NOT TO TALK TO THE SOUNDMAN

10. HE'S DEAF
9. HE'S NOT DEAF, HE'S IGNORING YOU
8. HE DOESN'T SPEAK ENGLISH
7. YOU DON'T SPEAK ENGLISH
6. HE'S STUPID
5. YOUR QUESTION IS STUPID
4. HE'S ON LOAN FROM:—
   A) BETTY FORD'S
   B) STAMFORD MENTAL EXPERIMENT
   C) BELLVUE
   D) ALL OF THE ABOVE
3. HE'S HITTING ON THE BLONDE
2. YOU ARE NOT A BLONDE

1. HE MIGHT ACTUALLY BE MIXING!

Note taped to the sound mixing board.
From the collection of Brian Nolan.

Model Sarah Brewer. Photo by Garrett Enloe.

There were so many proud moments with the magazine. We gave OK Go their first magazine cover; lead singer Damien Kulash's mom emailed me to send her a copy. Blue October asked for a blow-up of their *PLAYBACK:stl* cover to put on their tour bus. From a New York City stage, Semi Precious Weapons' frontman Justin Tranter called me out for the support they received in St. Louis. I was the moderator at a special screening of *Once*, fielding audience questions for actor/singer-songwriters Glen Hansard and Markéta Irglová who were in attendance.

My love for mixtapes also morphed into my love for concert lineups, as *PLAYBACK:stl* curated and sponsored shows at venues throughout St. Louis. We loved working with Mississippi Nights: setting up a table to the left of the bar, giving away T-shirts, lining up interviews, meeting new writers, creating a community. That's really what *PLAYBACK:stl* was: a community. We met so many people from many life and career paths, and we all came together through music.

That's what Mississippi Nights did on a grander scale: brought people together through music. I'll never forget the way it felt to be in that room, all of us dancing and singing along and living every note in every moment. Unfortunately, the St. Louis music scene lost an irreplaceable part of its soul when The Nights closed.

Cofounder, PLAYBACK:stl

Lapush, January 21, 2005. Photo by Brian Brinkley.

PRINCETON

ex-story of the year guitarist, greg haupt, returns, bringing a fury of rock and pop in his wake

ages 4 & up

november 23rd
THE NIGHT BEFORE THANKSGIVING
at
MISSISSIPPI NIGHTS
w/ Rushmore Academy & Blinded Black

go to www.myspace.com/princetonrocks for
more _____ _____ _____ downloads

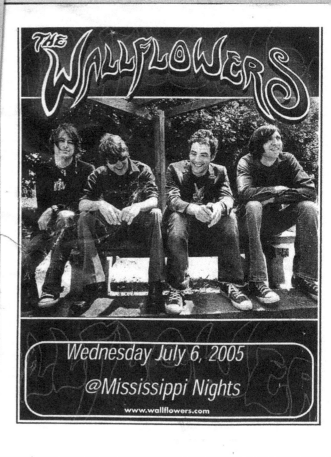

THE WALLFLOWERS

Wednesday July 6, 2005
@Mississippi Nights

www.wallflowers.com

© 2005 Moxie Bleep Loch / Bullet 339 Records.

Photo by: Patrick Vaughan

Brian Pearia
Drums

Scott Gertken
Vocals

Rock Davis
Guitars

Zach Broderick
Guitars

Rich Criebaum
Bass

226

moderndayzero
www.moderndayzero.com

BULLET339

uptoeleven.com

THE DECEMBERISTS
AND CASS McCOMBS

AT MISSISSIPPI NIGHTS
SUN. OCT. 16
ALL AGES 7PM

2006

Buckethead, September 14, 2006.
Photo by Garrett Enloe.

GARRETT ENLOE* REMEMBERS...

On September 14, 2006, I attended the Buckethead concert with my fourteen-year-old son Kyle. We were at the club early enough to get right up front by the stage. I knew this would be our last Mississippi Nights show, so I took many photos.

Buckethead is a guitar wizard who played with Guns N' Roses from 2000 to 2004. His playing features heavy metal, progressive metal, funk metal, and experimental rock. He wears a Kentucky Fried Chicken bucket on his head, hence the name.

Buckethead passed out toys to lucky people in the front during his concerts, so we decided to bring a gift for him. He put down his guitar in the middle of his set and showed off his nunchuck skills for a few minutes. Then, he picked up his bucket full of toys. He handed Kyle an octopus water toy, and Kyle gave him a Soul Descenders CD, which was Kyle's band at the time.

This concert was a fun send-off for us. When we left, I hugged the side of the building, saying my final goodbye.

*Author

Amanda de Agüero with Paul Waggoner,
Tommy Giles Rogers, Dustie Waring, and
Blake Richardson of Between the Buried and Me.
November 18, 2006. Photo by Karen de Agüero.

SCOTT CHURILLA* REMEMBERS...

Every time we played Mississippi Nights, I would run down to the river after the soundcheck and tight line for catfish. I always caught a few catfish and a few small sturgeons, as well.

*Drummer of Reverend Horton Heat

227

Anne Linders of School of Rock. (left) Anne Linders and other members of School of Rock. (right) Photos by Jane Linders.

Courtesy of Dan Reilly.

MISSISSIPPI NIGHTS
PLUS 44
www.plusfortyfour.com
ALL AGES * DOORS 7PM
$2 SURCHG FOR MINORS
SUN. DEC 3, 2006 8:00PM
GEN ADM 21.00

MISSISSIPPI NIGHTS
914 N. 1ST ST * ST LOUIS
ROB BELL
ALL AGES * DOORS 7PM
$2 SURCHG FOR MINORS
SUN. JUL 16, 2006 8:00PM
GEN ADM 10.00

MISSISSIPPI NIGHTS
914 N. 1ST ST * ST LOUIS
BUILT TO SPILL
ALL AGES * DOORS 7PM
$2 SURCHG FOR MINORS
SUN. SEP 17, 2006 8:00PM
GEN ADM 15.00

MISSISSIPPI NIGHTS
914 N. 1ST ST * ST LOUIS
COWBOY MOUTH
ALL AGES * DOORS 7PM
$2 SURCHG FOR MINORS
FRI. MAR 24, 2006 8:
GEN ADM 20

Courtesy of Daniel Durchholz.   Courtesy of Scott Gates.

Courtesy of Brian Nolan.

JASON VOIGT* REMEMBERS...

The only event I attended at Mississippi Nights was Joan Jett & the Blackhearts on October 27, 2006. Eagles of Death Metal opened. They rocked the house, but there were other things on people's minds that night; that was the same night the St. Louis Cardinals won their first World Series since '82. There were no TVs on, and this was before smartphones. Suddenly, people were yelling right in the middle of a song. Everyone knew it happened. I left the concert early and joined in on the fun outside as people were happily shouting and cheering on the Landing.

*Mississippi Nights patron

228

JOAN JETT and the BLACKHEARTS Live
with special guests:
Eagles of Death Metal
and
THROW RAG

Fri, Oct 27 - Mississippi Nights
914 NORTH FIRST STREET - St Louis, MO
all ages - 7pm - metrotix.com
JOAN.JETT.com

MICHAEL HAZER* REMEMBERS...

My younger brother, Daniel, had just turned twenty-one, and what better way to celebrate than a Rancid show at Mississippi Nights. We were standing at the edge pit, listening to "Olympia WA.," when suddenly a wall of sweaty human beings plowed into us. Daniel fell to the floor. As a stranger and I tried to help him up, some asshole saw us in a vulnerable position and purposely rammed into us as hard as he could. We fell hard on top of Daniel, and he let out a god-awful scream.

He told us he was hurt badly. So I asked the stranger to scoop him up and get him outside. He obliged.

Then, I searched the crowd for the face of the jerk who had violated the cardinal rule of the pit: "Never hit a man when he's down." I found him. I'm not proud of this, but I put one of the best sucker punches in the history of dirty fighting right into his face. I then slipped out through the crowd to find my brother.

Daniel was outside the club, violently puking. I knew I had to get him to the hospital. We spent the rest of the night at St. Anthony's Hospital. His X-rays came back showing he had two fractured vertebrae.

He recovered after a few months in a back brace, and from then on, he always stood at the back at shows. I always told him he was the most hardcore dude I knew. Breaking your back at a Rancid show is super punk rock.

Later, we found out that Daniel had an autoimmune disease that, among other complications, made his bones brittle, and he passed away in 2015. I have many memories from our lives, but that night at Mississippi Nights is one that's burned into my brain forever. [July 28, 2006]

*Mississippi Nights patron

New York Dolls, December 1, 2006.
Photo by John Wegrzyn.

Photo by John Wegrzyn.

Courtesy of Ted Hindes.

229

MATT ALBERS* REMEMBERS...

The only show I ever saw at Mississippi Nights was just before the venue closed in the fall of 2006: my first time seeing Less Than Jake, Catch 22, and several other bands that opened. I have seen Less Than Jake many times since, but at that point, I wasn't used to their antics. Like how frontman Chris DeMakes invited people up on stage to dance, make out, or chug beers (as he did with two of the bouncers), or when he made fun of the people watching the Cardinals game at the bar (during the playoffs), lying down on the stage to smoke a cigarette while he waited for them to stop watching the game.

It was my sophomore year of college at Saint Louis University, and I wrote a review of the show for my student radio station KSLU's newsletter. Looking back on it, that was probably one of the defining moments that set many things in motion for me. Being a part of radio and college journalism gave me the joy and confidence that helped me decide to study communication and broadcasting. Now I work in the field, which is challenging in the booming social and digital media age. [February 11, 2006]

*Mississippi Nights patron

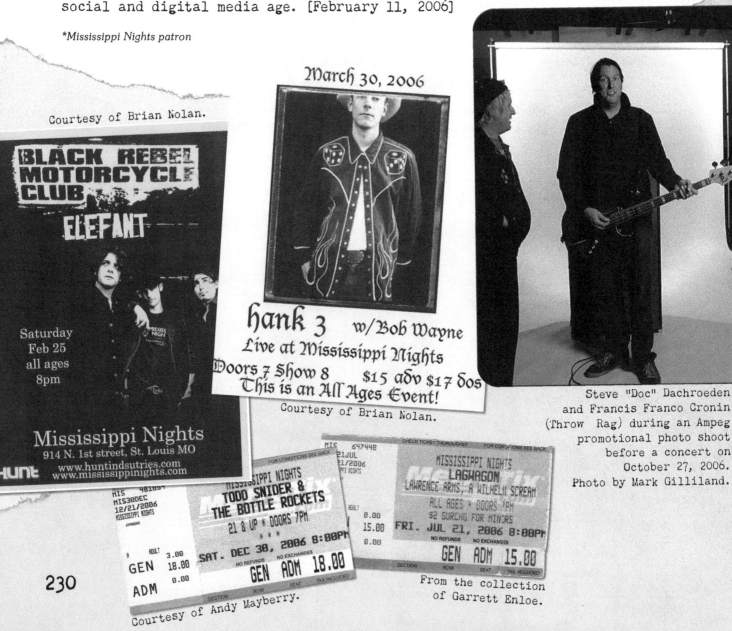

Courtesy of Brian Nolan.

BLACK REBEL MOTORCYCLE CLUB
ELEFANT

Saturday
Feb 25
all ages
8pm

Mississippi Nights
914 N. 1st street, St. Louis MO
www.huntindsutries.com
www.mississippinights.com

HUNT

March 30, 2006

hank 3 w/Bob Wayne
Live at Mississippi Nights
Doors 7 Show 8 $15 adv $17 dos
This is an All Ages Event!
Courtesy of Brian Nolan.

Steve "Doc" Dachroeden
and Francis Franco Cronin
(Throw Rag) during an Ampeg
promotional photo shoot
before a concert on
October 27, 2006.
Photo by Mark Gilliland.

MIS 481854
MIS30DEC
12/21/2006
Mississippi Nights

TODD SNIDER &
THE BOTTLE ROCKETS
21 & UP * DOORS 7PM
* * *
SAT. DEC 30, 2006 8:00PM
ADULT 3.00
GEN 18.00
ADM 0.00
NO REFUNDS   NO EXCHANGES
GEN ADM 18.00
SECTION ROW SEAT TAX INCLUDED
Courtesy of Andy Mayberry.

MIS 647448
21JUL
21/2006
ppi Nights

CHECK TICKET THOROUGHLY   FOR CONDITIONS SEE BACK

MISSISSIPPI NIGHTS
LAGWAGON
LAWRENCE ARMS, A WILHELM SCREAM
ALL AGES * DOORS 7PM
$2 SURCHG FOR MINORS
ADULT 0.00
15.00
0.00
FRI. JUL 21, 2006 8:00PM
NO REFUNDS   NO EXCHANGES
GEN ADM 15.00
SECTION ROW SEAT TAX INCLUDED
From the collection
of Garrett Enloe.

230

2007

MISSISSIPPI NIGHTS PRESENTS:
THE LAST NIGHT
AT "THE NIGHTS"

A SPECIAL BLOW-OUT BASH FEATURING A JAM SESSION WITH THE BEST ST. LOUIS MUSICIANS OF THE PAST THREE DECADES!

JANUARY 19, 2007

MUSICIANS INTERESTED IN PARTICIPATING NEED TO CONTACT TIM WEBER
(314) 421-3853 OR TWEBER@MISSISSIPPINIGHTS.COM

MISSISSIPPI NIGHTS 914 N. FIRST ST.
INFO- 314.421.3853 TICKETS- 314.534.1111
MISSISSIPPINIGHTS.COM • METROTIX.COM

Last Call

The final concert at Mississippi Nights, aptly named "Last Call," was on January 19, 2007. The event was hosted by Beatle Bob, a club regular known for his Beatlesque style and crazy dance moves, and featured The Movers, The Wicked, Slapdash, Greenwheel, Devon Allman, The Schwag, and members of The Urge. Last Call was a bittersweet reunion of employees, bands, and patrons from the venue's thirty-year run. That night marked an end to an extraordinary chapter in St. Louis music history.

The Cookie Lady

Barb "The Cookie Lady" Lutz was a fixture at Mississippi Nights, so of course she attended Last Call.

Lutz's passion for live music started while visiting her mother at work at the St. Louis Convention Center, then based under the Kiel Auditorium. She was able to go upstairs to see bands do their soundchecks. Lutz remembered, "After a while, my mom said, 'You know you're very good at baking. You ought to bring these guys something to show them how much you appreciate their music and their talent.' So, I started bringing them cookies."

Lutz started attending shows at Mississippi Nights and continued her ritual of bringing cookies to the bands. When asked about what made Mississippi Nights so special, she mentioned how new bands "cut their teeth in places like this."

Beatle Bob and Barb "The Cookie Lady" Lutz at Last Call, January 19, 2007. Photo by Brian Nolan.

She continued, "It's where the fans can get up and interact with the band and get up and stage dive and make eye contact and reach up and touch the guitar player's hand."

Lutz believed the homey family feel of Mississippi Nights was necessary for the bands to help them combat the loneliness of the road. She gave a big grin when she talked about her cookies being "a little touch of home while they are away from home."

STAFF

LAST CALL 1-19-07

WEBER	PRINCESS
ROCK	JETHRO
SUBWAY	LAUREN
GOOSE	CORKY
MULLEN	OSAMA
B	L L
GINA	ERICA
WACO	OSCAR
SIDESHOW	BECKY
DUCK	LING LING
BOO BOO	TONY
DANTE	BRIAN
DAYNA	ANIMAL
	EAZY

Shirt worn by the staff at Last Call. Courtesy of Brian Nolan.

DEREK KEHL REMEMBERS LAST CALL...

I was bartending at bar two [the small bar] and started drinking as soon as we opened. I think I left around 5 a.m.

ANGELA PRADA* REMEMBERS...

Last Call was sad and joyous in the same breath, a reunion of sorts for employees who had worked there over the years. I remember seeing most of the folks who were considered regulars and lots of local band members. Lots of memories were shared in that special place.

*Mississippi Nights server

PAT LACEY* REMEMBERS...

At Last Call, I sat up in the area by the bar and saw people as they came in. Everybody stopped to talk to me. It seemed like I knew almost everybody there. A wife of one of the two silent partners was standing next to me, and afterward, she said to me that she didn't realize how many people I knew and how popular I was.

*Mississippi Nights office manager

CHECK TICKET THOROUGHLY   FOR CONDITIONS SEE BACK

MISSISSIPPI NIGHTS PRESENTS
** LAST CALL **
914 N. 1st ST * ST LOUIS
DOORS AT 7PM * ALL AGES
$2 MINOR SURCHG AT DOOR
FRI. JAN 19, 2007 8:00PM

MIS 777358
MIS19JAN07
01/19/2007
MISSISSIPPI NIGHTS

ADULT 0.00
GEN 10.00
ADM 0.00

NO REFUNDS   NO EXCHANGES
GEN ADM 10.00
SECTION   ROW   SEAT   TAX INCLUDED

TIM WEBER* REMEMBERS...

[Beatle Bob was] like the cobblestones: annoying, but he added character to the place.

*Mississippi Nights manager

January 19, 2007. Photo by Cliff Schmitz. From the collection of Pat Lacey.

233

WALTER WRIGHT* REMEMBERS LAST CALL...

I was just drunk and crying.

*Supervisor for B&D Security (contracted by Mississippi Nights)

Jimmy Tebeau of The Schwag at Last Call,
January 19, 2007. Photo by Brian Nolan.

Mississippi Nights

'one last show'

featuring:
pomeroy
the upright animals
centerpointe
the cause
novella

January 12   **7pm**

Courtesy of Brian Nolan.

Tim Mullen, Mary and Rich Frame,
January 19, 2007. Photo by Brian Nolan.

Rich Frame and Tim Weber at Last Call,
January 19, 2007. Photo by Cliff Schmitz.
From the collection of Pat Lacey.

THE ROAD TO THE END

In 1966, the year after construction was complete on the St. Louis Arch, the City of St. Louis considered proposals for redeveloping Laclede's Landing between the Eads and Martin Luther King Bridges. Media coverage encouraged businesses to move into the area.

Rich Frame knew when he bought Mississippi Nights in 1979 that the city could snatch it away at any time. The building was in a redevelopment zone, and if the city decided to seize the property and pay Frame off, he'd be left with no recourse. The City of St. Louis was always looking for the next big thing to stuff the coffers at city hall with new tax dollars and raise the region's profile. In the 1960s, Disney even toyed with the idea of building Walt Disney's Riverfront Square Park St. Louis, recreating the historical riverfront of Laclede and Choteau in St. Louis, albeit a couple of miles west of the actual riverfront.

Not long after Frame bought the club, the city made the first of many plans to redevelop Laclede's Landing. The idea was to turn the property into the Jacques Cousteau Aquarium. Fortunately, it never broke ground. This pattern continued for the next two decades. The city consistently ignored Rich Frame and other business people's success on Laclede's Landing and kept looking for large developers with elaborate plans who had no connection to St. Louis' rich history.

In 1992, the city announced another deal that would potentially eliminate the club. Jumer Hotel and Casinos announced a $90 million development plan for Laclede's Landing to include two casinos, a hotel, and a rehab of the Switzer Candy building on 612 North 1st Street. But, again, nothing came of it, and Frame kept running Mississippi Nights.

Well-known and lesser-known developers came to Laclede's Landing with big plans that failed to materialize.

Two brothers concocted a plan to build Mississippi Nights Condos with residential space above the existing building and a parking lot sandwiched in between as a noise barrier. Unfortunately, although many music lovers would likely have loved living in the Mississippi Nights Condos with a stunning view of the Mississippi River, that project also stalled and died.

In the late 1990s, after almost two decades of scuttled plans and rumors, the City of St. Louis bought out the Mississippi Nights building for $1 million. Since Rich Frame no longer owned the building, he rented the club and the parking lot next door for one dollar a month. The city was not ready to kick him out and lose the club's tax dollars.

The club remained in limbo, paying the one-dollar monthly invoice without a word from the city about redevelopment until 2004, when Pinnacle Entertainment signed a contract with the City of St. Louis to open a casino on Laclede's Landing and invest an additional $50 million in revitalizing the area. The second phase included building retail stores and condos. So maybe Mississippi Nights would be turned into condos after all.

Finally, in October 2006, Rich Frame received a notice in the mail giving him thirty days to vacate the property. Plans were underway by Pinnacle Entertainment to start a new casino development in January 2007.

The parking lot where Mississippi Nights once stood. The front door would have been just to the right of where Max and Vaughan Kyle Enloe stand in the photo. Photo by Garrett Enloe.

Across from where Mississippi Nights once stood. Photo by Garrett Enloe in 2020.

Concerts were already booked into January, so Frame faced a dilemma. He contacted Pinnacle Entertainment and agreed to leave without any trouble with one stipulation: Mississippi Nights could remain open through mid-January to fulfill their obligations with the bands. Pinnacle agreed. However, concerned about public reaction to the closure, they obtained a gag order against Frame.

Despite the gag order, Frame's opinion about the casino slipped out during a magazine interview. Frame recalls his frustration, "Casinos are like giant vacuums. They come in and suck all the money for different elements: the hotel, entertainment, and the restaurants. They want the whole nine yards." Suppose the casino had pursued legal action against Frame; he could have been fined $20,000 for non-compliance with the gag order. But, instead, possibly fearing negative publicity, the casino never filed suit.

On September 20, 2007, the Mississippi Nights building was demolished.

Lumiere Place opened on December 19, 2007.

In 2007, the global financial crisis hit, and Pinnacle Entertainment canceled all plans for redevelopment on Laclede's Landing, which led to a long list of renegotiations and lawsuits with the City of St. Louis.

Without fulfilling their contract with the city to build stores and condos on Laclede's Landing, Pinnacle Entertainment sold Lumiere Place to Tropicana Entertainment in 2014.

237

THE END

Many music venues have dotted the St. Louis landscape throughout the years. Still, none of them managed the perfect mix of elements Mississippi Nights had, making it such a phenomenal place to see and play music. With its location on Laclede's Landing overlooking the Mississippi River, its intimate atmosphere, the fantastic sound system, the diversity of music genres, and especially, the family feel cultivated by the owner Rich Frame and office manager Pat Lacey, Mississippi Nights was an extraordinary music club.

Mississippi Nights is not just remembered but revered: by patrons, employees, and musicians alike.

Musicians still share their love for the venue. On July 20, 2008, Foo Fighters performed at Scottrade Center in St. Louis, and singer-guitarist Dave Grohl told a six-minute story about the night Nirvana played Mississippi Nights. They Might Be Giants wrote a song called "Mississippi Nights" where they assert, *"Nothing is like Mississippi Nights."*

Even musicians from across the globe remember the venue decades after playing there. Mississippi Nights fan Vance Watson says, "I wore my Mississippi Nights shirt recently out in Bangkok, and an older long-haired guy from Germany came up to me talking about playing there many years ago."

Employees still gather for reunions, where they often reminisce about the good times working at Mississippi Nights.

Remnants of the club are scattered across the St. Louis region. Fans and local historians cherish such items as sections of the bar, stage pieces, the building's awning, autographed drywall, posters, the T-shirt display, and bricks from the building itself.

In 2022, Laclede's Landing is a shadow of its former self. The modern casino complex with its vast parking lots north of the Martin Luther King Jr. Bridge harshly contrasts with the architecture of the historic buildings and cobblestone streets to the south. In 1985, thirty-five restaurants and bars and thirty-three shops, services, and attractions made Laclede's Landing a lively area. By 2013, only fourteen restaurants and bars were in operation. Cobblestone replacement, beginning in 2013 and continuing as of 2022, added to Laclede's Landing's difficulties. The Arch renovation project of 2014-2018 made accessing the area extremely challenging, further complicated matters. At this writing, only seven bars and restaurants make their home in Laclede's Landing's seventeen remaining historic buildings. The crowds are gone.

The nights when you could wander Laclede's Landing and see The Nukes at Kennedy's, Broken Toyz at All-American Saloon, Sinister Dane at Bernard's Pub, and end the evening at Mississippi Nights with Big Fun are long gone. Instead, the bands that used to arrive in tour busses along North 1st Street have headed west to the Delmar Loop or farther west to St. Louis Music Park.

Today, Laclede's Landing is a collection of For Lease signs and one-way streets ending in barricades. The northern section where Mississippi Nights once stood is dominated by the casino complex with its massive parking lots. Only the husk of Sundecker's gives any hint that a thriving nightlife once lit up that block.

The structure at 914 North 1st Street stood for over 150 years. The Great Fire of 1849 destroyed 430 buildings on Laclede's Landing, but 914 North 1st Street remained.

In 1896, an F4 tornado landed two blocks south on the Eads Bridge, but 914 North 1st Street remained.

The building housed a 1912 fireworks manufacturer, but 914 North 1st Street remained.

Fires raged through the building in 1954 and 1970, but 914 North 1st Street remained.

Sadly, the structure could not stand against the power of the casino and its wrecking ball.

As the Joni Mitchell song goes, "They paved paradise and put up a parking lot." Not only does a parking lot sit where Mississippi Nights once stood, but it is an *empty* parking lot, a barren testament to greed. They may have paved over Mississippi Nights, but they can never pave over our memories.

Long live Mississippi Nights!

MISSISSIPPI NIGHTS BY THE NUMBERS

Due to several missing calendars, bands or events missing from the calendars, and lack of advertising for the early and later years, the following numbers are probably inaccurate.

MOST SHOWS FOR LOCAL BANDS

1. BIG FUN (417)
2. THE URGE (100+)
3. FERRARI (88)
4. THE SHEIKS (57+)
5. THE UNCONSCIOUS (55)
6. DOMINO (49) tied with THE SCHWAG (49)
8. FRAGILE PORCELAIN MICE (47)
9. THE EYES/PALE DIVINE (46)
10. FAUSTUS (39)
11. MURDER CITY PLAYERS (37)

Note: Zane Gray and Arrow Memphis most likely should be included on this list.

Over 4,106 artists performed at Mississippi Nights.

MOST SHOWS FOR NON-LOCAL BANDS

1. BLUE DIXIE (48)
2. THE ELVIS BROTHERS (22)
3. THE SAMPLES (20)
4. BILLY GOAT (19)
5. THE BACK DOORS (16)
6. POMEROY (15)
7. THE BIG WU (14)
8. COLONY (13)
9. NIL8 (12) tied with THE RADIATORS (12)
11. BOCKMAN'S EUPHIO (11) tied with REVEREND HORTON HEAT (11)

Mississippi Nights
914 N. First St.
St. Louis, Mo. 63102

TOP TEN CRAZIEST SHOWS

(As voted on by the Facebook Mississippi Nights Fan Page)

1. THE URGE
2. VOICE OF GOD
3. MINISTRY
4. NIRVANA
5. GWAR
6. FISHBONE/RED HOT CHILI PEPPERS
7. MY LIFE WITH THE THRILL KILL KULT
8. RAMONES
9. SLAYER
10. SUICIDAL TENDENCIES/ EXODUS/PANTERA

TOP-SELLING MISSISSIPPI NIGHTS ALUM

Numbers denote millions of albums sold.

200: AC/DC
160: VANILLA ICE
100: EMINEM
 EMMYLOU HARRIS
 IRON MAIDEN
 LINKIN PARK
 THE POLICE

85: GREEN DAY
80: FOREIGNER
 MEAT LOAF
 RED HOT CHILI PEPPERS
75: NIRVANA

LOCAL BAND LONGEVITY AWARDS

Cumulative Years Played at Mississippi Nights.

1. THE URGE (13 yrs)
2. MURDER CITY PLAYERS (12 yrs)
3. JAKE'S LEG (11 yrs)
4. FRAGILE PORCELAIN MICE (10 yrs)
5. THE BOTTLE ROCKETS (9 yrs) tied with MAMA'S PRIDE (9 yrs)

THE BANDS

Artists listed performed at Mississippi Nights at least once during the indicated year. Numbers noted after the year reflect the total number of appearances in the indicated year or range of years. Again, due to incomplete records, the below list probably has inaccuracies.

#

+44: 2006

+850: 2000

10 Stories Tall: 1995 (2)

10,000 Maniacs: 1988, 1997

101 North: 1991

11th Hour: 1991

12 Gauge Blues: 2003

12 oz. Prophet: 2002 (2), 2003, 2005

12 Rods: 1996

12 Summers Old: 2003, 2004 (3)

13 After: 1998, 2001 (2), 2002, 2004

13 Lokie: 2003 (3), 2004

1369: 2000

15 Minutes Late: 2004

16 Down: 2002, 2003

16 Horsepower: 1995, 1986

19 Wheels: 1996 (2)

1932 Rhythm and Blues Band: 1976, 1977

2 Live Crew: 1990

2 Skinnee J's: 1999, 2000, 2002

20/20: 1979

22 Jacks: 1999, 2000

24-7 Spyz: 1989-1991, 1996

27 Various: 1992

3 Finger Cowboy: 1998

3 Foot Thick: 1990

3 Voices: 1994 (2)

3: 1988, 1993

311: 1994, 1999 (2)

360 Smile: 2005, 2006

38 Special: 1992

3JC: 2004, 2005

3rd Floor: 1993

3rd Shift: 2001

4 Against the World: 1994

4 Letter Lie: 2006

4 on the Floor: 1983 (5)

4 Real: 1994

40 Til 5: 2004

442: 2003

4th and Long: 2004

54-40: 1986

55 Clicks: 2001

6 Gauge: 2002

6 Star People: 2000

6 String Drag: 1998

7 Seconds: 1990, 1991

7 Shot Screamers: 2005 (2)

700 Miles: 1993

7D Funk: 1999

84-40: 2002

8Stops7: 2000

8th Day Band: 1986

9 Days Wonder: 1994

A

A Change of Pace: 2006 (2)

A Far Cry: 1991

A Full Moon Consort: 1994

A Great Laugh: 1996

A Lion in the Capital: 2006

A Little 2 Horny: 2004

A Perfect Fit: 1985, 1986 (5), 1987, 1988, 1991 (4), 1992

A Picture Made: 1986, 1987

A Reasonable Place to Park: 2002

A Tribe Called Quest: 1993

A Wilhelm Scream: 2006 (2)

A.L.F.A.: 2003

A3: 1998

A-440: 2002

Abandoned Pools: 2002

Abashanati: 1991

Abjeez: 1988

AC/DC: 1977

Academy is..., The: 2005, 2006

Accelerators, The: 1986

Accept: 1984

Acceptance: 2006

Acetone: 1994

Acoustic Trio: 1990

Acousticity: 1986, 1987, 1988 (2)

Action, The: 1982, 1983 (23), 1984 (4), 1988

Acts: 1982

Acute: 2006

Adair: 2003 (5), 2004, 2005

Adam's Farm: 1995

Adam's Off Ox: 2002

Adcock, C.C.: 1994

Addien: 2006 (4)

Adeline: 2005

ADHD: 2006

Adler: 2006

Adored, The: 2003 (3), 2004 (2), 2005

Adrastus: 1982

Aeuroline: 2006

Affair, The: 2003

Afghan Whigs: 1992

AFI: 2003

Against Me!: 2003 (2), 2005

Agatha Honey: 1994

Agent Athena: 1979

Agent: 1984 (3)

Agents of Good Roots: 1998

Aggravations, The: 1995 (2)

Airto: 1983

Akabu: 1990

Al Di Meola Project: 1993

Al Di Meola World Project: 1994

Alarm, The: 1985, 1988, 1989

Alaskan: 1998, 1999

Albright, Gerald: 1989, 1993, 1995-1997, 1999

Alcatrazz: 1984, 1986

Alchemy: 1992

Alcohol Ignition Switch: 1997, 1998

Alderaan: 1984

Aldo Nova: 1991

Aletta: 2006

Alexander, D.: 1989

Alice in Chains: 1990 (2), 1992

Alien Ant Farm: 2001

Alisdair: 2003

Alive: 2003, 2004

Alkaline Trio: 2001, 2003

All American Rejects: 2003 (2)

All Star Blooze Band: 1983 (3)

All: 1992, 1994, 1995

Allgood: 1994

Allison, Mose: 1987

Allister: 2005, 2006 (2)

Allman, Devon: 1992, 2002, 2007

Allman, Gregg Band: 1989

Allman, Gregg: 1978, 1985, 1986

Almost Joshua: 1994

Alpha Blondy and The Solar System: 1988

Alston, Gerald: 1989

Alternate Roots, The: 2005

Alternate Routes, The: 2005

Alvin Jett Band, The: 1994

Alvin, Dave: 1999

Amazing Crowns: 2000

Amazing Royal Crowns, The: 1998

Amber Pacific: 2006

Ambrosia: 1978

A-men: 1999

America is Waiting: 2003

America: 1994

American Blues Revival: 1996

Ammaretto: 1983 (2), 1984 (3)

Amos, Tori: 1992

Amsterband: 2005 (2)

Amusement Park: 1982

Anabel Evil: 2001 (2)

Anacrusis: 1987 (2), 1988-1993

Anastasia Screamed: 1991

Anchondo: 2002 (3), 2003 (3), 2004 (4), 2005 (2)

...And You Will Know Us by the Trail of Dead: 2003, 2005

Andreone, Leah: 1996

Andrew & the Upstarts: 1985 (2)

Andrew Tosh and the Andrew Tosh Band: 1988

Andrew W. K.: 2004

Andrews, Jeff: 1996

Andriano, Dan: 2003

Andy Sullivan Orchestra: 1992

Angelfish: 1994

Angelic Upstarts: 1985

Angry Salad: 1999, 2000

Angus Tweed: 1989

Answer No Answer: 1986

Antenna: 1983, 1992

Anthony, Eric: 1992, 1994 (2)

Anthrax: 1986, 1995, 1996

Antietam: 2004 (2)

Anti-Flag: 2003

Anubis: 2001, 2003

Anything but Joey: 2003 (4), 2004

AOK: 1996

Apartment 26: 1999, 2000 (2)

Apology Heard, The: 2006

Apostles, The: 1995

Apple, Fiona: 1997

Apples in Stereo, The: 1997

Appleseed: 2006

Aquabats, The: 1998

Aquarium Rescue Unit: 1994, 1996

Arc Angels: 1992 (2)

Arceneaux, Fernest: 1995

Are N' Be: 1991

Armageddon 1984

Armor for Sleep: 2005

Armored Saint: 1988 (2)

Armstrong, Dougie: 1984

Army of Freshmen: 2004, 2006

Arrow Memphis: 1978 (3), 1979 (7), 1981, 1982, 1985, 1983 (12), 1984 (8)

Ars Nova: 1983 (14), 1984 (20), 1993

Arsenic Orange: 1999

Art Thugs: 2003

Arythma: 2005

Asa & Eddie: 1979 (2)

Ashbourne: 2005

Ashtray Lizard: 2005

Asia Minor: 2003

Askin, Tom: 2002, 2003

Asleep at the Wheel: 1985 (2), 1990

Asphalt Ballet: 1993

Ass Ponies, The: 1995 (2)

Assailant: 1985

Astral Flight: 2001 (3)

Ataris, The: 2002, 2003

Ate My Young: 2005

Athena And the Hubcaps: 1986

Athena: 1995 (2)

Athenaeum: 1998 (2)

Atlanta Rhythm Section: 1989

Atlantics, The: 1979

Atomic Fossils: 1991

Atomicus: 2005 (2)

Attaway, Murray: 1993

Auk: 2003

Auset: 2005 (2)

Austin, Bryan: 2000

Autopilot Off: 2002 (2)

Autovein: 2006

Autumn Clock: 1994 (2), 1995, 1997

Autumn Sky: 2006

Ava, Wait: 2005, 2006 (3)

Avenue: 2006 (2)

Average White Band: 1979, 1996, 2001

Avex: 2003

Aviation Club: 1986 (3)

Avila, John: 1990

Avon Ladies: 1982

Axe Minister: 1987, 1989, 1991

Ayers, Roy: 1983, 1986 (2), 1988, 1997, 1998

Ayers, Will: 1983

B

B'zz, The: 1983

Babes in Toyland: 1990, 1992

Back Doors, The: 1992-1993 (2), 1995-2000 (2)

Back of Dave: 1995-1997

Backwards Day: 1989

Backyard Tire Fire: 2006

Bad Beau: 1983

Bad Brains: 1982, 1987, 1991, 1994

Bad Candy: 1992

Bad English: 1989

Bad Fathers: 2004

Bad Habits: 1978

Bad Manners: 1993, 1995

Bad Posture: 1992

Bad Religion: 1994, 1995

Badfinger: 1982, 1987

Badlands: 1989

Badlees, The: 1996 (2)

Badu, Erykah: 1997

Baez, Joan: 1993

Baghdad Jones: 1993

Bagga Bones: 1999

Bahr, Randy: 1995

Bailey, Phillip: 1993

Baird, Dan: 1993

Baker, Max: 1993

Balaam and the Angel: 1988

Balancing Act: 1987

Baldwin Brothers, The: 2001, 2004

Balkan Beat Box: 2006

Ball, Marcia: 1986, 1994, 1998, 1999, 2000

Ballcock Assembly: 2005

Banastre Tarleton Band: 1985

Bang Tango: 1989, 1990

Bankhead, Tommy: 1984, 1985, 1992, 1993

Banned, The: 1998, 1999

Barden Rd.: 1982

Bardo Pond: 2003

Bare Jr.: 1999-2001

Barefoot Revolution: 1999

Barenaked Ladies: 1998

Bar-Kays: 1993

Barking Aardvarks, The: 1989, 1990

Barking Spiders: 1990

Barnett, Billy: 1996

Basehead: 1992

Bash, The: 1989

Bass, Fontella: 1990, 1997

Bastards, The: 2001

Baton Rouge: 1990

Battalion of Saints: 1985

Battlefield Band: 1993

Bayside: 2004

Bazooka Joe: 1995

Beans: 2004

Bear Hug Jersey: 2005, 2006 (5)

Bears, The: 1987 (2), 1998

Beasley, Walter: 1996

Beastie Boys: 1992

Beat Daddies, The: 1992, 1993, 1994 (2)

Beat Farmers, The: 1985-1987, 1990-1993, 1998

Beat Patrol: 1989, 1990

Beat Rodeo: 1985

Beat, The: 1982

Beatnuts, The: 1999

BeauSoleil avec Michael Doucet: 1995

BeauSoleil: 1993, 1997 (2)

Beautiful Green: 1999

Beautiful Pale, The: 1992

Beck, Terry: 1982

Beck: 1994

Bedlam: 1992

Been, Michael: 1994

Beenie Man: 2001

Beer for Dolphins: 1996

Beer Nuts, The: 1992

Beggars Playground: 1993

Behind the Blindfold: 2005, 2006

Bel Airs, The: 1984 (2), 1985 (5), 1993

Béla Fleck and the Flecktones: 1992, 1993

Belew, Adrian: 1987

Belinda Chaire, The: 1992

Bell Tower: 1993

Bell, Bob: 2006

Bell, Tony: 1988

Bella Wolf: 1996 (4), 1997 (2)

Bellamy Brothers: 1984

Belly: 1993

Bellyfeel: 1996 (5), 1997 (2), 1998 (2), 1999 (2), 2000 (2), 2001, 2002

Below, Adrian: 1988

Benatar, Pat: 1979, 1997

Bender: 2000

Benders, The: 1987 (2), 1991 (2), 1992

Benet, Eric: 1997

Benevento/Russo Duo: 2004 (2)

Benny Green Trio: 1992

Bent: 1993 (5), 1994 (6), 1995 (3), 1996, 1997

Bentley, Dierks: 2004

Berlin: 1983

Bernhard, Sandra: 2002

Bernie Smith and the Sportsmen: 1994

Berry: 2005

Best Kissers in the World: 1992, 1993

Bettens, Sarah: 2006

Better Half: 2002 (2)

Better Than Ezra: 1995, 1996, 1998-2000

Bettie Serveert: 1993

Betts, Dickey: 1986, 1988, 2003

Between the Buried and Me: 2004 (2), 2006

Be-Vision: 1983, (7), 1984, 1986 (2), 1987 (5)

Bianchetta, Margaret: 1995

Big Ass Truck: 1993

Big Bad Smitty: 1992, 1993

Big Bad Voodoo Daddy: 1998

Big Band Review: 1994

Big Band with Larry Thurston, The: 1994

Big Bang Theory: 1991

Big Black: 1985, 1987

Big Blue Monkey: 1999 (2), 2001, 2002 (2)

Big Business: 2005

Big Chief: 1992

Big City Rock: 2006 (2)

Big Country: 1983, 1993

Big Fat Everything: 2005, 2006 (2)

Big Fun: 1985 (88), 1986 (69), 1987 (77), 1988 (62), 1989 (60), 1990 (54), 1991 (4), 1993 (3)

Big George: 1996, 1987

Big Guitars from Memphis: 1995

Big Head Todd and the Monsters: 1995, 1997, 2001

Big Mountain: 1999

Big Rude Jake: 1998

Big Sandy: 1996

Big Smith: 2004

Big Stick: 1995

Big Sugar: 1995

Big Twist and The Mellow Fellows: 1984, 1985 (2), 1986 (4), 1987

Big Will: 1983

Big Wreck: 1998

Big Wu, The: 1998, 1999, 2001 (3), 2002-2003 (2), 2004 (3), 2005, 2006

Bigga: 1994

Bigwigs: 2002

Bile: 1994, 2003

Bi-Level: 2000, 2001, 2002 (3), 2003, 2005

Bill Bruford's Earthworks: 1988

Billy and the Preachers: 1986

Billy Bragg and the Blokes: 1999

Billy Branch and the Sons of the Blues: 1994

Billy Engel Band, The: 1991, 1992 (2)

Billy Goat: 1991 (12), 1992 (2), 1994 (2), 1995, 1996 (2)

Bim Skala Bim: 1993

Biohazard: 1994 (2)

Bionica: 1994, 1995 (2), 1996

Bird, Andrew: 2006

Birdmen of Alcatraz: 1996

Bishop, Elvin: 1979, 1980

Bishops, The: 1987, 1988, 1990, 1991, 1992 (3)

Black 47: 1993

Black Crowes, The: 1990, 1998

Black Dahlia: 2004 (2), 2005

Black Flag: 1984

Black Keys, The: 2006

Black Lab: 1998 (2)

Black Market: 1984

Black Oak Arkansas: 1979, 1980, 1984

Black Pearl Mafia: 1992

Black Rebel Motorcycle Club: 2001, 2003, 2004, 2006

Black Sand Hand: 1994 (2), 1995 (2)

Black Train Jack: 1994

Black Uhuru: 1994, 2002

Black, Dave: 1995

Black, Frank: 1994

Blackboard Jungle: 1992

Blackeyed Susan: 1991

Blackfish: 1993

Blackfoot, J.D.: 1976, 1977, 1992

Blackmarket Flowers: 1994

Blades, The: 1985 (2)

Blake, Cicero: 1994

Blake, Kenny: 1992

Blakely, John: 1979

Blame Gary: 2003, 2004 (2), 2005

Bland, Bobby Blue: 1994

Blank Space: 1985, 1986 (5), 1987 (3)

Blast, The: 1985 (3), 1991, 1992

Blasters, The: 1981, 1985

Blastoids, The: 2000

Bled, The: 2003

Bleeding Through: 2005

Blessing, The: 1991

Blessthefall: 2006

Bleu: 2002, 2003

Blind Dates: 1985

Blind Idiot God: 1985

Blind Melon: 1992, 1993

Blinded Black: 2005 (4), 2006 (3)

Blindside: 2005

blink-182: 1998

Blitzpeer: 1991

Blood Brothers, The: 2003, 2005 (2)

Blood Red Skyline: 2005

Bloodhound Gang: 2000

Bloodline: 1994

Bloom, Luka: 1988, 1994

Bloque: 1999

Blow, Kurtis: 1998

Blue City Band, The: 1985, 1995

Blue Dixie: 1990-1991 (2), 1992 (14), 1993 (11), 1994 (10), 1997, 1998 (4), 1999 (3), 2005,

Blue Floyd: 2000

Blue Lightning: 1993 (2)

Blue Meanies: 1992, 1996

Blue Moon Ghetto: 1995

Blue Mountain: 1993, 1994, 1995, 1997

Blue Murder: 1989

Blue October: 2006

Blue Rags: 1997

Blue Riddim Band: 1981, 1983 (2), 1984, 1986 (3)

Blue Rodeo: 1992

Blue Shag: 1998

Blue: 2003

Blueground Undergrass: 2000, 2000

Blueprint: 2003, 2004

Blues Boys: 1978

Blues Handle: 1996 (2), 1997

Blues Machine, The: 1986

Blues Traveler: 1991, 1994, 2000, 2003

Bluesbusters: 1986

B-Movie: 1985

Bob and Tom Show Band: 1997 (2), 1999 (2)

Bob Mould Band: 2005

Bockman: 2005

Bockman's Euphio: 2001, 2002-2003 (4), 2004

BoDeans, The: 1986 (2), 1988, 1989, 1991 (2), 1999, 2001, 2002

Body Found: 1992

Bone Daddies: 1992

Bonfire: 1988

Bongos, The: 1985

Bonham, Tracy: 1996

Bonner Wells: 1996

Bonoff, Karla: 1980, 1986

Boo Boo Sis: 1991 (3)

Boogie Chyld: 1998 (2), 1999

Boomtown Rats: 1979

Boone, Mary: 1988

Boorays, The: 1991 (3), 1992, 1993 (3), 1994

Bootsy's Rubber Band: 1993

Border, Jordan: 1988 (2), 1990 (3), 1991

Boro City Rollers: 1998

Bosman Twins: 1988, 1995, 1997

Bottle of Justus: 2002 (2), 2004, 2005

Bottle Rockets, The: 1993 (3), 1994 (4), 1995 (4), 1996, 1997, 1998 (2), 1999, 2004, 2006 (2)

Bottom Ground: 2001 (3), 2002 (2)

Bouncing Souls: 1998

Bound: 2004

Bow Wow Wow: 1982

Bowen, Justine: 1994, 1995

Bowery Boys, The: 1987, 1991

Bowling for Soup: 2006

Boyfriend: 1988

Boys with Toys: 1985

Boyz, The: 1987

BR5-49: 1999, 2000

Bragg, Billy: 1989, 1990

Bramhall, Doyle: 1994

Bramlett, Bonnie: 1978

Branch Manager: 1995

Branch, Michelle: 2001

Brand New: 2002, 2006

Brannen, John: 1988

Brave Combo: 1983, 1994 (2), 1996, 1997, 2004-2006

Bravery, The: 2005

Breaking Benjamin: 2004 (2)

Breaking Point: 2001

Breaking the Faith: 2006

Breaux, Zachary: 1996

Brecker Brothers: 1993

Brecker, Michael: 1987, 1988, 1990

Brent Berry and the Roots Crew: 2002

Bret Michaels and the Hollywood Gutter Cats: 1991

Breuer, Jim: 2002

Brewer & Shipley: 1977, 1978, 1979 (3)

Brews, The: 2000-2003 (2), 2004

Brian & Tony Gold: 1995

Brian Auger's Oblivion Express: 1977

Brian Clark and the St. Louis Browns: 1994

Brian Jonestown Massacre, The: 2004

Brian Setzer Orchestra: 1998

Brian Vander Ark: 2004

Brian White Quartet: 1999

Briehan, Jeff: 1992

Brighten: 2006

Brisebois, Danielle: 1994

Brissett, Donovan: 1998, 1999

Britny Fox: 1990

Broadside Heart: 2006 (2)

Broadside: 2006

Broke: 1999 (4), 2000, 2001

Broken English: 1985

Broken Grass: 2004

Broken Homes: 1986

Broken Shadow: 2003

Broken Toyz: 1989 (3), 1990

Bromberg, David: 1979

Bronx Zoo: 1989

Brooklyn Deadwood: 2004 (2)

Brooks, Lonnie: 1979, 1986

Brooks, Paul: 2005

Brother Cane: 1993 (3), 1994, 1995

Brother: 1992

Broussard, Marc: 2004, 2005

Brown, Clarence "Gatemouth": 1979

Brown, Dennis: 1983, 1988, 1993

Brown, Junior: 1999

Brown, Tony: 1986 (3)

Bruce, Jack: 1988

Brunt Nervends: 1993 (5)

Bruntnell, Peter: 1999 (2)

Brutal Juice: 1995

Bryant: 1991, 1993

BT: 2000

Bubble Boys: 1997

Buchanan, Jay: 2006

Buchanan, Roy: 1985, 1987

Buck Acre: 1978

Buck Pets, The: 1989, 1991, 1992

Buckcherry: 1999

Buckethead: 2005, 2006

Buckner, Richard: 1999 (2), 2004

Buckout: 2006 (3)

Buckshot LeFonque: 1995

Buckwheat Zydeco: 1986, 1987, 1988 (2), 1989, 1990 (2)

Buffalo Bob & His Bedroom Blues Band: 1989

Buffalo Bob: 1993

Buffalo Tom: 1993, 1995

Buffalo, Grant Lee: 1993, 1994, 1998

Bugnon, Alex: 1990, 1992-1994, 1996, 1997, 1999

Bugsy & the Boys: 1991

Building Rome: 2005, 2006

Built to Spill: 2005, 2006

Bullens, Cindy: 1979

Bulletboys: 1988, 1991

Bullets: 1984 (4)

Burdon, Eric: 1982, 1989

Burn Rome Burn: 2005

Burning Spear: 1985, 1987-1989, 1991, 1995, 1996

Burnt Nervends: 1994 (2)

Burnt Ninja: 2006

Burton, Gary: 1977, 1979

Bus Boys: 1982

Bush, The: 1984

Bush: 1995

Buster, Brody: 2000

Butch Wax and the Hollywoods: 1993

Butler, Jonathan: 1996,1997

Butter Glory: 1994

Butthole Surfers: 1989

Buzzcocks: 1991

Buzzoven: 1994

By Name: 1992

Byrne, Martha: 1997

 C

C., Kevin: 1992

C.J. Chenier and the Red Hot Louisiana Band: 1990, 1992

Cabo Frio: 1986, 1987

Cabrera, Ryan: 2006

Cactus World News: 1986

Cadillac Tramps: 1994

Cagney: 1985 (2)

Cain is Able: 1990, 1991

Cake: 1997

Cale, J.J.: 1990

Cale, John: 1986

Calexico: 2005, 2006

Calico System: 2001 (2), 2002-2003 (3), 2006

Call Waiting: 1989

Call, The: 1986, 1989

Calling, The: 2001

Callison, Richie: 1984

Camden: 2004

Cameo: 1997

Campbell, John: 1991

Camper Van Beethoven: 1986-1989

Candiria: 2001

Candlebox: 1993

Candy: 1982, 1983 (2), 1992

Canned Heat: 1981

Cannibal Corpse: 1996

Captain Beyond: 1977

Carbon Leaf: 2006

Cardigans, The: 1997

Carillo: 1978

Carlisle, Brandi: 2005

Carlos: 1999

Carlton, Larry: 1994

Carlton, Vanessa: 2002

Carnival Strippers: 1994

Carpenter, Mary Chapin: 1999

Carrack, Paul: 1982

Carrasco, Joe "King": 1986, 1987 (2)

Cartel: 2006 (2)

Cartwrights, The: 2003

Caruso: 1985

Case, Bob: 1994

Case, Peter: 1986, 1989

Cash, Rosanne: 1981, 1988

Cassius Clay: 1995

Cast: 2006

Castor: 1997

Casualties of War: 1996

Casualties, The: 2002

Cat Heads, The: 1987

Catch 22: 2002, 2006

Cate Brothers: 1979

Cathedral: 1993

Caulfields, The: 1995

Cause, The: 2005, 2006 (5), 2007

Caution Horses: 1995, 1997 (2)

Cavanaugh, Tim: 1996

Cave In: 2002, 2003

Cavedogs: 1990, 1992

Cavo: 2003

CD Rom: 1997

CDawg: 2003

Celery: 1996, 1997 (3), 1998, 1999 (2)

Celldweller: 2004

Cellophane: 1997

Celtic Frost: 1987

Centerpointe: 2003, 2005-2006 (2), 2007

Chad and Jeremy: 1986

Chainsaw Kittens: 1994, 1997

Chalklit: 1998 (2), 1997

Champagne: 1979

Champion, Grady: 2000

Chapin, Tom: 1982

Chapman, Tracy: 1988

Chapterhouse: 1994

Charlatans, The (U.K.): 1992, 1997

Charlatans, The (U.S.): 1994

Charlemagne: 2006

Charlie Hunter Duo: 2002

Charlie Hunter Quartet: 2001

Charlie Sexton Sextet: 1995

Charms, The: 2006

Chasing Furies: 1999

Cheap Mink: 1978 (2), 1979 (12)

Cheap Trick: 1999

Checker, Chubby: 1982

Chemlab: 1997

Cher U.K.: 1993, 1994

Cherry: 1983

Chesnutt, Vic: 1994

Chesterfield Kings: 2006

Chia Band, The: 1997, 1998

Chick Corea Elektric Band: 1987, 1988, 1990, 1991, 1993

Chicken Scratch: 1992

Chicken Truck: 1989, 1990

Child's Play: 1990

Child's Play: 1979

Children's Audio: 2000

Chilton, Alex: 1987

China Crisis: 1987

Chiodos: 2006

Chixdigit: 1996

Chloroform: 1999

Chocolate Genius: 2002

Choice, The: 1992, 1993 (6)

Chosen Few, The: 1986

Chris Robinson and the New Earth Mud: 2003 (2), 2004

Chrome Nuns: 2002

Chuck and Ingrid Revue: 1991

Chucklehead: 1995

Chumbawamba: 1998

Church of the SubGenius: 1995

Church, The: 1988, 1994

Cibo Matto: 1999

Cinderella: 1995

Circa Survive: 2005, 2006

Circle Jerks: 1983, 1995, 2002 (2)

Circle of Fear: 1991

Cirrus: 1998

Citizen Cope: 2006

Citizen King: 1994, 1997, 1999 (2)

City A: 2003

City Limit Band, The: 2003

Civil Tones, The: 1996 (2), 1997

Clan of Xymox: 1991 (2)

Clarissa: 1996

Clark, Brian: 1983, 1984

Clark, Patrick: 1999

Clark, Stanley: 1994

Clark, W.C.: 2000

Clarke, Brian: 1990

Clarke, Gilby: 1995

Clarke, Stanley: 1985, 1990

Clarke/Duke Project, The: 1993

Classic Red: 1994

Claypool: 2005

Clayton, Willie: 1994

Clear Glass Religion: 1998, 2002 (2)

Clear: 2002

Clegg, Johnny: 1990, 1993

Clements, Vassar: 1979

Clever: 1998, 1999 (4), 2000 (3), 2001

Click Five, The: 2006

Cliff, Jimmy: 1988-1990, 1992

Climber: 2000

Clique: 1983 (2)

Clones: 1982

Closer: 1997

Cloud, Sarah: 1997, 1998 (2)

Clowns for Progress: 1998

Club Trini: 1998

Club Zero: 1986 (4), 1987 (3)

Clutch: 1994, 1995 (2), 1996, 1997, 1998 (2)

Coal Kitchen: 1977 (3), 1978 (4), 1979 (17), 1980 (4)

Coast, The: 1983

Coast to Coast Blues Band, The: 1988

Cobham, Billy: 1978, 1994

Coburn, Candy: 2005

Cockburn, Bruce: 1989, 1992, 1994

Cocker, Joe: 1982

Code Blue: 1985 (2)

Code Talkers, The: 2003

Code, The: 2003

Codie: 2003

Coe, David Allan: 1985, 1989, 1995, 1999

Coheed and Cambria: 2003

Coherent: 2006

Cohn, Marc: 1998

Cold Krush Crew: 1987

Cold Sweat: 1990

Cold Water Flat: 1995

Cole Tuckey: 1977 (2), 1978 (3), 1979 (28)

Cole, John: 1996

Cole, Jude: 1993, 1995

Cole, Lloyd: 2001

Cole, Paula: 1994, 1997

Coleman, Deborah: 1995

Colionne, Nick: 1995

Collaborateur: 1993, 1996, 1998

Collaboration: 2004

Collapsis: 2000

Collateral Insight: 2003 (2), 2006

Collective Soul: 1995

Collier, Terry: 1979

Collins, Albert: 1986-1988, 1990, 1992

Collinsville All-Stars: 2004

Collision: 1993

Colonel Bruce Hampton: 2003

Colony: 1994, 1995 (3), 1996 (4), 1997 (2), 1998, 2000, 2002

Color Blind: 1989 (3)

Colvin, Shawn: 1993, 1997

Coma: 2006

Commander Cody and His Modern Day Airmen: 1981, 1986

Commitments, The: 1996

Committee, The: 2003

Common Ailments of Maturity: 1985 (2), 1987

Common Rider: 2002

Company of Wolves: 1990

Compound Red: 1994

Con Alma: 1978

Con Funk Shun: 1996, 2005

Concrete Blonde: 1987, 1989, 1990, 1993

Condition 90: 1986 (2)

Conformists, The: 2001

Confusedirection: 1997

Connells, The: 1990-1993, 1996

Conquest: 1987, 1988 (2), 1989, 1990 (4), 1991 (3), 1992 (2), 1999

Cool for August: 1996 (2)

Cool Jerk: 1979

Coolidge, Rita: 1983

Cooper, Michael: 1996

Cope: 1999, 2000 (2)

Copeland, Johnny: 1984, 1988, 2001, 2006 (2)

Corduroy Jane: 1997

Core Project: 2001, 2002-2004 (2), 2005

Core: 1996

Cornershop: 1998

Coroner: 1989

Corporate Avenger: 2000

Corporate Humor: 1986 (2), 1987 (2), 1988

Corrosion of Conformity (C.O.C.): 1987, 1995, 1990

Cossu, Scott: 1987

Cotton, James: 1988

Counting Crows: 1994 (2)

Cour, Jonathan: 2006

Course of Empire: 1994, 1998

Cowboy Junkies: 1989, 1992, 1994, 1998, 2000, 2002

Cowboy Mouth: 1993, 1994, 1997, 1998 (2), 1999 (2), 2000, 2004, 2006

Cows, The: 1995

CPB: 2001 (3)

Crack the Sky: 1978

Cracker: 1992, 1994 (2), 2000, 2002

Cramps, The: 1992, 1994, 1997

Cranberries, The: 1993

Cranston, Lamont: 1979, 1982

Crash and Burn: 1986, 1989

Crash Kills Four: 1995

Crash Vegas: 1993

Crawlspace: 2002

Cray, Robert: 1985, 1986 (2)

Creature Comforts: 1999

Creeper Lagoon: 2001

Crenshaw, Marshall: 1983, 1987

Crescent Moon Connection: 2004

Crimson Addict: 2005, 2006

Critical Gopher: 1995

Croft: 1999, 2000, 2006

Cro-Mags: 2001

Crooked Fingers: 1999

Crosby, David: 1984

Cross Canadian Ragweed: 2004

Crosswind: 1982, 1983 (6)

Crow, Sheryl: 1993

Crowded House: 1991

Crowell, Rodney: 1981

Crowley, Kacy: 1998

Cruces: 1995

Crunge, The: 1998

Crusaders, The: 1985

Crush, The: 2006

Crushed: 1996

Crutch: 1997

Crutchfield, James: 1988

Cry of Love: 1994

Cry Wolf: 1991

Cryin' Shame: 1994

Crystal Method, The: 1997, 1998

Cubris: 2006

Culture Club: 2000

Culture Shock: 1986, 1987

Culture: 1984, 1988, 1990 (2), 1992, 1995, 1996

Cursive: 2002, 2003, 2006

Curve: 1998

Cute is What We Aim For: 2006

D

D Generation: 1996

D.P.F.: 2006

D.R.I. (Dirty Rotten Imbeciles): 1990, 1992

D'Urso: 1996

Da' Krash: 1988

Dada: 1993, 1994, 2003, 2004

Daisychain: 1999 (3), 2001

Dale, Dick: 2003-2006

Dali Automatic: 1995

Dambuilders: 1995

Damien, Max: 1979

Damone: 2006 (4)

Dan Reed Network: 1988

Dance Disaster Movements: 2005

Dance Hall Crashers: 1993

Dancing Hoods: 1986

Dandelion: 1994

Dando, Evan: 2003

Dandy Warhols, The: 1995, 1997, 1998

Danger Danger: 1991

Danger Girl: 1998

Dangerous Kitchen: 1998

Dangerous Toys: 1989

Daniel: 2005, 2006

Daniels, Chris: 1993

Danzig: 1989 (2), 1990

Dark Angel: 1989

Dark Horses: 1994-1998

Dark New Day: 2005

Dark Star Orchestra: 1999 (2), 2000

Dark, The: 1992

Darkest Hour: 2005

Darkwater: 2003

Darlahood: 1997

Darling Little Jackhammer: 1995

Darrah, Dan: 2003

Das Damen: 1991

Dash Rip Rock: 1996

Dashboard Confessional: 2001, 2002

Dave Edmunds Rockpile: 1978

Dave Glover Band, The: 2004

Dave Kalz and Impala Deluxe Band: 2004

Dave Matthews Band: 1994

Dave Matthews Cover Band: 2002

David & David: 1986

David Dee and the Hot Tracks: 1993

David Grisman Quintet: 1998

David Krull and the Cryin' Shame: 1995

David Lee and the House Rockers: 1989

Davis, Alana: 1997

Davis, Larry: 1993

Davis, Tyrone: 1997

Dawes, Simon: 2006

Day by the River: 1999

Day in the Life: 1998

Day, Howie: 2004

Daydream: 2006

Days Away: 2003 (2)

Days of the New: 1997, 1998

Dayton, Jesse: 2002

Dayton: 2006 (3)

Dazz Band: 1983 (2)

Dazzling Killmen: 1991, 1992, 1993 (2)

dB's, The: 1985, 1988

DC3: 1986

De La Soul: 1993

Dead 60s, The: 2005

Dead Boy & the Elephant Man: 2006 (2)

Dead by Tuesday: 2003 (2)

Dead Drive Fast, The: 2005, 2006 (3)

Dead Fucking Last (DFL): 1995

Dead Hot Workshop: 1995

Dead Kennedys: 1982

Dead Meadow: 2006

Dead Milkmen, The: 1987-1989, 1990 (2), 1992 (2), 1993

Dead Planet: 1989

Dead Reckoning: 1992

Dean Evans Band: 2005 (3)

Dear Fidelity: 2006

Dear Mom: 1992

Death Angel: 1988, 1990

Death Cab for Cutie: 2004

Death Ride 69: 1995

Death Row Bodine: 1997

Deborah Coleman Band: 1995

Decemberists: 2005

Deckard, Chris: 2000

Dee, David: 1985, 1992, 1994, 1997

Deep Banana Blackout: 2001

Deep Blue Something: 1995 (2), 1996, 2001

Deep Blue: 1995

Defiance: 1990, 1995 (2)

Deftones: 1995 (2), 2003

Degraw, Gavin: 2004

Del Amitri: 1995 (2), 1996

Del Fuegos, The: 1985

Del McCoury Band: 1999, 2003

Delaney, Brian: 2006

Delinquent Habits: 1996

Delirium: 2000

Deliverance: 1982, 1983 (6)

Del-Lords, The: 1985, 1986, 1988

Deluca, Rocco: 2005, 2006

Deluxe: 2000

Demolition Doll Rods: 1997

Demolition Hammer: 1991

Den of Thieves: 1991

Denali: 2004

Denim: 1977

Dennis Quaid and the Mystics: 1990

Dera, Cal: 1977

Derringer, Rick: 1986

Descendents: 1987, 1997

DeShay, James: 1988

Destroyer: 2005

Destruction Made Simple: 2003

Detachment Kit: 2006 (2)

Detarx: 1993

Deuce Project, The: 2003

Devastation: 1991

Devitto, Liberty: 1990

Devlins, The: 1994, 1998

Dexter Freebish: 2001

Di Meola, Al: 1985, 1987, 1990, 1998

Diamond Stud: 1986 (3), 1987

Dickies, The: 1988

Diddley, Bo: 1986, 2005

Didjits: 1986 (2), 1987 (2)

Dido: 2000

Die Kreuzen: 1992

Die Symphony: 1997 (3), 1998-1999 (2), 2000 (3), 2001, 2004

Die Trying: 2003

Diesel Band: 1981

Dieselhed: 1997

Diffuser: 2001

DiFranco, Ani: 1996

Dig: 1994

Digital Hitmen: 2001

Digital Underground: 1992

Dignitary Stylish: 1994

Dilcher, Cheryl: 1978

Dillinger Escape Plan: 2005

Dillion, Jimmy: 1999 (3)

Dillman Band, The: 1981

Dillon Fence: 1993 (2)

Dinosaur Jr.: 1992, 1993

Dio: 1994

Dionysia: 2001 (2), 2002 (3), 2003

Dirt Band, The: 1982

Dirt Merchants: 1995

Dirty Dozen Brass Band: 1990, 1996, 2000, 2003

Dirty Ernie's Greaseball: 2001

Dirty Looks: 1989

Dirty Vegas: 2004

Dirty Works: 1991

Disappear Fear: 1991, 1991, 1995

Disco Biscuits: 1992, 2001

Discord: 2006

Discount Firearm: 2006 (2)

Disferrence: 2003

Dishwalla: 1996 (2), 1998, 2002

Disober: 2005 (3)

Dissilience: 2000

Disturbing the Peace: 1997-1998 (2), 1999 (5), 2000-2001 (3), 2002 (7)

Ditch Witch: 1992, 1994

Divine Comedy, The: 2002

Divine: 1992

DiVinyls: 1983

Dixie Dregs: 1978, 1979, 2000

Dixon House Band: 1979

Dixon, Don: 1988

DJ Agile: 2000

DJ Alejan: 1998 (4)

DJ Destruction: 1992

DJ Digital: 2001

DJ Field Marshall: 2000

DJ Genaside: 1999

DJ Lily: 2001

DJ Logic: 1999, 2001

DJ Papa Ray: 2003

DJ Red Boy: 2002

DJ Skeletal: 2001

DJ Tim: 1998

DJ Track Star: 2005

DJ? Acucrack: 1998

DJ-Spin: 2001

DMC Band, The: 2000

Doc Powell: 1997

Doc Terry and the Pirates: 1991

Doder, Keith: 1995

Dog and Everything, The: 2002 (2), 2003, 2005 (2), 2006 (2)

Dog, The: 2004

Dog's Eye View: 1996 (2)

Dogfight: 1998 (3)

Dogtown Allstars: 2005, 2006

Dokken, Don: 1990

Dokken: 1984, 1995, 1997

Domani: 2005

Domino: 1976, 1977 (27), 1978, 1979 (17), 1980

Don Wasserman's Space Island: 2000

Don't Tell Ginger: 1995

Donna the Buffalo: 2003

Donovan: 1985, 1989

Doo Rag: 1997

Dope: 1999

Dorff, Andrew: 1997

Dorian Gray: 1995, 1996

Doro: 1990

Double Trouble: 2001

Douche Powder Factory: 2006

Doughty, Mike: 2002, 2004 (2)

Dovetail Joint: 1999

Dowell, Michael: 1995

Down to the Bone: 2002

Downflow: 2000

Downing, Will: 1991 (2), 1993, 1996-1998

Downstate: 2005

Downtown Quartet, The: 2000

Downtown Trio: 1991

Dozmary Pool: 2001, 2003 (2)

Dr. Dog: 2006

Dr. John: 1978

Dr. Zhivegas: 1996 (4), 1997 (11), 1998 (8), 1999 (2)

Drain STH: 1998

Dramarama: 1992

Drams, The: 2006

Drawpointe: 2000-2001 (2), 2002, 2003 (3), 2005

Dread Finks: 1986

Dread Zeppelin: 1991

Dread, Mikey: 1989

Dream Syndicate: 1986

Dream Theater: 1993, 2000

Dredg: 2001-2003

Dresden Dolls, The: 2004

Drew Emmitt Band: 2005 (2)

Drift: 1999

Drive-by Truckers: 2004-2006

Drivin' N Cryin: 1989, 1991 (2), 1993

Droge, Pete: 1998

Droners, The: 1994

Dropkick Murphys: 2001 (2), 2003, 2006

Dropping Daylight: 2005

Drown: 1994

Drums and Tuba: 2000

Drums of Fire: 1979

Drunks with Guns: 1985

Duarte, Chris: 1995, 1996, 1997 (2)

Dub Dis: 1998 (2), 1999

Dub Mystic: 1996

Dub Narcotic Sound System: 2002

Duckhills, The: 1992

Duke 45: 2001

Duke Tumatoe and the All Star Frogs: 1978 (3), 1979

Duke Tumatoe and the Power Trio: 1987

Duke, George: 1990, 1991, 1995

Duke, Mike: 1989

Dump Truck: 1987

Dunlap, Bob "Slim": 1997

Duya Duya: 1989 (2), 1990, 1991

Dyer Maker: 1989

Dynamite Boy: 2004 (2)

Dynatones: 1985

Dywer: 2005

E

E.J. Quit: 1991, 1992

Eagan, Walter: 1979

Eagle-Eye Cherry: 2001

Eagles of Death Metal: 2006

Earl Brothers, The: 1999 (2)

Earl Scruggs Revue: 1979

Earl, Ronnie: 1988

Earl: 2001, 2002, 2003 (2)

Earle, Steve: 1986, 1998, 1999

Early November, The: 2006

Earthworms: 2006

East Ash: 1991

East of Eden: 1989

Eastern Youth: 2003

Easton, Tim: 2002

Echo & the Bunnymen: 1992

Eclectic Fusion: 2006 (3)

Eclectic Midnight Grueve: 2002

Eddie & the Tide: 1985

Eddie, John: 2004

Eden Street: 1998 (2)

Edge: 1979

Edmonds, Dave: 1982, 1994

Edwards, Dennis: 1994

Eek: 1989-1991, 2005 (2)

Eels: 2003

Effic: 1982

Egypt: 1996 (2)

Eighteen Visions: 2004

Eighth Day, The: 1986

Einstein, Elizabeth: 1995, 1996 (2), 1997, 1998

Eisley: 2006

Ekoostick Hookah: 1995, 1996 (2), 2000 (3), 2001 (2)

El Caribe Tropical: 1992 (3), 1991

El Dopa: 1999

El Monstero y Los Masked Avengers: 1999

El Rayo-X: 1986 (2), 1988

Elán: 1986

Elastica: 1995

Elbow: 2002

Eleanor: 1995

Electrafixion: 1995

Electric Amish: 1996

Electric Sandbox: 1986

Electric Sun: 1985

Electric, The: 2003 (2)

Elefant: 2006 (2)

Eleventh Day: 1996

Eleventh Dream Day: 1991, 1993

ELI-STONE: 1998 (2), 1999 (3), 2000 (5), 2001-2002 (2)

Ellen James Society: 1991

Elliot, Richard: 1991, 1994

Elvis Brothers, The: 1982, 1983, 1984 (3), 1986 (6), 1985 (6), 1987 (3), 1993 (2), 1994

Elvis Himselvis: 1997

Ely, Joe: 1998

Emily & Ali: 2006

Eminem: 1999

Emmet Swimming: 1998 (2)

Emmett, Rik: 1991

End, The: 1987 (2), 1988, 1989 (2)

Energy Orchard: 1990

Engel, Billy: 1990

Engine Down: 2002

English Beat, The: 1982, 2002

Enormous Richard: 1990, 1991 (3), 1992, 1993

Enuff Z'Nuff: 1989

Envision: A Tribute to Yes: 2001

Epithet: 2005

Epoxies, The: 2005

Eric Gales Band, The: 1991

Eric Martin Band: 1987

Erma Whiteside and Blues Deluxe: 1994

e-Rockers: 2006

Escape Club, The: 1989

Escape: 2006

Escovedo, Alejandro: 1999

Esquires: 1986

Essence of Logic: 2003 (2), 2005, 2006 (2)

Essentials, The: 1985, 1986

Eternal Daze: 1984

Ether Project: 2005

Etheridge, Melissa: 1988, 1989

Ethiopian, The: 1987, 1990

Ethyl Meatplow: 1993

Eurogliders: 1985

Evans, Marsha: 1994, 1997

Evans, Scott: 1979

Eve 6: 1999

Eve's Plum: 1994, 1995

Everclear: 1997 (2)

Every Mother's Nightmare: 1990, 1993

Everything and Holden: 2004

Everything but the Girl: 1996

Everything: 1998

Evidence: 1990

Evinrudes: 1995

Excell: 1986

Exciter: 1984

Exies: 2005

Exit 159: 1999 (2)

Exit 161: 2001 (2)

Exit, The: 2004 (2)

Exo: 2002

Exodus: 1987, 1989, 1990

Exodust: 1984 (2)

Experience, The: 1996

Exploited: 1988

Explosion, The: 2001, 2003

Expressions, The: 2006

Extreme: 1990, 1995

Eyes Catch Fire: 2005

Eyes, The / Pale Divine: 1987, 1988 (2), 1989 (8), 1990 (14), 1991 (4), 1992 (9), 1993 (7), 1994

F

Fab, Scott: 1997

Fabulous Thunderbirds, The: 1979, 1985, 1989-1991

Face to Face: 1995 (2), 2000, 2002

Faceplant: 2002

Fad, The: 1986 (5), 1987 (10), 1988 (4)

Fafoglia, Tony: 1990 (2)

Failing English: 2002

Failsafe: 2002

Failure: 1996

Fairchild: 1979, 1988, 1990, 1992, 1993 (2)

Fairport Convention: 1989

Fairwell: 2006 (4)

Faith Band, The: 1977, 1979

Faith No More: 1987 (2), 1990, 1997

Falcon Eddy: 1985

Falcon, Billy: 1979

Fall Out Boy: 2004 (2)

Fallen on Deaf Ears: 2005, 2006

Fambooey: 1994

Famed, The: 2005 (3)

Fantasy: 1982, 1984, 1985 (2)

Fante, Ricky: 2004

Fantomas: 1999

Far Cry: 1991

Far: 1996

Farewell, Joan Bouise: 1986

Farm, The: 1994

Farmer: 1996

Farrar, Jay: 2002, 2004 (2)

Farwell: 2006

Fashion: 1987

Fast Break: 1979 (8)

Fastball: 1997, 1998

Faster Pussycat: 1989, 1992

Fat Cactus: 1999 (2)

Fat Trash: 1998

Fatkid Dodgeball: 2005

Fattback: 2006

Faustus: 1979 (4), 1980 (3), 1982, 1983 (13), 1984 (11), 1985 (6), 1994

Faze 3: 2002

Fear Before the March of Flames: 2006

Fear Factory: 1996

Feather: 2004

Feds, The: 1999, 2005, 2006

Feed the Flame: 2006 (2)

Feeding the Masses: 2005 (2), 2006

Feel: 2003

Fela Anikulapo Kuti: 1990

Felons, The: 1981 (2), 1983 (4)

Femme Fatality: 2005

Fenix TX: 2006

Ferguson, Maynard: 1985, 1986

Fern: 1998, 2000

Fernest Arceneaux and the Thunders: 1988, 1989

Ferrari: 1982, 1983 (38), 1984 (49)

Ferrell, Rachelle: 1995, 1998

Few and Far Between: 2002 (2), 2003 (2), 2004

Fiction Plane: 2003 (2)

Field of Grey: 2004, 2005

Fields, Lee: 1994

Fields, Marshall: 1987

Fiery Furnaces, The: 2006

Fifth Element, The: 2001 (2), 2002 (4)

Fifty-50: 2001

Figdish: 1995, 1997

Figgs, The: 1993

Fight Paris: 2005

Fight: 1994, 1995

Fighting Amish, The: 1998

Filet of Funk: 1988 (3)

Final Cut: 1992

Final Drive: 2004 (2)

Finch: 2003

Finger 11: 1998

Finger Paint Diary: 1998, 1999 (3), 2000

Finn Brothers: 1989 (6), 1990 (5)

Finns, The: 1990, 1991 (8), 1992 (4), 1993-1994 (3), 1995 (2)

Fire Theft, The: 2003

Firefall: 1983

Firehose: 1986, 1992

Firehouse: 1991

Firewater: 1998

First Aid: 1983 (2), 1984 (2)

First Light: 2004 (2)

Fishbone: 1986 (2), 1987, 1988, (2), 1989, 1994 (2)

Fishman, John: 2002

Five Block Shot: 2000

Five Block Street: 2001

Five Deadly Venoms, The: 1999 (2)

Five Feeler: 2000, 2002 (2)

Five for Fighting: 2002

Five of These: 1994, 1995 (2)

Five Point 0: 2000

Fixx, The: 1989, 1991, 2000

Flaming Lips, The: 1987, 1992 (2)

Flashlight Brown: 2006

Flat Duo Jets: 1998

Flee the Scene: 2005 (2)

Flesh for LuLu: 1989

Flick: 1997

Flickerstick: 2001, 2002

Flight 16: 1998

Flight of Mavis: 1991

Flinch: 2001, 2002 (2)

Flipoffs, The: 1997

Floating City, The: 2003 (3), 2004 (2), 2005

Floating Men: 1993

Flogging Molly: 2002

Flotsam and Jetsam: 1990, 1993, 1999

Flower: 1993

Flowerhead: 1993

Fluffers, The: 2005

Fluid Drive: 1987, 1990

Fly Everywhere: 1998, 1999

Flying Burrito Brothers, The: 1978, 1979

Flying Saucers: 1992

Flynova: 2001, 2002 (6), 2003

Focus North: 2003

Foghat: 1984, 1994

Folds, Ben: 2002

Follow, The: 1992, 2005 (3)

Fontenot, Allen: 1988

Foo Fighters: 1995

Food for Feet: 1990

Fools Face: 1983 (7), 1984 (5)

Footloose: 1981

For Sale: 2001

Forbert, Steve: 1979, 1982, 1987

Forbidden Young: 1990 (2)

Forbidden: 1989, 1990

Ford, Lita: 1988

Foreigner: 1991

Forest Green, The: 2005 (3)

Forgotten, The: 2002

Form Follows Failure: 2004

Format, The: 2006

Fortune, Sonny: 1979

Fortunetellers: 1987, 1988

Fossil: 1995

Foster, Jen: 2004

Foundation: 1989

Fountainhead, The: 1986

Four Horsemen, The: 1990, 1992

Foxx, Jamie: 1992

Fragile Porcelain Mice: 1992, 1993 (4), 1994 (7), 1995 (9), 1996-1997 (8), 1998 (5), 1999 (4), 2000

Frail Division, The: 2006

Frames, The: 1986, 2005

Framing Amy: 1999

Frampton, Peter: 1992

Frank Marino's Mahogany Rush: 1983

Frankie (aka Kingofthehill): 1986

Franks, Michael: 1979

Frans, The: 1996

Franti, Michael: 2002, 2004

Frayl: 2003, 2004 (3)

Freakwater: 1996

Freddy and the Dreamers: 1986

Freddy Freedom: 1987

Freddy Jones Band: 1992, 1993, 1995 (2), 1996-1999

Free Dirt: 1997, 1999

Free Radicals, The: 1999

Freeway: 1995

Freewheelers, The: 1992

Freeze the Hopper: 1996 (2), 1997

Frente: 1994, 1996

Fresh City: 1997

Fresh Water: 1978

Friendz: 1999

Friz: 2003

Frogpond: 1995, 1996

From Autumn to Ashes: 2002, 2003

From First to Last: 2005

From This Moment On (F.T.M.O): 1978, 1979

Front 242: 1991, 1993

Front Street: 1979 (7)

Front, The: 1989

Frosted: 1996

Frozen Food Section: 2005

Fu Manchu: 1996

Fudge Tunnel: 1993

Fuel: 1998, 1999 (2), 2000

Fugazi: 1991, 1993 (2), 1995

Full Day Affair: 2006 (2)

Full Fledged Ledge: 1995

Full Moon Consort: 1976, 1977 (5), 1978

Full On Venus: 1997 (3), 1998 (7) 1999

Full System Purge: 2001

Fun & Anguish: 1983 (2), 1984 (2), 1986

Fun Lovin' Criminals: 1996

Fundamental Elements: 2006 (2)

Fundamentals: 2005

Funhouse: 1991 (2)

Funkabilly: 1995

Funktion: 1977

Furtado, Nelly: 2001

Further Seems Forever: 2003

Fury: 1979

Fuse 12: 1998, 1999

Fuse: 2003

Fuzzy: 1993

FWTO: 1979

G

G. Love & Special Sauce: 1994 (2), 1996, 1997, 2000, 2005

Gaal, Linda: 2000 (3), 2001

Gadd, Steve: 2005

Gadjits, The: 1998

Gaines, Jeffery: 1994

Galactic Cowboys: 1996, 1998

Galactic: 1999, 2000 (2), 2002, 2004, 2005 (2)

Galactica: 1996

Galaxia: 1997, 1998

Galaxy Rock Meets William: 2000 (2)

Galaxy: 1987

Gale, Arlyn: 1978

Gales, Eric: 1993

Gallagher, Rory: 1978, 1979, 1985

Gametime: 2003

Gap Band, The: 1994 (2), 1996

Garage a Trois: 2003

Garage Girls a Go-Go: 2006

Garaj Mahal: 2004

Gargoyle Reign: 1994 (7), 1995 (4), 1997, 1998

Gas Huffer: 1994

Gathering, The: 2001

Gatsbys American Dream: 2005, 2006

Gaza Strippers: 2002

Gear Daddies: 1990

Geishamen: 1997 (6), 1998

Genaside 2: 2000

Gene Loves Jezebel: 1986, 1987, 1993

Generica: 1996

Gentleman Callers: 2003

George Clinton and the P-Funk All Stars featuring Parliament and Funkadelic: 1993

George Faber And Stronghold: 1978

George Thorogood and the Destroyers: 1979, 1991 (2), 1993-1994 (2), 1998

George, Sophia: 1990

George: 1978

Georgia Satellites: 1987

Get Smart!: 1985 (2)

Get Up Kids, The: 2003

Getaway Car: 2000

Getaway Cruiser: 1997

Ghetto Prenup: 2004

Ghost in Light: 2006

Ghost of an American Airman: 1993

Ghoul 5: 1997 (2), 1998

Giant People: 2001

Gibb Droll Band: 2005

Gigolo Aunts: 1994, 1999

Gilder, Nick: 1978

Gilmore, Jimmie Dale: 1992, 1993

Ginger Bay: 1997

Girl Next Door: 1985

Girl Talk: 1984-1985 (4)

Girls in Diners: 2006 (2)

Give Her a Lizard: 1993

Gizmo: 1983

Gizzae: 1999

Gladiators, The: 1983, 1984 (2), 1985, 1987

Glassjaw: 2002, 2003

Glory for Champions: 2000

Go Dog Go: 1991

Go Kart: 1995

Go, The: 2004

Gob: 2001

God Lives Underwater: 1995

God Street Wine: 1996 (2)

Godfathers, The: 1989

Godflesh: 1991

godheadSilo: 1995

Godspeed You! Black Emperor: 1994, 2003

Go-Go's, The: 1981

Gold Money: 1992

Golden Rockets: 1988

Golden Smog: 1996

Goldfinger: 1996, 2000

Gomez: 2006

Gone: 1986

Goo Goo Dolls: 1995 (2), 1996

Good Charlotte: 2002

Good Feelin': 1994

Good Night Ghost: 2003

Goodman, Jerry: 1986

Gordo: 2006

Gordon, Mike: 2002, 2005

Gordon, Robert: 1979

Gov't Mule: 1995, 1999, 2000, 2002, 2003

Government Cheese: 1987 (2)

Grabbers, The: 1995

Graduation, The: 2003

Grand Alliance: 1983 (2)

Grand Street Cryers: 1997, 1998

Granny's Bathwater: 1976, 1977

Grant, Fred: 1992

Grass Roots: 1982, 1984

Gratitude: 2005

Gravel Bone: 2001

Gravity Kills: 1996 (2), 1998, 2000

Gray, David: 1993

Gray, Macy: 2003

Grays, The: 1994

Great American Band: 1986

Great Big Everything: 1995 (6)

Great Harps of St. Louis: 1986

Great White: 1987, 1993, 1994, 1996

Green Day: 1994

Greenberry Woods: 1994

Greenhouse Effect, The: 2005

Greenwheel: 2001 (4), 2002, 2003 (2), 2005, 2006 (5), 2007

Greta: 1993

Griffin, Larry: 1993

Griffin: 1978 (4), 1979 (6), 1982

Griffith, Patty: 1999

Griffiths, Yabba: 1982

Grifters: 1993

Grill, Rob: 1982

Grim Reaper: 1984

Grinderswitch: 1978, 1979 (2)

Grip: 2003 (2)

Grisman, David: 1986, 1999

Grither: 1995

Grocery Sax: 1995

Grooveaholics, The: 2004

Groupers, The: 1993, 1994

Groupies, The: 1993

Gruntruck: 1992

Guadalcanal Diary: 1986, 1987, 1989

Guerry, Catherine Sarah: 1988

Guess Who, The: 1984

Gufs, The: 1996

Guided by Voices: 1999, 2001, 2003, 2004

Guild, The: 1994

Guitar Wolf: 1997

Gulliver: 1979, 1980

Gumball: 1993

Gun Club, The: 1982

Gunderson: 2004, 2005 (2)

Guster: 1998-2000

Guttermouth: 1995, 1997

Guy, Buddy: 1986

Guy, Vernon: 1997

Gwar: 1992, 1994 (2), 1995, 1996, 1997 (2), 1999

Gwen Mars: 1995

Gypsy: 1999 (2)

H

H.R.: 1990

H2O: 1997 (2), 2001, 2002

Hackensaw Boys, The: 2006

Hagfish: 1995 (2)

Haggard, Merle: 2000

Hairy Apes BMX: 1999, 2000

Half Pint: 2000

Halfway to Gone: 2002

Hall, James: 1996

Hall, Tom: 1986, 1990, 1992, 1993, 2006

Hallow: 2001

Hamell on Trial: 1997

Hamm, Stuart: 1991

Hammer, Jan: 1977, 1979

Hammond, John: 1986

Hancock, Herbie: 1979, 1995

Handsome: 1997 (2)

Hank: 1996

Hanover: 1986

Happy Endings: 2002-2006

Happy Jacket: 2005

Hard Knox: 1988

Hard-Fi: 2005

Harding, John Wesley: 1990, 1992, 1993

Harford, John: 1983

Harlot: 2006 (2)

Harp Attack: 1986, 1991-1993

Harp, Everette: 1996

Harper, Ben: 2000

Harris, Corey: 2000

Harris, Emmylou: 1997

Harrison, Jerry: 1988

Hart, Keith: 1992

Hart, Robbie: 2005

Hartford, John: 1981, 1982

Harvest: 2001

Harvey Danger: 1998, 2000

Harvey Mandell And the Mandell Machine: 1978

Harvey, Billy: 2002

Harvey: 2004, 2006 (2)

Haste: 1999

Hatch, The: 2005 (2), 2006

Hate Trip: 1992

Hatebreed: 1999

Hatfield, Juliana: 1992, 1993, 1995

Hathaway, Lalah: 1994, 1995

Hatton, Susie: 1991

Haunted, The: 1999

Havens, Richie: 1980

Hawthorne Heights: 2004

Haxton, Tom: 1983

Hazard to Ya Booty: 2004

Hazel Would: 2005

Hazy Malaise: 2003

He Said She Said: 1988

Head Candy: 1991

Head Swim: 1998

Heads Above Water: 1991 (24), 1992 (2)

Headtrip Window: 1995, 1996

Health and Happiness Show: 1996

Heart Like a Rabbit: 1987 (3)

Heartless Bastards: 2005

Heartsfield: 1977, 1978, 1999

Heaters, The: 1990, 1991 (2)

Heathers, The: 1992

Heaven's Flame:
1985 (2)

Heavy Rescue Band:
2006

Hed PE: 1998 (2), 1999,
2000

Heebie Jeebies:
1991 (2), 1992

Helena Handbasket:
1996 (3)

Helium Brothers: 1978

Helix: 1984, 1987

Hell in the Canyon:
2003-2005

Hello Dave: 1996

Hellogoodbye: 2006 (2)

Helmet: 1993, 1994,
1996, 1997

Helping Phriendly
Band, The: 2004

Helton, Darren: 1995

Helvetia: 2005 (3),
2006

Henderson, Bugs: 1978,
1979 (3),1986 (2),
1987, 1988

Henderson, Vondell:
1997, 1998 (2)

Henneman, B.: 1990

Henry Rollins Band,
The: 1987

Hensley, Ken: 1985 (2)

Henson, Doris: 2005

Hepcat: 1996, 1998

Her Majesty: 1992

Herb & Doris: 1991

Hero: 1983

Heroes: 1986

Heroic Doses: 1999

Hesher: 2001

Hewett, Howard: 1988,
1990

Hexum Brothers, The:
2004

Hexum, Zack: 2005

Hey Mercedes: 2001

Heymons, Richard X.:
1991

Heyward, Nick: 1994

Hiatt, Chris: 2003

Hiatt, John: 1994,
1996, 1997

Hibernauts, The:
2006 (2)

Hickman, Sara: 1989

Hidden in Plain View:
2005 (2)

Hi-Fi and the
Roadburners: 1991

Higgins, Billy: 1993

Highway 9: 2002

Highway Matrons: 1995,
1997, 1998, 2000,
2003 (2)

Highwaymen: 1990

Hill, Albert: 1996

Hill, Warren: 1993

Hillman, Chris: 1978

Himmelman, Peter:
1988, 1993, 1994

Hindsight: 1999

Hinojosa, Tish: 1989

Hi-Power: 1989

Hippie Crack Gas Tank:
1995, 1997

Hipsterphonic: 2005,
2006 (3)

Hiroshima: 1988

Hi-standard: 1998

Hit the Lights:
2006 (2)

Hitchcock, Robyn: 1990

Hobson, Ayanna: 2003

Hodder, Kane: 2005

Hogan, Kelly: 1992

Hoge, Josh: 2006 (2)

Hoge, Will: 2002, 2003

Ho-Hum: 1995

Holdsworth, Allan:
1984, 1986-1988

Hole: 1994

Holland: 1985

Hollow: 2002

Hollyfaith: 1993

Holmes, Carl: 1997

Holsapple, Peter: 1991

Homegrown Harvest
Band: 1980 (2)

Homegrown: 2002, 2003

Homestead Grays:
1990 (6)

Hometown Band: 1989

Homewreckers: 2000

Honorary Title, The:
2005

Honors English: 2005

Hoobastank: 2006

Hoodoo Gurus: 1987,
1989, 1991

Hooker, John Lee:
1978, 1979, 1986-1989

Hoosier Buddy:
1995,1996

Hooverphonic: 1998,
2000

Horns in the House:
1996

Hornsby, Bruce: 1996,
1999

HorrorPops: 2006

Hospital Life, The:
2005, 2006 (2)

Hot Club Canary: 1994

Hot Club of Cowtown:
2000

Hot House Sessions:
2003, 2004

Hot Rod Circuit: 2002

Hot Tuna: 1999

Hot Water Music: 2003

Hotel Faux Pas: 1995

Hotel: 1978

House of Assembly:
1989

House of Freaks:
1988 (2), 1989,
1991, 2005

House of Large Sizes:
1994, 1996

House of Love, The:
1992

Hovercraft: 1995

Howard, George: 1987,
1988, 1993,

1994, 1996, 1997

Howard, Miki: 1993

Howell, Miller: 2006

Hubbard, Freddie: 1979

Hudson and the Hoo
Doo Cats: 1998

Huey Lewis & The News:
1982, 1989 (played as
"Sports Section")

Huffamoose: 1997

Hum: 1995, 1997, 1998

Human Radio: 1991

Human Sexual
Response: 1982

Humble Pie: 1983

Hunt, Kelly: 2004

Hunter and Ronson:
1989

Hunter, Charlie: 1999

Hunter, Robert: 1979,
1980, 1984

Hurrah: 1987

Husbands, The: 1985

Hüsker Dü: 1985 (2),
1986, 1987

I

Ian Moore and Moment's
Notice: 1991, 1993

Ian Moore Band: 1995

Ian, Janis: 1993, 1997

Icon: 1989

Idle Wild: 2001

Ignition: 1987

Iguanas, The: 1999,
2000

Ikettes, The: 1991

Illett: 2002 (2)

Ima Robot: 2004 (2)

Image, The: 1986

Immaculate Machine:
2005

Imperial Blues Band:
1995

Imperial Teen: 1996

John, Andrew: 1994

Johnny Action Figure: 2000 (2)

Johnny Magnet: 1997, 1998, 1999

Johnny Quest: 1988, 1989

Johnny Reno and the Sax Maniacs: 1986, 1988

Johnny Socko: 1993

Johnson, Behan: 1997

Johnson, Brandy: 2000

Johnson, Drew: 1998, 1999 (3), 2001

Johnson, Eric: 1986, 1990 (3), 1997, 2005

Johnson, Freddy: 1993, 1994 (2)

Johnson, Jack: 2002

Johnson, Jaw Jaw: 1993

Johnson, Johnnie and the Magnificent Four: 1991

Johnson, Johnnie Band, The: 2005

Johnson, Johnnie: 1989, 1991 (2), 1993, 1999, 2000

Johnson, Luther: 1985

Johnson, Mike: 2005 (2)

Johnson, Robert: 1979

Johnson, Stacy: 1995

Johnson, Will: 2005

Johnson, Willie: 1994

Johnson, Wilma: 1997

Johnsons, The: 1986

Johnston, Freedy: 1997, 1999

Joint Jumpers, The: 1986, 1988

Joker: 1983

Jon Do: 1989, 1990

Jon Spencer Blues Explosion, The: 1997 (2), 2000, 2002

Jones, Joan: 1998

Jones, Marti: 1986

Jones, Oran "Juice": 1986

Jones, Steve: 1989

Jordan, Marc: 1978

Jordan, Montell: 1996

Jordan, Ronny: 1994

Jordan, Sass: 1992

Jordan, Stanley: 1994

Jovial Rouge: 2002

Joykiller, The: 1995

Jubilla: 2002

Jude: 1999

Judge Nothing: 1990-1993, 1994 (2), 1995

Judy Beats: 1994

Judybats, The: 1993

Juliana Theory: 2002, 2003 (2)

Juliette and the Licks: 2004

Jump, Little Children: 1999

Junction, The: 1993

June: 2006 (2)

Jungle Dogs, The: 1991 (7), 1992 (3), 1994, 1997, 1998

Junior Brown: 1999 (2)

Junior Varsity, The: 2005, 2006

Junkyard: 1989

Jupiter Jazz: 2005, 2006

Jupiter Sunrise: 2005

Just Add Water: 2001-2003 (6), 2004 (3)

Justus: 1978

K

k.d. lang: 1987

K.T.M.A.: 2001, 2002

Kadison, Joshua: 1993

Kalabash: 1989

Kamikaze Cowboy: 1993

Kamoze, Ini: 1988

Kansas: 1991

Kappus, Mike: 1979

Kaptain Jack featuring Ingrid Berry: 1977

Karl Denson's Tiny Universe: 2001 (2), 2002, 2003, 2004 (2)

Karlzen, Mary: 1995 (2)

Kârp: 1994

Katakis, Michael: 1977

Kaution: 1986

Kearney, Mat: 2006

Keating: 2006

Keely-Kimbrough Project: 1994, 1995

Keene, Tommy: 1986, 1992

Kelley, Josh: 2003 (2), 2004, 2005

Kelly, Sean: 1995, 2003

Ken Kase Group, The: 1996, 1997 (2), 1998, 2001

Kennedy, Bap: 1998

Kennett, Jimmy Lee: 1995 (2)

Kenny Brown Band: 2003

Kenny G: 1986

Kenny Shade and the Urge: 1987

Kershaw, Doug: 1977

Kevin McDermott Orchestra: 1989

Khaleel: 1999

Khan, Chaka: 1993

Kid 606: 1999

Kid Rock: 1999 (2)

Kid Tested Mother Approved: 2002 (2)

Kill Devil Blues: 1991

Kill Hannah: 1996, 2001 (2), 2002, 2003 (2), 2004

Killer Bees: 1984, 1985, 1988

Killer Dwarfs: 1987

Killers, The: 2004

Killing Floor: 1993

Killjoy 4 Fun: 2000 (2)

Kimball, Cheyenne: 2006

Kimbrough, Will: 2006

Kimock, Steve Band: 2005 (2)

Kimock, Steve: 2001

Kind, The: 1992

Kinetics, The: 1998

King Apparatus: 1993

King Diamond: 1987, 1998

King Missile: 1991

King Soloman's Grave: 2003

King Sonic: 1989

King, Albert: 1986 (2)

King, Jennifer: 1993

King, Joe: 1986

King, Kaki: 2005

King's X: 1991, 1992, 1994, 1996, 1998, 2000, 2001, 2002

Kingfish: 1978

Kingofthehill: 1991, 1992, 1994

Kings of Leon: 2005

Kirby, Scott: 1998

Kitsch: 1998

Klein, Jeff: 2006

KMFDM: 1990, 2003

Knitters: 2005

Know Boundaries: 2003

Koch, Geoff: 2006 (2)

Koch, Jeff: 2005

Koester: 2000

Kool Ray and the Polaroidz: 1986

Korn: 1996

Korova: 2002

Kottke, Leo: 2002, 2005

Kottonmouth Kings: 2000, 2002

Loeb, Lisa: 1995

Lo-fidelity Allstars: 1999

Logic, The: 2002 (2)

Logos: 2005, 2006 (3), 2003 (5), 2004 (2), 2005, 2006 (2)

Lokie: 2003

Lola and the Mouse: 2006

London Calling: 1986, 1987 (2), 1988, 1992 (9), 1993 (2)

London Quireboys: 1990

Long Beach Dub Allstars: 2000

Long Ryders, The: 1986, 1987

Longing for Providence: 2005, 2006 (3)

LoqueLa: 2004

Lorber, Jeff: 1984, 1987, 1993

Lord Baltimore: 2003

Lord of Word and the Disciples of Bass: 1995

Lords of Acid: 1995, 1997, 2000, 2002

Lords of the New Church: 1982, 1983, 1986, 1987

Los Lobos: 1992, 1996, 2000

Loser's Luck: 2003 (3), 2004-2006

Lost City Angels: 2004

Lost Parade: 2004 (2), 2005, 2006

Lost Prophets: 2004

Lost, The: 1991, 1992

Loud Lucy: 1995 (2)

Loudermilk: 2002

Loudmouth Angel: 2004

Love & Money: 1989, 1990

Love Brothers Band: 2006

Love Craft: 1978

Love Experts, The: 1989 (2)

Love Hogs, The: 1996 (2)

Love In Reverse: 1997

Love Scene, The: 2001

Love Spit Love: 1994, 1995, 1997

Love Tractor: 1985, 1986

Love, Clayton: 1997

Love/Hate: 1990

Loved Ones, The: 2006

Lovedrug: 2005

Low Pop Suicide: 1993

Lowercase: 2004, 2005 (5), 2006

LP Outsiders: 2001 (2)

Luce: 2002, 2003 (2)

Lucien, John: 1993

Lucky Boys Confusion: 2001-2002 (2), 2004, 2005 (3), 2006 (2)

Lucky Dube: 1989, 1990, 1997

Ludo: 2004 (5), 2005 (3)

Luna Halo: 1999

Luna Negra: 1995

Lunatic Calm: 1997, 1998

Lungbrush: 1999

Lungfish: 1994

Lunker Buzz: 1998

Lupins, The: 1994, 1995

Lush: 1994, 1996

Luther and Cody: 2003

Lynch Mob: 1991, 1992

Lynch, Stephen: 2003

M

M.I.A.: 1984

Mabarck, George: 1979

MacColl, Kirsty: 1993, 1995

Maceo Parker and Roots Revisited: 1991

MacGowan, Shane: 1995

MacGregor, Freddie: 1981

Machine Gun Kelly: 1993, 1995 (2)

Machines of Loving Grace: 1993

Mack, Jimmie: 1978

Mack, Lonnie: 1985, 1986

Mack's Creek: 1978

Macon, Q.T.: 1993

Madahoochie: 2000, 2002, 2005 (2), 2006

Madcap: 2002

Madder Rose: 1993, 1994

Mae: 2003 (3), 2005, 2006

Mafro: 2002

Magic Rockers, The: 1985

Magnolias: 1991

Magpies: 1994

Mahal, Taj: 1978, 1980

Mahal. Taj and the Phantom Blues Band: 2002

Mahlathini and the Mahotella Queens: 1991

Mahoney, Tim: 1998

Maids of Gravity: 1995

Mailman Bites Dog: 2005 (2), 2006

Majestics, The: 1982, 1984

Majesty Crush: 1994

Maker: 1985

Malcolm Bliss: 1995

Malevolent Creation: 1991

Malibu: 1986

Malkmus, Stephen: 2001

Malone, Michelle: 1993, 1994

Mama Rogers: 2006 (3)

Mama's Pride: 1977, 1978, 1979 (5), 1980 (2), 1983 (3), 1991, 1992 (3), 1993, 1994

Man Down: 2002

Man or Astro-man?: 1997

Man, The: 2006

Manana: 1977

Manchester Orchestra: 2006

Manhole: 1996

Mann, Aimee: 1993

Manowar: 1989

Manta Ray: 1986

Marah: 2000

March Hare: 1982

March, Steve: 1977

Marcy Playground: 1998, 1999

Marie, Teena: 1994 (2)

Marienthal, Eric: 1993, 1995

Marienthal Quartet, Eric: 1992

Marilee and the Boys: 1985 (2)

Marillion: 1992

Marilyn Manson: 1995 (2), 1996

Mark Tanner Band: 1979

Marks, Dave: 1992

Marley, Ziggy: 2003, 2004

Marquette Weekend, The: 2006 (6)

Mars Volta, The: 2003

Mars, Charlie: 2004

Marsalis, Brandford: 1995

Marsalis, Wynton: 1987 (2)

Martin, Marvin: 1992

Martin, Stephen: 1995

Martyr Ad: 2005

Marvin the Mandolin Man: 1992

Mary's Danish: 1989

Mas, Carolyne: 1979

Masekela, Hugh: 1993

Mason, Dave: 1982

Matchbook Romance: 2004, 2005 (2), 2006

Matches, The: 2005, 2006

Material Issue: 1991, 1992-1994 (2), 1995

Matisyahu: 2005

Matrix: 1979

Matt Pond PA: 2006 (2)

Matt's Dad's Basement: 2002, 2003 (2)

Max a Million: 1998

Maxd: 1986

Maxtone Four: 2004

Maxwell: 1996

Mayall, John: 1979 (3), 1986

Maybe Today: 2002-2004

Mayer, John: 2001 (2), 2002

Mayer, Peter Group: 1986 (3)

Mayer, Peter: 1985 (3), 1998

Mayfield Four, The: 1998, 1999

Mayfield, Curtis: 1986

Mayor Dan: 1997

Mazzy Star: 1994

MC 900 Ft. Jesus: 1992

MC Honky: 2003

McBride, Christine: 1993

McBride, Joe: 1992, 1994

McCain, Edwin: 1996, 1998 (2)

McCaw, Scarlet: 1983 (3)

McClinton, Delbert: 1993, 1998 (2), 2000, 2001

McCombs, Cass: 2005

McCoy, George: 1988

McCray, Larry: 1994

McDermont, Michael: 1993 (2)

McDonough, Rich: 1995

McGhee, Brownie: 1979 (2)

McGuinn, Roger: 2000

McIntyre, Joey: 2002

McLean, Don: 1981

Me First: 1986, 1987 (4)

Mead, David: 2003

Meadows, Marion: 1995

Meat Loaf: 1977, 1989, 1990

Meat Puppets: 1987, 1989, 1992, 1994

Medeski, Martin, and Wood: 1996, 1999, 2000, 2003, 2004

Medeski, Scofield, Martin & Wood: 2006

Media Darlings, The: 2005

Media: 1985

Meditations, The: 1984, 1985, 1988, 1995, 1997

Medussa: 1986

Meg & Dia: 2006 (2)

Megalith: 1984, 1985, 1986, 1989

Mel Cooleys: 1991

Melee: 2005

Meliah Rage: 1989

Melody Groove and the Movement: 2006 (3)

Melvin Seals and JBG: 1997

Melvins, The: 1992, 1995-1997

Men Without Hats: 1988

Men, The: 1992

Mend: 2001

Mendoza, Javier Band: 2001, 2002 (2), 2003 (4), 2004, 2005

Mendoza, Javier: 2000, 2001, 2004 (2)

Menthol: 1996

Mephiskapheles: 1997

Mercy Rule: 1995

Mercy Seat, The: 1988

Mercyful Fate: 1984, 1993

Merl Saunders and his Funky Friends: 2002

Merl Saunders and the Rain Forest Band: 1992

Mesh: 1997-1999 (3), 2000

Mest: 2000 (3), 2002 (4), 2004 (2)

Metal Church: 1985, 1989

Methney, Pat: 1977, 1993

Metropolis: 1982, 1983 (3), 1984 (6)

Mexico 70: 1997

Mia Vendetta: 2005

Michael Been and the Call: 1994

Michael Schenker Group: 1984

Michael Stanley Band, The: 1979

Michael, Louis: 1993

Mid August Night: 2006

Middle Rhythm Section: 2005

Midlife: 1995

Midnight Menthol: 1995

Midnight Oil: 1988, 2002

Midnite: 2002

Midtown: 2004

Midwest Avengers: 1995, 1998, 2002 (2)

Midwood, Ramsay: 2002

Mighty Big Band, The: 1997

Mighty Blue Kings, The: 1998

Mighty Diamonds: 1990

Mighty Joe Young: 1997

Mighty Lemon Drops, The: 1988, 1990-1992

Mighty Mighty Bosstones, The: 1991, 1992, 1994, 1996, 1997 (2), 2000

Mighty Striker, The: 1984

Mighty Wes: 1992

Mike Roche and the Diesel Boys: 1995

Mike Stern Trio featuring Dave Weckl: 1996

Mike Stern Trio: 1995

Milano, Tam: 1993

Miles of Wire: 2006

Millenium: 1979

Miller, Frankie: 1982

Miller, Rhett: 2002

Millions, The: 1995

Mills, Chris: 2003

Milon, Celtie: 1997

Mims, The: 1996, 1997

Mind Funk: 1991

Mind Go Flip: 2001

Mind Over Four: 1990, 1993

Mind Over Soul: 1998, 1999 (3), 2001 (2)

Mindbenders: 1986

Minders, The: 2006

Mindflow: 1998 (2)

Mindrive: 2004

Minerdi, Phil: 1988

Ministry: 1988, 1990

Mink DeVille: 1984

Minott, Sugar: 1991

Minus the Bear: 2005

Minutemen: 1985 (2)

Minutes to Midnight: 2005 (4), 2006

Miracle Legion: 1992 (2)

Misery Signals: 2006

Misfits, The: 1996 (2)

Misses, The: 2006

Missile Silo Suite: 2002, 2003 (3), 2004

Mission Mountain Wood Band: 1978

Missionaries: 1993

Mississippi Flapjacks: 2006

Misstakes, The: 1983 (2), 1984

Mix Mob: 2002

MJ 923: 1997

MK-Ultra: 1999

Moaning Lisa: 1999

Mobius Trip, The: 1998

Moby: 1995, 1999

Modelo: 1986

Models: 1986

Modern Day Hero: 2003 (2), 2004

Modern Day Saints: 1985-1988 (2)

Modern Day Zero: 2005 (4)

Modern Lovers, The: 1987

Modern Red: 2006 (6)

Modes, The: 1997, 1998

Mods: 1986

Moe: 1998-1999 (2), 2000

Mofro: 2002, 2003

Mogan, Teddy: 2000

Moja Nya: 1987

Mojave: 1996

Mojo Nixon & Skid Roper: 1986

Mojo Nixon: 1985, 1989-1992

Mojo Stew: 1990 (2), 1991 (3)

Moke: 2001

Molly Hatchet: 1979

Molly McGuire: 1994, 1995

Molone, Tommy: 2001

Moneen: 2002

Money, Eddie: 1977, 1993

Mongol Beach Party: 1991

Monkey Beat: 1994

Monkeyspank: 1992

Mono Puffs: 1996

Monroes, The: 1989 (2)

Monster Magnet: 1995 (2), 1999, 2004

Monster Voodoo Machine: 1995

Montgomery, Kevin: 1994

Montgomery, Monte: 2000, 2001

Montrose, Ronnie: 1988

Moon Seven Times, The: 1994

Moonlight Drive (The Doors tribute): 1983

Moore, Abra: 1995-1997

Moore, Chante: 1993

Mopeds, The: 1981

Morales, Michael: 1989

Morbid Angel: 1993

Morcheeba: 1997

Morgan, Steve: 1992

Morgantown: 1985, 1986

Morgoth: 1991

Morissette, Alanis: 1995

Morning Vision: 2005, 2006 (3)

Morningstarr: 1977 (2)

Morpheate: 2004

Morphine: 1995-1997

Morre, Vinnie: 1999

Morrells, The: 1982, 1984 (2)

Morris Day and the Time: 1996, 1997 (2), 1998, 1999

Morris, Gary: 1984

Morse, Steve: 1991, 1992

Mose Jones: 1978

Moses, Pablo: 1997

Moss: 1995

Motels, The: 1982 (2)

Mother Hips, The: 1995

Motion City Soundtrack: 2005, 2006

Motion featuring Jimmy Frink, The: 1986

Mould, Bob: 1990, 1997, 1998

Movement, The: 2006

Movers, The: 2007

Movie Star Kiss: 2006

Movielife, The: 2003

Moving Targets: 1987

Mowatt, Judy: 1989, 1991

Mower: 2004

Moxy Früvous: 1994

Mr. Big: 1989-1992, 1994

Mr. I: 2001, 2002

Mr. T Experience: 1998

MU300: 1992 (2), 1993, 1994 (2), 1996

Mud Puppies: 1990

Mud Sharks, The: 1995

Muffs: 1995

Mule: 1977

Mullins, Shawn: 1999

Murder by Death: 2003

Murder City Players: 1984, 1986 (10),1987 (6), 1988 (5), 1989 (3), 1990, 1991 (4), 1992, 1993 (3), 1994 (2), 2000

Murkin, Lance: 1992

Murmurs, The: 1995

Murphey, Michael Martin: 1984

Murphy, Matt: 1985

Murphy, Michael: 1980

Murphy's Law: 1991, 1992

Muse: 2004

Musselwhite, Charlie: 1978, 1995

Mustangs, The: 1987-1989

Mutabaruka: 1983

Mute Math: 2005

MxPx: 1997, 1999

My 2 Planets: 2000 (2), 2001 (5)

My Bloody Valentine: 1992

My Blue Life: 1996 (2), 1997, 1998 (2)

My Chemical Romance: 2003

My Gun Never: 1997

My Life with the Thrill Kill Kult: 1991-1993, 1995-1999

My Little Dog China: 1995

My Little Funhouse: 1993

My Morning Jacket: 2004-2006

My Name: 1992

My Other Self: 1992, 1993

My Sister's Machine: 1992

My Two Planets: 1999 (5), 2002 (4), 2003

Myles, Alannah: 1990

Mystic Voyage: 1985, 1998 (2)

Mystics, The: 1990

N

N.C.P. (No Commercial Potential): 1978, 1979

Nadine: 1997, 2001, 2003 (2)

Naess, Leona: 2001

Najee: 1987, 1988, 1991, 1992, 1994, 1996, 1999

Naked Groove: 2002

Naked Prey: 1986

Nalick, Anna: 2005

Nancy & Sluggo: 1985 (2)

Nantucket: 1983

Napalm Death: 1991

Napps: 1997

Nashville Pussy: 2002

Nasty Savage: 1990

Nathanson, Matt: 2006

National Lampoon
   Players: 1978

Natty: 1993, 1994

Nazareth: 1987, 1988

Ndegeocello, Me'Shell:
   1996, 1999, 2002

Neal, Eugene: 1994

Nebula: 2002

Ned's Atomic Dustbin:
   1993, 1995 (2)

Negative 90: 1991

Negatives, The: 2001

Neighborhoods, The:
   1986

Nelson, Rick: 1982

Nelson, Willie:
   2002 (2)

NEOxGEO: 2002, 2004,
   2005 (3)

Neptune Crush:
   2000 (6), 2001 (5),
   2002 (4), 2003

Nerf Herder: 1996,
   2000

Nerve, The: 1995 (4),
   1996 (3), 1997

Nervous Wrecks: 1998

Neurosis: 1995, 1999

Neuter the Stupid:
   2000 (4), 2001 (7),
   2002

NEV, The: 2005

Neverbent: 2001,
   2002 (2)

Neverland Express,
   The: 1989

Neville Brothers, The:
   1986-1988, 1992, 2005

New Amsterdams, The:
   2006

New Empire: 2002,
   2003 (4)

New Era Band: 1982

New Golden Rocket,
   The: 1989 (2)

New Patrons Saints of
   Husbandry, The: 1995,
   1997

New Pornographers,
   The: 2005

New Potato Caboose,
   The: 1992

New Riddem, The: 1991

New Riders of the
   Purple Sage: 1978

New Wave Enthusiasts:
   1978

New World Spirits:
   1992 (2), 1993 (3),
   1995 (4), 1996 (7),
   1997 (4), 1998 (6),
   1999 (2)

New York Dolls: 2006

New York: 1985

Newfound Glory: 2000

Newsboys: 1986 (3),
   1987 (6), 1988 (4),
   1989 (3)

Newspeak: 1984 (2),
   1985 (2)

Next Best Thing: 2005

Nick Lowe: 1982

Nickel Creek: 2003

Nickels: 1978,
   1979 (3), 1981, 1984

Nields, The: 1998

Nighthawks, The: 1979,
   1996

NIL8: 1991, 1995 (2),
   1997, 1998 (2),
   1999 (2), 2002,
   2004 (2), 2005

Ninekiller: 1996 (2),
   1997

Ninetrigger: 1998 (2),
   1999 (2), 2002

Nirvana: 1991

Nite Life: 1978 (3),
   1979 (12)

Nixons, The: 1995 (2),
   1996, 1997

Niyah: 1993

No Doubt: 1992

No Knife: 1996

No Motive: 1999, 2004

No Pain: 1993

No Slack: 1979

Nocturnis: 1991

NOFX: 1998

Noise to Go: 1982

Non Thought: 2006

Non-Billables: 2006

None More Black:
   2003 (2)

Norma Jean: 2003, 2006

North Mississippi
   Allstars: 2001,
   2002 (2), 2003,
   2004 (3), 2005, 2006

Northern Pikes: 1987,
   1992

Nosey Partner: 2003

Not on File: 1984 (2),
   1986 (3)

Not Waving But
   Drowning: 1999, 2002

Nothing Dream: 1995

Nothing Still:
   2003 (2), 2004 (3),
   2005 (5), 2006 (8)

Nov. 9: 1992 (2), 1993

Nova: 1984

Novella: 2005-2007

Novo Combo: 1981, 1982

NRBQ: 1988, 1990

NSYNC: 1985

Nuclear Percussion
   Ensemble: 1991

Nukes, The: 1987, 1988,
   1990, 1991 (3)

Nutt-Stalk: 1997

NY Loose: 1996

O

O.A.R.: 2001

O.J. Ekemode and the
   Nigerian All-Stars:
   1991

O'Kelley, Kim: 1978

O'Neal, Alexander:
   1985, 1994, 1995

O'Ryan Island: 1992 (7)

Oak: 1995, 1998

Oakley Hall: 2006 (2)

Oblivious: 1993

Ocean Blue, The: 1990-
   1993

Ocean Colour Scene:
   1992

Ocean Six: 2002 (3)

Ocküms Razor: 2005

October Fall: 2006 (2)

October Fraction: 1984

Odd Fellow: 2001, 2002

Ode II Anything: 2002

of Montreal: 2006

Off Broadway: 1979

Oglesby, Erskine: 1997

Ohio Players: 1993,
   1995 (2), 1999

OHM: 1983 (2), 1984

Oingo Boingo: 1988

OK Go: 2005, 2006

Old 97's: 1999, 2004,
   2005

Old Crow Medicine
   Show: 2006

Old Pike: 1999

Olson, Hans: 2003

Omar and the Howlers:
   1987

Omnisoul: 2006 (2)

One Down: 2004

One Drop All-Stars,
   The: 1990

One Less Reason: 2006

One Lone Car: 2005 (2),
   2006 (3)

One Man Army: 2003

One Part Human (OPH):
   1997 (2),

1998 (2), 1999

One People Band: 1996

One Tracy Lane: 2006

Open Skyz: 1994

Opium: 1999

O-Positive: 1990

Opus: 2001, 2002 (3), 2003 (2), 2004, 2006

Oral Defecation: 2000, 2001 (2)

Orange 9mm: 1994, 1996

Orange Punch Warfare: 2006 (3)

Orange Tree: 1997, 1999, 2000

Orbit: 1995

Orgy: 1999

Oriah: 2005

Orquesta La Solución: 1992

Orquesta Solución Latina: 1991

Osbourne, Joan: 1993

Other Side, The: 1992

Otis Clay and the Chicago Fire: 1992

Ottmar Liebert and Luna Negra: 1996

Otto's Revenge: 1990

Ouija: 2000

Our First Summer: 2006 (4)

Our Great Escape: 2005 (3)

Our Lady Peace: 1995 (3), 1997, 1998

Outfield, The: 1985

Outhouse: 1995 (3)

Outlaws, The: 1985

Outsiders, The: 1998 (3), 1999 (5), 2000 (5), 2003

Over the Rhine: 1998

Overkill: 1989

Owen: 2006

Owens, Ginny: 2006

Ozark Mountain Daredevils: 1978

Ozma: 2004, 2006

Ozomatli: 2002 (2), 2004, 2005 (2), 2006

Ozric: 1999

P

P.M.: 1986 (3), 1987-1988 (2), 1989-1992, 1993 (2)

P.O.D. (Payable on Death): 2000

P.O.L. (Parade of Losers): 1995

Pabulum: 1997, 1998

Pacers: 1993

Pacewon: 1999

Page Three: 1983, 1984

Page, Jim: 1998

Page, Martin: 1995

Painkillers: 1984 (3), 1985-1986 (5), 1987 (5)

Painscale: 2001

Paint the Earth: 1994 (4), 1995 (8), 1996 (5), 1997 (2), 1998

Pale Grey: 1998

Pale Hands Bound: 1999

Pallo Hide: 1994

Palmer, Robert: 1978, 1983

Pamper the Madman: 1996

Pandoras, The: 1986

Pangea: 2001

Panic Attack: 2002, 2003 (2), 2004 (3)

Panic! at the Disco: 2006

Pansy Division: 1994

Pantera: 1990 (2)

Papa Aborigine: 1996

Papa John Creach: 1977-1979

Papa Roach: 2004

Paradise Lost: 1993

Paradox: 1990

Paranoid Lovesick: 1995

Paris: 1983 (2), 1984

Park: 2005

Parker, Anders: 2004 (2)

Parker, Graham: 1988, 1995

Parker, Maceo: 1999-2001

Parkside: 2003, 2006 (2)

Particle: 2004

Passenger: 1985

Pat Hazel with the Mother Blues Band: 1979 (2)

Pat McLellan Band: 2005

Patrick Clark and the Murder Store: 1998

Patterson, Rahsaan: 1997

Paul Collins Beat: 1982

Paulson: 2006 (2)

Pave the Rocket: 1996-1997 (3), 1998, 1999

Pavement: 1994, 1997, 1999

Pavlov's Dog: 1983, 1984, 1989, 1990 (2)

Paw: 1993

Pay the Girl: 2003

Peachcake: 2006

Peacock, Alice: 2003

Pecaro, Steve: 1995

Pecorara, Steve: 1992

Peebles, Ann: 1992

Peek, Billy: 1986, 1997

Peg Boy: 1992

Peirson, Leroy: 1993

Penn, Michael: 1990

Pennies for Allah: 2002

People in Planes: 2006

Peoples, Theo: 1992

Pepperland: 1997, 1999, 2000 (2)

Peregrins: 1989

Perpetual Groove: 2003

Peter Holsapple and Chris Stamey: 1991

Peters, Mike: 1996

Petlover: 1999

Phantom Blues Band: 2001

Phantom Planet: 2004

Phantom Rocker & Slick: 1986

Phaze 3: 2001

Phillips and Wall: 1979

Phillips, Sam: 1992

Phillips, Shawn: 1985

Phillips, Simon: 1988

Phish: 1992 (2)

Phix: 2003

Phranklyn Project, The: 2006 (2)

Phunk Junkeez: 1998, 2003, 2004

Physical Therapy: 1992, 1998

Piano Slim: 1986

Piasa: 2003 (2)

Picture Made: 1986

Piebald: 2002

Pieces of a Dream: 1986, 1988

Pierson, Leroy: 1986

Pietasters: 1997 (2)

Pigface: 1991

Pihl, Gary: 1978

Pilate, Fenton: 1996

Pilfers, The: 1998 (2)

Pimps, The: 2005

Pinetop Seven: 2001

Pink Spiders, The: 2006

Pinkeye D'Gekko: 2004 (2)

Piranha Brothers Band: 1984

Pirenha: 1977

Pist on: 1996

Pistolas, The: 2000

Pit Er Pat: 2004

Pitchshifter: 2000

Plaid Cattle: 1990, 1991-1992 (2), 1993

Randy Raley and the Traffic Jam: 1986-1988

Ranier Maria: 2006

Rank and File: 1985, 1987

Rankin, Billy: 1984

Ranks, Shabba: 1993

Rapone, Al: 1988

Rapped in Color: 1995

Raspberry, Larry: 1980

Rasputina: 1997

RatDog: 2001, 2002

Ratt: 1984, 1990

Raunch Hands, The: 1986

Rave Band, The: 1982

Raw Fusion: 1992

Raw Knee Gnaw Knee: 1995

Ray, Goodman, & Brown: 1989

Raybeats, The: 1982

Ray's Music Exchange: 2002

Rayvon: 1995

Reach the Sky: 2001

Reacharound: 1996

Reaction, The: 2003 (4)

Real People, The: 1992

Realized Intention: 2004

Realm: 2000

Rearview Mirror: 2002

Rebel, Tony: 1996

Receiving End of Sirens: 2006

Recht, Rick: 1995 (2)

Records, The: 1979

Red Blues Band, The: 1995

Red Dog and Sassafras: 1980, 1981

Red Hot Chili Peppers: 1985-1988, 1989 (2)

Red House Painters: 1996

Red Rockers: 1982

Red Siren: 1989

Red Water Revival: 2006 (2)

Red Weather: 1991

Redbone, Leon: 1978, 1979, 1985

Redbone: 1979

Redd Kross: 1987, 1991, 1993

Redding: 2006 (2)

Redman, Joshua: 1993

Redrum: 1999

Redwalls, The: 2004

Redwood Landing: 1977

Reed, J.R.: 1992

Reel Big Fish: 1997, 1998 (2), 1999

Reeves, Dianne: 1991, 1997

Reggae at Will: 1989 (2), 1991 (3), 1992, 1993 (3), 1994, 1995 (3), 1996 (2), 1998

Reggae Revue Band: 1992

Reggie and the Full Effect: 2003

Regulators, The: 1992

Rehab: 2000

Reigning Heir: 2004

Relapse: 2006 (2)

Relayer: 1985

Release, The: 1986 (2)

Remaindrz: 1984

Rembrandts, The: 1993

Remedy: 2005, 2006

Renaissance: 1982, 1984, 1985

Rend: 2004

Rene & Angela: 1985

Renee Smith and the Little Dove Marks: 1994

Reno, Johnny: 1987 (2)

Rentals, The: 1996

Replacements, The: 1983, 1989

Resist All: 2002

Retros, The: 1979

Return, The: 2003

Reuben's Accomplice: 2001

Reuter, Bob: 1995

Reveille: 2000

Reverend Horton Heat: 1992-1994, 1995 (2), 1996, 1998-2000, 2003, 2006

Revival, The: 1985

Rewind: 2001

Rhino Bucket: 1991

Rhythm Corps: 1988

Rhythm Method: 1988

Rhythm Rockers: 1984

Rich Dalton and the Classics Band: 1989, 1991, 1995 (3)

Rich McDonough and Darren Helton: 1995

Richard Thompson Band: 1996

Richard, Zachary: 1991

Richman, Jonathan: 1982, 1987, 1990, 1991 (2), 1992

Riddlin' Kids: 2001, 2002 (2), 2003

Ridgeway, Stan: 1986, 1989

Rigor Mortis: 1988

Ring Cicada: 2000

Ringenberg, Jason: 2000

Riot Act: 1982, 1984

Riot: 1981

RIPD: 2003 (2)

Rippingtons, The: 1994

Rise Against: 2003

Ritter, Josh: 2005

River City Blues Band: 1996-1997 (3), 1998, 1999

River City High: 2001, 2003

River City People: 1990

River City Rebels: 2000

River Gypsy: 2004 (3), 2005

Riverton: 2005 (2), 2006 (3)

Road Apples, The: 1988, 1990 (2)

Roadmaster: 1979

Rob Rule: 1994

Robbie Fulks Band: 1997

Robert Bradley's Blackwater Surprise: 1996 (2)

Robert Cray Band, The: 2000

Roberto Randolph and the Family Band: 2003

Roberts, Marcus: 1991

Robillard, Duke: 1994 (2)

Rock God Superstar: 1999, 2001

Rock 'n' Roll Soldiers: 2006

Rock to Riches: 1983 (3)

Rockats: 1982

Rocket from the Crypt: 1993, 1996

Rocket Kirchner Band: 1985

Rocket Park: 2000 (3)

Rockets, The: 1979, 1982

Rock-four: 2002

Rockhouse Ramblers: 1998 (2), 1999

Rockhouse Trio: 2002, 2004

Rockin' Luckys: 1988 (2), 1992 (2)

Rockin' Sidney: 1988

Rocking Horse Winner, The: 2002

Rock-o-planes: 1998

Rod Piazza and the Mighty Flyers: 1995 (2)

Rodgers, Paul: 1993

Roger from the Dark: 1993

Roger Miret and the Disasters: 2003

Rogers, Jimmy: 1992, 1993, 1994, 1995

Rogers, Skeet: 1993

Rollins Band: 1992, 2000

Rollins, Henry: 1996, 1998

Rollins, Sonny: 1991, 1992

Rollover: 1994 (2)

Rondo's Blues Deluxe: 1983 (2), 1986, 1988, 1990

Ronnie Davis and Idren: 1997

Roomful of Blues: 1995, 1996, 1999

Rooney: 2003, 2004

Rooster Lollipop: 2000

Roots Radics: 1983, 1987, 1988 (2), 1989, 1990, 1996

Rosebud: 1979

Ross & Hunt: 1997

Roth, David Lee: 1994

Roth, Uli John: 1985

Roto the Wonder Band: 1977, 1978

Rough Cutt: 1986

Rough Squirrels, The: 1987

Rouse, Josh: 2000 (2)

Roustabouts, The: 1981

Roxy Music: 1979

Roy Loney and the Phantom Movers: 1979

Royal Court of China: 1987

Royal Crescent Mob: 1988, 1989, 1991

Royal Crown Review: 1998

Royal Fingerbowl: 1998

RTZ: 1991

Rubber Rodeo: 1983

Ruby Horse: 2002

Rude Pets: 1982, 1984 (2)

Ruffin, Lydia: 1997

Ruffner, Mason: 1987

Rufio: 2002

Rufus McNasty: 2005

Rugburns, The: 1987, 1996, 1997

Run-D.M.C.: 1998

Run Westy Run: 1995

Rundgren, Todd: 1985, 1995, 1997

Runner and the Thermodynamics: 2004

Runner Up, The: 2006 (2)

Rush, Otis: 1988

Rushmore Academy: 2004, 2005 (6), 2006 (2)

Russ Anderson and the Renegades: 1985

Russell, Leon: 1981, 1983, 1985, 1986

Rusted Root: 1994 (2), 1995, 2002, 2003, 2005, 2006

Rusted Shine: 2003 (3), 2004 (2), 2005 (5)

Rusted Skin: 2002

Rusty: 1995

RX Bandits: 2000, 2003

Ryan, Matthew: 1997

Ryder, Mitch: 1985 (2)

S

S.W.A.M.P.: 1987 (2)

Sable: 1989 (2), 1993

Sabre: 1985

Sac Lunch: 2005

Saccharine Trust: 1984

Sacred Heart Auto League: 2001

Sacrifice Isaac: 1995

Sacrilicious: 1996, 1997

Sad Cafe: 1979

Sadies, The: 2003 (2)

Saga: 1985

Sagittarius Band, The: 1990

Sahm, Doug: 1979

Saigon Kick: 1990, 1992, 1993

Sain, Oliver Revue, The: 1977

Sain, Oliver Soul Reunion: 1988-1997

Sain, Oliver: 2001

Saint Dog: 2004

Saints, The: 1987

Sako, Johnny: 1993

Salem 66: 1987

Sallee, Ron: 1996

Salt the Earth: 2002

Salt Vision: 2002

Salty Dog: 1990

Salty Iguanas: 1993

Sambistas: 1994

Same Club: 2003

Sammy and the Snow Monkeys: 1992, 1994

Sample, Joe: 1996

Samples, The: 1992, 1993 (2), 1994-1996, 1997 (2), 1998 (3), 2000, 2001-2002 (2), 2003, 2004 (2), 2006

Samsara: 2002 (2)

Sanchez, Paul: 1999

Sanctified Sister: 1999

Sanctuary: 1987, 1988, 1990

Sand Rubies: 1993

Sanford-Townsend Band: 1978

Sao: 2005

Satchel: 1996

Satori: 2005 (2), 2006

Satriani, Joe: 1988

Satyr: 1976

Savage St. Hubbins: 1999 (4), 2000 (3)

Savanna: 1977

Savatage: 1985, 1990

Save Ferris: 2000

Saved by Grace: 2002

Saved from Tomorrow: 2003, 2004 (2)

Saves the Day: 2001

Saving Boy Wonder: 2001, 2002 (2)

Savuka: 1990, 1993

Saxon: 1986

Say Goodbye: 2003, 2004, 2006 (3)

Says Who: 2002

Scatterbrain: 1990, 1991

Schenker, Michael: 1999

Schimmel, Robert: 2004

Schivo, Michael: 1994

Schleprock: 1996

Schneider, Bob: 2002, 2003

Schon, Neal: 1993

School of Fish: 1991 (2), 1993

Schooly D: 1987, 1988

Schoolz of Thought: 2003 (2)

Schwag, The: 1996 (4), 1997 (6), 1998 (2), 1999 (3), 2000 (5), 2001 (7), 2002 (20), 2005, 2007

Scofield, John: 1986, 1987

Scorched Earth: 2005

Scott, Brian: 1989

Scott, Tom: 1978

Scott-Heron, Gil: 1979 (2), 1986, 1988, 1995

Scrawl: 1997

Screamin Joe Neal: 1989

Screamin' Cheetah Wheelies: 1994, 1996

Screaming Jets: 1993

Screaming Trees: 1991, 1992

Screams, The: 1979

Scruffy the Cat: 1987

SCSI: 2001

Sea and Cake, The: 2003

Seagle, April: 1988

Seals, Frank "Son": 1979

Searchers, The: 1986

Season to Risk: 1991, 1993, 1995 (2), 1997

Second Wind: 1988

Secret Cajun Band: 1993 (3), 1994

Secrets, The: 1979 (2)

Seger, Shea: 2001

Selecter, The: 1993, 1995

Self Restraint: 2000 (2), 2001

Selfish: 1999

Semidivine: 2002

Semi-OK: 2006

Semisonic: 1996, 1998

Send the Reign: 2000

Sensafeelia: 1999

Sense Datum: 2001, 2002

Sense Field: 1996

Sensor: 1995

Sepultura: 1996

Serapis: 1995

Set Your Goals: 2006

Sets, Julia: 2000, 2003 (2)

Seven Days: 2000

Seven Mary Three: 1995-1997

Seven Shock Screamers: 1999

Seven Stitches: 2005

Seven: 2002, 2006

Sevenagainst: 2001

Sevendust: 1998

Sevenstar: 2002 (3), 2003 (9), 2004 (4), 2005 (2)

Seventeen & 7: 2004

Seventh of Never: 1995

Sever: 2005

Sexsmith, Ron: 1996

Sgt. Carter: 1988

Shabba Ranks: 1993

Shadowfax: 1988

Shadowland: 1990

Shag, The: 1995

Shaggy: 1995

Shaheen, Michelle: 1994

Shakers, The: 1985

Shaking Family: 1990

Shaman's Harvest: 1999, 2002-2003 (2), 2005 (3)

Shame Club: 2003, 2005

Shame on Those: 2006

Shampoo Sharks: 2001, 2002 (3)

Shangoya: 1985

Shanti Groove: 2004, 2005

Sharp, Bree: 2000

Sharp, Dave: 1993

Sharpies, The: 1991, 1996

Shattermask: 2004

Sh-boom: 1987, 1988

She Means Business: 2006

She Wants Revenge: 2005

Sheer: 1996

Sheik, Duncan: 1996, 1997, 1998

Sheiks, The: 1977 (24), 1978, 1979 (24), 1983 (2), 1984 (2), 1985 (4)

Shelly, Michael: 1998

Shepard, Vonda: 1998, 1999

Shifted: 2004

Shiloh: 2006

Shine: 2001 (2), 2002 (6), 2003 (2), 2004

Shiner: 1996, 1997 (2)

Shiny Tim: 2000

Shock Opera: 1993

Shocked, Michelle: 1994, 1996, 2002

Shoes, The: 1982

Shooting Star: 1985, 1993

Shore, Susan: 1990

Show of Hands: 1989

Showbread: 2005

Showdown, The: 2005

Shrinking Violets: 1996

Shudderbug: 1999

Shurman: 2003

Shy Talk: 1985

Sick Life: 1999

Sick of It All: 2001, 2006

Side of Fives: 2002, 2003 (4), 2004, 2005 (4), 2006 (3)

Sidewinders, The: 1989, 1990

Siegal, Dan: 1993, 1995

Signal Earth: 1984

Signal the Sirens: 2006 (2)

Silos, The: 1995

Silverchair: 1997 (2)

Silvercloud: 1991

Silverfish: 1991

Silvertide: 2005

Simeon: 2006

Simms Brothers Band: 1979

Simon & Bard: 1985

Simones: 1997

Simple Mary's Diary: 1999-2000 (4)

Simple Plan: 2002, 2004

Simple Simon: 1990 (2), 1991, 1992 (3)

Sin Drone: 2001, 2002

Sincola: 1995

Single Bullet Theory: 1979

Single File: 2006

Sinister Child: 1992

Sinister Dane: 1988, 1989, 1990 (2), 1991 (6), 1992 (3), 1993 (2), 1994 (5),1995 (8)

Sister Carol: 1992

Sister Double Happiness: 1991

Sister Hazel: 1997, 1998, 2006

Six by Silver: 2005 (2), 2006

Six Percent: 1999

Sixpence None the Richer: 2003

Sixteen Down: 2001

Skabs, The: 2001

Skaggs, Ricky: 1981

Skatalites, The: 1993. 1998, 2000

Skavoovie and the Epitones: 1993

Skeleton Key: 1996

Skeletones, The: 1994, 1996, 1997

Skeletons: 1979 (3), 1991 (4), 1992 (2), 1993

Skerik: 2003

Skid Roper: 1989

Skillet Sisters: 1995

Skills of Ortega, The: 2004

Skin Flick: 1992

Skinny Puppy: 1990, 1992

Skulls, The: 1986

Skunk: 1993

Sky Bop Fly: 1996 (3), 1997

Skylars, The: 1997

Skyline: 2003, 2004 (2)

Skywalk: 1986

Slackers, The: 2002

Slackjabber: 1997

Slammin' Gladys: 1992

Slammin' Watusis: 1988, 1989

Slapdash: 1997, 1998 (2), 1999 (4), 2000 (2), 2001, 2006 (3), 2007

Slash's Snake Pit: 1995

Slayer: 1984, 1994, 1996, 1998

Sleater-Kinney: 2005

Sleazy Lee: 1992 (2), 1993 (2)

Sleeze Beez: 1990

Slick Nickel: 1993

Slick, Venus: 1997

Sliders, The: 1999 (2), 2000 (3)

Slip, The: 2002 (2), 2004

Slosh: 1995

Slow Runner: 2005

Slowfall: 2006 (3)

Slugworth: 1992

Small Ball Paul: 1991 (2), 1992, 1994 (2)

Small Brown Bike: 2002

Smarties, The: 1997

Smashed Gladys: 1988

Smashmouth: 1997

Smiling Assassins, The: 2003

Smith, Bennie: 1992, 1995, 2006

Smith, Benny: 1991

Smith, Darden: 1988, 1993

Smith, Lonnie Liston: 1983, 1997

Smith, Michael A.: 1988

Smith, Patti: 2000

Smith, Renee: 1994, 1996

Smith, Steve: 1983

Smithereens, The: 1986, 1988, 1990, 1991, 1994

Smoke or Fire: 2005

Smoke Stick: 2002

Smoking Popes: 1995, 1998

Smooth, The: 1999

Smudge: 1993

Snail: 1978

Snapcase: 2001

Snider, Todd: 1998, 2006 (2)

Sniff'n the Tears: 1979

Snobank: 2002

Snopek, Sigmond: 1979

Snot: 1998 (2)

Snow, Phoebe: 1989

So Far Gone: 1999 (2)

So Many Dynamos: 2003, 2005

So They Say: 2005, 2006

Soak: 1997

Sobule, Jill: 1997, 2001

Social Blunder: 1997 (2)

Social Distortion: 1989, 1992, 1996

Social Offense: 1985 (2), 1986

Soda Jerk: 1999 (3), 2000 (5)

Sofachrome: 2003-2004 (2), 2005 (3), 2006

Soil: 2004

Solar Trance: 2001

Solas: 1999

Solex: 1999

Solicitors, The: 1998

Solo: 1996

Solution a.d.: 1996

Solvin, Shawn: 1993

Soma Holiday: 2000

Somerville-Scorfina Band: 1981

Something Brothers, The: 1989, 1990 (5)

Something Corporate: 2001, 2003 (2), 2005

Somnia: 2000, 2001, 2002 (2), 2003, 2004 (2)

Son of Starchild: 1996 (4), 1997, 1998

Son Seals: 1993

Son Volt: 1995, 1996 (3), 1999 (5), 2004 (2)

Sonia Dada: 1993, 1995 (2), 1996 (2), 1997, 1998 (2), 1999

Sonic Joyride: 1998

Sonic Reducer: 2002, 2005, 2006

Sonic Reduction: 2003

Sonic Youth: 1986, 1990

Sonny Terry & Brownie McGhee: 1977, 1978

Sons of Mass: 1996

Sons of Regret: 1995

Sophomore: 2002, 2003, 2005

Soul Asylum: 1986 (2), 1987, 1988, 1991, 1992, 1997

Soul Brains: 2001

Soul Coughing: 1994, 1997, 1998

Soul for Silver: 2005 (2)

Soul Funktion: 1991, 1996

Soul Kiss: 1995 (2), 1996, 1997 (3), 1998 (5), 1999 (4), 2002

Soul Reunion: 1990, 1991

Soulard Blues Band: 1981-1983, 1986, 1990 1991, 1994, 1996

Souled American: 1988

Soulfly: 1998 (2), 1999

Soulhat: 1993, 1994 (2)

Souls at Zero: 1995

Souls of Mischief: 1993

Sound System: 2002

Soundgarden: 1990 (2), 1991

Sounds, The: 2004, 2006

Soup Dragons: 1992 (2)

Soup Kitchen: 1999

Sourpatch: 1995, 1996

Souther, J.D.: 1986

Southern Culture on the Skids: 1994, 1997

Southgang: 1991, 1992

Southpaw: 2003

Southside Johnny and the Asbury Jukes: 1978, 1979

Souvenirs, The: 2001

Soviettes, The: 2005

Space Age Palmer: 1998

Spacehog: 1998, 2001

Spam Paris: 1993

Spankin' Rufus: 1990, 1992

Sparkle Horse: 1995

Sparland: 2005

Sparta: 2002, 2003

Spatik: 2005, 2006 (2)

Spatz: 1985

Speak No Evil: 1999

Speakeasy: 2003 (2), 2004

Spearhead: 2002, 2004

Special Beat: 1992, 1993

Special EFX: 1985, 1987

Specials, The: 1996

Spelunkers: 1998, 1999

Spent: 2003 (2)

Spheeris, Jimmie: 1978, 1983

Spillway: 1996

Spin 54: 2001

Spin Doctors: 1991

Spirit: 1979, 1984, 1991

Spirtles: 1987

Spitalfield: 2005 (2)

Sponge: 1995, 1996

Spontaneous
Combustion: 1990

Spookie Daly Pride:
2002 (2), 2003

Spoons: 1987

Spot 1019: 1987

Spring Heeled Jack:
1998 (2)

Spring Loaded: 2003

Spud: 1999

Spur: 2005

Spyra Gyra: 1979

Squirrel Nut Zippers:
1996, 1998, 2000

SR-71: 2000, 2001

St. Corner Symphony:
1979 (11)

St. Croix
Philharmonic Steel
Orchestra: 1983

St. Louis Blues Band,
The: 1991

St. Louis Kings of
Rhythm with Ike
Turner Jr.: 1986

St. Louis Sambistas:
1992

St. Stephen's Blues:
1992-1993 (2), 1995,
1996 (3), 1997

Stabbing Westward:
1993, 1996

Stacey Johnson and
Skeet Rogers with
the Kosmic Blues
Band: 1995

Stage Dolls: 1989

Stain of Mind: 2003

Staind: 1999

Stamey, Chris: 1991

Stand, The: 1989

Standing Still: 2006

Standpointe: 2006 (4)

Stanley Clarke &
George Duke: 1983

Star Apple Theory:
2005

Star Nineteen: 1999

Star People: 1999

Starr, Belle: 1998 (3),
1999

Starr, Garrison: 2002

Stars of Track and
Field, The: 2006 (2)

Start, The: 2003

Starting Line, The:
2003, 2004, 2006

State of Mind: 1992,
2006 (2)

State of Shock: 1986

State, The: 2006

Stateside: 2004

Static X: 2000, 2004

Stavesacre: 1997

Steadfast: 2001

Stealin' Horses: 1987,
1988 (2)

Stealth: 1999 (2), 2000

Stedfast: 2002

Steel Band: 1983

Steel Train: 2005

Steelheart: 1991 (2),
1992

Stendek: 2005 (6)

Steppin' Out: 1982,
1983, 1984 (6)

Steps: 1988

Stereo Fuse: 2003

Stereophonics: 2004

Steriogram: 2004

Stern, Mike: 1993

Stern, Robert: 1990

Steve Ewing Band,
The: 2005

Stevie E. (Steve
Ewing): 2002

Steve Schenkel
Quartet, The: 1988

Steve Stevens and the
Atomic Playboys: 1989

Steve, Bob & Rich:
1984 (2), 1985 (6),
1986 (2)

Stevens, Corey: 1998,
2001

Stevens, Sufjan: 2005

Stevenson, B.W.: 1977

Stewart, Al: 1976

Stick People, The:
1991

Stickfigure: 2002

Sticky Fingers: 1997,
1998

Stiletto: 1984, 1985

Still Life: 1990, 1991

Stillwater: 1995 (2),
1997, 1999 (2)

Stillwell, Tommy: 1997

Stimulus X: 1991

Stir: 1994 (7),
1995 (2), 1996 (3),
1997, 1999, 2000 (2),
2002

Stockholm Syndrome:
2004

Stolen, The: 2001

Stone Deep: 1995,
1995, 1997 (2)

Stone Ground: 1978

Stonebraker: 1994

Stonecutters, The:
1993, 1994 (2), 1995

Story of the Year:
2002

Straight Jacket Lucy:
1991 (2)

Stranded Lads, The:
1986 (3), 1987 (6),
1988, 1989, 1991 (2),
1992 (3), 1993 (2)

Strange Brothers, The:
1994

Strangefolk: 2002

Stranglmartin: 1994

Stratford 4: 2003

Straw, Syd: 1989, 1996

Stray Cats: 1982, 1989

Straylight Run: 2004,
2005 (2), 2006

Street Terry Corner
Symphony: 1982

Street to Nowhere:
2006

Streets: 1983

Stretch Armstrong:
2003, 2004

Strictly Isaac: 1998

Strike Anywhere: 2003

String Cheese
Incident: 1998 (2)

Stroke 9: 2005

Stroke: 1999

Strokes, The: 2001

Strong, Marcel: 1994,
1995

Strung Out: 1995

Stryck9: 1999 (2)

Stryper: 1985

STS Horns, The: 1994

STS9 (Sound Tribe
Sector 9): 2004 (3),
2005

Stubblefield Band,
The: 1996, 1997 (2),
1998, 1999

Stuck Mojo: 1998, 1999

Studebakers, The:
1986, 1989

Suave Octopus: 1989,
1992 (2), 1993 (5),
1994 (4)

Subdudes, The: 1990,
1991, 1993, 2003

Subject to Change:
1986

Substitute Heroes:
1985, 1986

Substitutes: 1986

Suede Chain, The:
1991, 1992 (5),
1993 (3), 1994 (8),
1995 (5), 1996 (2)

Sugar Coated: 2002 (2)

Sugar Ray: 1995, 1997

Sugar: 1994

Sugarbomb: 2001 (2)

Sugarbuzz: 1995

Sugarcult: 2002, 2006

Sugardaddy: 1996-
1997 (2), 1998

Sugarstickygirl:
1995 (2), 1997

Suicidal Tendencies:
1987 (2), 1988, 1990

Suite 13: 2001 (2),
2002

Sullen: 2000, 2003

Sum 41: 2001

Sumlin, Hubert: 1993

Summer, Henry Lee: 1988, 1992

Sun City Girls: 1984

Sun Sawed in ½, The: 1990, 1991-1992 (2), 1993 (5), 1994 (4), 1995 (2), 1996, 1998

Sundays, The: 1990, 1993

Sunny Day Real Estate: 1999

Super 8: 1996

Superchunk: 1993, 1994, 1999 (2), 2000, 2002, 2003

Superdrag: 1996

Superfunk Fantasy: 1996, 1997

Supersuckers: 1992, 2002, 2006

Supertramp: 1985

Supervillain Zero: 2002 (2), 2003

Supreme Love Gods: 1993

Surge: 1995

Surkamp, David Band: 1998

Surkamp, David: 1985 (8), 1986 (2), 1991

Surreal: 2003 (2)

Survivor: 1981

Susan Voelz Band: 1993

Swaggin' Dickies: 1987

Swales, The: 1996

Swamp Boogie Queen: 1998

Swan, Brian: 1983

Sweet 75: 1997

Sweet, Mathew: 1992 (2), 1994 (2), 1995, 1997 (2)

Sweetwater: 1992, 1993

Swift Kixx: 2002

Swing Set: 1992, 1994 (2)

Switch III: 2003 (6), 2004, 2006 (2)

Sword, The: 2005

Sybris: 2006 (2)

Syd Rodway Trio, The: 1996

Symptoms, The: 1978

Synergy: 2001

System of a Down: 1998 (2)

T

T.H.U.G.S.: 1994

Tad: 1995

Taft, Bill: 1992

Tail Stories: 1992

Tailgators: 1986 (2)

Tainted Wisdom: 2004, 2005

Takemura, Nobukazu: 2001

Talas: 1984

Talking Heads: 1979

Tall: 2001

Tally Hall: 2006

Tanjent: 2002

Tapeworm: 1992

Target Market: 2005

Tastes Like Chicken: 1994, 1995 (5), 1996 (4), 1997 (4), 2000

Taylor, Dan Lee: 1996

Taylor, Koko: 1986, 1987, 1992, 1999

Taylor, Livingston: 1982

Taylor: 1998

Team Tomato: 2005

Teddy Boys: 1983, 1984 (3)

Teenage Fanclub: 1992

Television: 1993

Ten Story: 1983

Ten Years Gone (Stevie Ray Vaughan tribute): 2000

Tenderloin: 1993, 1994 (2)

Tentacles: 1999

Terror: 2004

Terry, Doc: 1988

Terry, Sonny: 1979 (2)

Tesla: 1987

Testament: 1988-1990, 1992, 1999

Texas Instruments: 1991

Texas: 1994

TGL: 2006

That Hope: 1986 (2)

That One Guy: 2006

Thelonious Monster: 1986, 1988

Theos: 2004, 2006

Therapy: 1993, 1994

Thermadore: 1996

Thermals: 2006 (2)

They Came in Droves: 1993

They Might Be Giants: 1990, 1992, 1995, 1996, 1997 (3), 1998, 1999, 2004

Thick: 1993

Thimes, Denise: 1998 (2)

Thin Lizard Dawn: 1997

Thin White Rope: 1986

Think Thank Thunk: 2005 (6)

Third Eye Blind: 2003

Third Floor: 1993

Third Stone: 1993

Thirteen Days: 2002

Thomas, Butch: 1990

Thomas, Chris: 1990

Thompson, Richard: 1985, 1991, 1992, 1994, 1999

Thompson, Teddy: 2006

Thorns, The: 2003

Thos: 2005 (2)

Those Guys: 1977, 1978 (2)

Those Who Stay: 1986 (2)

Thought Industry: 1992

Thousand Yard Stare: 1992

Thrashing Doves: 1987

Three Dog Night: 1984

Three Fried Men: 1997

Three Merry Widows: 1990-1991 (3), 1992 (5), 1995

Thrill Hole: 2001

Thrillseeker, The: 2002

Throw Rag: 2006

Throwing Muses: 1991, 1992, 1995

Thrush Hermit: 1997

Thug Murder: 2001

Thumper: 1986

Thunders, Johnny: 1986

Thunders, The: 1988

Thursday: 2002

Tiara: 1997

Tiger Army: 2001

Tiger Mountain: 1997

Tilbrook, Glenn: 2005

Timbuk 3: 1988

Times Beach: 1985

Timmys, The: 2005

Tinfoil Antenna: 1997

Tinhorn: 1997, 1999, 2000

Tiny Buddy: 1994

Tiny Town: 1997

Tiorah: 1999

Titanic Love Affair: 1988

T-Model Ford: 2001, 2002

TNZ: 1992

Toad the Wet Sprocket: 1990, 1992, 1997, 2003

Toadies, The: 1995 (3)

Toasters, The: 1991, 1993 (2), 1994 (2)

Toback, Jeremy: 1997 (2)

Tobi Kai and the Strays: 2005, 2006 (3)

Today is the Day: 1997

Todd on LSD: 1994 (4), 1995

Tolerance: 2002

Tom Steiger Seven: 1999

Tommy Conwell and the Young Rumblers: 1988

Tomorrow's Rumor: 2006

Tone Loc: 1998

Tongue and Groove: 1993

Tonic: 1996, 1997, 1999, 2000

Tonight at Seven: 2006 (5)

Tony Furtado Band: 2001 (2)

Tony Williams Quintet: 1992

Too Bad Eugene: 1999

Too Much Joy: 1991, 1992

Tool: 1992

Toots and the Maytals: 1987 (2), 1989

Tora Tora: 1989, 1992, 1993

Tornader: 1977

Torsion: 1992

Tortoise: 2001, 2004

Tossers, The: 2006

Tovar, Mike: 1990

Tower of Power: 1993, 1994, 1996

Townsend, Henry: 1986, 1988, 1993, 1997

Toxic Reasons: 1986

Tracy + the Plastics: 2002

Tragically Hip, The: 1993, 1996

Trailer: 1996

Train: 1999

Trance Logic: 1989 (4)

Trans-Lux: 2001

Transparents, The: 2002

Trapezoid: 1990

Travers, Pat: 1984, 1985

Travis, Michael: 2005

Traxx: 1982

Treat Her Right: 1989 (2)

Tree: 1997

Treehouse: 1997

Trees: 2004

Tremulis, Nicholas: 1987

Tres Amigos: 1988

Triage: 2002

Triangle: 1995

Tribe After Tribe: 1991, 1993

Tribes with Knives: 1992 (2), 1994

Trick Shot: 1982, 1983

Trickster: 1978

Tricky: 1998, 1999

Trinidad Exotic: 1983

Trip Daddys, The: 1999, 2002, 2006

Trip El Ecks (XXX): 1997, 1998 (3), 1999

Trip Shakespeare: 1990-1992

Triple Clamp: 1999, 2000, 2003

Triple Fast Action: 1995, 1997

Tripp, Gregg: 1991

Tripping Daisy: 1994, 1995, 1998

Tripstar: 2001, 2006

Trixter: 1990

Tropical Storm: 2001

Tropix: 1984

Trouble: 1987

Trout, Walter: 1999

Trower, Robin: 1985, 1985, 1986 (2), 1994, 1997-2000

True Believers: 1986

True Blue: 1994

Truman's Water: 1994

Trust Company: 2004

Truth, The: 1987

Trynin, Jennifer: 1995, 1997

Tryptophane: 2002-2004

TSOL (True Sounds of Liberty): 1986 (2)

Tubes, The: 1987

Tubring: 2006

Tucker, Bill: 1997

Tucker, Tanya: 1978, 1979

Tuff Nutz: 1989, 1990-1991 (2), 1993

Tupelo Chain Sex: 1986 (2), 1989

Tupperville, Charles: 1977

Turning Curious: 1984

Turnstyles, The: 2000

TV 50: 1997

Twain: 1991

Twilight Jump: 1996 (2)

Twilight Singers, The: 2006

Twilley, Dwight: 1977, 1984

Twin Bullet Band: 1983

Twinkle Brothers: 1985

Two: 1998

Type O Negative: 1996

U

U.D.O.: 1988

UB40: 1983

UFO: 1995

Ugly Duckling: 2000

Ugly Kid Joe: 1991-1993, 1995

Ulcer Inc.: 2003

Ulcer: 1994, 1995 (3), 1996 (2), 2004

Ultima Thule: 1995

Ultimate Fakebook: 2002, 2003

Ultra Bidet: 1995

Ultra Blue: 2002, 2004 (2)

Ultra Vivid Scene: 1990

Ultrablue: 2002-2004, 2005 (2), 2006

Ultrafink: 1997 (2)

Ultraman: 1987-1990, 1991 (3), 1993 (2)

Ultraspunk: 1998

Ultraviolet: 1989

UltraViolets, The: 1998, 2001

Ultravox: 1979

Umphrey's Universe: 2004 (2)

Umphrey's McGee: 2002-2003 (2)

Unanimous: 2005

Unchained: 2000 (2), 2001-2002 (4), 2003 (2)

Uncle Albert: 1997 (2)

Uncle Tupelo: 1988, 1989 (2), 1991 (3), 1992 (2), 1993, 1994 (2)

Unconscious, The: 1986, 1987-1988 (5), 1989 (26), 1990 (18)

Uncut: 2005

Undecided Noyz: 2000, 2001

Undercover: 1984

Uninvited, The: 1998

Union Station: 1993

United States Three: 1995

United States: 1996

Unsane: 1996

Unseen, The: 2003

Until December: 1986

Until Tomorrow: 2004

Ununbium: 2003

Unwritten Law: 1995, 2001

Upright Animals, The: 2005 (5), 2007, 2006 (2)

Upside: 2005

Urban Grind: 1998

Urge Overkill: 1987, 1991, 1993

Urge, The: 1989 (2), 1990 (6), 1991 (12), 1992 (13), 1993 (12), 1994 (9), 1995 (10), 1996 (6), 1997 (3), 1998 (2), 1999-2000 (8)

Uriah Heep: 1982, 1990

U-Roy: 1983,1989

Used, The: 2003

UTI (Under the Influence): 1998

V

Vacation, The: 2006

Vagrant Across America: 2001

Vai, Steve: 1993, 1996

Valium, The: 1997, 2000, 2001

Vallejo: 1997, 2000

Vampire Moose: 2000 (3)

Van Zant, Johnny: 1982

Van Zant: 1984, 1985

Vanilla Ice: 1998

Vanished, The: 2005

Vargas Swing: 1998 (8), 1999 (3), 2000 (2), 2001

Varnaline: 1998

Vatos, Johnny: 1990

Vaughan, Jimmie: 1994

Vaughan, Stevie Ray: 1983

Vaughn, Ben: 1988

Vedera: 2006

Vega, Suzanne: 1985, 1996

Vegas to Verona: 2006 (2)

Veldt, The: 1990, 1991

Velvet Elvis: 1988 (2)

Velvet Jones: 1997

Vendetta Red: 2003

Vent: 1996

Vents, The: 1997

Verbow: 2000

Verlaine, Tom: 1988

Verlaines, The: 1993

Vernon Burch Group: 1977

Vertical Horizon: 1999 (3), 2003

Veruca Salt: 1994 (3), 1995, 1997, 2000

Verve Pipe, The: 1994, 1997

Victims, The: 1986

Vida Blue: 2002

Videodrone: 1999

Vigilantes of Love: 1994

Village Idiot: 2004 (2)

Villanova Junction: 1996

Vinnie Vincent Invasion: 1988

Viogression: 1991

Violence: 1987, 1988, 1990

Violent Femmes: 1990-1994

Virginia Coalition: 2005

Vital Information: 1987

Vitamin A / Vitamen A: 1992 (2), 1993, 1994 (4), 1996 (4), 1995 (2), 2001 (2), 2002

Vivid Aura: 2000 (2)

Voeks, Erik: 1994

VOEX: 1991

Voguel, Steve: 1995

Voice of God: 1991, 1992-1993 (5)

Void: 2006

Voivod: 1990, 1994

Vonray: 2003

Voodoo Glow Skulls: 1996

Voyager: 2006

W

W.A.S.P.: 1997

Waco Brothers: 1996

Wagoneers, The: 1988, 1989

Wailers, The: 2003-2005

Wailing Souls: 1993

Wainwright III, Loudan: 1990

Wainwright, Rufus: 2002

Wait: 2005

Waite, John: 1982

Waitresses, The: 1982

Wake Up Report: 2005

Wake: 2000 (2)

Wakefield: 2003 (2)

Wakeling, Dave: 2002

Waldman, Steve: 1993

Walk the Earth: 2005

Walk the West: 1986 (2)

Walker, Jerry Jeff: 1980

Walker, Joe Louis: 1995

Wall of Voodoo: 1983

Wallets, The: 1985-1987

Wallflowers, The: 1997, 2005

Walnut Park AC: 1982

Walsh, Brock: 1980

Walsh, Joe: 1992

Walt Mink: 1992

Walter Trout Band: 1999

War: 1988, 1993, 1994 (2), 1995, 1982, 1983

Warlocks, The: 2001, 2005

Warrant: 1995

Warren Zevon and the Patrician Homeboys: 1988

Washington, Carlos: 2001

Water Brothers, The: 1977

Watershed: 1996

Waterworks: 1994

Watt, Mike: 1995

Watts, Ben: 1996

Wave Band, The: 1982 (2)

Wax: 1995

Way Moves, The: 1990

Wayne, Bob: 2006 (2)

Wayne: 2002

Weapon of Choice: 1994

Weber, Zach: 2006

Weckl, Dave: 1993, 1994

Weckl, Dave (clinic/ performance): 1993, 1994, 1998

Wedding Present, The: 1994

Ween: 1995, 2000

Weezer: 1994, 1996

Weir, Rusty: 1977

Welch, Gillian: 2004

Wells, Jr.: 1986

Weltman, Sandy: 1995

Wernee, David: 1979

Werner, Carla: 2003

Wertz, Matt: 2006

West, Red: 2003

Westcott: 2005 (2)

Westenhoefer, Suzanne: 1997

Westerberg, Paul: 1993, 1996

Wheat: 2003

Wheatus: 2000

Wheel, Catherine: 1992

When Sorrow Fails: 2006

Whild Peach: 2005

Whispers: 1996

White Animals: 1984, 1985

White Hassle: 2000

White Pride: 1983

White Star Line: 1979, 1983

White Suburban Youth: 1984, 1985

White Trash: 1992

White Wolf: 1985

White, Billy: 1995

White, Karen: 1987

White, Lenny: 1978

White, The (Tribute to Led Zeppelin): 1983

Whiteside, Erma: 1993

Whitfield, Mark: 1991

Why Store, The: 1996 (2)

Whydown: 2006

Wicked, The: 2007

Wickerman: 1996

Widespread Panic: 1991 (2), 1992, 1995

WIK: 2005

Wilco: 1994, 1995 (2), 1997 (2)

Wild Colonials: 1996

Will & The Kill: 1987

Williams III., Hank: 2006 (2)

Williams, Dar: 1998

Williams, Dave: 1986

Williams, Greg: 1994

Williams, Julius: 1988

Williams, Keller: 1998-2000, 2001 (2), 2002

Williams, Lucinda: 1992, 1999

Williams, Saul: 2002, 2003

Williams, Tony: 1979 (2)

Williams, Vesta: 1989 (2)

Willing, The: 1992

Winbush, A'ngela: 2005

Windows, The: 1982

Winger: 1993

Winningham, Mare: 1992

Winston County: 2002

Winter Hours: 1987, 1989

Winter, Edgar: 1986

Winter, Johnny: 1978, 1982, 1989, 1992-1994, 2000, 2002

Wishbone Ash: 1983

Wolfgang Press, The: 1992

Wolfmother: 2006

Wolfsbane: 1989

Womack, Bobby: 1994

Wonder Band, The: 1977 (4)

Wonder Stuff, The: 1994

Wood, Tom: 1987

Wood: 1999

Woods: 1988

Wookiefoot: 2003

Wooten, Victor: 2002, 2003

Working Title, The: 2005 (2)

World Party: 1997

World Sinfonia: 1990

Wrathchild America: 1989

Wyle E.: 1992, 1993

Wynn, Steve: 1990

X

X: 1982, 1983, 1993

X-Cops: 1994

Xscape: 1995

XYZ: 1990, 1991

Y

Yakity Tracks: 1992

Yanks, The: 1985

Yard Squid: 1996

Yellow Afternoon: 1994, 1995 (2)

Yellowcard: 2003

Yellowjackets: 1986, 1989, 1991, 1994

Yellowman: 1982, 1983, 1989, 1990

Yer Majesty: 1999

Yesterday and Today: 1977

Yo Dawg: 1991

Yo La Tengo: 1988, 1990, 1991, 2004

Yoakam, Dwight: 2003

Yohimbe Brothers: 2002

Yohn, Todd: 1996

Yonder Mountain String Band: 2000, 2001 (3), 2002

Yorn, Pete: 2002

You Am I: 1995

You Were Spiraling: 1999

You, Yabby: 1985

Young Conservative: 1986

Young, Jesse Collin: 1985

Young, Kristeen: 1993, 1997 (4)

Your Mom: 2004

Z

Zamudio: 2005, 2006 (3)

Zane Gray: 1980

ZANG!: 2006

Zap Mama: 2003

Zapp and Roger: 1994, 1995

Zapp Band: 1985

Zazz: 1977, 1978

Zebrahead: 1999 (2)

Zeller, Martin: 1995

Zero Boys: 1993

Zero Degree: 1983

Zero Principle: 2003, 2004

Zeros: 2002

Zevon, Warren: 1978, 1990, 1992

Zilla: 2005

Zito: 1997, 1999

Znowhite: 1985

Zodiac Mindwarp: 1988

Zoo People: 1995

Zoo: 1984

Zox: 2006

Zulu Spear: 1997

Zuvuya: 2003

THIS CONCERT BROUGHT TO YOU BY...

This list was compiled with the help of owners, management, and the Mississippi Nights Fans Facebook page. Unfortunately, it is impossible to include everyone. We thank all who brought us the Mississippi Nights experience.

Adena Roche (server)

Alan Bates

Al Banks (door, security)

Al Slivinksi (door)

Alicia Hamilton (server)

Amanda "Ava" Butler (security, server)

Andy Mayberry (manager, booking, bartender, door)

Andy Trommler

Angie Italiano Askew (server)

Anthony "Pookie" Cappello (bartender, tech staff, runner)

Anthony "Hawk" Hawkins (door)

Airika Neugent (server)

Bea Christopher Toft (lighting tech)

Beth Clements (server, office)

Beth Italiano (server)

Beth Signorelli (server)

Bill Matthews (door)

Bob "Doc" Hyait (door)

Brad Gorman (bartender)

Brian Nolan (sound engineer, production manager, booking)

Brian "B" Teal (security, barback, bartender, office)

Brooks "Panty Dropper" Robertson (runner, door, staff)

Bud Evans (barback)

Chad Haferkamp

Charlie Johnson (bartender)

Charles "C.J" Jones (door)

"Cliff [Schmitz], our maintenance guy, was invaluable," says Rich Frame. Before the remodel, Schmitz spent a good portion of his work shift making sure the residential toilets in the bathrooms stayed functional for the patrons, and he never complained about it. In addition, he kept a good sense of humor about his job. Schmitz named the rats, as well as set the traps for them. The rats were so enormous that the alarm company recommended Mississippi Nights reset the alarm to allow for the size of a small dog.

Cheryl Tebbe (server)

Chris Glacin (door)

Chris Reisa

Christopher "Chef" Ellis (runner)

Christopher "Farva" Schwab (security)

Cindi Correale (server)

Cindy Fehmel (publicist)

Cindy Mikulait (server)

Clancy Brady (door, security)

Cliff Schmitz (maintenance, receiving, barback)

Cody "Corky" Cook (door)

Dan Binggeli (bartender)

Dan "Dan-Fred" Traum (bartender)

Dan Utterson (asst. manager)

Darrel Martin

Dave "Gig Butt" Butzler (lighting tech)

Dave Hill

Dave King (security)

David "Ike" Eisenhower (crew, sound engineer)

David "Osama" Jafari

David Planitz (security)

Dayna Godfrey (server)

Debbie Brown

Dee "Edwin" Blanton (monitor tech)

Deirdre Clements (security, server, bartender)

Demetrius Blanton (montitor engineer)

Dennis Coon (bartender)

Denny Fanger (door)

Derek "Waco" Kehl (barback, bartender, promotions director, cleaning crew)

Diana "Dirty D" Harris (server)

Don Long (security)

Donna

Doug Preston

Elaine

Elliot "Boo Boo" Bradshaw (bartender)

Eric "Goose" Burns (security)

Eric Holshouser (security)

276

Cliff Schmitz and Tim Mullen were both buried in Mississippi Nights shirts, and lighting technician Tony Creamer's ashes were spread where the venue once stood.

Photo of Mary and Cliff Schmitz.
Courtesy of Pat Lacey.

Fran Italiano (server)

Gary Lamonte (security)

Gary Wheatly (production manager, sound engineer, lighting tech)

Gary Zambrzuski (stagehand)

Gene Glass (crew, lighting tech)

Glen Weindel

Glenda

Greg Angell (door)

Greg Bender (runner)

Greg Jackson (lighting director)

Greg Kenney (bartender)

Harley Duffy (door, security)

Ira Bill Cox (door, security, barback)

James Stull (sound engineer)

Jamie Welky (front-of-house engineer and production manager)

Jan Roberts (server)

Janice

Jarrod "Subway" Eiden (head of security)

Jason Eric (security, barback)

Jason Hopkins (security)

Jason Nico (security, barback, merch)

Jeff Byford (manager, door, bartender)

Jeff Howatt (manager)

Jennifer James (runner)

Jeremy Johnson (security)

Jesse Raya (media & marketing director)

Jess Bahl Jennings (server)

Jill Oldham (server)

Jim Ferlisi (bartender)

Joe Barrett (barback)

Joe Krassinger

Joe "Connie Joe" Pavia (door, bartender)

John Green (bartender)

John Cavanaugh (bartender)

John Hancock (security)

John Heimburger (door, bartender, asst. manager)

John Lundgren (security)

Julie Moore (server)

Justin Bisher

Kathy McLeod Alexander (server)

Ken Krueger (stage production, lighting tech, expansion construction)

Kim Lucas (server)

Krissana Allen (runner)

Kurt Dolan

Lance (monitor engineer)

Larry "Hammie" Gronemeyer (front-of-house engineer and production manager)

Larry Stricklin

Laura

Lee "Eclipse" Campbell (door)

Lenny Lindsey (lighting tech)

Lizzie Griffith (server)

Mark Andrews (manager)

Marc Beffa (bartender)

Margie Drury (server)

Mark Kellog (monitor engineer)

Mark "Joker" Lightle

Mark Slivinski (door)

Marshall Stacy (sound engineer and monitor tech)

Martha Bollman (server)

Mary Frame (server)

Mary Hessler (server)

Matt "Sideshow" Siewert (bartender, barback, security)

Michael Ames (door)

Michael "Big Mike" Chance (security)

Michael Jackson (door, bartender)

Michelle Hopkins (server)

Michelle Raleigh-Cross

Mike Fairbanks (manager)

Mike Kleb

Mike McLaughlin (busser)

Mike Resendez (door)

Mike Wisdom (staff, popcorn)

Mike Witt (door)

Miles Ogilvie (stage crew)

Mitch Shelton (security, asst. manager)

Myron Reynolds (head bartender & asst. manager)

Nate Hill (promotions director, asst. manager, bartender)

Pat Hagin (bartender, manager, booking)

Pat Lacey (office manager, ticket taker, everything)

Paul Acsay (security)

Paul Summers (lighting tech)

Paula Kiel

Perry Cochran (security)

Perry Preston

Phil

Quintin Washington (security)

Ralph

Randal Cochran (door, barback, office)

Randy Anderson (monitor engineer)

Randy Dinnella (door, bartender)

Randy Phillips (door)

Randy "Animal" Martin (production manager and front-of-house engineer)

Randy "Little" Noldge (sound engineer)

Regina Schniers Teal (security, server)

Rich Dickinson (door, barback, bartender)

Rich Frame (owner)

Richard Wolf (runner and stagehand)

Rick O'Drissel (door)

Rick Schroeder (door, security)

Rick Turner (bar manager)

Robin Duncan (server, bartender)

Ronnie Gamble

Ross

Ria Askew (security)

Ryan Mackley (runner)

Sam Lance (door)

Scott "Duck" Bryant (security)

Sarah Jane "Double D" Voss (server, runner)

Shane Richmond (door)

Shane Valconi (door)

Sharon Frankwicz (server)

Sharon Rall (server)

Sharon Schmitt (server)

Sharon Weeks (server)

Steve Carruth

Steve Duebelbeis (owner)

Steven "Rock" Black (doorman, asst. manager)

Steve Frank (security)

Steve "Pac-man" Pack (door, bartender)

Steve Pulley (door, barback)

Sue Thro (server)

Tim DePung (door)

Tim Farmer

Tim "Coach" Mullen (barback, bartender, head bartender, catering)

Tim Rodgers (production, monitor engineer)

Tim "Hootie" Simmons (barback)

Tim Weber (head of security, manager, marketing director, talent buyer)

Terry Welty (sound engineer)

Tom Duffy (owner)

Tom Tiger (stagehand, expansion construction)

Tommy Damron

Tommy Wieprecht (bartender)

Tom Whittacker (door)

Tony "Pookie" Cappella

Tony Creamer (lighting tech)

Tony P. Pona (stagehand, security

Tony Valenzuela

Tracy Duebelbeis Fowler (office, ticket sales)

Tyrone

Walter Wright (security)

Wendell Bule (security)

Wes Stillman (stagehand)

Instead of hiring an outside caterer, bartender Tim Mullen catered for the venue. "He thought it added a personal touch for the bands," says Rich Frame. The first band he catered for was The dB's in 1986, and he continued providing homey meals to groups at Mississippi Nights throughout the club's run.

279

ERIC LYSAGHT* REMEMBERS...

Tim [Mullen], the bartender, made these great lemon drops. I've never had a lemon drop as good as the ones he made. He just did something special. I think it was because he just shook the hell out of it in the shaker, and when he poured it out into the shot glass, it was frosty. Just delicious. He cared about it. He took pride in it.

L.O.V.E., Neuter the Stupid, Full On Venus, Neptune Crush, Salisbury, Superjam

Tom Whittaker and Pat Hagin camping for the VP Fair in the Mississippi Nights parking lot. Photo by Andy Mayberry.

GARRETT AND STACY WOULD LIKE TO THANK...

Kathy Shelton (for taking us to the auction that started this journey), John and Angela Sebben and St. Louis Classic Rock Preservation Society (for having that auction, and all your help and guidance), Rich and Mary Frame, Steve Duebelbeis, Tom Duffy, Pat Lacey, Pat Hagin, Andy Mayberry, Tim Weber, Brian Nolan, Ron Stevens, Kim and Rob Wagoner, Greg Kessler, Julia Gordon-Bramer, Josh Stevens of Ready Press (for your advice), Walter Wright, Jason Ross (rerunrecords.com), John Wegrzyn, Merril Barden, Gary and Pam Wheatley, Mike Glader, Ken Krueger, John Neiman, Steve "Doc" Dachroeden, Pat Liston, Jeff Herschel, Steve Pick, Patricia Fitzgerald, Harry Pilkerton, Jeff Smith, Max Enloe, Angela Prada, Thomas Grady, Paul Ebenreck (for inspiring the Mississippi Nights diagram), Lauren Gornik (for making the Mississippi Nights diagram. Lgornikart.com), Andrew Wanko and the Missouri History Museum, Adele Heagney and St. Louis Public Library, and the Missouri Historical Society. Thank you to the band members, promoters, roadies, patrons, Mississippi Nights managers, and staff who provided stories. Thank you to all the collectors who sent photos, flyers, tickets, posters, and other memorabilia. And a big thank you to all the members of our Mississippi Nights Fan Page on Facebook; without your inspiration and support, this book would not have been possible.

CPSIA information can be obtained
at www.ICGtesting.com
Printed in the USA
BVHW011918071222
PP14395300001B/15

9 781737 203100